The Poetry of Pop

The Poetry of Pop

ADAM BRADLEY

Yale UNIVERSITY PRESS/NEW HAVEN & LONDON

Published with assistance from the Louis Stern
Memorial Fund.

Yale University Press books may be purchased in
quantity for educational, business, or promotional
use. For information, please e-mail sales.press
@yale.edu (U.S. office) or sales@yaleup.co.uk
(U.K. office).

Designed by Mary Valencia.
Chapter titles designed by Justin Francis.
Illustrations by Leland Chapin.
Set in Century and Gotham type by Westchester
Publishing Services.
Printed in the United States of America.

Library of Congress Control Number: 2016956986
ISBN: 978-0-300-16502-9 (hardcover : alk. paper)

A catalogue record for this book is available from
the British Library.

This paper meets the requirements of ANSI/NISO
Z39.48-1992 (Permanence of Paper).

10 9 8 7 6 5 4 3 2 1

To Ava, who loves to dance.
To Amaya, who loves to sing.
To Anna, who loves them both.

Contents

The Poetry of Pop

Introduction

M ost of us live with a shifting soundtrack, songs that fill our ears as we go about our days: a workout mix, a drive-time playlist, the songs we hear in stores, the music we dance to at parties. The songs themselves are secondary; they call us to experiences rather than being experiences. We half listen, but our attention is elsewhere.

Some of us also listen in a different way. We obsess over a certain song, even over individual words and sounds in the song. We play songs in remembrance or in celebration. We listen live at concerts, or learn to play favorite songs for ourselves. Sometimes we choose these encounters; at other times they surprise us, commanding thought and feeling. Such songs comprise another soundtrack, a collection of memories accessible only through sound. These are some of mine:

I'm three years old, listening to "Little April Shower" from the movie Bambi. *I haven't seen the film because my mother says it's too scary. But I have the picture book and I have the LP. I clutch the album cover close to me as the music plays. The song is confusing. It makes me sad, yet I want to hear it over and over again. I'm captivated by the voices—of women, then of men, in haunting harmony. I recognize only a few words: "Drip drip drop little April shower." These repeat more times than I can count. The melody summons a strong and unfamiliar emotion in me. Now I'd call it wistfulness. All I knew then was that this was the first song that ever made me cry and made me long for it at the same time.*

I'm twelve years old, playing air guitar to Guns N' Roses' "Welcome to the Jungle." No one else is at home, so I choreograph a performance in front of the living-room speakers. First I'm Slash because he's biracial like I am, then I'm Axl Rose because he's a badass. I love the noise, the keening guitar, and Axl's straining voice. I'm drawn to the contrast between the cacophony of the chorus and the calm of the bridge, where Izzy Stradlin strums chords as Axl sings, "And when you're high you never / Ever wanna come down. / So. Down. So. Down. So. Downnnnn. Yeah!" Axl's "yeah" melts into Slash's bended note until they are a single sound. There's wonder in this noise, then quiet, then noise again. Like a lot of tweens and teens in the summer of 1987, I listen to Guns N' Roses because something about their music feels like me, or maybe just the me I want to be.

I'm a twenty-three-year-old graduate student, about to take a three-hour oral exam on the history of Western literature before professors whose names appear on the spines of Norton anthologies. I spend the night before the exam in the bathroom, vomiting from stress. In the morning I leave my dorm room and walk to the test, my oversized headphones blasting the Wu-Tang Clan's "Triumph" on repeat. "I bomb atomically, Socrates' philosophies and hypotheses / Can't define how I be droppin' these mockeries / Lyrically perform armed robbery." Listening to these lines, I'm conscious of their poetry: the figures and forms, the rhythm patterns and rhyme schemes that I've been studying are here just as they are in Beowulf *and T. S. Eliot's* The Waste Land *and Elizabeth Bishop's "Roosters." I'm mindful of how effortless the poetic patterns sound in the song's raw beats and hard rhymes. I take my headphones off as I reach the exam room door. I pass the test.*

I'm thirty-six years old, a first-time father, and my infant daughter won't stop crying. I sing her lullabies to no avail, then switch to pop songs. I try the Beach Boys' "Don't Worry Baby," Bob Marley's "Redemption Song," Joni Mitchell's "Both Sides Now," and the entire Beatles songbook. Nothing works. Desperate, I sing Hall & Oates's "Private Eyes." It does the trick. As soon as I finish the song she starts to cry again. To soothe her I sing Billy Joel's "Just the Way You Are," Kenny Loggins's "Danny's Song," and Christopher Cross's "Arthur's Theme (The Best That You Can Do)." She settles happily to sleep. I reluctantly face the truth: my three-month-old daughter loves soft-rock hits of the seventies and eighties. So at least once a day for nearly half a year I perform a cappella concerts for her. I'm no singer, but singing these songs helps me to appreciate their careful construction, the way they work in spite of my voice. As I hold her small body against me, dancing slow circles in near-darkness, a simple fact dawns on me: Almost all songs have a spark of magic in them.

This is a book about the magic of pop songs and how a significant part of that magic resides in the language of the lyrics, both on the page and in performance. Few of us first encounter song lyrics on the page as poetry or as sheet music; instead, we experience lyrics in sound, sometimes live but usually recorded. Lyrics, no matter how artfully conceived and constructed they may be, rarely matter much alone; they exist in relation to the voice that enchants them through rhythm, melody, and harmony; in relation to the instruments that intensify their language or obscure it entirely; and in relation to the experience of pop songs when heard alone or in a crowd.

The Poetry of Pop offers the license to look unabashedly at these lyrics. It asks you to take pop songs seriously without being too serious about it.

There's something irresistible about words set in song. In fact, songs are among the most powerful forms that words take. If all art aspires to the condition of music, as Walter Pater once observed, then it does so because music achieves a register of feeling unmatched by any other mode of expression. Words in song can elicit emotions that plain speech cannot. Some songs render words percussive and melodic, nearly divested of symbol and meaning. Other songs enshrine words' complex sense, building images and narratives so durable that they live on for millennia.

Situating literary matters in the dynamic space of popular songs promises new attention to old concerns. It builds a bridge between the poetic acts, both humble and sublime, taking place around us in pop music every day and those that can seem distant and forbidding when encountered in novels and plays and poems. The result is a mutually sustaining connection between disparate creations, united by a poetic practice that does not artificially discriminate between "low" and "high" culture, between the popular and the canonical. The pop music I'm talking about isn't a narrow genre, but a broad descriptor that encompasses everything from Broadway musicals to country ballads, from obscure soul sides to *Billboard* Hot 100 hits. It reaches back to the dawn of recorded music in the early decades of the twentieth century and forward to the ever-evolving soundscape of our digital present.

I choose to use "pop" instead of "rock" or another term out of a considered choice, though not an easy one. Pop comes closest to the descriptive range that I seek. The term stands both for genre and for culture and commerce writ large. Some endeavor to use "rock" in such a way. The Rock & Roll Hall of Fame makes an implicit claim to universality, enshrining rap groups like Public Enemy, Run-DMC, and N.W.A.; country acts like Carl Perkins and Brenda Lee; blues artists like Muddy Waters and Etta James; and pop groups like ABBA and the Bee Gees; not to mention rock and rollers like Buddy Holly and Chuck Berry, who headlined the Hall's inaugural class back in 1986. The first rock and roll was rhythm and blues by another name. It began as a term of convenience, a way of distinguishing the music white artists were making from the music black artists were making, though the sounds and styles were often nearly the same. Today, using the term "rock" to describe the vast body of popular music since the 1950s unduly whitewashes a vibrantly mixed catalog of sounds.

In contrast, pop is inclusive, multiracial, and global in its appeal. Certainly, it carries its own baggage, including assumptions that all pop is bubblegum music intended for preteens, that it is mass-produced and indifferently crafted. However, the virtues of the term outweigh these detriments. Pop is encompassing and capacious. It is popular music. It is the *Billboard* charts, which reach across genres. Pop invites rather than excludes. At the same time, pop allows insurgency and opposition and stubborn isolation.

Writing in his introduction to *Listen Again*, the 2007 collection of essays from the EMP Pop Conference, Eric Weisbard offers the following defense of pop as a cross-genre term: "If, as now seems increasingly clear, rallying terms like folk, jazz, blues, rock and roll, soul, hip-hop, and so on are more confining than illuminating, what should take their place? Perhaps an expanded view of pop, which has numerous meanings, but, as the catch-all music fan's term for sticky sounds, inauthentic identity, and commercial crazes of every sort, remains the best word for all that is heard, loved, and yet rarely ennobled." This book shares Weisbard's impulse. Following the novelist Nick Hornby, I use "pop" to "encompass just about anything that isn't classical music."

Think of this book, then, as a strange sonic dinner party at which Taylor Swift sits beside Richard Hell, who sits beside Aretha Franklin, who sits beside Jay Z, who sits beside Loretta Lynn, who sits beside Ozzy Osbourne, and so on around the table. This strangeness is by design. The artists I quote and the songs I analyze don't reflect any one genre or sensibility; they don't even reflect my own taste. They all simply perform music in English, and this music is pop in the broadest sense of that term: everything but classical.

Writing this book required conducting an enormous amount of research and compiling a massive amount of data. I combed through close to three hundred artist memoirs, gathering notes on matters of compositional practice and performance style. I transcribed hundreds of lyrics, scanning their rhythms and marking their rhymes. I surveyed every *Billboard* Hot 100 hit since the advent of the charts in 1958, cataloging songs by genre, song structure, and a dozen other matters of lyric form. I listened for hours, really for years, to the detriment of my ears and the betterment of my being. Though this book is rarely about me in any overt sense, it is the closest thing I've ever written to a memoir in that it comprises my life in listening. My listening experience is, of course, far from comprehensive. The lyrics and recordings I cite throughout are not exhaustive, only exemplary. I hope engaged readers will apply the principles in this book to the music of their minds.

The book is organized into three parts. Part I offers a primer on why and how to analyze song lyrics as poetry. Part II addresses pop music's poetic forms. Part III engages pop music's poetic functions. Finally, an appendix gathers together annotated playlists that explore everything from a selection of page-born poems that inspired pop songs to a collection of memorable whispers, screams, and laughs in recorded pop. The chapters center on big concepts (such as rhythm and story) that winnow themselves down to the particulars of individual lyric lines. Of course, all of the subjects of the book's sections entwine with one another through performance. One rarely fixates solely on rhyme when listening to a song. Having a chapter on voice doesn't mean that voice fails to come up in other chapters. In fact, we experience pop's poetry most directly when we lose sight of where one element ends and another begins.

For pop music fans, *The Poetry of Pop* offers a glimpse into the aesthetic labors of language and performance that create the recordings we cherish or despise, and in doing so offers a new means of thinking and feeling about popular music. For lovers of literature, *The Poetry of Pop* equips you with the tools to unlock the particulars of language in song lyrics by fostering a literacy that moves readily between the page and performance, between words as written and words as sung. Awareness of such acts of creation isn't compulsory, but it can prove transformative. It can change how we credit the craft of popular entertainers, how we appreciate the marriage of language and voice, and how we understand that our tastes are rooted not in mystery alone but in concrete particulars that live side by side with that mystery and enchant us all the more.

My goal is not to dignify or defend pop lyrics; they are their own best defense. Rather, my goal is to open points of entry for those who wish to engage deeply and analytically with forms of language and sound that we often uncritically consume as entertainment. Applying the tools of poetics to song lyrics is itself great entertainment. Part of it is the pleasure of the puzzle, of understanding how disparate elements fit together to fashion an aesthetic experience. Part, too, is the pleasure of situating art that is often considered ephemeral in the firmament of tradition, of underscoring the continuity in culture and practice that connects the seemingly disconnected. It is invigorating to be able to trace the connection between the four-beat lines of *Beowulf* and the four-beat lines of Biggie, not because it ennobles one or debases the other, but because it reaffirms continuity across lyric creation.

This book relies on two things: readily acquired skills of literary analysis, and common practices of close listening that are already part of how most of us listen to music. It does not require extensive musical knowledge, nor does it require preexisting experience with poetics. Instead, it takes a functional approach, rooted in the belief that all songs have some mystery to share with those willing to give patient attention, and that exploring this mystery—often hiding in plain sight—will enrich listening pleasure. Singers' and songwriters' conscious creations in language, music, and performance affect us intellectually and emotionally. Their craft is the poetry of pop.

Part

I

Chapter One

Lyric & Song

R ihanna singing "Diamonds" is my idea of poetry. Of course, "Diamonds" is a pop song first, a 2012 global hit that gave Rihanna her twelfth number-one single in just over six years—bested only by the Beatles and the Supremes. It is a 3:45 pop ballad and a music video, an object of culture and of commerce. Chances are neither Rihanna nor the scores of writers, producers, engineers, label executives, radio programmers, DJs, and consumers responsible for the song's success ever once stopped to think of it as a poem.

But "Diamonds" is a poem. Without the poet's tools, the song could not exist. The poetry lives in the lyrics that the Australian singer-songwriter Sia is said to have composed in fourteen minutes while in a New York studio. It lives in how those lyrics nest themselves in the StarGate- and Benny Blanco–produced instrumental. Most powerfully, it lives in the rhythms and intonations of Rihanna's voice as it lays its own art atop the art of others.

The poetry of pop demands both eye and ear. Part of the poetry is visible in word alone. The first thing Rihanna sings on "Diamonds," "Shine bright like a diamond," is a serviceable though not particularly inventive simile. Sia's lyrics soon reimagine it: "We're like diamonds in the sky." Now the diamonds have become a metaphor for stars, which in turn becomes a simile for two people in love. Later in the song diamonds are beauty and shooting stars are a "vision of ecstasy," both the drugged state of romance and the drugged state of the drug itself.

The poetry is also in repetition, the signal quality of all poetic form. On the page, this repetition soon surrenders to redundancy. In the ear, the repeated hooks and choruses become occasions for anticipation, of the familiar and also of unexpected departures in rhythm and harmony. Rihanna closely follows Sia's vocal pattern from the demo recording, a fact of which most of the listening public is likely unaware and, if made aware, probably wouldn't care. As Sia conceives it and as Rihanna executes it on the studio recording, the song's melodic character is enchanting, full of unusual vocal ripples and eddies that always bend back to the flow.

Of course, we don't need poetics to find pleasure in listening to "Diamonds," or to any other pop song for that matter. The poetry of pop matters inasmuch as our curiosity demands that we understand why and how the song affects us—why we know the lyrics without giving them conscious thought, why the melody ends up running through our heads, why we tire of the song, or even why it leaves us cold. Poetic analysis helps to identify patterns in the language, figures and forms, rhythms and rhymes familiar from the study of poetry meant first for reading. When directed at a recorded song, poetic analysis reveals what happens when words leave the page and go to live in the air, in the ear.

Saying that "Diamonds" is a poem is not meant to elevate it as high art. It makes no value judgments. A poem need not be profound to bear the name; the same holds for song lyrics. The lyrics to "Diamonds," which *New York Times* critic Jon Caramanica characterizes as "insipid," are also purpose-built: they are meant to carry a melody and evoke familiar feelings and common associations so as to reach the broadest possible audience. Pleasing poems are often made of unsturdier stuff.

Thankfully, "Diamonds" need not rely on lyrics alone. Pop's poetry always lives in the space between word and music. It follows different rules than those that govern most page-born poetry. Sometimes a song's poetry expresses itself best in the craft of a well-wrought lyric whose value is most apparent on the page. Leonard Cohen's "Hallelujah" is such a song, as is Lauryn Hill's "Final Hour," both of which have an effortless sound that belies the complexity of their construction. Often, though, a song's poetry is better heard than seen—or, rather, better seen and heard together. This is the case, for instance, with Nirvana's "Smells Like Teen Spirit" and Joanna Newsom's "Book of Right-On," both of which rely on the emotive clarity of their performance to counterbalance the cryptic quality of their lyrics. Once asked about being a poet, Newsom responded equivocally: "I don't exactly know how poetry is defined. I don't write poetry that's not meant to be sung."

"Diamonds" is a poem meant to be sung. The song's performance makes its poetic form palpable. Though its lyrics respond in small ways to poetic analysis—a rhyme here, a simile there—the preponderance of its poetic splendor is apparent only in performance. Hearing the lyric as part of a recorded song, one finds a balance of repetition and difference, and patterns of diction that underscore the heightened state of love's first flush. The bright assonance of "i" sounds knits tight in the ear threads of words that are only loosely tied in the mind. Shards of image that appear oddly mixed on the page fit in clear composite on the recording. One finds, in other words, a poetic act that is also a musical one. One finds an art in equipoise.

Take "Diamonds" or Rihanna's number-one hit from the previous year, "We Found Love," or the Beatles' "Let It Be," or Bob Marley's "No Woman, No Cry"—take all of the songs you'll encounter in this book—and you'll find that their shapes derive in no small part from the craft of their poetry. Rhythm, rhyme, figurative language, voice, style, story, abound here just as they do in different measures across a Homeric epic, a Modernist lyric, and an experimental poem written yesterday. The poetry of the page and the poetry of performance equally animate the poetry of pop. Listen and read. Read and listen. Though these are pop songs more than poems, they wouldn't be the songs they are without their poetry.

When written on the page, song lyrics look a lot like poems. The lines break, as the lines in poems often do. As with poems, the syntax of song lyrics usually diverges from the patterns of casual speech; language is rendered ritual. Rhythm bends lyrics into uncommon shapes, percussive breaks that dance with the lines across the page. Figures and forms of speech and thought abound in ways they rarely do in daily conversation. Then there is rhyme, often at the ends of lines, just as one might expect of poetry from an earlier time.

The *Oxford English Dictionary* defines a poem as "a piece of writing or an oral composition, often characterized by a metrical structure, in which the expression of feelings, ideas, etc., is typically given intensity or flavour by distinctive diction, rhythm, imagery, etc.; a composition in poetry or verse." Very little about this definition is prescriptive; poetry is "often characterized by a metrical structure" and is "typically given intensity or flavour" by elements of its form. It may be written or recited; it may express "feelings, ideas, etc." Put simply, a poem is possibility.

To fulfill this possibility, poems generate feeling through direct emotive appeal, through accretion of image, and, more subtly, through the play of sound. Song lyrics outsource much of that emotive work to the music and to how the singer's vocal inflections color the words. Both music and singing have more direct access to our emotions than does the written word. As a consequence, the language of lyrics need not work as hard and, in fact, is often better served by doing less than the language of page-born poetry. Song lyrics still do work, though that work is often different from that done by poetry meant for the eye: the sound-supporting effort of linguistic play, for instance, and the winnowing of words to fit the melody.

Reading song lyrics as poetry invites cognitive dissonance. We know from the listening experience that a song is emotively powerful, even if in reading the words on the page little of that power comes through. A Great Big World's surprise 2013 *Billboard* number one, "Say Something," is a deeply affecting song. The contrast between Ian Axel's vulnerable, uneasy lead vocals and Christina Aguilera's uncharacteristically restrained but strong background vocals, combined with the delicate piano melody and vibrant strings, fashions an emotive experience that is as close to operatic as a 3:49 song can muster. Precious little of that feeling, however, is apparent on the page:

> Say something, I'm giving up on you
> I'll be the one if you want me to
> Anywhere, I would've followed you
> Say something, I'm giving up on you

As lyric, these lines are limited. The first and fourth lines are identical, as are three of the four end words; the fourth end word relates to the others in a rather pallid rhyme ("you" and "to"). More limited still is the third line, an awkward syntactical inversion that would make Yoda proud ("Anywhere, I would've followed you"). For all that is redundant and plain about these lines, however, their construction follows sound poetic practices. Writing them down reveals the care with which they are crafted. Scanning the lines' rhythm exposes an underlying order:

> *Say* something, / *I'm* giving / *up* on you
> *I'll* be the / *one* if you / *want* me to
> *Anywhere,* / *I* would've / *fo*llowed you
> *Say* something, / *I'm* giving / *up* on you

The entire verse is written in dactylic trimeter, a stressed syllable followed by two unstressed syllables, repeated three times per line. The measured cadence imbedded in the line gives birth to the measured qualities of the melody and performance, working in an uncredited supporting role to the rhythm and feel of the song. For all its obvious deficiencies and incompletions as a freestanding poem, its poetry nonetheless accounts for some of the lyric's success as a recording.

Pop songs take much of their form from such unseen acts of lyric craft, a craft we readily ascribe to poetry and often fail to acknowledge in song lyrics. We generally accept that poetry is a concise and precise art, the right words in the right order. The dominant poetic mode of the moment certainly leans that way: slender lines that abstain from rhyme and insist on their interiority. Such art demands rumination that is voiced, when voiced at all, in a cloistered concert of the mind. By contrast, song lyrics revel in rhyme of all types and invite performance and communal engagement. Tap your toes. Stomp your feet. Bob your head. Dance and sing, and you need not do it alone.

Pop lyrics are also carefully calibrated. A good pop song, like a good lyric poem, demands the right words in the right order, even if those words are "Oooowh! I feel good!" or "Oh, na na. What's my name?" We can recognize the *poetics* of pop songs even if we resist the urge to identify the lyrics as poetry. Accepting the poetics of pop songs simply admits that lyrics are made of much the same stuff and respond to the same kinds of attention generally reserved for poems on the page. Reading songs, or, to borrow a phrase from N*E*R*D, seeing sounds, reveals the patterning and organization at work, as well as the breaks in form and flights of fancy that define the best art in any genre.

The musicologist Lawrence M. Zbikowski observes that "despite their differences, words and music work together in song. . . . Music can breathe the breath of life into poetry or create a poem on a poem." Creating a poem on a poem, as "Diamonds" and "Say Something" do, is an apt way of describing both the challenge and the possibility of songwriting: How do you conjoin one aesthetic artifact with its own rhythm and logic and a second aesthetic artifact with its own rhythm and logic to create a third aesthetic artifact that somehow reconciles the two and improves on both? In some instances, songs make lyrics legible; in others, the two achieve a delicate equipoise; in others, they work in tension; in still others, the music is either so inconsequential or so artfully inconspicuous as to intensify the natural effects of the lyrics as poetry. In still other instances, the lyrics are obscured or occluded by the sound, either in performance or in production. "In music, some notes are accented relative to others, by virtue of their pitch, loudness, or rhythm; these accents constrain the words that will fit well with the melody, and help establish the musical mannequin on which the lyrical clothing will be hung," explains the sound engineer turned neuroscientist Daniel J. Levitin. Language carries its own constraints; a line of lyric has its inborn patterns of accent and pitch, rhythm and loudness. A song must resolve these two into one; in moments of conflict the music usually prevails.

Imagine song lyrics existing on an expressive continuum, on which some lyrics are almost entirely subservient to their music, while others approach independence from it. At one extreme, the words to songs can work as pure sound, another kind of music. At the other extreme, they can achieve an expressive singularity, with the recorded song providing an aural setting for the music and meaning of the words. Think of the difference between jazz singer Ella Fitzgerald's rendition of "One Note Samba," where her scat singing distills language to its phonemes and its expressive power largely shifts from the semantic to the sonic realm, and Public Enemy's "Fight the Power," where the Bomb Squad's "Wall of Noise" production attunes the listener's ear to the language of Chuck D's lyrics as political act. As the Barbadian poet Kamau Brathwaite reminds us, noise too is part of meaning. In the first instance, the lyrics shape an entrancing music; in the second, the music serves the lyrics as rhetoric and poetry.

Most song lyrics lie somewhere in the middle of this continuum, neither unmoored syllables nor clear and emphatic expression. The music gives the lyrics a mandate, which often includes the following: (1) support the sound; (2) do not detract from the song by becoming overcomplicated; and (3) capture the audience's attention through a catchy hook or other lyric device. The vast majority of pop lyrics abide by these rules most of the time. The resulting language is mostly composed of preexisting parts; like a prefabricated home, pop lyrics are often economical, serviceable, and undistinguished. The best that can be said about most of them—and this is no small thing—is that they do their job.

But every lyric will steal a moment, small though it may be, where it incites a revolution against the tyranny of music, where it commands attention to the recording primarily as language. This doesn't compromise the song's identity as song; what it does, though, is complicate blanket pronouncements about the servility of lyric. For this reason, a pop lyric almost always provides close readers and listeners with something upon which to exercise their skills in poetic analysis. It might be a surprising disruption in the rhyme pattern or a particularly vivid image; it could be a playful moment of alliteration or a hidden exercise of assonance. Poetics, with its emphasis on the mechanics of language, patterning, and arrangement, is a useful body of knowledge to put to work in song lyrics because the lyrics invariably respond, sometimes in surprising and delightful ways.

Even still, people make good arguments for why song lyrics should not be considered poetry. Poems are meant for the page, while song lyrics lose their vitality when read in cold print. "I respect poetry and I try to write subtly, but lyrics really aren't poems. Printing them like poems can make them seem silly," Marvin Gaye told his biographer, David Ritz. Song lyrics need music, voice, and performance to give them life. "Lyrics by definition lack something," writes Stephen Sondheim; poetry is complete unto itself. Good songwriters leave room in their lyrics for the marriage with melody by consciously constraining the effects of rhythm, rhyme, and image. The sociomusicologist Simon Frith explains this succinctly: "Good song lyrics are not good poems because they don't need to be."

Some differences between song lyrics and print-based poetry are obvious. Songs are social; a community must generally come together to compose lyrics and music and produce a recording for commercial release. Poetry, by contrast, is usually the work of an individual writing words meant to be read silently by another individual. "A completed poem is self-sufficient," notes the songwriter Sheila Davis. "A finished lyric, however, is an unfinished product; it is half a potential song." The poet Glyn Maxwell amplifies Davis's point: "The other half of everything for the songwriters is music. For the poets it's silence, the space, the whiteness."

Though we might draw any number of reasonable distinctions between poetry and song lyrics, strong evidence suggests that our brains do not. "The auditory arts of music and poetry hold a privileged position in human history, and we see this reflected in our own time in neurological case studies," observes Daniel J. Levitin. "Individuals suffering from Alzheimer's disease, victims of strokes, tumors, or other organic brain trauma, may lose the ability to recognize faces, even of people they've known their entire lives. They may lose the ability to recognize simple objects such as hairbrushes or forks. But many of these same patients can still recite poetry by heart, and sing songs that they knew as children. Verse—whether spoken or sung—appears to be deeply encoded in the human brain."

The neuroscientist Oliver Sacks observed that cursing, singing lyrics, and reciting poetry might equally be understood as instances of automatic speech, as distinguished from the propositional speech that constitutes most everyday conversation. This lifeline to language and song extends even to those suffering from dementia. "Music is no luxury to them, but a necessity," writes Sacks, "and can have a power beyond anything else to restore them to themselves, and to others, at least for a while."

I can attest to the power of poetic and musical memory. In my grandmother's last years, when so much of who she once had been was slipping away due to Alzheimer's, I often sat by her bedside and read aloud from her battered copy of Robert Frost's *Poems*. Sometimes she closed her eyes, letting the rhythms and rhymes engulf her. From time to time, drawing from deep within her ravaged memory, she would speak a word or phrase or even a complete line. In every case, her voice seemed driven by the shape of the sounds rather than the denotation of the words alone. She seemed, in other words, to be singing.

How do we classify the pop song, that aesthetic amalgam of music and words? Our answer to that question has considerable implications for the kind of cultural capital we confer on pop, for how—and even if—we study it, for where we play it and whether we pass it down or just throw it away. Pop songs are neither music nor poetry and yet both. I mean by this that pop songs often fuse elements of music and of poetry—sometimes the one before the other, sometimes both at the same time. It matters little what comes first because the successful song is inevitably the product of an ongoing mediation of difference. "The simple truth," according to the songwriter Jimmy Webb, "is that anyone who has had 'hands-on' songwriting experience knows that the process is fluid and that to be successful it must be mutable and words and music mutually adaptable." To say that a pop song is a poem makes just as much sense as to say that a pop song is only music. Both claims are partial truths.

No, song lyrics are not the same as print-based poetry, but that does not rob them of their claim to the name. We extend the name "poetry" to other forms that reject easy categorization. Slam poetry bears the name "poetry," yet, like the song lyric, it relies on performance for its full meaning and impact. Various forms of visual poems are considered poetry, though they rely on nonlinguistic matters of arrangement and design. Sound poetry is poetry, too, though it abjures conventional forms of poetic meaning, privileging the phonetic and aural qualities of words over their semantics, as song lyrics sometimes do. Poetry is a much wider field than arguments over the poetic identity of song lyrics ever allow it to be.

The contested boundary of poetry and song lyric made headlines in October 2016 when the Swedish Academy awarded Bob Dylan the Nobel Prize in Literature "for having created new poetic expressions within the great American song tradition." In an interview after the announcement, Professor Sara Danius, the Permanent Secretary of the Swedish Academy, made the case for Dylan's award. "He is a great poet," she said, calling attention to his "brilliant way of rhyming," his "putting together refrains," and his "pictorial thinking." Looking back across millennia, Danius cites Homer and Sappho as writing "poetic texts that were meant to be listened to . . . often together with instruments." Like those ancient counterparts, Dylan too writes lyrics that, though meant to be performed, are at home in the silence of the page. Take away his inimitable voice, his signature phrasings, and what remains still merits praise and attention. "He can be read and should be read," Danius concludes, "and he is a great poet in the English tradition."

In recognizing Dylan, the Nobel committee might well have imagined itself doing its best imitation of Led Zeppelin: trashing the hotel room and throwing the television out the window in defiance of their own past practice and the rigid barriers separating the popular and the canonical. But selecting Dylan was actually a fairly safe move. His literary bona fides are unimpeachable. For over half a century now his lyrics have garnered extensive scholarly attention even as other great singer-songwriters have been overlooked. Witness the nearly fourteen-pound collection of lyrics edited by literary critic Christopher Ricks in 2014, presenting Dylan's words as if they were torn from the pages of Wordsworth and Coleridge's *Lyrical Ballads*. One could make the case that in the public eye Dylan is now just as much a poet as he is a pop star.

The story of how we arrived at such a narrow vision of the poem is now overfamiliar: Poetry retreated to the page in the age of sound recording and began favoring a procrustean poetics that submerged songlike qualities to achieve a more complex ideal. Taking a broad view of poetry's history, the literary poetry of today has fallen further out of phase with poetry through the ages than has contemporary song lyric. Transplant an ancient Greek and an Elizabethan to the present day and place before them John Ashbery's ". . . by an Earthquake" and a transcription of Taylor Swift's "Blank Space" and they'll more readily recognize Swift's lyrics as the poem. This doesn't mean that Swift is the superior poet, only that at the level of form pop-song lyrics capture the poetic eye. Where Ashbery abjures end rhyme and an aesthetics of economy, Swift offers ample end rhyme and a measured lyric line.

The lyrics to pop songs and most poetry differ in this: Pop lyrics are asked to dance to someone else's music, while poetry dances to a music all its own. A poetics of pop must account for this dual existence of lyric as word and sound. In privileging the denotational meanings of song lyrics over their sonic function in a recording, we radically mismeasure pop's poetry.

The rock critic Greil Marcus, certainly no fan of song-lyrics-as-poetry, comes close to admitting the possibility, with a necessary caveat. "Of all the nonsense that has been written about the poetry of Neil Young, Paul Simon, or even Bob Dylan," Marcus writes in *Mystery Train*, "no one has ever said anything about Jimi Hendrix's 'Little Wing.' The poetry question, especially when we are dealing with a song, has to do with how a writer uses language—

and his music will be part of his language—to make words do things they ordinarily do not do, with how he tests the limits of language and alters and extends the conventional impact of images, or rescues resources of language that we have lost or destroyed."

Marcus does not reject Young, Simon, and Dylan as artists; he rejects the myopic critical assessment of them that imputes poetic value to their lyrics in silence. Such a poetics of pop neglects an artist like Hendrix, whose poetic appeal in a song like "Little Wing" relies on a full accounting of the language of the lyric in recorded music. The way Hendrix sings the word *anything*, from 1:33 to 1:36 of "Little Wing," for instance, is just as worthy of poetic attention as an exalted Dylan line imbricated in rhyme.

A functional poetics of pop acknowledges how song lyrics "make words do things they ordinarily do not do" when language is under the sway of song. The reason that some people prize certain singer-songwriters as poets often has less to do with the merits of craft than with the complacency of literary critics who are unwilling or unable to develop a new poetics to account for the double life of song lyrics as word and music. Resolving "the poetry question" when it comes to pop music begins with cultivating a poetics that is alive to the richness of lyric as contextualized in performance.

There's a long history, dating back to the birth of rock and roll and reaching into the 1970s, of books about the poetry of pop lyrics, falling broadly into two categories: hagiographies of individual songwriters and polemical efforts to equate—and in these critics' minds, to elevate—pop songwriting by comparing it to the craft of the Western poetic tradition. The best example of the former approach is pretty much every book ever written about Bob Dylan. The best example of the latter is David R. Pichaske's *Beowulf to Beatles: Approaches to Poetry*, an anthology first published in 1972 that intersperses rock lyrics by songwriters such as Jim Morrison and Joni Mitchell with poems by canonical poets like William Blake and Robert Frost. The flaw in Pichaske's book isn't that it goes too far in putting forward song lyrics for close analysis. Rather, Pichaske doesn't go far enough in asserting his chosen lyrics' aesthetic autonomy. By insisting on a scaffolding of canonical poems, the book underestimates the capacity for song lyrics to stand on their own with and without their music, as a hybrid tradition worthy of study and demanding a particular kind of analysis distinct from that commonly directed at print-based poetry. Behind such earnest efforts as Pichaske's is a desire to ennoble pop music and to rationalize our obsessive attention to it. The problem is that it often comes across as contrived, seeking sanction from a high literary authority when rock never much cared for authority in the first place.

The Poetry of Pop offers something different. The end of analysis isn't enshrining pop lyrics in the Western poetic canon but, rather, figuring out what makes them work structurally and sonically, what makes them beautiful, and what makes them move us so. Such analytical labor is best accomplished by listening to the lyrics in the context of their performance as music; however, a small but critical part of the work can be done only by looking at the lyrics on the page.

Certain song lyrics stand up on the page better than others; they comport themselves well as poems. "I like 'Across the Universe,'" John Lennon told *Rolling Stone* in 1970. "It's one of the best lyrics I've written. In fact, it could be the best. It's good poetry, or whatever you call it, without chewin' it. See the ones I like are the ones that stand as words, without melody. They don't have to have any melody; like a poem, you can read them." When the interviewer asked Lennon if that was "his ultimate criterion" for great songs, he replied, "No, that's just the ones I happen to like."

Finding out that a great song lyric also makes a great poem is akin to finding out that your car can double as a boat—kind of cool, but hardly the foremost thing on your mind during your morning commute. Nora Ephron once asked Bob Dylan if he was a poet, by which she meant if he thought his words "could stand without the music." Dylan responded, "They would stand but I don't read them. I'd rather sing them." Elsewhere, though, Dylan insisted: "It ain't the melodies that are important, man, it's the words." So what matters most—the words, the music? The more compelling consideration is whether a song lyric's capacity to stand alone in print makes it somehow better to sing. Could better poetry mean better recorded songs?

In the eyes of some, looking like a poem on the page renders a song lyric poetry—or, more damning, "poetic," that amorphous adjective one often hears used to describe the overadorned, the inscrutable, and the meaningless. Such has been the fate of the work of certain songwriters who write lyrics that are easily metabolized as poems—Bob Dylan, Joni Mitchell, Leonard Cohen, and Lou Reed all come to mind. People who describe these songwriters as poets (sometimes, in fact, the songwriters describe themselves as such) are using the term "poet" as an honorific. Taken this way, being a poet means being a member of the cultural aristocracy, an artist rather than a craftsperson. Not everyone buys in. "I don't think that rock & roll songwriters should worry about art," Keith Richards asserts. "I don't think it comes into it. A lot of it is just craft anyway, especially after doing it for a long time. . . . Art is the last thing I'm worried about when I'm writing a song. I don't think it really matters. If you want to call it art, yeah, okay, you can call it what you like. As far as I'm concerned, 'Art' is just short for 'Arthur.'"

Keith is onto something. Some of the reasons that a song lyric works well as a poem are the same reasons that it works well in a recorded song: lyric concision, perhaps, but also occasional superfluity; imagistic beauty, but also an artful ugliness. At the same time, some of what makes for a good poem can get in the way of a good lyric—assonance, for instance, which can create a small, beautiful music on the page, might clash with the music in performance as song; or a rich accretion of image, which might choke out the space necessary for the music to breathe. One only discovers this, however, by applying the principles of close reading and close listening to a song, as both lyric and recording. One only discovers this after learning to read and to listen again.

Chapter
Two

Reading

R eading song lyrics is not the same as reading *into* song lyrics. The former is a neglected practice, the craft of being an active observer capable of negotiating words and phrases, tone and meaning. The latter is a favorite pastime of teenagers, weedheads, and rock critics—and certainly of teenage weedhead rock critics.

The lyrics to pop songs are routinely the subject of close scrutiny, often of the wrong kind. "Louie Louie" merited its own FBI file, investigating the purportedly salacious content hidden in the near-indecipherable mix. The Eagles' "Hotel California" has been read as an allegory of good and evil and as a metaphorical account of experiences in drug rehab. Don McLean's "American Pie" is about Buddy Holly, or the Vietnam War, or who knows what. Many people assumed that Peter, Paul & Mary's "Puff the Magic Dragon" couldn't really be about a magical creature that frolics in the autumn mist in a land called Honalee, as the singers and the songwriter themselves averred, but is a drug allegory suitable for a sing-along. These instances, and countless others in the pop canon, attest to the fact that one can think hard about pop music without thinking smart. They prove that there's a difference between looking closely at the way a lyric is constructed, considering what accounts for its emotional appeal, and using song lyrics as an occasion to prove how clever one is, or to see some secret symbol.

The approach to reading espoused here differs fundamentally from hagiographic attention to the "hidden meanings" in songs; the act of "decoding" toward a pure text; the smart-aleck certitude maintained by many who parse lyrics. Rather, it is invested in cultivating a less conjectural reading practice, one that is descriptive rather than prescriptive, that responds to what songwriters and singers, and the host of others responsible for turning a song into a recording, have actually done rather than to what they may have been thinking or feeling while doing it. This analytical practice looks to the evidence of the reader's own eyes and ears rather than relying on supposition.

The act of analysis often requires temporarily isolating interrelated elements from one another to understand better the workings of the aesthetic whole. Is looking at the lyrics to Joni Mitchell's "Big Yellow Taxi" the same as hearing the song? Of course not. Is it as full an aesthetic experience? Not by half. But do we stand to gain a clearer understanding of her art, art in general, and our own aesthetic and emotional responses by looking at the lyrics alone? I argue that we do.

Analysis also requires moving from that temporary isolation to synthesis. Pop songs are always created and experienced in relation; they extend and complicate multiple traditions, quote scraps of lyric and sound from other songs and other places, and engage the culture in the broadest possible sense. "Like the novel, rock & roll operates by means of heteroglossia, the free and democratic mixing of a wide variety of voices, and that openness to other traditions, genres, sounds, worlds, is both what's best and what's most challenging about the rock & roll that matters," the literary critic Kevin Dettmar observes. Pop music—call it rock and roll, or hip hop, or any old thing you choose—demands critical attention that can toggle between the particular and the relational.

When it comes to reading song lyrics, the first question to ask is *why* you are reading lyrics in the first place. What do you hope to find? I suggest the following: Read for patterns and breaks in patterns of language, for a taxonomy of form. Read for the struggle between poetry and song, the verbal and the musical in antagonistic cooperation. Read for the transformative exercise of performance on that which is composed as it expresses itself in the voice and in the emotion of a given recording. Read for the stories that songs often tell.

The next question concerns *how* to read lyrics. One may, for instance, read a song lyric as one reads a page-based poem these days—in complete silence with a sense of duty and mild foreboding. Few song lyrics stand up to that particular brand of attention. Instead, try reading song lyrics aloud. What kind of music do the words themselves make, irrespective of the music? The experience will be different, of course, if you know the song than if you don't. If you know the song, your mind will undoubtedly fill in the melody and performance in spite of your best efforts to tamp them down. So try reading a lyric to a song you've never heard. Do you read it quickly or slowly? What words make you stumble? What sections flow? Does the repetition seem overmuch? (It usually will.) What about the rhymes? Are they perfect or slant or absent entirely? Are they patterned in a sequence of couplets, or are they organized more idiosyncratically across the page? What mood does the lyric conjure on its own? What needs does the lyric satisfy, and what does it leave you wanting? Reading a lyric like this, aloud but apart from its performance, creates a template against which to understand the essential function of the music in completing the lyric and making the song whole. Music often serves a clarifying purpose for lyric, on the levels of meaning and of emotion, just as the lyric often does for the song.

Reading song lyrics aloud is almost never the same as reading poems aloud. A poem, as acknowledged above, brings its own music, while a song lyric knows that much of its music comes from somewhere else. The lyricist Noël Coward explains it this way: "Unless the reader happens to know the tune to which the lyric has been set, his eye is liable to be bewildered by what appears to be a complete departure from the written rhythm to which his ear has subconsciously become accustomed. . . . In many instances, the words and rhythms he reads, divorced from the melody line that holds them together, may appear to be suddenly erratic, inept or even nonsensical." Coward overlooks the fact that it is precisely in such departures that a lyric announces its craft. A great lyric will hint at its music; we should have a feel for the music's presence even though we can't hear it. So when reading a lyric aloud, note the moments when the lyrics seem to miss the melody for guidance, where they seem most lacking, or where they build their own energy. Returning to the song in performance, you'll find occasions for surprise, particularly if you were previously unfamiliar with the song.

Another way of reading lyrics is to try performing them. I'm no singer, but while I've been writing this book I'm sure that passersby have heard my voice coming from behind my office door as I struggled to reach that high note at the beginning of Al Green's "Love and Happiness." You need not be a great singer to practice this method; it's all in the name of analysis. As with reading silently, there's a substantial difference in practicing this kind of reading with a tune you know and with one that you don't. When you know the song, you are already acquainted with what the singer must do to translate the words to performance. When you don't, you are left to intuit as best you can, given the scant clues imbedded in the language, what the song might sound like. Can words themselves suggest their proper melody? Perhaps not. But they can certainly conjure music, if only through their rhythm and the collision of sounds.

Finally, the most powerful method of all, and the one to which these other methods naturally lead, is reading a lyric while listening to the recorded song. Doing so stages an encounter between two common ways of taking in art—through the eye and through the ear—that results in generative moments of tension and resolution. Things fall into place, and things that seem familiar and natural in one context suddenly become revealing and strange.

One could conceive of other analytic practices, such as listening to a song without the transcribed lyric but with a conscious focus on language, or reading a lyric after having recently heard the recording. A method that I found surprisingly helpful during the composition of this book was analyzing a performance entirely from recollection. Recapitulating a remembered performance of a song from silence opens up a new way of perceiving the interrelations of words and sounds. I'd often wake up with a song running through my head, conjured by my subconscious, which my conscious mind then had to puzzle over to discover why the song had come to me.

Each method has its inherent virtues and limitations. Toggling among perceptual positions helps one to appreciate that the song extends from the sheet music to the lyrics to the recordings. Amoebic in its shape, the pop song can easily shift from poem to performance, from lyric to music, to the territory in between. All this variety begs the question: Where does the song actually exist?

I borrow this question from the poet Stephen Dobyns's query of poetry. Does the song exist "in the air" as sound and performance, on the page as text (as sheet music, musical notation, or lyric), or in the mind, "nonexistent until it is perceived"? What is the primary aesthetic object under consideration when it comes to a song? The lyrics? The sheet music? A specific recording? Or is a song reinvented with each successive performance? Answers to these questions condition how to approach the process of analysis.

In this book, I take as the primary aesthetic object the particular recording to which I refer, understanding that the conclusions one can draw about a song will differ depending on the iteration of the song, lyric, or recording. At times, however, my attention turns to the song itself—to the process of composition and to the lyric artifact, what might be termed the "script" for the song's arrangement, performance, and recording. In other words, attention shifts between the product of particular performers (the recorded track) and the aesthetic object of songwriters (the song itself, as lyric and music).

Pop music is often the product of creative people with little or no formal musical training. Traditionally, songs are written before the recording process begins, but this is not always the case. Sometimes in pop music the studio becomes the site of creation. When the post-punk band Joy Division was first taking shape in the mid-1970s they were driven largely by intuition. "Back then we didn't know rules or theory. We had our ear, [lead singer] Ian [Curtis], who listened and picked out the melodies," recalls the band's bassist, Peter Hook. "He always had his scraps of paper that he'd written things down on and he'd go through his plastic bag. 'Oh, I've got something that might suit that.' And the next thing you knew he'd be standing there with a piece of paper in one hand, wrapped around the microphone stand, with his head down, making the melodies work. We'd never hear what he was singing about in rehearsal because the equipment was so shit. In his case it didn't matter because he delivered the vocal with such a huge amount of passion and aggression, like he really fucking meant it. It was great. Who cared what he was saying as long as he said it like that." "Saying it like that" is the way a pop *recording* can sometimes save a pop *song*, the way a band's feeling, conviction, and creative impulses can overcome almost anything, even the song itself.

The language that most band members speak to one another when it comes to making a recording is not primarily one of technical musicianship, but mostly of emotion and feel. "As a singer and a writer—or cowriter—I find that it's often my responsibility to say, 'Look, this song is very aggressive.' Or, 'This is a touching sequence that *becomes* aggressive,' or whatever. They don't want to know what the words are but they want to know what the mood is," Mick Jagger says in explaining the importance of feeling over lyrics during recording sessions with the Rolling Stones. Or, as Elvis Costello quipped: "You don't really need musical notation for rock and roll. I always said it was all hand signals and threats."

Songs never settle into fixed forms; they remain in a state of perpetual evolution and reinterpretation with far greater range than most any other art. Analyzing the Rolling Stones' "Wild Horses," originally from 1971's *Sticky Fingers*, one might hear different qualities in the song if one were working from their live version on 1995's *Stripped*, or one of the numerous concert versions available on YouTube, or Alicia Keys and Adam Levine's 2005 live cover version. Yes, songs come to states of rest with definitive recordings that fix particular performances in the imagination. But even these signature renditions always leave open the possibility of their reinscription in another voice for another time.

Song lyrics' most enduring place might not be in performance at all, but in composition. "Song lyrics exist independently of their performance in the practice of songwriters," observe the songwriter Peter Astor and the musicologist Keith Negus in a joint essay. "Songs can no more be reduced to their performance than to their lyrics, a recording or sheet music. Song lyrics live and endure between and beyond all these interpretations, transcriptions and renditions." Song lyrics are mutable things, coalescing into fixed forms only to shift shape and reappear as something different, though somehow also the same. This asks much of us as readers; it promises much in return.

In isolating a lyric, one temporarily relinquishes the experience of a recorded song in full so as better to comprehend and appreciate the many ways that language dances with music. "A record is, above all, a richly textured surface, which we apprehend only as a sensory, temporal, and complete experience," the musicologist Albin Zak writes. "All of its parts must be present in order to grasp it. As soon as we section off some part of it—the lyrics, the chord changes—we are no longer dealing with the record." For the times throughout the book when we shall not be dealing with the record, it will always be in the spirit of returning to that record with a keener ear and a finer attunement to the richness of the recording in full.

I should take a moment here to clarify some terminology. When I refer to "song" I mean the musical composition in full as rendered in sheet music or a lead sheet, inclusive of lyric and music; when I refer to "lyric," I mean the words alone. When I refer to "recording," I mean a specific version of a given song as produced and distributed for commercial consumption. When I refer to "performance" I mean a live concert that I attended; "live" performances released as recordings are recordings, subject to many of the same processes that produce studio recordings. As the musicologist Theodore Gracyk reminds us, names matter because they help us be sure that we are talking about the same things.

I take as my primary text the song lyric, the studio recording, and perhaps other recordings of the song as well. Most of the book's listening attention will be directed at studio recordings of songs rather than live recordings or songs that I personally heard live in concert. The reasons for this are many, most significantly because the studio recording is usually— though certainly not always—the most authoritative version, and because it is the one most readily available to any reader. The focus on the studio recording should not, however, dissuade one from applying the principles of pop poetics to the vast range of recordings and live performances you might experience.

I direct secondary attention to the melody (inasmuch as it gives shape to and sometimes finds itself in tension with the lyric) and the sheet music (inasmuch as looking at how the song is rendered on the page in words and musical notation reveals something about the language of the lyric). In studying a song lyric like "Killing Me Softly with His Song," one might consider the Grammy-winning Roberta Flack recording from 1973, Lauryn Hill and the Fugees' cover from 1996, and Lori Lieberman's 1972 original, as a means of illuminating the form, feeling, and meaning of the song.

A web search for "Killing Me Softly lyric" yields over 25,000 entries. Among those are dozens of different presentations of everything from the song's words to the way the lyrics are broken into lines. Even published versions of lyrics in liner notes, sheet music, and books provide no consensus. Deciding which version to use becomes imperative once we begin applying the tools of poetic analysis to our chosen song lyric. Literary poetry is a graphic medium in which lineation, typesetting, and even typeface have traditionally played important roles in the design of the aesthetic object. They provide explicit and implicit instructions for reading. The same holds for analyzing a song lyric.

What makes song lyric transcription so difficult, of course, is song's dual identity as language and as sound. Words in song are bound both by the conventions of language, which make them easy to transcribe, and by the conventions of sound, which make them nearly impossible to transcribe with elegance and specificity. "Writing about things heard is particularly difficult because so much of the inner life of sound dwells below conscious thought," writes Seth Horowitz, a neuroscientist who studies human hearing. "At first thought, it seems easy—many of the sounds we pay attention to in daily life are words. You can transcribe conversations or lyrics into written form in a straightforward fashion because words are bound by the conventions of language. But go a bit below the basics of the written and spoken word and you find that the rules of written language only give you a piece of the richness found even in plain speech of a nontonal language such as English."

The dual identity of song lyrics not only renders the practice of transcription fraught with challenge, it also leaves even the most assiduous text a mere approximation of the lyric as it lives in sound. This limitation is most exposed in moments when the music and the singing voice move language beyond conventional expression. Transcribing Stevie Wonder's "Don't You Worry 'Bout a Thing," you might reasonably write out the first and second chorus in the same way. After all, they use the same words. Lost in such a transcription, though, is that on his second time through Wonder stretches the word "out" into a seven-second melodic run (from 1:39 to 1:46), a beautiful embellishment that defies all attempts to set it down on the page.

Though the perfect lyric transcription is unattainable, this does not mean that transcriptions aren't worth doing, and doing well. Even the best transcriptions are functional documents, meant to be used to explore the song from new angles, not as an end in themselves. Before one can attend to the practice of close reading and listening, it is essential to have a reliable transcription on which to work. This will allow us to make observations about the poetic functions of the lines (the relation of rhymes, for instance, or the balance of syllables and stress) as well as the musical functions (the structure of the musical sections as they map on to the lyrics).

The goal is to respect the integrity of the poetic line while underscoring its identity as language imbedded in musical performance. Doing so means discerning the relation of the lyric line to the musical measure. "Lyrics are written according to the phrasings of music; they are not written in stanzas, but (usually) in eight-bar units," observes the songwriter Gene Lees in his indispensable *Modern Rhyming Dictionary*. "Within a given eight-bar unit," he continues, "the melody may call for four, five, six, or more lines of lyric." In singing, the melody dictates the proportion of lyric lines to musical bars. The number of notes in the melody will dictate the number of lines in the lyric; these will often be marked by a pattern of end rhyme. In most Tin Pan Alley compositions, for instance, an eight-bar musical section will take four lines of lyric. Hoagy Carmichael's 1927 classic, "Stardust," illustrates this:

> Sometimes I wonder why I spend
> The lonely nights dreaming of a song
> The melody haunts my reverie
> And I am once again with you

Much contemporary lyric adheres to this pattern of four lyric lines per eight musical bars, though one also finds five lyric lines and more. Rap traditionally calls for eight full lines of lyric to correspond to eight musical bars, with sixteen-bar/sixteen-lyric-line sections as the standard unit of measure. This longer line is necessary because rap more closely approximates speaking than singing.

A transcribed song lyric, of course, presents certain obvious differences from a page-born poem. The first is the authority of the written text. Can we trust that the words we see are the ones the writer intended, presented in the right order on the page? Poets usually oversee the way their words appear in print. By contrast, songwriters rarely vet published lyrics, be they the transcriptions that commonly appear in the inner sleeve of LPs and CDs or the countless lyrics now available online. Transcriptions of song lyrics vary wildly in the texts they present; readers cannot presume that the lyrics approximate the way the songwriters would want their words seen.

There is no stable state for printed lyrics; either they portray a written record of their compositional process, as in the case of Dylan's handwritten draft of "Like a Rolling Stone," which sold at auction for over $2 million back in 2014; or they capture a listener's—or, in the case of online lyrics, a crowd-sourced community's—transcriptions of utterance. Only rarely will songwriters prepare lyrics for publication as text alone, and even in those rare instances when they do—as part of a poetry collection, for instance, or interspersed throughout a memoir—one finds a shocking lack of care and consistency. In the era of the LP, many artists, including the Beatles, incorporated printed lyrics to their songs on the album liner. More recent decades have witnessed the proliferation of books that collect song lyrics as poems, often with the artist's putative involvement. Surprisingly, neither liner-note lyrics nor lyrics-as-poetry books follow consistent practices when it comes to matters like line breaks or section structure. Most read as if they were prepared by underpaid interns at the record label or the book publisher, which in fact might often be the case.

Music fans write out lyrics in various idiosyncratic ways. For those of us who wish to explore a lyric's construction with greater care, however, another kind of transcription is required, one that stands up to the rigors of close reading and close listening combined. For a lyric to be usefully analyzed on the page, a few conditions must be met.

First, make sure the transcription underscores rather than obscures the structural organization of the song. It should clearly demarcate the moving parts of verses, choruses, bridges, and any other features that songwriters construct when composing a song. Without structural clarity, the patterning and repetition that comprise the defining qualities of a lyric's formal shape are hidden. Most websites, for instance, will transcribe the chorus only the first time through, thereafter simply writing "Chorus," even in instances of small but significant differences of language. In his illuminating account of the songwriter's craft, *Tunesmith*, the prolific songwriter Jimmy Webb describes how he and many other songwriters he knows will actually use tracing paper to ensure that the formal structure of rhyme, line length, and rhythm pattern are consistent across the verses in a song. This kind of attention is quietly at work in many songs, without listeners' knowledge. There's a value in attending to it, both to extol the songwriting craft and to come to terms with the formal puzzle each lyric presents.

Second, ensure that the transcription expresses a clear and consistent relation between the rhythmic structure of the music and the rhythmic structure of the lyric as rendered in the lyric line. For a lyric transcription to have integrity it must clarify and codify the relationship between the length of a lyric line and the span of a musical bar. A reader must be able to look at a lyric and know that each line represents the same period of musical time. This will allow a reader to experience the songwriter's lyric play and dilation of time when one line is significantly longer or shorter than others, or the constancy that results when the lines are essentially the same length.

A brief example may be helpful here. Consider the children's nursery rhyme "Twinkle, Twinkle, Little Star," which is based on Mozart's musical scoring of the French nursery rhyme "Ah! Vous Dirai-Je, Maman," first published in 1761. Two other well-known lyrics in English have been set to this tune, "The Alphabet Song" and "Baa, Baa, Black Sheep." In the transcriptions below, I've followed the same practice with all of the lyrics, where the four lines represent eight musical measures. I've written the number of syllables per line along the side to demonstrate how each lyric dilates its language to fit the same musical space:

Ah! Vous dirai-je maman	7
Ce qui cause mon tourment?	7
Papa veut que je raisonne	8
Comme une grande personne	8
Twinkle, twinkle, little star	7
How I wonder what you are	7
Up above the world so high	7
Like a diamond in the sky	7
A, B, C, D, E, F, G	7
H, I, J, K, L, M, N, O, P	9
Q, R, S, T, U, V	6
W, X, Y and Z	7
Baa, Baa, black sheep, have you any wool?	9
Yes, sir. Yes, sir. Three bags full	7
One for my master and one for my dame	10
And one for the little boy who lives down the lane	12

Moving from "Ah! Vous Dirai-Je, Maman" to "Baa, Baa, Black Sheep," we notice a striking expansion of syllable count. Seven seems to be the ideal number of syllables each line will naturally take (both in French and in

English). "Twinkle, Twinkle, Little Star" fits that form exactly, both in the section I've transcribed and in most of the lines of verse that follow. The melody remains; however, each lyric demands a different number of syllables in the same space of musical time. The shortest line, "Q, R, S, T, U, V," fills the same space as the longest, "And one for the little boy who lives down the lane," because the former includes a medial caesura (an internal pause at the middle of the line that looks like this: "Q, R, S // T, U, V") and the latter accelerates the pace of the singing to fit in the added syllables before the end of the measure. This is only a simple illustration of something that is going on in every song we hear.

Most songwriters carefully calibrate their rhythmic durations per line, down to the syllable; a reader should be aware of this patterning in the same way that a listener is implicitly aware of the push and pull of the lyric as performed in relation to the beat. Additionally, the concordance of line length and musical time will reveal important details about rhyme patterning. A poor transcription will obscure the play of internal rhyme, particularly if a transcriber assumes that the line must always break whenever a rhyme crops up.

Third, endeavor to make the transcription as faithful as possible to the particular language of the lyric as performed. This is an obvious point that often proves challenging, due to either the inattentiveness of the transcriber or the unintelligibility of the recording. Pop recordings run the gamut from careful articulation of language to conscious obscuring of the voice. Sometimes, too, the absence of clear enunciation is a key element of the performer's style. Elton John, for instance, cultivates a stylized slur on much of his *Goodbye Yellow Brick Road* LP. "Saturday Night" and "Bennie and the Jets" both draw much of their appeal from the messiness and the implicit emotional urgency of expression that such slurring communicates. The lack of certainty about particular words does nothing to diminish the impact of these songs. On the contrary, it builds mystery and empowers the listener to fill in the gaps of comprehension that remain. Of course, one should work to get every word right in a transcription, but the first two conditions for transcription are more important when it comes to the work of analyzing and appreciating the lyric craft.

Finally, no matter how successful the transcription is at achieving the above aims, it should always be understood as a provisional document. Lyrics by themselves are rarely the aesthetic end of a song. Even in the case of

Beck's *Song Reader,* a set of sheet music he released in 2012 as an invita-
tion to other artists to record their own versions of his songs, Beck conceived
of the written document as a means to a future end. Transcriptions of song
lyrics are purpose-driven documents; certainly, they may bring aesthetic
pleasure on their own, and they may even communicate ideas and feelings
in ways different from the song as performed, but they achieve their true
value in providing engaged listeners with another point of entry into the re-
corded song. A faithful transcription is a celebration of the songwriting
craft, as well as a working document that a listener, now a reader, may use
to gain a greater understanding of the poetic and musical structures at work
in a recording.

Analyzing the poetics of a song on the page naturally privileges a certain
kind of lyric and a certain kind of listening. It showcases keenly crafted lines
of patterned rhythms, rhymes, or the two combined. It engages the eye for
analysis while forestalling temporarily the ear for emotion. This is why read-
ing lyrics is never an end in itself, but always part of a process of defamil-
iarization and refamilarization with the song in full. Appreciation for all
songs will benefit from the process of looking at their lyrics on the page,
though some songs will benefit more than others. The Beatles' "Revolution"
and "Revolution #9" are both fascinating, but there's simply more to say
about the poetics of the former than those of the latter.

Yes, poetic analysis favors certain kinds of lyrics over others. So does lis-
tening to music in a state of distraction, or of rapt attention, or inebriation
or celebration or jubilation or perambulation or any combination of these
states. Whether we know it or not, all of us already subject the songs we hear
to all kinds of filters: analysis and emotion and attention and so on. This
battery of de facto experiments in musical cognition is every bit as denatur-
ing as looking at lyrics on the page, with and without the benefit of the music.
Through it all, the song survives. Songs are made of sturdy stuff.

So, when reading the poetry of pop, the beauty of certain songs will inten-
sify, while the beauty of other songs will diminish in the gaze of the reading
eye. The important thing is to know this and to account for both transforma-
tions as best one can in the analysis. This means realizing the limits of each
critical practice and allowing space for the mystery of things beyond our
grasp. Every analytical approach has blind spots, and certain songs will
prove inscrutable to the methods described here. For instance, poetic analy-
sis might not account for what is most appealing about a rap freestyle, in

which extemporization undercuts the kinds of formal patterning that poetic analysis rewards. The same might be true for songs, and there are many of them, where the beauty of the sound exceeds sense and structure.

Accepting these limitations, the poetic analysis of song lyrics is a marvelously adaptable method, capable of capturing and communicating to others some of what is so moving and remarkable about the songs that stay with us, and those that pass us by. Poetic analysis reveals the inner workings of a lyric as simple as "I Want to Hold Your Hand," and one as textured as "A Day in the Life." Poetics is sensitive to sound and to sense, as well as to the many places in between.

A great deal of the fun in reading the poetry of pop is in the way that it can reveal brilliance and conscious craft in places where they might not be apparent in the listening alone. Pop tends to wear its poetics lightly, with raffish disregard that belies the careful tailoring that goes into its construction. Many pop songs are better poems than they need to be to satisfy their listeners and to do the job that their music demands. So much of the pleasure of analysis, then, comes in the surprise of finding just how much is going on—not beneath the surface of the lyric, but on the surface itself.

The surfaces of songs take shifting shapes. Just look at the t-shirts you may have seen people wearing over the years, bearing lists of common song structures. As these t-shirts attest, pop songs are modular, composed of formal units that can be assembled and reassembled to fashion innumerable patterns of repetition and difference. The terminology and notation used to name the parts have shifted over time, though the constitutive elements of a pop song have remained essentially the same for a century: the sing-along familiarity of the chorus, the narrative drive of the verse, and the digressive energy of the bridge.

Choruses are usually fixed, repeated with little or no change twice or more during the song. They tend to be short, six or eight bars in duration. They often contain the song's primary hook, the most memorable or "sticky" section of melody and lyric. Verses, by contrast, are the domain of difference. They are longer than choruses, often stretching to twelve, sixteen, or many more bars in duration. They are the primary space for narrative in pop songs, where singers and songwriters mark development from the chorus's point of relative stasis. Finally, bridges furnish the unexpected; usually played only once, the bridge marks a sonic, lyric, and emotive shift from the song's established pattern. "From Stevie Wonder to Steely Dan," Pharrell Williams told students at NYU, "bridges are everything."

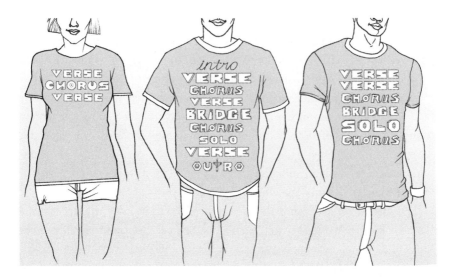

"We all wrote to the same formula in the beginning," recalls the singer Paul Anka of his late 1950s–early 1960s apprenticeship in the Brill Building, hallowed shorthand moniker for the hundreds of music publishers and songwriters who occupied space in and around the Brill Building's 1619 Broadway and 49th Street address in Manhattan. "The structure of the music was also simpler, it was just the classic AABA format," continues Anka. "A" stood for the verse, and "B" stood for the bridge, which was intended as a compelling sonic and lyric departure from the pattern the verses established. One might also find a refrain, or repeated tagline, imbedded in the verse, which would satisfy the sing-along function now common to the chorus. The Shirelles' 1960 hit "Will You Still Love Me Tomorrow," written by Brill Building luminaries Carole King and Jerry Goffin, is an elegant example of the simple beauty of the AABA form. The two verses that open the song establish a pattern of expectation in the listener that the bridge subtly subverts, only to close with a final verse that reestablishes the pattern and offers resolution.

Most pop songs, however, follow patterns with more moving parts than the AABA form. The most common of these is probably the ABABCB form, where "A" is the verse, "B" is the chorus, and "C" is the bridge. The overall principle is the same as it is with the AABA pattern: establish expectation (with a verse alone in the shorter form, or the verse followed by a chorus in the longer), disrupt that expectation (in both cases, with a bridge), and arrive at resolution (either with a concluding verse or with a chorus).

A fine example of this form is "Nothing Compares 2 U," a Prince song that Sinéad O'Connor took to the top of the global charts in 1990. Prince employs the ABABCB structure to capture the emotional stages of heartache, putting the constitutive formal parts to their optimal uses. The two verses narrate the singer's mournful state. Verse one commences in striking fashion: "It's been seven hours and thirteen days / Since you took your love away." The inversion of temporal order combined with its exacting specificity speaks to the lived experience of love lost. The remainder of the verse celebrates the freedoms of being unencumbered by a relationship, rejecting each of them in favor of the blues-drenched sadness of loss.

The second verse extends the narrative of the first, rejecting the consolation of some other romance and even a doctor's prescription to go have some fun. Following each verse is a simple, powerful chorus that gradually unfurls the words of the title. The halting repetition of the title phrase is in tension with the soaring melodic line, just as the singer's emotional state is caught between heartache and passion. The bridge, which begins "All the flowers that you planted," is a departure both sonically and substantively from all that comes before it. The singer, now addressing her beloved, admits even in the face of having been left behind that she's willing to try it all again. When the chorus returns, it is charged and changed by this small possibility of reconciliation. O'Connor sings the lines with a heightened passion that sounds both hurt and hopeful. Take any element of the ABABCB form away from "Nothing Compares 2 U" and the song is not the same; the musical and emotional heights it reaches are unattainable.

In recent years, popular music has seen a shift in the song's center of gravity away from the verse and toward the chorus. Many pop songs today do not include a bridge at all, ceding the space in the song to a hook-driven chorus. But the story of the pop song's formal transformation isn't just one of simplification. Quite the contrary—one is more likely now than ever before to find an array of song structures that depart from established norms. At least part of this is attributable to the modes of pop production. Contemporary pop songs are more often than not the work of producers rather than songwriters alone, so fixed lyric forms are often supplanted by ornate patterns that reflect the exigencies of sound recording rather than the dictates of written composition. A producer moves a few bars here, then copies them and moves them there as well, and now the song has a pre-chorus. An artist needs a big radio hit, so the producer ensures that the chorus repeats a half dozen times instead of only three.

Even songs that seem formulaic often reveal unexpected complexity hiding on the surface of the sound. Beyoncé's "Single Ladies (Put a Ring On It)" appears straightforward enough; it follows the same ABABCB form as "Nothing Compares 2 U" and thousands of other pop songs. The verses are still narrative ("Up in the club, just broke up," the first verse begins), the chorus is certainly catchy ("'Cause if you like it then you should have put a ring on it" became a cultural catchphrase), and the bridge offers a striking key change and a lyric assertion of self in the face of her lover's lack of attentiveness. "Once I got the bridge, I thought the song could become iconic," the song's lead writer and producer, The-Dream, told Genius.com. "Without the bridge, it would just be this melodic hip-hop record. I believe that's why it got Song of the Year."

"Single Ladies" is, in many ways, the perfect pop song. Transcribing the lyrics, one finds a downright Byzantine architecture comprised of small repeated units and surprising departures from established pattern. The song is fitted with parts that must be given names other than "verse," "chorus," or "bridge." There's the "All the single ladies" phrase that repeats numerous times at the beginning of the song that I suppose you could call an "Intro," as Genius.com does, except for the fact that it repeats again near the song's end. Then there's the "Wuh uh oh uh uh oh oh uh oh uh uh oh" section that comes after the first chorus, a prominent part of the recording that the Genius transcription excludes. Call it a post-chorus, or a pre-chorus to the chorus that follows it? "Single Ladies" is the work of two preeminent pop producers, The-Dream and Tricky Stewart, which might help account for the fact that the form reflects the shifting sonic textures of production more than it does a logic of lyric.

Though traditionalists might wish to write the story of pop music as one of decline—the only variance being the high-water mark to which the critic clings, be it Tin Pan Alley or Brill Building or 1960s and 1970s rock troubadours or something else—the nature of song structure tells a different story. One finds today, in fact, a profusion of forms with more elements of lyric and sound, more variations, more ways of fitting parts to a whole. This doesn't mean better songs than in the past. What it does mean, though, is that pop music constantly challenges us to hear it and to read it in new ways.

Chapter
Three

isten to this: Guns N' Roses' "Paradise City" begins with a chorus, clear and anthemic. "Take me down to the Paradise City/Where the grass is green and the girls are pretty." Axl Rose's vocal cadence, layered with harmonies, follows the natural rhythmic contours of the lyric language. We hear each word and we know how it relates in the sentence to the words around it.

By contrast, the first verse opens something like this: "Suta urcha nana nun on the street, um ahh." It is a sonic and rhythmic event, not a clearly discernible semantic one. Rose's singing erodes the boundaries between individual words, loosing syllables from one another and inviting them to forge new unities in sound. The lyrics actually read "Just an urchin living under the street, I'm a . . ." Listening back to the recorded song with Rose's real words in mind, the opening line snaps into focus. We now know where one word ends and the next begins.

But are we any better for the knowledge? Not necessarily. The same edge and urgency come across in Rose's singing and in the music whether we can decipher the language of the lyrics or not. Why, then, study lyrics at all? Because many songs call attention to specific meanings in ways that "Paradise City" does not. And because many of the tools of poetics work just as well on "Suta urcha" as they do on "Just an urchin."

The poetry of pop concerns both language and performance, both the semantic and the sensory. Part of the pleasure stems from listening closely to the recorded song and applying analytical tools to that experience in sound. This act of analysis considers language as it lives in the air, evading efforts to capture it in print. Part of the pleasure, as well, derives from attending to the lyrics on the page—as a script for performance, and as relations visible only in the provisional space of print. Though the latter kind of critical attention is more commonly associated with poetics, the former is equally the domain of poetic analysis.

Listening to pop songs with a critical ear begins by attending to language, sound, and style as they imprint themselves on feeling. Deep listening is only possible once we invite emotions into our analysis. When listening, imagine your whole body as a seismograph of sorts, except instead of registering the earth's vibrations, you're capturing your own sympathetic engagements with sound. What does the song make you feel, and precisely when does it make you feel it? Can you account for specific qualities of the recording that inspire those feelings?

"Music has the power to stop time," observes Ahmir "Questlove" Thompson, the drummer and musical director of the Roots. "When I listen to songs, I'm transported back to the moment of their birth, which is sometimes even before the moment of my birth. Old songs, rock or soul or blues, still connect with me because the human emotions in them, whether jealousy or rage or hope, are recognizably similar to the emotions that I'm feeling now. But I'm feeling all of them, all the time, and so the songs act like a chemical process that isolates certain feelings at certain times: maybe one song helps illuminate the jubilation and one helps illuminate the sorrow and one helps illuminate the resignation."

This kind of close listening is a process of emotional reciprocity, of recognizing shared impulses and feelings of others through the language of song. Most all of us listen to music, at least at times, in the way that Questlove describes, temporarily ceding our emotional compass to the inexorable pull of someone else's sound. The only difference between this kind of listening and the deep listening I propose is that the pleasure or pain the song inspires in you is the beginning rather than the end of analysis. Close listening almost always moves from an apprehension of feeling to an apprehension of form.

Most of us are far more comfortable listening to a song than reading a novel or a poem; we're better practiced at it, and our critical guard is down because most of us understand listening to songs as play rather than work. In addition, the cultural barriers put in place over the years to bar entry to, or at least to exact a toll of attention from, those engaged in literary conversations have never been successfully replicated in discussions of popular music.

To paraphrase the folk historian Bruce Jackson, pop-music audiences are no different from literary audiences; they're just less pretentious about what they do. Though Jackson was writing about folk poetry, his distinction holds for pop music as well. Unlike literary audiences, folk audiences and pop-music audiences "do not pretend their decisions are based on high and immutable aesthetic values; they do not pretend they have no gut reactions to things; they do not pretend to like things which make no sense to them. In a way they are the harshest of audiences, for they are intolerant of what bores them and tend to discard boring things quickly and to reject boring performers immediately."

Like folk poetry, the poetry of pop exhibits an aesthetics of immediacy. More often than not, pop songs do not require their audience to pull back the integuments of meaning, like unfurling the buds of an artichoke to reach its heart, in the way that page-based poetry often demands. Instead, pop recordings luxuriate in surface effects that include everything from rhythm to rhyme to rhetorical figures and forms. In other words, they call upon tools used by students of literature, augmented by an intuitive or trained ear for music.

Though pop songs sometimes carry complex meanings, those meanings are rarely hidden insights into the human condition. A great deal of the language is prefabricated; a great measure of the emotion is canned. Lyrics come to aesthetic life in action: in performance, and in the way that the music animates listeners' lives. The meanings of pop lyrics are contextual and active; they live on the surface of the language, in the minds of the people who listen, and in the spaces in between. "I have often found careful listening to be repaid with delight even when the song and the performances are not to my taste," remarks the musicologist Albin Zak. "I also find that the harder I listen, the more I am aware of how much there is to hear and how much the record artfully withholds from me." This artful withholding is a call to deeper listening—not for hidden meanings, but for those qualities that reside, evanescent, ephemeral, on the surface of the sound.

The *Oxford English Dictionary* defines "ephemeral" as "in existence, power, favour, popularity, etc. for a short time only; short-lived; transitory." Pop music is ephemeral, not primarily in the sense that it is something that soon passes out of notice, but in the sense that it is meant to entertain us *right now*. All but the most ponderous pop songs appeal in some way on first listen. Though returning to them can clarify and intensify their meaning, pop songs generally expose their splendors from the start. Of course, the entertainment pop music provides also supports a multibillion-dollar industry. The fact that pop songs are engines of commerce, however, does not negate the fact that their primary function must always be to entertain; if they fail at that, then nothing else follows. To understand the source of pop songs' entertainment, it's best to look to the surface. What one is likely to find there is not just ease of articulation but also a certain obstruction. Both define the poetry of pop.

Poets often seek a way to provide just enough obstruction and just enough direction to guide readers through their work. The pleasure to be found in a great many poems is, after all, in the labor of them, more so than in their outward effects of sound or the dance of their lines on the page. So much about poetry can be explained by this simple insight: Poems are the product of the poet's necessary labor, which in turn creates necessary labor for the reader. We see it in the derangement of syntax, in the fashioning of image, in the disruptions and misdirections brought on by line and enjambment, in the artifice of poetic diction. All of these qualities and more stand between the reader and pure—if there can be such a thing—meaning. What distinguishes most poetry from everyday speech is the ritual that the former demands of its reader. Be it through incantatory rhythm, patterns of repetition (from alliteration to assonance to rhyme), shifts in voice, games with structure, or any number of other techniques, poets endeavor to control the pace of cognition so as to create pockets of epiphany.

Songwriters referred to as poets achieve this distinction in large part because their lyrics satisfy common preconceptions of the poetic, the most important of which is this idea of obstruction. We need to puzzle over Jim Morrison's lyrics to the Doors' twelve-minute opus "The End," so therefore it must be poetry. The central image in Bob Dylan's "Tangled Up in Blue" is so charged, the temporality so strange, that it must be poetry. However, this approach creates inherent bias against certain genres of music—namely, dance- and rhythm-driven music, which is to say the vast majority of African American and Latin American music—that often achieve their complexity through the alchemy of sound and language. Accepting a broader definition of "poetry" or "poetic" means including aesthetics that privilege qualities other than semantic difficulty. Such inclusion broadens and deepens pop's poetic heritage and directs attention to the qualities that predominate in genres beyond the folk/rock singer-songwriter of the 1960s and 1970s. What is the poetics of an artist like Johnny Cash? Or a group like the Ramones? What is the poetic aesthetic of Michael Jackson or Madonna? Of Nicki Minaj or the Weeknd? Answering these questions leads to a rich and varied appreciation of what words can do in the minds and in the mouths of pop singers.

Popular songs don't always offer much cognitive obstruction on the level of the lyric, although they often generate other kinds of obstructions on the musical and performance levels that end up impacting the lyric. When the Beatles sing "I want to hold your hand," the words themselves demand no deep thinking. That said, it would be a mistake to dismiss them without reflection. In performance, that simple statement conveys longing. For scores of young fans, it permitted a safe and attainable desire. The counterpoint of harmony underscores the union promised by the speech act.

Much of the mismeasure of pop music is a consequence of misplaced interpretive frameworks. A listener critiquing a Rick Ross club banger for its absence of lyric nuance is missing both the point of the song and the point of serious criticism. Of course, one is certainly within his or her rights to find such a song unappealing or objectionable. However, it's left to those listeners with knowledge of the song's genres and conventions to speak with nuance about the value and quality of the performance. This isn't to establish an aesthetic hierarchy; music, and popular music in particular, is defiantly democratic, even against oligarchical business interests that seek to control it. It is, rather, to assert the power and agency of an informed and active listener, one willing to judge a song against the terms it announces for itself.

A song announces itself most palpably in emotional terms. Poems generate emotion through direct emotive appeal, through accretion of image, and, more subtly, through the play of sound. Song lyrics often outsource much of this emotive work to the music and to how the singer's vocal inflection colors the words. Both music and singing have far more direct access to emotions than do words alone. Song lyrics still do a great deal of work, though the work is different from that done by the words of print-based poetry.

Understanding how language functions differently in song lyrics than it does in print-based poetry means grappling with the matter of emotional inflection. In song lyrics, words can be emotionally shaded in many ways: through the tone or timbre of the vocalist; through the tone or timbre of the accompanying music; through the melody, harmony and rhythm of the singing, rapping, or speaking; through the melody, harmony, and rhythm of the accompanying music; and through the qualities of sound engineering and production that result in the finished recording. These sonic effects on language are interrelated and often experienced simultaneously. As with speech, song lyrics rely on the fact that most people have the equipment to process multiple stimuli, deriving meaning and feeling from them all at once. As with instrumental music, music with words also depends on a more primal impulse to draw meaning directly from the experience of sounds.

Performances of a song charge words with meanings they might not carry in reading. Singers often endow the songs they sing with their own aesthetic perspective within the interpretive space that the song allows. Singers make meaning in a song through phrasing, holding and clipping words, or pausing and accelerating the lines; emphasizing words that neither the poetics nor the music suggests for emphasis; changing or cutting words outright; taking liberties with the melody; introducing vocal harmonies; and creating dramatic contrasts. "The best pop songs . . . are those that can be heard as a *struggle* between verbal and musical rhetoric, between the singer and the song," Simon Frith observes. Struggle can potentially express itself on several different levels as well: the struggle, for instance, of performance with poetics, or between the individual artist's sense of time and the sense of time embodied in lyric and song.

On Pearl Jam's "Even Flow" one hears the push and pull of singer with song. Eddie Vedder extenuates and accelerates syllables as he sings. Single words stretch across entire measures, and a dozen or more syllables jostle against one another in the space of a single line. This can't be rendered apparent on the page without deranging the words, like writing "Freezin'/Rests his head on a pillow made of concrete" as "Freeeeeezin'/Rests his head onapillowmadeofconcrete." Vedder's performance stages a small drama, conjuring a dynamic emotional mood. Of course, this can only be experienced fully in the listening.

Lyrics express their meaning and exert their feeling in several ways: through sound (rhythm, rhyme, and other patterns of repetition and difference), through story (the narrative voice and action that command heightened attention to detail), through the ways that individual words and phrases alight on our consciousness (opening lines, choruses, hooks, or other memorable parts of the whole), and through the ways that the sum of the words comprise ideas and elicit emotional responses through the song in full. The poet Adrian Matejka once told me that he believes the emotions in pop music are almost always predicated on language first. "Song lyrics can take a vague feeling brought on by the melody or an instrumental solo and make that vague feeling tangible for the listener," he said. "Music has a visceral power, but lyrics pinpoint feeling." Though instrumental music is a potent tool for eliciting emotion, the lyric usually carries the specificity of that emotion. Lyrics are the emotional compass pointing the listener in a direction of feeling.

Consider two songs that take on love, pop's greatest theme: Hank Williams's "I'm So Lonesome I Could Cry" and Stevie Wonder's "I Was Made to Love Her." Though their respective music situates the listener in an emotive field of melancholy and joy, respectively, the lyrics direct us more precisely to a sense of desperation in the former and of new romance in the latter. This is accomplished both through the songs' narratives and, more subtly, through their registers of diction—the patterns of words that the songwriters have selected to help foster a feeling. Williams, for instance, underscores the lyric's sadness with words like "blue," "low," "night," "crawling," "moon," "die," and "falling." Wonder captures the excitement of first love with words and phrases like "sweetheart," "hand in hand," "inspiration," "appreciation," "sweet," "blossomed," "worship," and "adore." Of course, these constellations of meanings account for only part of the life of the language. The rest lives in the tone and timbre of the words rendered through the singing voices.

One song can express divergent emotional meanings through different performances, though the words remain the same. When performed by Willie Nelson (the songwriter) and by Patsy Cline (the singer of its most definitive rendition), the lyrics to "Crazy" summon distinct emotional responses. Nelson's phrasing extenuates then attenuates the lyric line, establishing small patterns of anticipation and release. "My phrasing is peculiar to me," Nelson writes, recalling his recording of "Crazy." "I'll lay back on the beat or jump ahead. I'm always doing something funny with time because, to me, time is a flexible thing." By contrast, Cline phrases more securely in the pocket of the beat, emphasizing words that the poetics and the music also stress. Cline's rendition is measured and melancholy; Nelson's, rueful and even a bit wry. Whichever version you prefer, critical attention to language in relation to music and performance provides a vocabulary for supporting your taste and explaining it to others.

Besides being vessels for a song's emotion, lyrics also function in the act of storytelling. Music by itself carries narrative only by analogy; a song can build to a climax, can devolve, can explore alternate paths and return to its main thematic thoroughfare, but we only understand this as narrative in the associative act of metaphor. Many pop songs structure themselves as stories, with characters and climaxes and tensions familiar from narrative art forms like short stories, novels, plays, and certain kinds of poetry. Lyrics often expand to fit their stories, as in rap where the lyric line is long enough to contain complex narratives. When song lyrics function as narrative, it requires no analogic leap or critical translation to apply the tools of narrative analysis as practiced in other literary genres. Of course, these tools must be tailored and sometimes reinvented to account for the particularities of the story's expression in song, but they nonetheless retain their basic structures and critical practices.

Lyrics announce their importance to pop songs in the antagonistic cooperation between words and song, in the emotions they carry and help to clarify, and in the stories they tell. But we've yet to consider one final factor in how the poetics of pop songs function: you. How do you listen? How does the language of lyrics enter into that listening?

Some songs ask to be experienced in isolated moments, musical phrases and inflections, scraps of lyric, particular riffs and sounds. Others demand attention to the whole, a sonic flow washing over you without clear differentiation of words from other sounds. All songs invite attention both to their particulars and to their wholes, and each song usually suggests an inclination for its own analysis. It's the difference between listening to James Brown's "Funky Drummer" with its solos, breaks, and howls, and listening to Ike and Tina Turner's Phil Spector–produced "River Deep, Mountain High," with its Wall of Sound production rendering instruments and voices at times indistinguishable. Some pop lyrics achieve a state of transparency where they can be metabolized so cleanly as sound and feeling that one forgets their materiality as language. Other lyrics bear an expressive density where the substance and structure of the language and meaning demand active attention.

The song lyric and the lyric poem share a capacity to be appreciated when only partly understood, or to be understood at multiple levels by different individuals, or even to be understood by the same individual in different ways at different times. Pop songs and poems also share an implicit appeal to audience, a call to empathy and to recognition. The literary critic M. H. Abrams calls this process the "imaginative transformation of the self." In poetry, it manifests itself most plainly when we read a poem aloud and become, if only for the duration of the recitation, the "I" of the speaker. We inhabit the haunting condition of Emily Dickinson's speaker when we read these lines: "Because I could not stop for Death/He kindly stopped for me;/The carriage held but just ourselves/And Immortality." In pop music, empathetic identification makes itself most apparent when we sing along to a song. Singing the lyrics to Simon & Garfunkel's "Bridge over Troubled Water" means accepting an intimate relationship with an unnamed person in need of comfort: "When you're weary, feeling small/When tears are in your eyes/I will dry them all."

To understand what listeners expect from the language of pop songs, it is useful to begin by exploring exactly what happens to those words once they enter our consciousness. Scientists have recently posited that song lyrics are processed in the right hemisphere of the brain, in the "primitive" limbic system. The limbic system, and specifically the amygdala, records the emotive connotations of words rather than their precise denotations. When research subjects listen to song lyrics while connected to a neuroimaging scanner, the amygdala lights up. This suggests that song lyrics are experienced in the brain's domain of automatic speech and nonpropositional thinking, which houses other speech acts like counting, cursing, and conventional greetings. By contrast, propositional thinking—creating original expression by stringing together words in syntactical structures—happens in the left hemisphere of the brain.

The human brain is hardwired to attend to the language of song lyrics in a markedly different way than the way it attends to the language of everyday conversation or even to the language of literature. It is not a lesser form of attention, nor is the distinction absolute. In general terms, though, it is fair to say that when we listen to song lyrics, we are likely to comprehend the emotion and conviction (in other words, the connotations) behind the words more readily than we do the denotative meaning of the words themselves. That is why it is possible to love a song and to be able to play it back in your head, but not be able to recite all of the lyrics or even to recognize a given lyric line when it is presented out of context. Though song lyrics sometimes demand repeated attention akin to the close reading required of literary texts, they almost always reward our first listening as well.

Words in song are never just words, of course, in large part because of the dictates of the melody and the inflection given them by the singing voice. Sound has syntax. Song lyrics are memorable because of their distance and their difference from conversation. It is the difference between the statement "The ballerina danced on the beach" and Elton John singing "Ballerina, you must have seen her / Dancing in the sand." It is the difference between reading the words "Somewhere over the rainbow / Way up high" and hearing them sung to a melody that demands that the singer jump up an entire octave from the first to the second syllable in the space of that opening word: Some-*WHERE*. Words in song have the capacity to become unforgettable when the singer finds a way of extracting something from the constituent sounds of words that might otherwise remain locked up. Sometimes this happens by accentuating sounds in unexpected ways; sometimes it happens by juxtaposing certain sounds with others through rhyme or alliteration or assonance; sometimes it happens by deranging the sound entirely, rendering a familiar word strange. The very sounds of words, even when divorced from sense, communicate meaning through emotion.

Take this example. In the mid-1980s the British duo Wham! was one of the biggest groups in the world. They had a string of number-one hits before splitting up. The lead singer, George Michael, would go on to a solo career with an even longer string of number-one hits. Wham! epitomized a certain strain of 1980s pop by combining elements of soul singing with New Wave instrumentation on songs almost always about love. Perhaps the best example of this style is their 1984 million-selling, chart-topping hit "Everything She Wants." Written, produced, and sung by George Michael, it embodies his singular vision of how a pop song should sound.

"Everything She Wants" is clearly legible as a song of longing and lament even when the lyrics glide past awareness. A good deal of this has to do with the melodrama of the music and the clarity with which the music and the voice, including the lyrics, communicate a particular emotional state. It also has to do with Michael's plaintive tone, starting with the ad-libbed moan that begins the record before the lyrics come in, unleashing a flood of connotative meanings. It also has to do with the lyric moments that the song highlights, the words that seep into conscious awareness, the ones we might sing along to or that might crop up unbidden in our head. These could be the words of the song's title, for instance, or the chorus, or the interjection near the song's end when Michael blurts out, "My God! I don't even think that I love you." Together, these discrete moments build an impression of the song's meaning, its various states of being.

Pop songs encourage such gestalt listening, where the "essence or shape of an entity's complete form" is clearly understood, though the particulars may not be. This way of knowing a pop song is different from the way we generally come to know a lyric poem, where the act of reading stipulates a basic attention to individual words on the page. It's the difference between looking and seeing, hearing and listening. "This is the power of the song lyric," writes Daniel J. Levitin. "The mutually supporting forces that bind rhythm, melody, harmony, timbre, lyrics, and meaning in a song allow some of the elements to fill in for others when there is ambiguity, contradiction, or outright opacity." Any uncertainty in the particulars is made tolerable by our relation to the whole.

Gestalt listening may be the predominant way that listeners' relate to pop music, but it is certainly not the only way. At the other end of the attentional spectrum is what I call acute listening: those sparkling, singular moments of linguistic concentration that result in heightened awareness of individual words or phrases in a lyric. These specific lyric moments, be they single words, entire lines, or even larger passages, are not matters of objective fact; each listener's relation to a song is unique, and even distinct with each listening. However, if enough people's ears are drawn to the same scrap of lyric, it can start to show up in the culture as a whole. One can then begin to build a case for given instances of acute detail that are more generalizable than the predilections and particular tastes of an individual.

Listen to Pharrell Williams's Oscar-nominated pop confection "Happy" and, beyond the joyous feel of the song (the gestalt), what stands out in the minds of many listeners are these lines from the chorus (the acute): "Clap along if you feel / Like a room without a roof." These are the lines that may even last beyond the pop life of the song itself. People think they are profound or silly or clever or playful, but they *think* about them. One listener tweeted Williams to ask him what the lines meant. "Heya @Pharrell," she wrote, "why is a room without a roof happy? #lyricalriddle." Williams responded: "Hi Kate. It is metaphorical for one's space w/out limit." He might have added that the power of the line resides both in figurative language and in what that poetic figure demands of the mind: connecting an abstract concept, happiness, with a concrete if unfamiliar image, a room without a roof. For Williams, that connection embodies the idea of limitlessness, but the interpretive range of the simile is broad enough to allow other readings as well, such as the act of opening up something that is traditionally closed, or letting fresh air into a previously confined space, or the freedom one feels in letting the sun or the rain touch the skin.

Pharrell's "room without a roof" simile's effectiveness and its wide appeal rest in the fact that the meaning is not singular. Though its cognitive complexity might not rise to the level of a riddle, it nonetheless causes one to puzzle, if fleetingly, for a way of connecting the parts. In a song that is not primarily grounded in its lyrics, this object of acute listening attention generates a small moment of startling imagistic beauty. The song concentrates its themes of defining and owning happiness in this single simile. It isn't that one doesn't hear or even know the other lyrics; they just somehow recede into the gestalt. We're left both with an overarching feeling and with a couple of acute images from the song to attach to that feeling.

Lines like these from "Happy" are the lyric equivalent of what scientists call involuntary musical images and most of us just call earworms. Whereas an earworm is generally understood as a catchy tune that runs continually through the mind, with the emphasis on the infectious melody, the moments I describe here are primarily based in language, with the melody as the vehicle for delivery. Undoubtedly, there will be instances where the two types meet somewhere near the middle, where the melody and language both capture attention. It is also worth isolating those lyric moments in which the emphasis bends toward language rather than melody for acute recognition.

Pop's most memorable words may derive their staying power from their meaning, from their performance, or from other factors both internal and external to the song. There is, for instance, the category of indelible opening lines. Take this example: "Just a small town girl. . . ." For listeners of a certain generation, a particular taste, or both, this will automatically set off a near-eidetic recreation of Journey's "Don't Stop Believing," sung in the mind's evocation of Steve Perry's plangent voice. The words themselves are unremarkable, except inasmuch as they commence the narrative. The timbre and emotive quality of Perry's delivery—impassioned, even theatrical—make this line memorable. Perry wrings poignancy from prosaic words, the emotion propelled by a melody and piano figure that create a mood of nostalgia and longing. Even if you haven't heard the song in years, your mind will likely set the song to playing with that single line.

Another category that calls attention to specific lyrics is the play of poetic figures and forms. In its simplest manifestation, this may take the shape of sound play; in more rarified forms, it becomes simile, metaphor, or other figurative constructs. Play with sound abounds across genres, in the form of ad libs or in lyric substitutions where sounds take the place of semantics. A surprising number of these substitutions arise in songs about love, partly because most pop songs are about love, and also because the experience of being in love often defies expression. Whether it is 1960s soul grooves like the Delfonics' "(La-La) Means I Love You" or contemporary pop tunes like Lady Gaga's "Bad Romance," love often drives singers and songwriters to abstraction.

Minnie Riperton's "Loving You" raises this kind of lyric substitution to an art form; the most evocative lines in the song are the ones that transcend words and edge into the upper registers of the human voice, toward squeals and ecstatic sighs. Here's how one online lyric site attempts to transcribe the song's closing lines:

> Lovin-ughhhhh. la-la-la-la-la-la-la.
> And doot-doot.dootin.doot-do.
> b.doom.doom.doom.
> mya.mya.mya.mya.mya.mya.mya.
> la.la.la.b.doom.b.doomb.doom

Good luck giving voice to that. This song, and this section of the song specifically, has endured because it resides somewhere beyond words, expressing the ecstatic confusion of being in love.

This kind of play with sounds is only the most obvious example of the ways that pop songwriters and performers use poetic strategies to activate the audience's acute listening. Among the varieties of figurative language in pop music, the simile predominates. It may be most obvious in rap, which makes it a staple of its poetics, though it thrives across the pop-music spectrum. Entire songs sometimes function as experiments in figurative language, as in the song "Black Swan" from Radiohead frontman Thom Yorke's solo album, *The Eraser* (2006). From metaphor ("I'm your black swan, black swan") to simile ("People get crushed like biscuit crumbs"), lyric derives its force and energy from the transitive quality of juxtaposition and identity. Yorke's simile comes across with a swagger more naturally associated with hip-hop, an attitude underscored by the spare drum accompaniment and Yorke's vocal syncopation. This lyric invites close inspection even as it allows listening to the song in the gestalt as groove and as mood.

Sometimes songs dissuade acute lyric attention by making the words difficult to discern. Even nearly incoherent lyrics, though, like those on My Bloody Valentine's "Only Shallow" or almost every song on Radiohead's *Kid A*, tend to clear up a bit in the chorus. On Pearl Jam's "Yellow Ledbetter," for instance, Eddie Vedder's famous warble goes from incomprehensible in the verses to barely interpretable in the chorus. Pearl Jam's most commercially successful tracks, like "Alive" and "Even Flow," are clearer still, offering listeners a strong chorus where they can sing along and attach words to abstract feelings. Many pop songs invite such sing-along, some mainly in the chorus, others throughout. At a Jimmy Buffett concert, you're more likely to spend the night hearing an old white guy in a Hawaiian shirt singing in the crowd next to you than hearing an old white guy in a Hawaiian shirt singing to you from the stage. By contrast, most of Vedder's songs play like invitations to shut up and listen, with occasional concessions in the chorus to the audience's unmet desire to join in the song. The gestalt and the acute are both part of the pleasure of the song, both necessary to the practice of close listening.

The best place in song to explore the confluence of the acute and gestalt, the semantic and the sensory, is the hook. "Hook" is a mutable term in popular music, commonly used and variously applied. In its narrowest definition, a hook is a repeated portion of lyric often imbedded in the chorus and frequently containing the song's title. "The hook brings you back/On that you can rely,"

John Popper sings on Blues Traveler's 1994 single "Hook," a song that lampoons pop music's formulaic structure even as it exploits that structure to climb up the *Billboard* charts (the song peaked at number 23 on the Hot 100 chart). The opening lines of the first verse set the tone: "It doesn't matter what I say / So long as I sing with inflection." As it turns out, the phrase "the hook brings you back" is in fact the song's hook, repeated six times, twice in each of the three turns of the chorus. The line is catchy, both melodically compelling and ironically self-knowing. The song was a hit because it captured two distinct audiences: those upon whom the hook worked its practical magic, and those amused by the lyrics' ironic critique of pop's formulas.

A functional understanding of the term "hook" allows for its various applications in the parlance of songwriters, producers, and performers of popular music today. In this broad definition, a hook is one or more catchy passages in a song, be they lyric, melodic, or harmonic. "The hook can be the track itself," says Ryan Tedder, the songwriter, producer, and frontman for the pop group OneRepublic. He points to Coldplay's "Clocks," where the opening piano figure functions as the sonically sticky element of the song, the part that excites listener anticipation. The hook might be a portion of the chorus or the title of the song; it might equally be a guitar riff, a seductive sample, a stutter, or a scream. Rather than restricting the hook to a prescribed portion of the song, it is best to understand it as a quality defined retrospectively. A hook is that which asserts itself on the listener's consciousness, inviting anticipation and providing pleasure with each return.

Hooks in this expansive sense of the word dominate contemporary popular music. This isn't to say, however, that today's singers and songwriters invented the hook-heavy single. Writing of the Eurythmics' 1983 *Billboard* number one "Sweet Dreams," Dave Stewart, the instrumental half of the duo beside the vocalist Annie Lennox, remarked that they consciously composed the song to blur the lines between verse and chorus. "There is not one note that is not a hook," Stewart boasts. In his 2015 exploration of the business of pop-song craft, *The Song Machine*, the journalist John Seabrook identifies what he calls the "track-and-hook" method of pop-song production. "In a track-and-hook song," he writes, "the hook comes as soon as possible. Then the song 'vamps'—progresses in three- or four-chord patterns with little or no variation. Because it is repetitive, the vamp requires more hooks: intro, verse, pre-chorus, chorus, and outro hooks. 'It's not enough to have one hook anymore,' [the producer] Jay Brown explains. 'You've got to have a hook in the intro, a hook in the pre, a hook in the chorus, and a hook in the bridge, too.'" Citing Brown, Seabrook argues that successful pop music must provide a hook at least every seven seconds to account for the fickle nature of listener attention. What does a song with a hook every seven seconds sound like? It sounds like Taylor Swift's "Shake It Off."

"Shake It Off" was the lead single off of Swift's fifth album, 2014's *1989*. It debuted at number one on the *Billboard* Hot 100 chart, only the twenty-second single to do so, joining such pop megahits as Michael Jackson's "You Are Not Alone," Celine Dion's "My Heart Will Go On," and Lady Gaga's "Born This Way" in that distinction. "Shake It Off" was nominated for Record of the Year, Song of the Year, and Best Pop Solo Performance at the fifty-seventh Grammy Awards. Like other songs on the album, "Shake It Off" was born of the creative collaboration between Swift and two Swedes, the superproducer Max Martin and Martin's protégé, Shellback.

"Shake It Off" delivers its first hook before Swift even utters a word, in the syncopated drum pattern that begins the song. Rather than following the predictable hook-heavy ploy of commencing with the chorus, as Martin does on *NSYNC's "Tearin' Up My Heart" and as Swift and Martin do on one of *1989*'s other hits, "Bad Blood," "Shake It Off" begins more conventionally with a verse, which is generally the section of a song lightest on hooks. For the most part, the verse vamps in the manner that Seabrook predicts in his "track-and-hook" formula, though even in the verse hooks abound. Several distinctive supporting elements stand out as strange and compelling, working together to call attention to one another. The first of these is the synthesized horn that lays down a sonic bed for Swift's vocals; the second is Swift's "ad-libbed" (though they must certainly have been composed) endings to phrases: "That's what people say, *um hum*," she sings, then repeats the line. The horns drop out for each of the four "um-hums" in the first verse and subsequently during the four utterances in the second verse, setting them apart from the rest of the verse's lines. It's a small sonic move that calls attention to the casual phrase and helps define Swift's attitude of joyful indifference to her detractors. All of this transpires in twenty-three seconds, before the verse gives way to the hook's native domain: the chorus.

In a song of hooks, the chorus delivers the biggest hooks of all:

> Cause the players gonna *play, play, play, play, play*
> And the haters gonna *hate, hate, hate, hate, hate*
> Baby, I'm just gonna *shake, shake, shake, shake, shake*
> I *shake* it off, I shake it *off*

The descending repetition of the end words becomes the song's signature; it's the portion that makes you want to sing along. All that repetition leads to the crowning repetition of the chorus in a final hook, the line of the title. Both musically and rhetorically, Swift has constructed this hook to deliver repetition with a difference. As the pianist and part-time pop-music theorist Chilly Gonzales observes, the phrase ends musically with an instance of rhythmic displacement. The musical phrase repeats but achieves resolution by displacing the rhythmic emphasis from the beginning to the end of the phrase. A parallel process transpires in the language of the lyrics, where Swift's voice registers a small but significant shift in stress from the first part of the phrase to the second. In music and lyric, these shifts bring the chorus to a pleasing resolution even as they underscore through repetition the dominant meaning and motif.

"Shake It Off" repeats the chorus three times, augmenting it with three pre-chorus sections and a post-chorus section, each with their respective hooks. Perhaps the most hookish section of the song outside the chorus, though, comes in the spoken interlude between 2:18 and 2:28. This brief section incited a great deal of commentary on social media, most of it centered on Swift's concluding phrase, "this sick beat." That phrase functions as a hook all its own. Recognizing as much, Swift's team actually applied for a trademark on it. Vocally, Swift slyly moves from speaking to chanting in the bridge, then back to singing through a melodic outburst that lands back in the familiar chorus, the hook of all hooks.

The singer-songwriter Ryan Adams's audacious cover of Swift's entire album is instructive in many ways, not least of which in its handling of "Shake It Off." Swift's ballads, like "Blank Space" and "Wildest Dreams," are more readily assimilated by Adams's acoustic sensibility, more responsive to Adams's implicit theory that if you strip away Swift's pop veneer you'll be left with solid songs. "Shake It Off" presents something of a problem for this approach. So much of what makes "Shake It Off" appealing is its artifice, the play of its surface rather than the deep structures of the song. Stripped down by Adams, "Shake It Off" simmers but never boils. The "haters gonna hate" section with its joyful repetitions is foreshortened. The line hangs in silence, leaving the ghost appendage of Swift's repetition echoing in our memories. Other hooks are eliminated entirely. In fact, the only hook that remains from Swift's original is the repetition of the song's title in the chorus, which Adams performs with Springsteen-level world weariness. More than any other song on the album, "Shake It Off" resists Adams's efforts and doggedly demands its original recorded form, with its profusion of pop hooks, its surface delights, its sense of fun and play, and even its disposability.

The poetry of pop is finally this: a poetry that relies on form—patterns of rhythm and rhyme, and figurative language—as a means to transcend form. Analyzing pop songs means moving from pleasurable but often unreflective listening, to directed and attentive listening, then back to pleasurable listening enhanced by the new pleasure of understanding. It means reading with your ears and listening with your eyes. It is a poetry whose success lies in getting you to forget that it is poetry at all.

Part

II

Chapter
Four

Rhythm

Rhythm matters. I'm picking up my two daughters, both under the age of five, from preschool. I buckle them in, kiss their foreheads, and supply them with snacks for the five-minute drive to the house. But when I turn the key in the ignition, the music I forgot to shut off—Drake's "Hotline Bling"—blares from the speakers. It could have been worse. The song before had been Future's "Fuck Up Some Commas"; the song before that, Pusha T's "Crutches, Crosses, Caskets." The problem is that the girls, particularly my four-year-old, love the few seconds of the song that they hear. After I shut off the stereo, my older daughter begins belting out the only lyrics she understood, the first line of the chorus—"You used to call me on my cellphone!"—and doesn't stop singing it until we pull up to the house.

Now "Hotline Bling," aka "The Cellphone Song," is on their request list, right beside "Let It Go" and "The Wheels on the Bus." Out of desperation I discover Kidz Bop, the successful series of cover-song compilation albums with kids singing sanitized versions of pop music's latest hits. I play them Kidz Bop's "Hotline Bling" and both girls seem satisfied. My ear, though, can't help fixating on the small emendations made in childproofing the lyrics. "You used to call me on my cellphone / Late night when you need my love" becomes "You used to call me on my cellphone / Anytime you need to talk." It's a serviceable substitution, erasing all implications of after-midnight assignations. Like the original, the new line is seven syllables long. None-theless, something's wrong with the rhythm. In Drake's performance, the line rests on a series of stressed syllables—"need my love"—that emphasizes a sense of longing. That same stress on "need to talk" seems out of place. Even more disruptive is Kidz Bop's substitution of the multisyllabic word "anytime" for Drake's balanced phrase "late night when." Both are three syllables long, but pronouncing "anytime" requires crowding the syllables together, whereas Drake's three separate words luxuriate in their collective sound.

It's a subtle disruption, and a small price to pay for getting my girls the song they want in a manner that my wife and I can allow. It's also an impor-tant reminder that no single analytical tool can account for the many rhythms at work in a pop song. Merely counting syllables and stresses, Drake's line and Kidz Bop's line are interchangeable. Close listening to the actual recordings, however, underscores their differences. A full accounting of the complex rhythms in the poetry of pop demands attention not simply to the stressed and unstressed syllables, but to the microrhythms that define the texture of the sound.

Rhythm is the sequence of sounds over time. Before song lyrics are anything like poetry, they exist as sequenced sounds. "If you don't have the sound right," Paul Simon observes, "it doesn't matter if you have the words right, because the ear isn't available to hear them." The sounds of lyrics express themselves most apparently as rhythmic pulse—a binary code of stressed and unstressed syllables set to music that itself is a binary code of stressed and unstressed sounds. Stripped to its essence, pop music is the dance of the rhythmic pulse of the lyric over and against the rhythmic pulse of the music. Jimi Hendrix put it more succinctly: Music is "nothing but rhythm and motion."

Three distinct rhythms and motions govern pop songs: the rhythm of the music, the rhythm of the lyric language, and the rhythm of the singer's performance of that language to the music. Rhythm, therefore, is the lingua franca of music, poetry, and performance in song. These three elements, distinct but interrelated, come together in dynamic tension to achieve a single emotive effect in the listener. One can study each element in isolation, but the full meaning of a recording's rhythm lies in the space that they inhabit together.

Most of us are comfortable with the concept of rhythm in music, even if we lack the formal training to explain how it works. What is a song's time signature? What kinds of rhythmic and polyrhythmic textures are developed in the instrumental performance? Not everyone can answer these questions, but just about everyone can tap their toe or bob their head to a beat. "Music is a foreign language which everyone knows but only musicians can speak," explains Stephen Sondheim. "The effect is describable in everyday language; how to achieve it is not." The rhythm of a song expresses itself in the quantifiable—the meter of the composition—and in the ineffable—each instrumental performer's distinctive interpretation of the music's meter and the interplay of rhythmic impulses and instrumental voices across a given track. "The control and perception of form in any music involves recognition of two basic musical activities—repetition (or similarity) and change (or contrast)—plus an activity that combines these two. This latter activity is referred to as 'development' and provides contrast within similarity," observes Jack Perricone, professor of songwriting at Berklee School of Music.

As repetition with a difference, the rhythm of a musical composition defines the territory in which lyrics traverse the space of sound.

The second measure of rhythm, the rhythm of the lyrics, is governed by the laws of poetic meter. How many stressed syllables appear in the lyric line? Do the stressed and unstressed syllables coalesce into any discernible metrical patterns? For all its chaos and cacophony, Nirvana's "Smells Like Teen Spirit" settles comfortably into iambic tetrameter in the language of the lyrics: "Our *lit*/tle *group*/has *al*/ways *been*// And *al*/ways *will*/un*til*/the *end*." Kurt Cobain singing these lines deranges this strict formal structure, but the rhythmic regularity of the syllables still counterbalances the defiant indeterminacy of the lines' meaning. Lewis Turco observes in his *Book of Forms* that the terminology used when scanning accentual syllabic lines of poetry in English borrows from ancient Greek, whose poetry was, by contrast, quantitative—"(that is, like musical notes, syllables were assigned 'lengths'—full note, half note, quarter note, etc.)" rather than differing in volume or stress, as in English prosody. "Smells Like Teen Spirit" offers a wonderful confluence in the language of the lyric imbedded in song between accentual syllabic stress and quantitative duration of emphasis.

Song lyrics are words under pressure, compressed in a space that the music defines. "They are reinforced, accented, blurred, belied, inspired to new meaning, in a continual interplay," writes the literary critic Mark W. Booth. The rhythm of the music situates the rhythm of the lyric. It defines optimal expression: Words will fit best here, at this tempo, in this rhythmic pattern, even to this specific melody. Melody, after all, is just pitch set to rhythm. The rhythm of the music and the rhythm of the lyrics often line up. In rap, for instance, we generally find lyric lines of four stressed syllables for every 4/4 musical bar. However, words are never completely governable. Though they fall under the sway of the song, they push and pull and sometimes break free. When that happens the rhythms of music and of language clash, through carelessness or conscious design.

The final measure of rhythm in pop music is the rhythm of the performing voice, which relates to both the rhythms of the music and those of the lyrics. In fact, it is often the bridge between the two, reconciling the rhythms of music and lyric in a single performance. This performative rhythm, though bound by the rhythmic possibilities that the music and the lyrics allow, is otherwise free to express itself in accordance with the distinctive rhythmic sensibility of the singer. The performative rhythm might cleave closely to the imbedded rhythms in the lyrics by obeying the laws of poetic meter; it might abide by the prescribed rhythms of the music by staying in the pocket of the beat. More often than not, though, the performative rhythm expresses a distinct sense of time that reflects the style and sensibilities of the performer.

For all their differences, Frank Sinatra, Willie Nelson, Ray Charles, and Aretha Franklin all tend to dilate and contract the lyric phrase when they sing. The way they syncopate and swing, playing on and off the beat, charges every song they sing with reckless brilliance. One always fears that they will take it too far, breaking rather than merely bending the rhythmic integrity of the song. It is a testament to their craft that they rarely do so.

The interplay and tension of these three rhythms account for a great deal of what makes pop music appealing to hear and compelling to analyze. On a November 2015 episode of *Switched On Pop*, the podcast in which the craft of songwriting meets the science of musicology, one of the hosts, Charlie Harding, led a guest, the comedian Chris Duffy, through a game called Name That Song, Name What's Wrong. Harding read a few lines of lyrics and played a few seconds from the recorded song, then asked Duffy to identify the song and to point out what was strange about the snippet. Harding started with the beginning of Taylor Swift's "Bad Blood," the Grammy-nominated fourth single from her 2014 album, *1989*:

> Did you have to do this?
> I was thinkin that you could be trusted
> Did you have to ruin
> What was shiny? Now it's all rusted

Duffy correctly guessed that it was Swift singing, but whiffed on the song's title. He also could not discern what Harding thought was wrong, even after Harding read the lyrics to him again in a robotic voice. "The em-*pha*-sis is on the wrong syl-*lab*-ble," Harding quipped. "The rhythm is completely wrong!" Swift's diction in "Bad Blood" is undeniably strange—stylized and clipped. Something unusual is going on in the song's prosody, the way that the words imbed themselves in the music. It strikes the ear as artificial, if not exactly robotic.

Surely this isn't the product of poor song craft, though—not from an artist as polished as Swift. Why, then, would Swift and her production team seek out such strangeness? Answering this is a job for the poetics of pop.

Beginning with a simple syllable count, the song's two verses establish an alternating pattern of a short line of six syllables followed by a long line of nine or ten syllables. The same pattern holds for the number of stressed syllables per line, which alternates between two stresses in the short lines and three in the long:

Did you *have* to *do* this?	6/2
I was *think*in' that you *could* be *trus*ted	10/3
Did you *have* to *ru*in	6/2
What was *shi*ny? *Now* it's all *rus*ted	9/3

Even before listening to the recording, one can already glean from the lyrics that the performance will have a herky-jerky rhythm to it. The lyric language all but guarantees it. With more empty sonic space—more "air"—around the words in the shorter lines, we experience the longer lines as a kind of release, a flood of language that gets dammed up by the short line that soon follows, only to be released again when the long line returns.

This pattern of short line then long line becomes the dominant order of the verses, supplanting natural syntactic order. In lines three and four, for instance, retaining the short-long pattern means sharply enjambing the third line, cutting Swift's question (Did you have to ruin what was shiny?) in half and rendering it less clear. Rhythmic logic has replaced semantic logic here. An even more dramatic instance of the obscuring influence of the song's rhythmic imperative comes in the next two lines: "Did you have to hit me/Where I'm weak? Baby, I couldn't breathe and. . . ." Here the line break, which Swift registers in her performance through an extended pause, momentarily leads the listener to believe that the syntactical unit has closed, that Swift is asking a troubling question about physical abuse (Did you have to hit me?) rather than employing a metaphor of violence to underscore an emotional violation (Did you have to hit me where I'm weak?). The patterned rhythm of the lines and the rhythm of Swift's performance conspire here to leave both questions resonating in listeners' minds. If Swift had sung her lyric question in a continuous, flowing phrase it would have registered as a pallid cliché rather than as the unsettling query it is by virtue of its studiedly stilted delivery.

Scanning the lyrics again while the song plays, it becomes clear that Swift's performance further exaggerates the syllabic and stress differences imbedded in the language itself. Here is my scan of the lyrics, followed by a scan of how I hear the stresses falling in Swift's performance:

Did you *have* to *do* this?	6/2
I was *think*in that you *could* be *trus*ted	10/3

Did you *have* to *ru*in	6/2
What was *shi*ny? *Now* it's all *rus*ted	9/3
Did you have to *do* this?	6/3
I was *think*in that *you* could be *trus*ted	10/4
Did you have to *ru*in	6/3
What was *shi*ny? *Now* it's all *rus*ted	9/4

The striking difference between the rhythm of the lines as poetry and the rhythm of the lines as Swift sings them rests in the way that she stresses naturally unstressed syllables. Each line has one more stressed syllable when Swift sings it than it does when read on the page. Not only does she augment the stress in the lines, she also relocates it. She begins the first line, for instance, by according almost equal stress to the first two words ("did" and "you"), whereas neither word gets heavy stress in the language of the lyrics. In line two, Swift displaces the natural stresses and instead emphasizes the pronouns ("I" and "you"), a fitting move in a song about betrayal and recrimination.

The liberty Swift takes with the inherent syllabic emphasis of the lyrics gains authority through her singing's rhythmic relation to the music. Her vocal performance, particularly in the short lines, plays on and off the rhythm of the track. On the first and the third lines, she places emphatic stress on the opening word, falling on the downbeat, then she locates the remaining stresses in rhythmic counterpoint on unexpected beats in the measure. Swift's combination of stressing syllables that the natural flow of syntax leaves unstressed and placing those same stresses in counterpoint to the rhythm of the track accounts for what some listeners hear as her robotic tone. It also accounts for the unsettling energy that helped make the song a hit.

Reading rhythm in popular music is never just one thing. When multiple musicians assert their rhythmic sensibilities, whether inside or outside the confines of the song's demands, anything is possible. At their best, rhythm and motion cohere with purpose and direction. "Just like the rising and falling of a poem, the music also travels, and you have to feel it," Gregg Allman writes of playing in a group. "It's like traveling on a train, rolling through the hills. It's a journey with your partners, and they're all going with you, and some of them make the same turns, and a couple may go a different route, but they all meet you on the other side. I know that's a strange way of describing how the arrangement to a composition works, but it's like a musical journey."

Rhythm is fundamental to pop music, both in obvious ways like the prominence of percussion and in subtle ways like the cadence of the lyric line as expressed in the singer's delivery. Each pop song constitutes its own rhythmic network, a series of relationships in constant flux. Given that the focus of this book is on song lyrics, of particular interest is how the small rhythms of language relate to the big rhythms of the music and of the singing. How much of the rhythmic information native to the words and their specific order finds expression in the song as performed? Does the performance of the song follow the natural rhythmic inclinations imbedded in the written lyric, or does the performance transform them, push against them, subvert them?

RHYTHM DEFINED

Pop is synonymous with rhythm, which is to say it is synonymous with repetition. The *Oxford English Dictionary* defines "rhythm" as "relating to a regular repeated pattern of sound or movement." Rhythm, therefore, is organized, predictable, and replicable. In pop, this can mean anything from a hip-hop break beat to a rock and roll backbeat. Rhythm expresses itself in sound and in movement, although the term "movement" alone might be enough to describe it given that sound itself is the product of movement (the vibration of vocal cords or strings) and sensed through movement (the displacement of air and the vibration of cochlea in the ear).

Rhythm is also a primary quality of language. The OED further codifies rhythm as "the measured flow of words or phrases in prose, speech, etc." A specific form of this is prosody in verse, the metrical divisions of stressed and unstressed syllables that comprise syllabic feet. Rhythm has a parallel meaning in music, as the OED defines it: "the systematic grouping of musical sounds, principally according to duration and periodical stress; beat; an instance of this, a particular grouping or arrangement of musical sounds." Rhythm is found in nature and even in human physiology; as the dictionary observes, rhythm can refer to "the recurrence at (normally) regular intervals of the heartbeat, breathing, or other physiological process; periodicity."

In poetry and music, rhythm takes the form of art. "The word has retained throughout its history an aesthetic aspect, suggesting a movement or spatial arrangement that exhibits some degree of regularity without being mechanical," explains the literary scholar Derek Attridge in *The Princeton Encyclopedia of Poetry and Poetics*. He goes on to describe rhythm's defining features, which include regularity (that is, delivered at expected intervals), repetition (of the same stimuli), variation (which enhances rhythm's enjoyment by staving off monotony), hierarchy (the privileging of some beats over others in gradations of emphasis), and grouping (or the organization of those hierarchal sequences into relational units). Writing in *The Harvard Dictionary of Music*, the musicologist Harold S. Powers amplifies many of these literary qualities in defining rhythm for music. Put simply, rhythm is "the pattern of movement in time." Most Western music, like most Western poetry, follows an accentual rather than a durational rhythm. In 4/4 time, the heaviest emphasis is on the first beat, with secondary emphasis on the third. Similarly, in English prosody a dactyl places the heaviest emphasis on the first syllable of a three-syllable sequence. Instead of counting rhythmic units like a Japanese haiku (a poem of seventeen syllables, grouped 5-7-5) or an Indian raga (a melody comprising a fixed number of notes, usually five to nine), pop songs express themselves—both in lyric and in music—as an arrangement of varying weights of rhythmic emphasis.

Rhythm's form is one thing. It must also have a function. The neuroscientist Daniel J. Levitin posits that the rhythm of group song served a practical purpose of social cohesion and protection among our early human ancestors. "Rhythm in music provides the input to the human perceptual system that allows for the prediction and synchronization of different individuals' behaviors," Levitin writes. "Sound has advantages over vision—it transmits in the dark, travels around corners, can reach people who are visually obscured by trees or caves. Music, as a highly structured form of sound communication, enabled the synchronization of movement even when group members couldn't see each other." In 1964 the R&B singer Major Lance scored a minor hit with an ebullient song called "Rhythm" whose lyrics illustrate Levitin's ideal:

> What's that sound? (That rhythm)
> Everybody around (Likes rhythm)
> There can be no beat (Without rhythm)
> Makes me wanna move my feet (That rhythm)

Rhythm abounds in these lines and in this recording: in the call-and-response between Lance and his backup singers; in the repetition of the word "rhythm" at the end of each line; in the laid-back, layered groove. All these rhythms underscore the elemental force and the communal connection rhythm conjures, and they all emphasize structured repetition, a pattern of rising and falling. Rhythm is sonic, social, ordered, and bodily.

In pop music, repetition asserts itself most apparently in the rhythmic backdrop of the music known as the groove, established through some combination of drums, bass, keyboards, rhythm guitar, and background vocals. "The rhythm section sets the groove, the steady repetitive accompaniment against which the singer(s) and any soloists may have much more varied rhythms," writes the musicologist Walter Everett. "The drummer pretty much controls the pocket, the repetitive pattern basic to the groove."

Alex James, the bassist for the English rock band Blur, recalls one particular groove from their first album. On "I Know," James looped a two-bar bass line and repeated it throughout the entire recording, creating a propulsive groove that defines the sonic feel of the track. "The fundamental unit of groove is the riff," he writes. "If the riff is good, the groove is good. A groove is usually the same riff played again and again with subtle variations. With a looped groove, you're actually hearing exactly the same thing over and over. The bass player jams along with the drums and a small section of the performance, usually eight beats long, is cut and pasted together to make the bassline for the whole track." James's bass groove dominates "I Know," demanding a near-reflexive physical response from a listener. It's a minute in before you hear a human voice—and that's just fine.

The regularity of the groove liberates solo instruments and voices to explore a greater range of rhythmic textures. These two rhythmic impulses, the (relatively) fixed and the (relatively) free, are mutually sustaining. "There is something very earcatching about the same thing repeating, a hypnotic perfection. Eight beats is quite a small amount of time, but it is actually long enough to change the course of popular history, if you get it exactly right," James continues. "Making good loops is no easier than playing well through the whole song. In fact, it puts even more emphasis on the 'feel.' 'Feel' is the subtle quality that separates the great players from the ordinary ones. It's largely innate, like a person's way of walking or talking. A hundred different guitarists will all play the same riff in exactly one hundred slightly different ways. The subtle pushing and pulling at the rhythm, the exact length of the notes and how hard the strings are hit and bent, mean that no riff is ever quite the same in different hands. Things played with clinical accuracy often sound quite lifeless and mechanical. If it feels good, it is good." At its most transcendent, the groove fashions a syncopated space of dance and reverie. Or, as Prince once slyly observed, "There's joy in repetition."

Propulsive rhythms are a soundtrack for active listening, accompanying everything from dancing to driving to exercising to having sex. Whether in hip-hop or in electronic music, rhythm carries associations of a Dionysian departure from the conventions of polite culture. "In song and in dance man expresses himself as a member of a higher community; he has forgotten how to walk and speak and is on the way toward flying into the air, dancing," writes Friedrich Nietzsche in *The Birth of Tragedy*. "His very gestures express enchantment." Whether at an early-morning revel in Ibiza or a suburban spin class, rhythm can conjure a trancelike state among listeners. Rhythm has the capacity beyond any other quality of music to hold listeners under its sway.

Rhythm can also alienate. Rhythm's perceived overabundance in pop is the very thing that makes the music objectionable to some tastes. To the ears of pop music's detractors what has always been missing, no matter the era or the style, is proper attention to music in full, beyond the beat alone. A thumbnail history of the last century of popular music must sound something like this to the ears of those who reject a primacy of rhythm—a primacy, in particular, of rhythmic syncopation, whose displacement of rhythmic expectation has fomented sonic revolutions. First there was jazz, with its licentious, primal cadences. Then there was rhythm and blues and rock and roll, which held melody in thrall to the driving rhythms of drum, bass, piano, and rhythm guitar. After that came disco, whose 4/4 beat turned all who heard it into dancing, drug-addled automatons. Then came hip-hop, a music so rhythm-obsessed that some wondered if it qualified as music at all. To bring the story up to the present, electronic dance music (EDM), which draws liberally from a panoply of pop sources, especially disco and hip-hop, may have finally apotheosized the beat. Where critics once feared the rhythm-crazed flappers of the Jazz Age or the dancing queens and kings of disco, they now denounce another generation for bobbing their heads and waiting for the beat to drop.

Of course, this is only part of the story. Each of these musical styles has always been more textured and varied than critics would admit. However, this caricature underscores a fundamental sonic truth. Pop music *has* treasured rhythm as a defining element of its form. The reasons for this are many, though certain themes endure.

Rhythm begins in our bodies. Humans are among the few creatures on the planet born with rhythm. As I've been writing this book, I've been playing a lot of music for my two young daughters. I've seen my two-year-old spin herself dizzy to Fred Astaire's jaunty 1952 rendition of Irving Berlin's "Puttin' On the Ritz." My four-year-old has stared transfixed at a video of Beyoncé's choreographed dance moves to her 2008 hit "Single Ladies (Put a Ring on It)" before getting down on the floor to try them herself. "The rhythmic properties of language and music may well be unique to humans: informal observations suggest that no other primate can easily be trained to move to an auditory beat, as in marching, dancing, tapping the feet, or clapping the hands," writes the experimental psychologist Steven Pinker. This process, called unconscious entrainment, helps to set the brain's metronome. "Rhythm turns listeners into participants, makes listening active and motoric, and synchronizes the brains and minds (and, since emotion is always intertwined with music, the 'hearts') of all who participate," writes the neurologist Oliver Sacks. With all due respect to these esteemed researchers, my daughters are the only proof I need that the physical urge to respond to musical rhythms is born in us.

Pop music inspires what the sociomusicologist Charles Keil terms "kinesthetic listening." In other words, pop music, or almost any form of music, activates a physical response; audiences feel "the melody in their muscles." When we listen, we are inspired to embody the performance as if we were in fact making the sounds. "Across repeated listenings," explains the literary critic Elizabeth Hellmuth Margulis, "the particular sonic and temporal trajectory of the piece grips and regrips motor circuitry, solidifying a kind of motor routine that makes the music increasingly feel like a familiar way of moving, rather than merely a familiar series of sounds. The more this happens, the more the music seems to dissolve boundaries, occupy your subjectivity, and connect your inner sensibilities with the outer world: important parts of the pleasure of repeated listening." Repeated sounds, such as beats, over repeated listenings begin to manifest themselves in our nervous system, inciting responses that we only partly control. "The reason why rhythm is particularly significant for popular music," writes Simon Frith, "is that a steady tempo and an interesting patterned beat offer the easiest ways into a musical event; they enable listeners without instrumental expertise to respond 'actively,' to experience music as a bodily as well as a mental matter."

Beyond the biological connection, rhythm carries culturally coded meanings specific to communities of the music's origin. In the United States, rhythm-dominated genres—from jazz and R&B to salsa and hip-hop—have been most closely associated with black and Latino performers and, at least at first, with black and Latino audiences. A surfeit of rhythm caused suspicion among listeners who assumed the song must have something to hide. A glance at the rhetoric of music censorship in the United States reveals a surprising antipathy toward rhythm- and dance-oriented music. Critics associated such music with corruption and even madness. "Jazz was originally the accompaniment of the voodoo dance, stimulating half-crazed barbarians to the vilest of deeds," asserted Ann Shaw Faulkner, president of the General Federation of Women's Clubs, which launched its attack against the moral ravages of jazz in 1921. The steady beat of the tom-tom in 1920s jazz music would become the backbeat of early rock and roll, the 120 beats per minute of disco, and finally the boom-bap of rap and blips and pulses of EDM. The beat meant sex and drugs and excess. It meant the loss of control and, perhaps, a kind of revolution. Of rap, William Bennett of Empower America offered the following fatalistic claim: "I think that nothing less is at stake than preservation of civilization. This stuff by itself won't bring down civilization but it doesn't help."

In the antebellum South, the drum was indeed an instrument of insurrection, if not one of physical liberation then at least a liberation of the mind. Recognizing this, the South Carolina Slave Code of 1740 banned "using and keeping of drums, horns, or other loud instruments, which may call together or give sign or notice to one another of their wicked designs and purposes." The talking drums offered a way for enslaved Africans to communicate across distance in coded cadence. That code would fit itself to language through work songs and spirituals that drew on Old Testament stories of the Israelites' deliverance from bondage to map salvific potential onto soul-crushing everyday realities. Fast forward to the middle of the twentieth century, and the sly calypso rhythms of Harry Belafonte's "Banana Boat Song (Day-O)" made dancers move even as it helped make a movement as an anthem for civil rights activists. Even today, pop music, particularly the rhythm-rich music that inspires dance, elicits wariness and skepticism from some, often for nothing more than an unspecified sense of threat communicated through the beats. For others, though, rhythm is life.

Unpacking the complex interrelatedness of rhythms in pop songs means coming to terms with the dynamics among the three rhythmic forces at play in most recordings: musical rhythm (the rhythmic identities of the instrumentation), poetic rhythm (the patterns of stress in the language of the lyrics as identified through the process of scansion), and performative rhythm (the idiosyncratic way that a singer interprets a lyric in a given performance).

MUSICAL RHYTHM

When musicians talk about rhythm, it sometimes sounds as if they're talking about poetry. "Rhythmic content means how you accent, where your accents are, and how they fit in with different types of rhythm," the jazz trumpet great Dizzy Gillespie explained to the *Paris Review* in 1965. "You can't notate it for them; they have to be able to hear it. You can come close, but you can't really write jazz." Though speaking of jazz, Gillespie illuminates an essential distinction of category for both music and poetry: the difference between rhythm and meter.

Meter is what you *can* notate. Meter is the syntax of musical rhythm analogous to the syntax of language. Indeed, music, language, and dance are all connected in the brain as common modes of communication. Meter is the stuff of sheet music, of quarter notes and sixteenth notes. It is the metronome and the time signature. It is, in other words, the ideal. Rhythm, by contrast, is the real. It is human breath, its flaws and frailty beside its inspiration and invention. Gillespie understood this as "rhythmic content," the conscious assertion of an individual rhythmic sense atop a given metrical pattern. The result for the studied ear is a palimpsest, where the stylized rhythm of the performer, who chooses what and when to accent, shares space with the prescribed meter of the composition.

The most danceable songs find a balance between the reassuring and the surprising. A great example of this is Pharrell Williams's "Happy." "The song is layered with predictable beats and complex, syncopated ones," argues the neuroscientist Maria Witek, principal author of a 2014 study on what makes a song danceable. "The drums, the piano, the clapping and even Pharrell's voice create inviting gaps." Out of the interplay of predictability and novelty, of structures and gaps, is born syncopation—stress where one would expect rest, and rest where one would expect stress. A talented singer, like a talented percussionist, knows when to rush forward and when to lay back. "Knowing when not to play is in some ways more important than actually playing," the percussionist Sheila E. observes. The same could be said for singing. Out of this manipulation of time style is born. But none of that exists without the foundation of meter.

"One can't have rhythm without meter," explains Walter Everett. "Meter is the imaginary background grid of regularly recurring pulses against which performed rhythmic patterns are heard and interpreted. Meter provides a constant flow of inaudible beats, some of which (or some parts of which) are manifested in the actual rhythms of a song, and some of which pass silently by. In many songs, the drums simply beat out the meter, marking every beat uniformly on the snare for a hard-driving effect; this is true in the Rolling Stones' '(I Can't Get No) Satisfaction.'" With Charlie Watts banging out beat for beat, Bill Wyman's bass line dancing around Watts's pattern, and Jack Nitzsche creating rhythmic counterpoint on the tambourine, the song fashions a fertile field for Mick Jagger's alternately smooth and jerky vocal delivery. Whether the performers outline or elide meter, its presence is defining. "Rhythms often align with meter, or they can syncopate against it by emphasizing normally weak beats (or their parts), thus creating the great off-balance, propulsive tension typical of rock music," continues Everett. This rhythmic arrangement was unusual for the Stones; Watts usually followed Keith Richards's guitar, and Wyman typically hit his notes slightly behind the drumbeat. Richards would also often use acoustic guitar as an additional percussive instrument, but in "Satisfaction," that acoustic rhythm is mixed so low that it becomes nearly indecipherable from the cymbals and tambourine.

In poetry, meter serves an analogous function. Skilled poets syncopate over and against the rhythmic patterns they invoke. Meter is the ideal against which metrical poets assert their rhythmic sensibilities. William Shakespeare wrote his sonnets predominantly in iambic pentameter, which is to say that most of his sonnets follow the rhythmic pattern of iambic pentameter *except* when the language itself resists it, or when he artfully deviates from the form to achieve a desired effect of sound or feeling. Sometimes he subverts his readers' rhythmic expectations from the start, as he does in the opening lines of Sonnet 130:

> My mistress' eyes are nothing like the sun
> Coral is far more red than her lips' red
> If snow be white, why then her breasts are dun
> If hairs be wires, black wires grow on her head.

When scanned, the lines maintain the expected iambic impulse, the upswing of the voice, albeit with some striking departures. Most notably, the second line disrupts the meter by beginning with a trochaic substitution (a falling rather than a rising inflection): "*Coral*/is *far*/more *red*." This small metrical inversion alters the music of the sonnet, drawing the eye to the idea at the center of the lyric: that these conventional comparisons of beauty are a poor fit to describe the object of the speaker's affections, just as the poetic line itself bridles against the beauty of iambic conformity. Rhythm here is an engine of both sound and meaning. This is the same sensibility—the art of rhythm rather than the science of meter—that Gillespie understood. In both music and poetry, the distance between rhythm and meter often holds the mystery of emotion and meaning.

Not surprisingly, both pop songs and poetry have evolved systems of analysis intended to domesticate rhythm, through notation and critical terminology that help creators and critics to systematize an unruly and mysterious force. Musicians notate time from left to right on a staff, with pitch delineated by a note's vertical position along the staff and bar lines dividing the notes on the horizontal plane. The time signature designates tempo. Poets and literary critics have developed their own notation through scansion, marking stressed and unstressed syllables in lines of poetry that in metrical verse fall into familiar patterns. Asserting that a given line is written in dactylic trimeter is nothing more than an approximation, a functional fiction. The true identity of these lines in rhythm, their subtle gradations of stress, their orchestration of breath and articulation, exceed our capacity to contain them in neat categories. Linguists have developed more accurate measures that account for finer grains of emphasis (setting out four or eight or more gradations of stress), but these systems fail to suit the poet and the critic because their complexity renders them unwieldy for composition and close reading.

"Of course," writes the inimitable English wit Stephen Fry in his customary tone of assuredness, "it is fundamentally daffy to scan lyrics . . . since it is the musical beat that determines emphasis, not the metrical stress. You could never guess the very particular emphasis on 'get no' just by reading the lyrics of 'Satisfaction' unless you knew the tune and rhythm it was written to fit." Fry is partly correct. Though it is decidedly daffy to imagine that one could resuscitate the idiosyncratic and rich rhythmic textures of the Stones' recording from the lyrics alone, it is not daft in the least to identify rhythmic dynamism in the language by comparing transcription and performance, and by locating instances where the natural impulse of the scanned poetic line is in tension with the dominant rhythmic impulse of the music.

Below I've first scanned the lyric as I would a poem meant for the page, and next as I hear Mick Jagger singing the lyric on the studio recording of the song:

I can't / *get* no / *satis* / *faction*
I can't / *get* no / *satis* / *faction*
Cause I *try* / and I *try* / and I *try* / and I *try*
I can't / *get* no, / I can't / *get* no

I can't get no-*oh satisfac*tion
I can't get no-*oh satisfac*tion
Cause I *try* and I *try* and I *try* and I *try*
I can't *get* no, I can't get no

Scanned as page-based poetry, two lines of trochaic tetrameter (a sequence of four stressed/unstressed syllabic pairs) precede one line of anapestic tetrameter (four instances of two unstressed syllables followed by a stressed syllable) and another line of trochaic tetrameter, albeit one that lends a feel of irresolution through its failure to close the sentence in the same way that it does in the first two lines. Scanning Jagger's performance, the most striking departure is in the way he spaces the first three words from one another, which lends them almost equal stress. He makes a two-syllable word out of "no," which endows it with a rising impulse. The multisyllabic "satisfaction" remains largely unchanged from its natural state in the language, save for a small flourish at the end of the word. In his singing of the third line, Jagger gives himself up entirely to the rhythmic impulse of the anapests. The final line is instructive for the way Jagger charges the same words with a subtly but significantly different rhythmic pulse, pushing the emphasis to the middle of the phrase the first time (I can't *get* no) and to the front the next (*I* can't get no). Depending on which "get no" Fry means, he may be right: You can't imagine the rhythmic energy Jagger gives this last line without hearing the performance. Part of the urgency of Jagger's tone, in fact, comes out of his choice to push against the natural metrical inclination of the language. Equally instructive are the moments in the lyric where Jagger's performance cleaves to the dictates of poetic meter, emphasizing the ease and elegance of the rhythm.

Comparing the lyrics as scanned apart from their music and the lyrics as recorded results in a kind of prosodic syncopation, an imposition of verbal stress governed by the rhythms of the musical performance rather than by the conventions of natural speech. This is the site upon which close comparative analysis of language on the page and language in performance is most richly rewarded. As a reader of song lyrics, then, we should make what use we can of these domesticating efforts of meter in poetry and music while understanding that rhythm really roams wild beyond their bounds.

POETIC RHYTHM

If we can gauge the meter of the music and the meter of the lyrics, then composing a song would seem to boil down to making sure those meters are in sync with one another, or at least don't awkwardly clash. Imagine a musical composer, a lyricist, and a singer as three separate individuals, each exerting as much control on the song as their positions allow them while collaborating with one another in the act of creation. Now imagine that the composer has written the musical instrumentation and the melody, which the lyricist then supplies with lyrics to create the song that the singer performs. Who exercises the greatest control of the rhythm? "When you put words to a melody," notes the songwriter Sheila Davis, "the meter is all laid out with its strong and weak accents, its pauses, its peaks and valleys of emotion. A gifted writer simply fills in the blanks. Well, almost." So the composer makes the lion's share of the rhythmic decisions, the lyricist exercises some small measure of influence in the placement of syllables along the line, and the singer exerts an even further attenuated rhythmic influence through choices in phrasing within the limited frame provided by the melody. At least that's one way a song becomes a recording.

"Lyrics are 'married' to music," explains Pat Pattison. "Whether the lyric is written before the music, at the same *time* as the music, or *after* the music, its syllables are intended to fit with notes. Music is, by its nature, rhythmic. So you must arrange syllables into rhythmic patterns, either to *prepare* them for music or to *match* music that has already been written." For some songwriters, the process is more organic. "It seems that the words and the melody come at the same time with me," Johnny Cash said. "I always have it in my head before I can ever find a pencil and a piece of paper. It's always running through my mind. . . . I don't know, I think it's God. They come from Him through me." Songwriting is rarely as neat a process as someone composing the music, then another person writing a lyric, and another interpreting that lyric in performance. Songwriting can get downright messy.

The greatest claim for music's primacy over lyrics might be scrambled eggs. "He didn't have the words yet. He was calling it 'Scrambled Eggs,' and singing 'Scrambled eggs . . . Everybody calls me scrambled eggs,'" recalls Eric Clapton. So goes the myth of Paul McCartney composing "Yesterday," the Beatles' classic 1965 ballad that would go on to become one of the most covered songs in music history. Clapton is close. McCartney's actual dummy lyrics were "Scrambled eggs / Oh, you've got such lovely legs" or "Oh, my baby how I love your legs," depending on whom you trust. McCartney even developed the theme to complete the lyric—"Scrambled eggs / Good for breakfast, dinner-time or brunch / Don't buy six or twelve, buy a bunch"—which might explain why the song languished for a time before McCartney thought to return to it. In his biography of McCartney, Peter Carlin picks up the story of the song's lyric evolution: "Riding in a car to the southern coast of Portugal, with his girlfriend snoozing at his side, a restless Paul thought back to the 'scrambled eggs' song and began kicking around words to fit the three-beat opening riff. Then, somewhere in the hot, barren fields, the opening word arrived: yesterday. And that was it. Something about the word encapsulated the melody perfectly: reflective, melancholy. The rest came in a rush, the words of a man reflecting on his emotional isolation."

The final lyrics McCartney wrote clarify the emotion already present in the melody. McCartney would later second-guess the song, troubling over its indefinite meaning. "They're good," McCartney told *Playboy* of the lyrics, "but if you read the whole song, it doesn't *say* anything; you don't know what happened." Misgivings aside, that indeterminacy is in keeping with the emotional state the music implies. This is a song that rejects easy answers and clever consolation. Carlin puts it succinctly: "Yesterday" is "a plainspoken description of heartbreak." It's fitting that McCartney would record the song alone with his guitar, backed only by a string quartet, with the rest of the band sitting the session out.

The story of McCartney's "Scrambled Eggs" is now a standby when lyricists want to explain the creative process of composing through dummy lyrics. It ennobles the humble and messy craft of songwriting and sustains hope that even the silliest lyrics might one day become sublime. "I use nonsense words until I get the right ones—the way Paul McCartney used 'Scrambled Eggs' before he came up with 'Yesterday,'" writes Paul Anka. "You scat, you go da da da, just keeping the basic idea in mind. The words are generally tweaked later. Like a house, you need that foundation to build on. You need the music. The words are only as good as the notes under it. That's where the magic comes in, when you have that real strong melody."

It isn't that words in pop songs don't matter, it's that they often matter in different ways than words in conversation and in writing usually do. Because listeners almost always experience the language of pop in performance, the sonic quality of a given word, or of a cluster of words, is usually of greater importance than the semantic meaning alone. Derangement of language can occur at any number of points during the process of a song's creation—during composition when a songwriter might favor a logic of sound over sense, during vocal recording when a singer might choose stylized pronunciations or melodic choices that render spoken idioms strange, and during recording and production when producers and sound engineers sometimes consciously bury the language of the lyrics in the mix.

Pop songwriting and performance most always celebrate language, enshrining certain words and their constitutive sounds. Creedence Clearwater Revival's blistering "Born on the Bayou" vividly illustrates the ways that words matter both as meaning and as sonic texture and mood. The band's singer and songwriter, John Fogerty, recalls in detail how the language of the song started in feeling and only later coalesced into meaning:

> I'm screaming nonsense vowels and consonants—*"AEEEE ewwaaaaAAAaaaaaAAA."* Random words and sounds lead me into something, and every once in a while it sounds like an actual word. I always tried to pick words that were really cool-sounding to sing. That's a lot different from the way many songwriters write, but it's because I'm the singer too. I'm a rock and roll guy. There are words that are really just cool-sounding to sing, and I'd find that word. "Puppy," "doggy," or ... *"hound dog"*? "Shazam"—now there's a cool word. This was an important ingredient, along with pronunciation of the word itself, which was almost like a musical instrument to me.

Fogerty's compositional practice privileges rhythm and sound as the source of his song's language, while also understanding that some words carry rich associations. Finding words that are "just cool-sounding to sing" is no less a conscious poetic act than choosing words for their profundity or allusive reach. At the same time, Fogerty articulates the singer's prerogative to reshape those words in performance, using his voice as an instrument to bend and distort just as reliably as an electric guitar's whammy bar.

For all the concern that songwriters direct at their language, the vestigial remains of dummy lyrics often find themselves in songs that make it on the radio, even songs that become big hits. In most instances, listeners don't perceive these lyrics as scaffolding that hasn't been stripped away from the final structure. On the contrary, these dummy lyrics—often nonsense words and phrases—can end up becoming the most memorable parts of the song, even the reason the song becomes a hit. Hal David, the lyric-writing half of a songwriting duo with Burt Bacharach, reveals that "Raindrops Keep Falling on My Head" was a dummy lyric that Bacharach had put in as a syllabic placeholder to guide David's composition. When David couldn't come up with something that could fit Bacharach's intricate melody as well or better than the dummy lyrics, he capitulated to the absurdity of the line and worked to make semantic sense to go along with its sonic sense.

In other instances, the songwriter makes little or no effort to resolve the absurdity of the lyric holdover. When Phil Collins was working on his post-Genesis solo album, he had an idea for a melody without the requisite words to phrase it. In their place he simply said "a kind of nonsense thing that just sounds nice."

> There's a girl that's been on my mind
> All the time. Su-su-sussudio. Oh-oh-oh . . .
> Now, she don't even know my name
> But I think she likes me just the same
> Su-su-sussudio. Whoa-oh-oh . . .

"I kinda knew I had to find something else for that word," Collins recalls, "then I went back and tried to find another word that scanned as well as 'sussudio,' and I couldn't find one." I remember being ten years old in 1985, watching the "Sussudio" video on MTV and giving surprisingly little thought to what the word actually meant. I just knew it seemed cool. It had to be. It was on MTV, and I was ten years old. In pop music, that's more than enough. Throwaway lyrics and detritus of the compositional process can become a source of wonder and mystery, or they can simply be absorbed without resistance. So much relies on their delivery, the way the words sit in the song. Steven Tyler of Aerosmith describes the process of scatting or using dummy lyrics this way:

> I would listen back, along with the rough of the song, and I would
> hear lyrics. Every time. Tapped right into my own subcontinent. It
> would jump right out at me from the scat. I could play you scats and
> if you listened close enough, you would hear the lyrics that I wrote.
> Not unlike psychoacoustics. If two people are playing, you hear things
> in the middle. If two notes are played or people are singing . . . there

is a tone on the in-between. Harm-onics-slash-psychoacoustics-slash-vibe. The scat kink became Pink. The scat to the Beatles' classic "Yesterday" was scrambled eggs. Fucking magic.

A song, Tyler asserts, begins with emotion, and emotion communicates in sound more than meaning. It requires entering a nonliteral state of mind. Marvin Gaye's biographer, David Ritz, describes Gaye's methods of composition as "subconscious." "Watching him record," Ritz continues, "I noticed that usually no lyrics were written before he started singing. . . . 'I mumble things into the microphone,' Marvin told me. 'I don't even know what I'm saying, and I don't even try to figure it out. If I try, it doesn't work. If I relax, those mumbles will finally turn into words. It's a slow, evolving process, something like the way a flower grows.'" This method of lyric composition is largely done behind the scenes, with the exception of rap freestyles where the process of sonic association and stream of consciousness is the aesthetic end of the art. Grandmaster Caz, one of the architects of the art of MC-ing, describes the process as moving "from lines to sentences to paragraphs to verses to rhymes." Songwriting follows a similar progression; the difference is that rap sometimes makes the method its meaning.

"A good MC has to ride the beat. And a really strong beat will eat a wack MC alive," the poet Kyle Dargan, a child of the hip-hop generation, tells me. We're listening to Timbaland's pulsing "Jigga What, Jigga Who" beat, which Jay Z flows atop with casual virtuosity. When given a beat like that, an MC's goal is to figure out how not to get run over by it. An MC must have something to say and must fit it in the rhythmic space the beat allows. Where does Jay Z stay with and where does he stray from the rhythm of the track? Sometimes he goes double time. Sometimes he finds his way securely in the pocket. Sometimes he lags a little behind or jumps a little ahead. His capacity to find the beat's elasticity without stretching it to attenuation is one of the hallmarks of his rhyming skill. This virtuosity expresses itself almost entirely through rhythm. We marvel at the rhythmic ingenuity; that's the first thing that catches our attention. "An MC can get away with saying just about any old thing if the rhythm is right," Dargan concludes.

Long before hip-hop, James Brown was doing some freestyling of his own. Over the course of his career, he would follow essentially the same recording practice in the studio: establish his band's groove, then start extemporizing jive on top of it. "So much of his stuff comes out of a process of recording in

the studio, which is live jamming, with a tremendous amount of spontane-
ity, proto-rapping, verbal riffs like 'mo' peas,' 'get on the good foot,' 'popcorn,'
just like horn riffs," notes the anthropologist Steven Feld. ". . . And because
he's going from the sound to the sense—'mother popcorn,' 'mama come here
quick, bring me that lickin' stick'—it's the pops and the clicks, the /p/s, the
/k/s, the sounds of the words, not that they mean anything particular to
James, either when he utters them, or later. It's the sound of those words
together." Just as sound often leads sense in rap, it does the same in other
pop genres as well.

Lyric improvisation is a practice that cuts across genres. In her acclaimed
memoir *Just Kids*, Patti Smith relates an exchange she had with Sam Wag-
staff, an art curator and Smith's benefactor:

> "Say anything," he said. "You can't make a mistake when you im-
> provise."
> "What if I mess it up? What if I screw up the rhythm?"
> "You can't," he said. "It's like drumming. If you miss a beat, you
> create another."

Smith touts this moment as initiating her into the "secret of improvisa-
tion," which she would draw upon throughout her career. One hears it on
"Gloria" in the slurring conversational tone of the lines "I'm movin' in this
here atmosphere where anything's allowed/And I go to this here party and
I just get bored," which leads to the more melodically structured lines that
follow, "Until I look out the window, see a sweet young thing/Humpin' on
the parking meter, leanin' on the parking meter." These lines might equally
be the product of studied labor or in-the-moment invention. What matters
here is the effect—the contrast and play between chaos and order.

One of the most amazing live performances I ever witnessed came in the
early 2000s at Black Lily, the New York–based musical happening, often
hosted by the Roots. A young R&B singer named Jaguar Wright took the
stage to perform extemporized lyrics with all the feeling of a vintage soul stir-
rer and all the look-ma-no-hands swagger of a battle rapper. To watch her
keep the beat and craft a melody atop the Roots' rhythms and chord progres-
sions, all while furnishing rhymes and fashioning a narrative, was nothing
short of miraculous. Only in retrospect, though, did I become conscious of
the feats of her lyric technique. In the moment of performance, I was too
captivated by what her voice was doing to give much thought to what her
brain was pulling off.

When a composer furnishes a lyricist with music in need of words, as was almost always the case in Tin Pan Alley days and remains a common practice of popular music today, some of the lyricist's decisions are already made. The song's time signature dictates the points on each lyric line that will receive a strong beat and therefore command the most emphasis. The melody will even dictate rhyme: "It is a mark of skill in a lyricist when he uses a lot of open rhymes on long notes at the ends of musical phrases," writes Gene Lees in his songwriter's bible, *The Modern Rhyming Dictionary*. The melody will also draw the ear to particular moments in a song by elevating pitch or otherwise generating sonic drama, even before language renders those moments concrete. In this regard, the composer asserts a greater share of control over a song than either the lyricist or the performer. Stephen Sondheim explains this dynamic:

> Performers can color a lyric with phrasing and rubato (rhythmic fluidity), but it's the melody which dictates the lyric's rhythms and pauses and inflections, the accompaniment which sets the pace and tone. These specific choices control our emotional response, just as a movie director's camera controls it by restricting our point of view, focusing us to look at the details he wants us to notice. For the songwriter, it's a matter of what phrase, what word, he wants us to focus on; for the director, what face, what gesture. An actor singing 'Oh, what a beautiful mornin'' might want to emphasize 'beautiful,' but Rogers forces him to emphasize 'mornin'' by setting the word on the strongest beat in the measure and the highest note in the melody.

Consider the aforementioned chorus from Rodgers and Hammerstein's *Oklahoma!* The rhythm of the accompaniment and the shape of the melody set the following words in sonic spotlight:

> *Oh*, what a *beautiful morning*
> *Oh*, what a *beautiful day*
> *I've* got a *wonderful feeling*
> *Everything's going* my *way*

Poetic scansion reveals that the lines are charged with a dactylic pulse (a pattern of one stressed syllable followed by two unstressed syllables) that lends a rhythmic feel akin to a waltz. The first two metrical feet in each line are dactyls; the third is truncated into trochees (one stressed followed by one unstressed syllable). This imbalance in the poetics, however, is resolved in the melody, which extenuates the syllables of the last word in each line. Notice that the syllables emphasized by the arrangement of language echo the emphasis accorded by the melody:

> *Oh*, what a/*beau*tiful/*mor*ning
> *Oh*, what a/*beau*tiful/*day*
> *I've* got a/*won*derful/*feel*ing
> *Everything's*/*going* my/*way*

A great deal of the success of this elegant song is a consequence of the coordination of rhythm and emphasis in the music and lyric. "Melody should mirror the natural rhythm of the language as much as possible," according to Jimmy Webb, a pop songwriter with experience writing for Broadway. As one can see above, the natural accents of the language and the accents conjured by the music overlap in a mutually supportive way. The result is a song in which the melody gains resonance and inspires memory through the words, and the words gain emotive depth through the music.

Musicians use the term "prosody" to capture the way that a lyric sits in a musical context. An ideal space exists in which a prosodically matched lyric fits "correctly" into the rhythms of the music. The relation of musical bars to metrical feet is rarely one for one; for instance, if a line of lyric scans as iambic tetrameter, it is likely to require more than just four musical beats, a single bar, to fit it. Effective lyricists write with a sense of the line as performed; in other words, they anticipate that a single syllable might sustain itself over an entire musical measure or more, that lyric lines will expand and contract as the melody requires or as the performer dictates. "In songwriting, uniformity in the length of lines creates monotony and works at cross-purposes to the fluidity and diversity that interesting music requires and that the composer will want to achieve," writes Webb. "From a songwriting standpoint 'nursery rhyme' predictability is not only annoying but debilitating. The best lyrics have an element of asymmetry in the length and positioning of the different lines."

Lyrics can flood the line or leave it wanting. Often lyrics written before the music are simply too wordy, which is why poems intended for the page rarely work well as lyrics. Given a blank page, a poet or a song lyricist will be hard pressed not to fill it. "Composers, on the other hand," writes Sheila Davis, "instinctively think of held tones, and they tend to carve out melodies with some open spaces between the notes." The necessary economy of song lyrics is perhaps more readily born of writing to a melody and rhythm that defines spaces for language. "It would appear that composers have the rhythmic edge," Davis continues. "To state the obvious: they use notes for the musical framework of a song, whereas lyricists must struggle to make musical structures with mere words." The words of song lyrics have their intrinsic rhythms that don't always match up precisely with the rhythms in the music. One can see and hear the sway that music has over language at those times, for instance, when a singer holds a single word, even a single syllable, over an entire measure or more. Think of Whitney Houston sustaining her "I" in the triumphant final chorus of "I Will Always Love You." These moments of difference, however, generally work as part of a system in which the rhythm of lyrics and the rhythm of music accord.

This is not to say that lyrics must always follow music. The process is rarely as clear-cut, given the necessity of working back and forth between language and music in songwriting. "There is nothing about beginning with a lyric that prohibits the careful development of a beautiful chord structure," Webb reminds us, "and chord structure directs melody into areas of grace and originality at least as much as the form and meter of a lyric." Billy Joel, speaking of his contemporary Elton John, observed the following about the lyric-or-music-first question: "Now, I've seen him write to Bernie's [collaborator Bernie Taupin's] lyrics. He looks at the lyric, and he sits down and starts writing music. I do it the other way around. I write music first, and then I jam lyrics on top of it. So there's a totally different dynamic to how we work."

Willie Nelson, one of the most prolific American songwriters of all time, prefers to write his lyrics before the music. "Melodies are the easiest part for me, because the air is full of melodies," he writes. "I hear them all the time, around me everywhere, night and day. If I need a melody, I pluck one out of the air." He tells the story of sharing the lyric to one of his most famous songs, "On the Road Again," with a group of friends, including the filmmaker Sydney Pollack, before he had written the music to accompany it.

"How about the melody? What does it sound like?" Sydney asked.

I said I didn't know, I would work on the melody later. I didn't give any more thought to the melody until months later, the day before I was going into the studio to cut it. I saw no reason to put a melody to something I wasn't ready to record. I knew I wouldn't have any problem pulling the melody out of the air.

Not every songwriter can simply pull melodies out of thin air, of course. The anecdote underscores the fact that the dominion of melody and song over lyric is far from absolute. The relationship is dynamic, involving intuitive moves on both the composer's and the lyricist's parts. Gil Scott-Heron, who wrote some of his best-known songs with his musical collaborator Brian Jackson, describes the creative process in exquisite detail. It's worth quoting him at length:

> I had an affinity for jazz and syncopation, and the poetry came from the music. We made the poems into songs, and we wanted music to sound like words, and Brian's arrangements very often shaped and molded them. Later on when we wrote songs together, I'd ask Brian what he had on his mind, which sometimes I could more or less intuit from the music, because it carried an atmosphere with it. Different progressions and different chord structures brought a certain tone to mind. Sometimes I'd ask him and he'd convey in words what sort of feeling he was trying to bring about with that particular chord and that helped me get into it.

The melding of music and language that Scott-Heron describes is a testament to his songwriting partnership with Jackson and to the mutually constitutive relationship pop music at its best can achieve. Across the pop-music landscape, one comes across countless instances in which the laws of prosody are trampled, tarnished, or otherwise violated, often without compromising the song. Certainly, pop music is a space in which matters of rhythm and form are less scrupulously governed than in Tin Pan Alley songs or in today's musical theater. "The metronomic cadences of classical rhythm must give way, certain notes must be elongated, space must be allocated for the singer to take air, long musical phrases may call for more metric feet in one line than another, other musical lines will be abrupt and attenuated, etc.," notes Webb. "In other words there is a nonregimented quality to most nonmilitary melody. This calls for a compromise between regular rhythm and anarchy on the part of the lyricist and composer." Turn on the radio right now and listen for five or ten minutes and you'll likely hear half a dozen instances where words and music clash in rhythm, either through error or conscious design.

I felt this rhythmic tension even before I had the words to express it as such. Listening to Toto's "Africa" as a seven-year-old in 1982, I can remember being unsettled by the word "Serengeti"—or, more specifically, by the way that "Serengeti" sounded in the song. I'll quote several other lines from the verse so you can see it in context:

> The wild dogs cry out in the night
> As they grow restless longing for some solitary company
> I know that I must do what's right
> As sure as Kilimanjaro rises like Olympus above the Serengeti

As performed, it always sounded awkward to me. Part of it has to do with the pattern of the melody, as reflected in the poetics of the lyric. The lines establish a pulsing short/long/short/long structure, with the first and third lines coming in at a compact eight syllables apiece, while the second and fourth lines dilate that length, with sixteen syllables in line two and a whopping twenty-one syllables in line four. In addition, the rhythmic and melodic structure of the line forces the lead singer, Joseph Williams, into circumlocutions of stress that end up mangling the final word of that longest line; instead of "Seren*ge*ti," the rhythm and melody of the song force him to pronounce it as "*Se*rengeti."

The melody also subjects the last word in line two, "company," to a similar distortion, though it is less severe, perhaps because the word naturally carries a stress on its first syllable and perhaps because it doesn't come in quick succession after "Kilimanjaro" and "Olympus" in a line already packed with syllables. In any case, I understand this moment now as an unhappy, though fleeting, collision of contrary rhythms. The song still moves me, however, all the more now for this small window into the world of its rhythm.

Certainly there are instances in pop music in which a studied tension or unexpected clash between the rhythms of music and lyric produces a great song. Tension on the level of rhythm doesn't always register as a mistake. A common practice in popular music is introducing rhythmic variation and complexity after establishing regularity throughout most of the song. Crosby, Stills & Nash's "Marrakesh Express" is a rhythmically ordered song that generates much of its mood and energy from the lilting lightness of its melody and cadence. The song contains three verses, of which the first two are as close to rhythmically identical as they could be: Each five-line verse rhymes AABBC with the stressed-syllable count of 6-6-4-4-5. Even the total syllable count per line is nearly identical across the verses. The third verse, however, introduces a subtle rhythmic subversion. The third line of the third verse includes an additional unstressed syllable, for a total of eight syllables instead of the seven in the third lines of the previous verses. This leads to syncopation in the singing. I've transcribed the third line of each verse below:

First verse: *Ducks* and *chicks* and *pigeons call*
Second verse: *Hope* the *days* that *lie ahead*
Third verse: *Col*ored *cottons hang in* the *air*

It's a small disruption, one that nonetheless calls attention to itself in the listening. The result is repetition, but with a difference. The ear registers both the now-familiar pattern and the slight departure not as an accident, but as a small embellishment that the song's otherwise strict formal adherence earns for it.

The relation of musical to poetic rhythms is both an art and a science. "A song," writes Webb, "is a magical marriage between a lyric (some words) and a melody (some notes). It is not a poem. It is not music. It is in this gray area of synthesis between language, rhythm and sound that some of the most acute of all sensors of human emotion lie." This "gray area of synthesis" finds definition and clarity in one place: performance.

PERFORMATIVE RHYTHM

The language of lyrics divorced from song is a language of pure rhythm. It is sequenced syllables accorded different levels of verbal stress in keeping with the natural inflections of speech and the ordered imposition of art. It behaves, in other words, like poetry. There's music to lyrics when read in this way, though that music is primarily percussive. For all their rhythmic character, however, words are never simply sound. "Words hold meaning—they serve as vessels for it—whereas musical sounds, by some accounts, are the meaning," writes Elizabeth Hellmuth Margulis.

Melody casts a spell on language, rendering it wondrous and unpredictable. One often finds a generative tension at work between the way a line appears on the page and the way it is performed in relation to the musical accompaniment and the vocal melody. How singers inflect a given line—what syllables they emphasize, where they pause or extend a sound—shapes the melody and, in doing so, maps a dynamic relationship on the lyrics as written.

For analytical purposes, it is useful to draw a distinction between lyrics at rest—that is, as fixed composition on the page, where they exist as a set of relations in rhythm—and lyrics in motion—that is, as interpreted by a singer in the context of a performance, in which the words are shaded with melody and idiosyncratic emphasis that defy the iterative logic dictated both by the habits of pronunciation and by the practices of poetic convention. The melody often overtakes the small rhythm of the words, and the melodic line exercises a linguistic logic all its own, one that works with and against the inborn impulses of the words themselves. Melody leaves no footprint in the lyrics as rendered on the page. To put it another way, melody charges the words in ways impossible to discern simply with a lyric transcription.

Consequently, one might be tempted to assume that lyrics in motion render lyrics at rest superannuated, but that is not the case. Attending to the resting state of a song lyric offers an unexpected window into the lyric in motion, one that suggests both a simple causal relationship between the two versions and an imbricated linkage that attests to the subtle ways that skilled singers command the language.

The relationship between the lyrics as written—the lyrics as poetry—and the lyrics as performed is defining for pop songs. Where are the two qualities in sync and where are they disjointed, and what effect, whether conscious or not, do they achieve together? Do poor songs tend to create certain relations between text and performance in the way that they do with poor prosody? Do poor singers make mistakes that can be better understood in the relation between lyric and performance? Equally, do great songs and great singers evince certain habits that are apparent in this relation between the lyric as text and the lyric as song?

Consider Van Morrison's "Into the Mystic" both as lyric and as recorded performance. Where does he follow as a singer the natural course of the language as he composed it, and where does he resist it? Do these moments reliably correspond to certain emotive effects, certain feelings of tension or ease, that he wishes to conjure in the listener? Two versions of the first verse of "Into the Mystic" follow, one scanned for its poetic stresses, the other marked with the stresses Van Morrison accords the language in his original studio recording of the song:

> We were *born* be*fore* the *wind*
> *A*lso *young*er *than* the *sun*
> *Ere* the *bonnie boat* was *won*
> As we *sailed* in*to* the *mys*tic

> We were *born* be*fore* the *wind*
> *A*lso *young*er than the *sun*
> *Ere* the *bonnie boat* was *won*
> As we *sailed* into the *mys*tic

The lyrics themselves fall into four-beat lines of iambic trimeter, with an important exception in the fourth line of the verse, which opens with an anapestic foot (two unstressed and one stressed syllables) and includes only three stressed syllables, creating a sense of resolution for the verse through this small rhythmic variation. In performance, Morrison underscores the rhythmic shape of his lyric through glissando and tonal shifts. The differences are few but instructive: augmenting the level of stress in certain syllables ("bonnie boat") and diminishing the level of stress in others ("into" from the fourth line). This sometimes subtle, sometimes seismic shifting of the patterns of language as expressed from how they are written is one of Van Morrison's defining elements of style.

"Van Morrison is interested, *obsessed* with how much musical or verbal information he can compress into a small space, and, almost conversely, how far he can spread one note, word, sound, or picture. To capture one moment, be it a caress or a twitch," observed the famed rock critic Lester Bangs. The poetics of the lyric in "Into the Mystic" is not ancillary to Van Morrison's music and performance; it is defining. His pushing and pulling at the syllables relies on them having an expected place in our minds, a place cemented by their poetic arrangement. If the lyric were less soundly constructed and less rigorously patterned Van Morrison would not enjoy the performative freedom that he does, and the song would not be as great as it is.

The move from lyrics on the page to performance is an act of translation. It requires attending to the specific shape of the song as rendered in the abstract as well as to the song's spirit. Communicating that spirit may at times mean complicating or even contradicting the lyrics and music as composed. "I get to a point where I would make so much out of a single line," recalls Bruce Springsteen on his early days as a singer-songwriter. "And if there would be a word or two in there and you're just not singing that word right, you get pretty crazy about it." The process of moving from page to performance is taxing. At least part of the success of a song, though, relies on the poetic construction of the lyric. Contrastingly, a singer can compensate for certain deficits or elisions in the lyrics through interpretation and performance.

Certain songs carry reputations among singers. "The Star-Spangled Banner," for instance, is notoriously difficult to sing because of the vocal range it requires; it was written, it seems, with little regard for the poor souls who would have to sing it at sporting events across the United States every night. Certain songs are known to be easy to sing, both because the range of the melody suits most voices and because the lyrics ease the process of performance. Short melodic lines generally make for smoother singing. In analyzing the declarative vocal performance style of the Kinks' Ray Davies, for instance, Steven Tyler of Aerosmith offered the following compelling proposition: "You know why they sang it like that? Shel Talmey, their producer, thought that Ray Davies couldn't sing, so he told him to blurt it out in short little telegraphic outbursts. That way you don't have to sing the melody. Fucking genius, because every word hammers at you, every word is percussion in that song. I love that."

Sometimes producers and songwriters do the opposite, purposely composing songs that are rhythmically difficult to sing. "'Backdoor lover always hiding 'neath the covers.' You can't SING that unless you're a drummer or have some major sense of rhythm," Tyler writes, using one of his own lyrics to set his own sense of rhythm against that of Davies. Another famous rock singer with a drummer's pedigree, Don Henley, argues that a drummer's intimate knowledge of rhythm can enhance both songwriting and vocal performance.

> It helps define the meter of the lyrics. It teaches me how to sing in the holes, and it helps my phrasing a great deal. When I used to play and sing at the same time I would sing around my playing, and vice versa. I try to write conversationally; I try to write like people speak and put the emphasis on the right syllable. I hear a lot of songwriters who put emphasis on the wrong syllable of a word and it drives me up the wall. When you're singing a word, the emphasis should be on the syllable that it's normally on. Sometimes songwriters and singers forget that. They get a melody in their head and the notes will take precedence, so that they wind up forcing a word onto a melody. It doesn't ring true.

Henley's rhythmic sensibility, as a singer and a songwriter, seeks out the inborn rhythms in the lyric line, aspiring to a conversational sound. Of course, a great melody can sometimes supersede the interests of conversational lyric expression. The melody of the great pop-song-turned-jazz-standard "Tenderly," for instance, forces the emphasis in the title word to the final syllable rather than the first, as we would expect in normal usage. We forgive it, though, because the elegance of the melody overpowers the inelegance of the wrenched word.

Most often any rhythmic tension between language and melody, between composition and performance, is hidden from listeners' ears. On occasion, though, songwriters seek ways of making the difficulty apparent in a bravura gesture of rhythmic play. Nile Rodgers describes writing Diana Ross's "Upside Down" using "excessively polysyllabic words like 'instinctively' and 'respectfully' in the lyrics, because we wanted to utilize Diana's sophistication to achieve a higher level of musicality. Along with the complicated verse, we deliberately made the chorus rhythmically more difficult to sing than the catchier, one-listen song hooks for Chic [Rodgers's band, which scored its biggest hit with "Good Times" in 1979]." With a particular aesthetic aim in mind, Rodgers crafted a song to showcase Ross's virtuosity, as well as his own.

Song lyrics at rest follow a Newtonian logic and doggedly insist on staying at rest. Certain lyrics are difficult to put in motion as song. These lyrics are often composed before the melody and then retrofitted to music. One might think here of the "raps" that are often written by those with only the most rudimentary and incomplete knowledge of rap itself. Think, too, of amateur lyrics written without respect to the limits of normal vocal range, or to the necessity for space where the music can reside. These are lyrics at permanent rest, lyrics that make sense only on the page and fail to lend themselves to performance.

The other Newtonian claim is equally true: Lyrics in motion tend to stay in motion, which is to say that once we hear a song it is nearly impossible to read the lyrics without referencing their performance in our head. Try reading the lines to "Respect" without an Aretha Franklin concert breaking out between your ears. For our purposes, though, it is not necessary and not even desirable to achieve some sort of naïve and impartial relation to the lyrics we analyze. The vestiges of performance that stick to the lines on the page provide useful information for analyzing the poetics of the lines as well. They invite a hybridized process of close reading that engages by turns both ear and eye. Together, it helps explain the practice of phrasing.

RHYTHM AND PHRASING

There's a difference between reading a novel or a poem or a speech aloud and performing a lyric from sheet music. Both involve the act of reading, though the means of articulation is dramatically different. Some of those differences are obvious: A reader of prose has only the rudiments of syntax and punctuation to govern the pace and structure of vocalizing. A reader of a poem generally has more direction, through line breaks that signal subtle pauses or clusters of rhythms that invite a certain ordered phrasing. But for the most part, readers have little more than their own sensibilities and the page.

By contrast, singers have an abundance of instruction when it comes to performing song lyrics. Sheet music provides the tone and the tempo, even sometimes the mood. When recording vocals in a studio, a singer generally has producers, sound engineers, fellow musicians, and a host of hangers-on ready to provide input on matters of pitch, cadence, and inflection. For all of this, though, singers also have to read a lyric; even when that lyric is performed from memory or improvised on the spot, there's a silent negotiation between the language as conceived and the language as voiced. In this regard, at least, a singer shares the same burden as any reader. Writing of poetry, the literary critic David Caplan observes that "a reader who silently mouths these words fails to experience them fully. Instead, he or she must perform them, interpret the written document as a script for verbal articulation." This holds doubly true for song lyrics.

If lyrics are a script for verbal articulation of the lyric phrase, then singers must attain facility as readers and interpreters as well as vocalists. Reflecting on his apprenticeship as a country singer under Chet Atkins, the father of outlaw country, Waylon Jennings, recalls the hard lesson of learning how his voice could—and why his voice should—interpret a written lyric. "Words are so important to country music, you need to hear every one," Jennings writes. "[Chet] always tried to get artists to enunciate clearly, and I agreed with him. There are at least three different ways of saying the words 'beautiful' and 'darling,' and each has a different meaning." Jennings's observation extends across genres. The quality of stress and vocal inflection a singer imparts to a word or phrase can have a radical impact on the audience's understanding, emotional connection, and enjoyment of a song.

Phrasing measures the exercise of performance on poetry over and against the dictates of music. The lyrics are the poetry, the melody is the music, and the performance resolves whatever differences exist between the other two. No singer has full autonomy when it comes to performing a song. She must attend to the dictates of the lyrics, in the particulars of the words as well as in the way that those words' arrangement dictates everything from where the singer can breathe to where the stresses naturally fall along the line. She must also situate her performance in relation to the music, both the accompaniment and the melodic line, which dictate where the voice rises and falls along the scale, where one finds pockets of breath, and how the song shades emotions. Singers can take certain liberties both with the lyrics and with the music, but they do so in a prescribed interpretive frame. Stray too far from the melody and the song is lost, rendered unrecognizable to the audience. Break the lyrics or even the phrasing established by the poetics and the music of the line and one risks exposing the inherent vulnerabilities of the human voice—the gasping for breath, or the fumbling to fit words in a measure.

When a young Quincy Jones was arranging for Frank Sinatra, he marveled at the quality of Sinatra's phrasing. "Some singers like to work in front of the beat. Some lag a little behind it. Frank did it all: in front, dead center, and slightly behind, as though it were inevitable," recalls Jones.

> Just like Billie Holiday and Louis Armstrong, whom he adored, Frank had grown up singing with the big bands and learning how to sound like a horn, so he knew exactly where the beat was at all times. He swung so hard, you could've turned him upside down and shaken every piece of change out of his pocket, and he would have never missed a beat. He grooved through the first sixteen bars of "Come Fly with Me," then took a long drag on his cigarette just before the bridge. When he hit the bridge and sang, "When I get you up there, where the air is rare . . . ," he turned his head so that a pinspot of blue light onstage would catch his profile, and finally blew a stream of smoke out of his mouth. It was incredible. He had every delicate nuance down. He wasted nothing—not words, not emotions, not notes. He was about pure economy, power, style, and skill.

The many rhythms of a song meet in a singer's phrasing: lyric, music, and performance all relate in balance, and sometimes imbalance. How much leeway a singer takes with the rhythmic and melodic structure of a song depends on the particulars of individual style. Sinatra, for instance, pushed the limits of how a given lyric line can fit in the musical measure, while his contemporary Johnny Hartman favored a style that adheres more strictly to the lyric's prescribed place. In *How Music Works*, David Byrne offers a helpful description of how singers' rhythmic invention recasts the relationship between performers and audience:

A good singer will often use the "grid" of the rhythm as something to play with—never landing exactly on a beat, but pushing and pulling around and against it in ways that we read, when it's well done, as being emotional. It turns out that not being perfectly aligned with a grid is okay; in fact, sometimes it feels better than a perfectly metric fixed-up version. When Willie Nelson or George Jones sing way off the beat, it somehow increases the sense that they're telling you the story, conveying it to you, one person to another.

The producer Jerry Wexler invokes the term "tempo rubato," or "stolen time," which was coined during the Baroque era, to describe this play with the rhythmic grid. A singer robs time from one measure and gives it to another when he speeds up and then slows down, or vice versa, to render a greater sense of expressive freedom and invention. Singing in this style requires an intrinsic sense of time so that the singer understands how much he or she can "steal" while still respecting the structure of the melody and the integrity of the lyrics. Stealing time demands breath control, a sense of how best to shape a phrase, and an understanding of the emotive potentialities one can expose through rhythmic variation. "The three masters of rubato in our age are Frank Sinatra, Ray Charles and Willie Nelson," Wexler writes. "The art of gliding over the meter and extending it until you think they're going to miss the next actual musical demarcation—but they always arrive there, at bar one. It's some kind of musical miracle."

People sometimes criticize Nelson for singing off rhythm; indeed, his way of rendering a lyric was strikingly out of phase with his contemporaries when he first broke into Nashville's country and western scene. In one of his several memoirs, Nelson reflects on shattering the generic expectations for vocal phrasing in country music. "Even though I was writing a country song," Nelson recalls, "I wasn't singing it in the traditional way. Not that I couldn't. I just wanted to phrase it the way I felt like phrasing it. I could sing on the beat if I wanted to, but I could put more emotion in my lyrics if I phrased in a more conversational, relaxed way." By destabilizing the expected balance of rhythms across lyric and song through his distinctive phrasing, he could generate emotional tension and energy, teasing out anticipation and, at the last minute, delivering fulfillment. Too much precision in vocal rhythm can rob a performance of its humanity and vitality; equally, though, too much license can render the music muddled and inexpressive.

Nelson explains his innovation in phrasing this way: "I found I could get ahead of the beat or fall behind the beat and still make it all work out in the end without breaking meter. . . . I never intentionally broke meter, but I did intentionally phrase dangerously close to it." "Phrasing dangerously close" to the break is one element that makes Nelson's singing so unmistakable. His voice—its timbre, its measured twang, its calibrated vibrato—is a rich instrument.

Nelson's phrasing also satisfies the inborn human desire for both rhythmic regularity and difference. Writing in *The Atlantic*, Derek Thompson reported on a 2011 Harvard study that demonstrated that listeners found robotic rhythms too precise. "There is something perfectly imperfect about how humans play rhythms," Harvard physics researcher Holger Hennig told Thompson. "The lurches and hesitations are internalized through performance, and after a while everyone knows when they'll happen," observes David Byrne. "The performers don't have to think about them, and at some point that becomes part of the band's sound. Those agreed-upon imperfections are what give a performance character, and eventually the listener recognizes that it's the very thing that makes a band or singer distinctive."

Nelson is nothing if not distinctive. His phrasing accounts for how he can make even other people's songs his own. You can hear it on Nelson's cover of the country classic "Always on My Mind," where the background singers abide by the traditional dictates of the rhythm while Nelson wanders off and on, drawn by his own sense of musical time and space. You can hear it, too, on Nelson's rendition of the Cindy Walker song "You Don't Know Me." "You Don't Know Me" was originally released in 1956 by the country singer Eddy Arnold, then again later that same year by Jerry Vale, whose version peaked at number fourteen on the pop charts. It settled into the space of a standard; it has now been recorded numerous times by artists in and out of the country genre.

Perhaps the two finest versions of "You Don't Know Me" belong, not coincidentally, to two singers who employ a high degree of rubato: Nelson and Ray Charles. Though the shape and emotional impact of their two performances are striking in their own ways, they share a similar approach to the song. Contrast that with Arnold's original, which more faithfully adheres to Nashville's standard performance practices, and one understands what Nelson means when he attests to the emotive power one can generate through calculated suspension and release. The simple song, which consists of only a few chords, and straightforward lyrics convey a sense of vulnerability and intimacy that the words alone only partly suggest. Both Nelson's and Charles's performances render the song richer in their emotional shading of Walker's words. Both performers exploit the space between the bars, the pulse that separates the end of the fourth beat of one measure and the beginning of the first beat of the next. Rather than a space for breath, a pause to acknowledge the end of the bar and the close of the lyric line, Nelson and Charles fill it instead with melody, finding their breath in the midst of the measure where the pause is unexpected.

How much of that power can be attributed to the fact that Nelson and Charles both bend but never break the meter? For an instructive contrast, look no further than Michael McDonald's overembellished version of the song. Redolent of melisma (several notes strung across a single syllable) and a surfeit of vibrato (the pulsating change of pitch), McDonald's version comes across like a display of technique rather than an emotional appeal. He breaks the meter, repeatedly, and with great prejudice. As a consequence, he draws attention away from the simple beauty of the song and its emotionally naked lyrics and, instead, calls attention to his overdressed stylizing and vocal showboating. With Nelson's and Charles's versions one always knows who is singing the song, but one never loses sight of the song itself.

Phrasing is closely tied to the structure of the lyrics on the level of the syllable. Although a vocalist's improvised decision to sing a certain line a certain way can come across as an idiosyncratic consequence of performance, the improvisation is frequently a result of the lyrics themselves. Like a Judd Apatow film where audiences often assume the humor is the product of the actors' improvisations, the funny lines are most often in the script itself. So it is with a good song; those qualities we might attribute to the singer's idiosyncratic sensibility are often written right into the language of the lyric. The same is often true of poetry. Listen to Gwendolyn Brooks reading her most famous poem, "We Real Cool," aloud and the shape it takes on the page seems preordained. She bites off the end of each "we" to mark the sharp enjambments that define the poem's form ("We real cool. We / Left school. We"). Like a great vocalist, Brooks luxuriates in the artful tension between her listener's expectations of how a semantic unit should unfold and her distinctive, disruptive phrasing (registered on the page through enjambment) that endows the poem with its rhythm and meaning. The shape of the lyric, be it in literary poetry or in song, does far more to encode and to inform its performance than we usually give it credit for doing. Sometimes the silent lyrics on the page reveal secrets about the song that no manner of listening could ever do.

It is instructive to see a gifted singer at work interpreting a familiar song. One can hear the assertion of style in elements like rhythm and tone as well as the singer's restraint and respect for the song itself. The performed rhythm and tempo of a song lyric are not identical to its meter, nor to the measure of its music. Often, a singer's performance works against the implied meter of the line, the rhythm of the music, or both. Aretha Franklin is such an interpreter. Gifted with a powerful vocal instrument, she also understands the liberties she can take with melody without compromising the integrity of the song. My friend Andy Schneidkraut, longtime proprietor of Boulder's Albums on the Hill and repository of musical knowledge, likes to say that Franklin does not so much sing a note as she locates it. In that seeing-eye method of finding the notes, Franklin creates small dramas in places where no drama naturally exists. This can be maddening to some. When balanced right, though, it can achieve a pitch of emotional intensity unmatched by other styles of singing. At base, Franklin's approach to singing relies on destabilizing the rhythms of both language and song. In this regard, she shares something with an eclectic assortment of other singers from Ray Charles to Willie Nelson to Frank Sinatra who, for all their obvious differences, share one big thing in common: They know how to exploit the elasticity of the lyric phrase in the context of the music's rhythm.

Overdetermined rhyme schemes and rhythm patterns require the elasticity of the human voice to move them toward natural speech. The end result is artifice without being artificial, stylized but not stilted. That's why we can still read aloud with pleasure the metrical verse of Coleridge, which plays on and off fixed patterns, but Longfellow's near-perfection of artificial forms makes it difficult to voice his lines without resorting to singsong. This holds as well for song lyrics. Many songs, though certainly not all, strive for the natural, albeit ordered, voice. Think of artists as far removed from one another as James Taylor and Jay Z, each of whom seeks a conversational tone. Contrast them with Thom Yorke and Rihanna, who consciously stylize their deliveries and accentuate the sharp edges of lyric. Rather than reaching for the conversational, they seek the confrontational, challenging assumptions of how a word or sequence of words should sound. Many have observed, for instance, that Rihanna stretches the three syllables in the word "umbrella" into four—*um-bur-el-la*—in a way that makes something familiar exciting and strange. No one, not even Rihanna, speaks like Rihanna sings.

In reading prose, readers govern the tempo; beyond punctuation, paragraph breaks, and the dictates of the page, readers are free to set the words to their own pace. Songs present the structure of the music, the duration of the musical measure, the time signature of the tune, and the span in which a certain lyric line must be expressed. These constraints are also opportunities, and skilled singers find ways to assert personal style and feeling in the space the song allows. Writing of Otis Redding, the musicologist Allan F. Moore calls attention to the ways that Redding would dilate the lyric line. "Perhaps Redding's most effective tool in terms of playful voicedness is his sense of rhythmic play," Moore notes. "He routinely breaks up lines by inserting rests between words that would normally, both in speech and song, flow together. This is often augmented by the repetition of a word on either side of the rest. The net result of such effects is to convey the notion of halting speech, indicating that the singer is getting so emotionally overcome that he is unable to generate smooth, flowing 'normal' linguistic utterances, just as commonly happens with real people in real life during emotionally loaded moments." Redding "reads" the lyric through his distinctive phrasing of the song, endowing it with emotion that it might not otherwise communicate in the voice of another singer.

On "Try a Little Tenderness," for instance, Redding voices the lyrics in clustered phrases that coil up and release their emotive energy. Compare the following transcriptions, the first from the Ray Noble Orchestra's original 1932 recording of the song with vocals by Val Rosing, and the second from Redding's 1966 studio recording:

> You know she's waiting
> Just anticipating
> Things she may never possess
>
> > (Ray Noble Orchestra)

> You ... know ... she's waitiiiing
> Just ... an ... tiss ... uh ... pay ... ting
> A thing ... that she'll never-never-never-never-possess
>
> > (Otis Redding)

Rosing's voice glides in easy syncopation with the rhythm of the music and the metrical inclination of the lyric line, while Redding's phrasing pushes and pulls and finally breaks the bounds of the lyric's rhythmic and poetic dictates. In the first line, Redding sets the two opening words apart from one another, separating but not severing their semantic link. In the second line he revels in the multisyllabic possibilities of "anticipating," creating space around every syllable so as better to charge each with emphasis. Finally, in the third line, he catches on that single, central word, "never," holding it up before us to let it refract the light of multiple meanings, containing them all in prismatic splendor. The song remains more or less the same, but the singer's sense of time and language and feel has rendered it reborn, renewed.

In addition to considering two singers' renditions of the same song, it is useful to consider one singer's version of the same song at different times. In 1937 a twenty-two-year-old Billie Holiday recorded "I've Got My Love to Keep Me Warm"; it was one of her first recordings. More than twenty years later she recorded the song for the last time, just before her death in 1959 at the age of forty-four. The words are the same, though Holiday's voice and her vocal approach to the song have markedly changed. Think about the young Holiday's clarion-clear tone set against her ravaged voice on the late recording. More than the tempo has changed. With the transformation of voice comes a transformation of meaning and emotion in the lines. Listen for the points of emphasis, the words and syllables that take a stress in her phrasing of the lyric. Is one better than the other? Certainly the vocal tone on the first recording is technically superior. But what about the emotional content? What about the conscious ways that Holiday exploits the expressive capacities of her damaged instrument? We're wont to impute greater feeling to the later recording, a knowingness and hard-won wisdom. Part of that is undoubtedly romanticization, the myth that the artist in pain is always the superior artist. That's not necessarily true. One can't deny that, better or worse or just different, Holiday's late recording of the song charges the lyrics with deeper emotional shades, rewrites the song while hardly altering a word.

When a great pop singer "reads" a song lyric, that song ceases to be the sum of its language and music. Even the silly becomes sublime. Writing of opera, Adriana Cavarero observes a tension between the denotative meanings of lyric language and their expression in vocal performance. "According to [Catherine] Clément, therefore, the libretto, the words, count," writes Cavarero. "They count precisely because their meaning is erased by a singing voice that makes even those who know it forget the text. Without the musical emotion, opera would be ridiculous—not only because of the literary style of the libretto, but also because of the stereotypical banality of the misogynist story that it stages. Sung by a voice that challenges human possibilities, this story becomes sublime."

One could say the same of so much pop. The Ronettes' "Be My Baby" is little more than a collection of trite words and canned sentiments. But Phil Spector's production and Ronnie Spector's passionate vocal performance make it electric. "When I'd sing a lyric, I'd close my eyes and try to feel the truest emotion I could find," she explains. "And I'd keep pushing myself until I got there. Then Phil would add that sound to the sounds of all the other singers, musicians, and engineers. And the result would be a wonderful combination of textures and personalities and genius that people started calling the wall of sound."

Like the librettos of Italian opera, the language of pop songs is at times ridiculous, simplistic, stereotypic, and misogynistic. Billie Holiday's lament that her man is gone is charged with sexist assumptions that deny her agency and power, but her performance wrests that agency and power back from the lyrics. Ronnie Spector's lovelorn longing is charged with dignity as well as desperation. Song lyrics on the page often betray their absurdity or triviality. We read them, though, to understand better what happens when a sublime voice enchants them. We read them to understand better why, despite their limitations, they still move us so.

Two final examples will suffice. The melody of the Police's 1980 hit "Don't Stand So Close to Me" conjures a sense of temptation and forbearance befitting a song about a teacher grappling with a schoolgirl's crush. From the verses to the chorus, this is a song about restraint and release. Sting sings the first verse in the hushed voice of a rumor, building tension with his overdubbed vocals halfway through, and building further with his falsetto harmonizing coming in on the critical final words of the verse: "this girl is half his *age*." The energy meted out so carefully throughout the verse finally comes busting out in the chorus, in ecstatic tones and contrapuntal harmonies.

A closer look at the lyric reveals a micro version of this macro pattern of restraint and release. The lines of the verses alternate between bifurcated phrases, split by a medial caesura (a slight pause in the center of the line), and whole lines that Sting performs in a single breath. The bifurcated lines are split in two through natural syntactical divisions (a comma, a colon) and through stylized pauses in phrasing that Sting employs to shape the line to fit the song's rhythmic pattern. In the quatrain that follows, you'll notice that Sting pauses briefly in the first and third lines—in the first, to signal the natural syntactical break of the comma, and in the third, to continue the stylized effect of phrasing that contrasts the line with the one that precedes it and the one that follows it. I've used a double slash mark to signal the medial caesura born of how Sting performs the line:

> Young teacher, the subject
> Of schoolgirl fantasy
> She wants him // so badly
> Knows what she wants to be

The first and third lines lurch and reach, while the second and fourth easily unfurl. The contrast and tension between these lyric states of being embody the speaker's conflicted emotion, rendered in syllable and sound.

In the song's chorus, the restraint-and-release pattern expresses itself in the halting, repeated phrasing of the song's title line. Here the language acts out in sound and semantics the resistance of the teacher to the allures of student. For all this, the song leaves the narrative unresolved, unrequited, and unconsummated. The end rhyme further accentuates the herky-jerky denial and fulfillment of the rhythm, following an alternating rhymed/unrhymed ABCBDEFE pattern in the first two verses. The rhyme intensifies in the final verse through alternating rhymes in the first half of the octet as ABAB instead of the expected ABCB. "Don't Stand So Close to Me" is a rich example of the ways that the lyrics on the page both reflect the performance and, in fact, dictate the terms of the performance they demand.

Similarly playing with this alternating pattern of restraint and release is Soundgarden's "Black Hole Sun." Like "Don't Stand So Close to Me," its lyrics' imbedded rhythmic structure conditions the song's performance. "Black Hole Sun" was a surprise summer hit in 1994 for the Seattle-based alternative rock group. The band's frontman, Chris Cornell, married brooding lyrics and a somber theme with a simple, delicate melody. Boasting a big, memorable chorus, one can understand how so many made space for it on their summer playlists beside anodyne hits like All-4-One's "I Swear" and Ace of Bass's "Don't Turn Around." Cornell's performance distinguishes "Black Hole Sun," his rich tenor gliding along a pulsing melodic line. There's something bluesy about the performance, in Cornell's tasteful moments of rhythmic departure and in the repetitions. The lyric begins with a series: "*In* my eyes, *in*disposed/*In* disguises no one knows." In the span of a rhyming couplet, Cornell plays a game of repetition with a difference. "In" dances across the lines, shifting shapes even as it creates an emphatic pattern of rhythm and sound.

A broader pattern establishes itself in these first two lines as well, one that will govern both verses in the song. It is imbedded in the song's linguistic DNA and does not announce itself, but it nonetheless shapes the song and the singing. This pattern is the back and forth between a line of six syllables followed by one of seven. The first verse matches this pattern to precision: 6/7/6/7/6/7/6/7. The missing syllable in the lines of six syllables is given over to a medial caesura. In all but the penultimate line of the verse, this caesura corresponds to a natural separation of syntax as well, like this: "Boiling heat, summer stench." After the six-syllable line, we experience the seven-syllable line as a kind of release—an uncoiling, if subtle—in Cornell's phrasing.

The song's phrasal patterning is particularly intriguing, however, because of what Cornell does in the second verse. Rather than simply duplicating the strict adherence to the 6/7 syllable pattern, he introduces a few instances of targeted departure from it. These departures are slight enough that they subvert without surrendering the form. In each of the three instances of the eight-line verse where he departs from the pattern, he does so by extending the syllable count. After beginning with the 6/7 pattern in the first two lines, he dilates the next two to 7/8 syllables, strictly speaking, though his performance of the lines downplays the difference as he partly swallows the extra syllables. You can hear—and see—this play out most prominently in the second verse, where I've marked his elision of the extra syllables by according the line a half syllable:

Stuttering, cold and damp	6
Steal the warm wind, tired friend	7
Times are gone for honest men	6.5
And sometimes far too long for snakes	7.5
In my shoes, a walking sleep	6.5
In my youth I pray to keep	7
Heaven send Hell away	6
No one sings like you anymore	8

Finally, in the last line of the verse Cornell decidedly enunciates all eight syllables ("No one sings like you anymore"), which conjures a tone of wistfulness and longing. The chorus comes in, but, as if to reassert the pattern of the verses and remind us that the divergences from the pattern were no accident, Cornell offers something of a coda: two lines that resume the 6/7 syllable count. Instead of leading into a third verse, the rhythm pattern returns again to the rousing strains of the chorus, getting swallowed up, as it were, in the black hole sun.

Chapter
Five

What rhymes with "liberty"? In 1832 Samuel Francis Smith, a twenty-three-year-old student at Andover Seminary, agreed to write lyrics for a patriotic song to be performed at a children's Independence Day celebration at Boston's Park Street Church. Cribbing his melody from a tune collected in a German songbook for children, which had borrowed its melody from the British national anthem, "God Save the King," Smith soon fitted words to song. "Seizing a scrap of waste paper, I began to write," he later recalled, "and in half an hour, I think, the words stood upon it substantially as they are sung to-day." Smith would title his song "America," though most of us now know it by its famous first line—which also contains the rhyme he found for "liberty"—"My Country 'Tis of Thee."

Rhyming "liberty" with "'tis of thee" might seem like surrender. After all, rhyme is generally understood as the concordance of sound and of stress in the endings of two *words*. "Cat" rhymes with "bat," and "power" rhymes with "shower" because the words begin differently and end the same. Given a multisyllabic word like "liberty," however, one-word rhyming options are few. Charlotte Brontë rhymes "liberty" with "tyranny" in her poem "Preference," and Shakespeare, with "injury" in Sonnet LVIII. Needless to say, neither of those words would have suited Smith's patriotic occasion. One can imagine Smith working backward from the word he knows he wants to use, planting a rhyme in an earlier line that will let him use it. Just a few lines later we see him doing it again, devising a pair of rhymes for the multisyllabic word "mountainside"—a word that has no single-word rhyme partner:

> Land where my *fathers died*
> Land of the *pilgrims' pride*
> From ev'ry *mountainside*

Multisyllabic words like "liberty" and "mountainside" all but demand that the songwriter rhyme single words with phrases instead of other single words. The phrase immeasurably expands one's semantic options while still satisfying rhyme's sonic requirements. Since we experience song lyrics through the ears rather than the eyes, any awkwardness and artificiality of such rhymes that might be exposed on the page are muted: sounds, after all, are sounds, whether drawn from one word or from many.

In the poetry of pop, rhyme frequently expresses itself in the relation of words with phrases. Because a multisyllabic rhyme word takes up considerable space on a line, it also necessarily implicates itself in that line's rhythm. What results are rhythm-rhyme units in which the sonic echo binding phrases extends beyond the narrow constraints of the rhyming pair to the words around them. On the Beatles "Michelle" from 1965, for instance, Paul McCartney sings:

> I love you, I love you, I love you
> That's all I want to say
> Until I find a way

The rhyme here is full and simple: "say" and "way." But the pattern of rhythmic stress extends past those two words, securing the lines in rhythm as well:

> That's *all* / I *want* / to *say*
> Un*til* / I *find* / a *way*

Both lines are written in iambic trimeter, with the heaviest stresses falling on the final accented syllables "*want* to *say*" and "*find* a *way*." You'll hear this same joining of rhythm and rhyme on Smokey Robinson and the Miracles' "Tears of a Clown," where Robinson writes (and sings) the following couplet: "Just like Pagliacci did / I try to keep my sadness hid." The lines are a wonderful collusion of the high cultural (the reference to the pagliacci— Italian for "clowns"—from the 1892 Ruggero Leoncavallo opera of the same name) and the colloquial contrivance of the second line ("sadness hid"). As with the Beatles example, Robinson offers a simple rhyme ("did" and "hid") that he imbeds in parallel rhythmic phrases ("Pa*gliacci did*" and "my *sadness hid*"). As a consequence, we experience rhyme in these lines not simply as a connection between two words but as the union of two phrases in rhythm and rhyme. "I think that a song should be poetic," Robinson told the *Detroit Free Press* in 1966, around the time he wrote "Tears of a Clown." "I want to hear something that rhymes."

In instances of such asymmetrical rhyming—where a multisyllabic word is paired with a phrase—the attendant rhythm pattern plays an even greater role. A compelling rhythmic echo across lines underscores the connection between rhyming units, rendering that which might come across as artificial in print seem natural in sound. Joni Mitchell's "Both Sides Now" is a study in rhyme's fluidity of form. Almost any lines from the song will do to illustrate this. Look at these from the beginning:

> Rows and floes of angel hair
> And ice cream castles in the air
> And feather canyons everywhere
> I've looked at clouds that way

These four lines set the AAAB rhyme pattern that all the song's verses will follow. They also model the collaborative work of rhythm and rhyme to erase any awkwardness of rhyming "angel hair" and "in the air" with "everywhere." Save for the trochees that dominate the opening lines of each verse, the song is structured entirely in the rising rhythm of iambs—iambic tetrameter, with iambic trimeter in the concluding line of each verse. Mitchell's ordered rhythmic universe in "Both Sides Now" creates a fixed form against which to play with patterns and disruptions in end rhyme, befitting a song about the loss of innocence in the face of life's experience.

Almost all pop songs contain rhyme, at the ends of lines and sometimes inside of them as well. End rhyme keeps time. It governs the rhythmic flow of the language, marking units of sound and of thought. Rhyme is the defining aesthetic demand on the song lyric, something that cannot be said for poetry written for the page. It's ironic that rhyme, the quality that once defined poetry, now clearly distinguishes poetry from song lyrics. We live in "a rhyme-drenched era" where "strong rhyme breathe[s] again" through rap and other forms of popular song lyric, not to mention advertising jingles, catchphrases, and political slogans. "As all those songs stuck in our heads confirm," writes the literary critic David Caplan, "the nature of rhyme has changed. It has grown more confident and assertive; it claims the airwaves and Internet; it swaggers and seduces." For all the variety of rhyme sources, song lyrics are by far the richest archive of rhymes of all types—full, slant, multisyllabic, and many others.

The story of rhyme's flight from contemporary lyric poetry is a familiar one, having to do with twentieth-century poets' conscious retreat to the page and studied submersion of the songlike qualities that once predominated in poetry meant for the ear as much as for the eye. "One 'discards rhyme,'" Ezra Pound wrote in his influential 1915 essay "Affirmations: As for Imagisme," "not because one is incapable of rhyming neat, fleet, sweet, meet, treat, eat, feet but because there are certain emotions or energies which are not to be represented by the over-familiar devices or patterns." Rhyme begins as surprise, a coincidence of sound that spans differences of sense. Overfamiliarity of particular rhyme pairs (the "moon" and "June" that songwriters often bemoan) threatens stagnation.

For most poets today, and for their patient readers, rhyme is a vestige of the past. "And now," writes the English poet Glyn Maxwell, "your kinsfolk think rhyme is sepia, Modernism stark black-and-white, and whatever he or she did this morning high-definition colour." Contemporary poets often eschew rhyme entirely or choose subtler sonic devices such as assonance, which *The Princeton Encyclopedia of Poetry and Poetics* defines as "the repetition of a vowel or diphthong in nonrhyming stressed syllables near enough to each other for the echo to be discernible." Songwriters sometimes do the same. Robert Plant substitutes assonance for rhyme in the following lines from "Stairway to Heaven": "When she gets there she *knows*/If the stores are all *closed*." The long "o" sound binds the end words in the successive lines, albeit not as tightly as a full rhyme would do.

It is possible that this rhyme-deprived period of poetry will be looked upon generations hence as an anomaly. Though one is not likely to make a strong claim for the cultural permanence of the rhyme-rich lyrics found on the *Billboard* Hot 100 chart, one can nonetheless argue for their continuity with the long-standing poetic tradition of rhymed verse. "A striking feature of the history of rhyme is that even when, as in our own era, rhyming does not dominate poetry, the use of rhyme, continuing or renewed, does not acquire an archaic cast," observes the poet and critic Susan Stewart. If anything, rhyme today is at the cutting edge of culture—at the very least, it is at the cutting edge of popular culture.

Rhyme's history in pop music has been far from fixed. Quite the contrary, the story of rhyme in twentieth- and early twenty-first-century pop songs is one of revolution and dramatic change. That story begins with Tin Pan Alley, which cultivated a catholic rhyme aesthetic that required full rhymes at all times. Within that rhyme constraint, songwriters sought novel pairings to display their wit and skill. Ira Gershwin, who handled many of the lyric duties for his brother George's tunes, went to great lengths to find a rhyme for "enjoyment" on the jaunty "Nice Work If You Can Get It" from 1937: "The fact is, the only work that really brings enjoyment/Is the kind that is girl and boy meant." A generation later, Johnny Mercer devised unusual—though still perfect—rhymes like "Parcheesi" and "real easy." This tradition survives to this day on Broadway. Witness these lines from "Right Hand Man," a song from Lin-Manuel Miranda's *Hamilton*: "Now, I'm the model of a modern major general/The venerated Virginian veteran whose men are all/Lining up . . ." A sharp enjambment between the second and third lines puts Miranda in position to rhyme "general" with the unexpected phrase "men are all." On the page, it looks contrived; in performance, it flows fluidly.

Early rock and roll eroded but did not entirely efface the practice of perfect rhymes. The 1960s rock revolution, which changed so much about the pop song, changed rhyme as well. Recalling his days with the British beat band the Hollies, Graham Nash describes the new rhyme perspective like this: "We abandoned the trite moon-and-June rhymes, the hold-your-hand and just-one-kiss fluff that had governed lyrics for so long, in order to express ourselves musically. As songwriters, everyone's perspective was expanding, and with it their imaginations, their command of language, their facility with rhyme." The Hollies' 1966 song "Stop Stop Stop," for instance, includes conventional full rhymes like "door" and "floor" as well as textured slant rhymes like "breathe" and "leave" and instances of assonance like "week" and "street."

Increasingly, popular music has taken a more relaxed approach to rhyme or, to put it in the active sense, it has expanded the rhyme palate for the purposes of sound, sense, and feeling. Indeed, many pop music performers now unmoor their lyrics entirely from rhyme. On Alison Krauss and Robert Plant's marvelous *Raising Sand* (2007), they recorded a Rowland Salley composition called "Killing the Blues" that largely avoids rhyme. Instead, it relies on patterned repetition of sound and phrase; the chorus repeats four times and grounds the song in its familiar diction. But that song is an anomaly on the album, a promise of what a lyric without rhyme can achieve.

Rap music, emerging in the 1970s and reaching pop-music saturation by the turn of the century, apotheosized rhyme—indeed, "rhyme" became synonymous both with the product of the rapper's composition (a rhyme is a rap lyric) and with the act of rapping itself (to rhyme is to perform a rap lyric). In its early years, rap favored neat couplets and full rhymes. As the art expanded, it embraced a far broader rhyme palate. In the process, it breathed life back into ancient rhyme practices while developing rhyming techniques without precedent. "Who now, in *your* now, makes the strong rhyme breathe again?" asks Maxwell. "The rap artist, for one. Rap rhymes for show, for fun, for power. Why is rap the shape it is? Why doesn't it pause for breath? Because it's an urban form, it formed with others standing close, itching to interrupt it, to break it, best it, it won't stop till it's had its say: *This-and-hey-this-and-how-about-this-and-then-this-and-also-this-and-hell-yes-this!* It wants you to feel it was conjured into life, whipped up under pressure, not handed down, owing nothing, made up *right now*." Maxwell has much of this right, though he overstates the degree to which rap is breathless in its expression, flooding the lyric line with words, rhyming and otherwise. "Rap—so many words, so little said," Keith Richards quipped to the *New York Daily News* in 2015. But rap can also be deliberate and measured. Now that rap is in its fifth decade, one can also see the many formal influences it has exercised on other genres, particularly when it comes to rhyming.

Simply pointing out that rhyme lives in pop songs, however, gets us nowhere beyond curiosity. I could spend the rest of the chapter diagramming a menagerie of rhyme varieties, linking them up with those of print-based poetry, and call myself quite clever. For analysis of these rhymes to matter, though, for it to offer something useful for our larger analysis of the poetry of pop songs, we need to focus on rhyme's reason for being in a song lyric. Is it possible to discern patterns in how the lyrics to pop songs use rhyme that suggest something about the development of the song form? What does it tell us that rhyme has continued to thrive in recorded music when it has withered in poetry? What is it about rhyme that serves the needs of our contemporary culture, and how, if at all, do those needs differ from the needs of the past?

This chapter is dedicated to exploring these questions. It posits that, though rhyme serves numerous functions, we can usefully identify three core purposes. The first of these is rhyme's relation to pattern. Rhyme, like rhythm, satisfies an inborn human desire for repetition with a difference. The small music that rhyme makes, especially when conjoined with rhythm, pleases us on a deep, neural level. This is tied up equally in rhythm's and rhyme's oft-touted mnemonic effects. After all, we remember lines with rhythm because they fashion a pattern that the mind fills with the right words; we remember lines that rhyme because rhyme is addictive, compelling us to find more instances that echo the same sound across distance and difference.

Everything from nursery rhymes to Kendrick Lamar verses stick to the mind because of their particular patterning of rhythm and rhyme. "How much such recitation depends on musical rhythm and how much purely on linguistic rhyming is difficult to tell," writes the neurologist Oliver Sacks, "but these are surely related—both 'rhyme' and 'rhythm' derive from the Greek, carrying the conjoined meanings of measure, motion, and stream. An articulate stream, a melody or prosody, is necessary to carry one along, and this is something that unites language and music, and may underlie their perhaps common origins." The patterned music of rhythm in rhyme in song is perhaps the primary pleasure to be taken from the language of pop music.

The second function of rhyme is its specific expression in recorded song: the way that songwriters harness rhyme's capacity to govern the flow of rhythm and melody in vocal performance. The distance or proximity of rhyme is the most obvious way that rhyme helps control a song's rhythmic flow. A rhyme marks a resolution; its deferral can prompt either excitement or frustration depending on how the lyric accounts for that span of absence. The rock-rap group 21 Pilots begins their 2015 song "Stressed Out" with a rhyming couplet that sets up the expectation of another couplet to follow. Rather than satisfying that pattern, though, they subvert it to illustrate the content of the lyric:

> I wish I found some better sounds no one's ever *heard*
> I wish I had a better voice that sang some better *words*
> I wish I found some chords in an order that is new
> I wish I didn't have to rhyme every time I sang

The result is jarring, but the effect is temporary; the next two lines restore the couplet with a perfect rhyme, "shrink" and "think." Though resisting rhyme both in form and meaning, the song ultimately accedes to rhyme's implacable force.

Finally, rhyme is perhaps the songwriter's greatest creative constraint, and this constraint is the songwriter's greatest opportunity to put virtuosity in evidence and, importantly, to underscore thought and feeling. In the Broadway tradition, for instance, one finds lyricists working to resolve the tension between their desire to expand the language of their lyrics and the responsibility of maintaining perfect rhyme pairs. When Hal David wrote the lyrics to Burt Bacharach's music for "I'll Never Fall in Love Again" from the 1968 musical *Promises, Promises*, it seems as if he chose some words precisely because they would prove difficult to rhyme. In the first verse, for instance, he pairs "bubble" with one of its few perfect rhyme pairs: "trouble." In the second verse, he offers this couplet in response to the question "What do you get when you kiss a girl?": "You get enough germs to catch pneumonia/After you do, she'll never phone ya." The rhyming pair "pneumonia" and "phone ya" satisfies the need for a sonic echo even as its artificiality embodies the sardonic tone of the song.

Most often, though, songwriters seek to resolve rhyme's challenge in more naturalistic and conversational ways. The Australian singer-songwriter Courtney Barnett's playful "Elevator Operator" from her 2015 debut LP *Sometimes I Sit and Think, and Sometimes I Just Sit* is a study in conscious constraint and creative evasion in rhyme. The opening lines sound rich in rhyme when performed without including perfect rhyme at all: "Oliver Paul, twenty years old / Thick head of hair, worries he's going bald." "Paul," "old," and "bald" roughly relate to one another through assonance, while "old" and "bald" connect even more securely in a slant rhyme. The effect is a pleasing difference with a reassuring unity.

Not all songwriters, of course, are thrilled with the expectation of rhyming their lines. "I'm not a big believer in rhyme," says Tori Amos. "Who decided that rhyming was the way to do it? Who was that guy? Let's go find him and have a little chat, because this has really cramped writers for a long, long time. It's about content, it's not about the rhyme." Billy Joel, though a very different kind of artist from Amos, concurs with her. "I hate the tyranny of rhyme," he says. "But if you're going to be musical and you're going to make something work, nine times out of ten you do have to rhyme because it would be as if you ended a musical phrase in a different key with no relation to anything else that had happened before." This resignation to rhyme speaks as much to audience expectation as it does to tradition and songwriting craft. When it comes to pop songs, rhymes just sound right.

Working with and against the posited ideal of the perfect rhyme pair, songwriters stretch and bend rhyme's capacity, and sometimes even break it, in the name of making sound, feeling, and meaning through their songs. An effective rhyme pair or rhyme scheme both entertains and instructs the listener. Song lyrics are by far the most robust living repository of rhymed words, so it seems fitting to look here to discover just why rhyme matters so much to us, what cultural and aesthetic functions it serves, and the many ways that it lives in lyrics.

RHYME DEFINED

Rhyme is the amity of sounds. In its perfect form, it consists of the repetition of the last stressed vowel sound and all the sounds following that vowel (such as in "demonstrate" and "exonerate"). "Rhyme is a play with words and its first effect is pleasure," writes the poet and critic Jeffrey Wainwright. "It comes from delighted surprise as words, remote from each other in meaning but which happen to sound alike, are made to coincide." Rhyme, therefore, works on a principle of expectation and surprise. The mind is tasked with linking the familiar (in sound) with the unfamiliar (in meaning), resulting in a pleasure akin to what one feels in completing a puzzle.

A taxonomy of rhyme begins with the division between "masculine" and "feminine" rhyme. Masculine rhymes terminate in stressed syllables, such as "can" and "man." Feminine rhymes add an additional unaccented syllable after the accented rhyming syllable, as in "mountain" and "fountain." Often songwriters will fashion multisyllabic patterns that echo both rhyme and rhythm across multiple syllables. Consider the opening lines from Graham Nash's "Marrakesh Express," recorded by Crosby, Stills & Nash:

> Looking at the world through the *sunset in your eyes*
> Traveling the train through *clear Moroccan skies*

This couplet is bound by the simple masculine end rhyme of "eyes" and "skies" and also by the five-syllable rhythmic pattern of stressed-unstressed-stressed-unstressed-stressed syllables. Rhythm and rhyme combined produce a lilting tone in keeping with the electric guitar and Hammond organ instrumentation and the exotic train ride the lyrics describe.

So far, it might seem that rhyme functions almost identically in song lyrics and in poetry. The difference, of course, is that songwriters express rhyme solely in sound; the secondary pleasure that poets employ of patterning for the eye is unavailable to them. Rhyme in song lyrics is an aural expression that makes no necessary distinction in orthography or even, at times, in the placement of the rhyme along the line. "Songs are made for ears, not eyes," writes Pat Pattison. "Because people listen to songs, you must learn to write for eyeless ears. Rhyme creates a sonic roadmap: it tells those eyeless ears where to go and when to stop. It shows them the way." In this regard, rhyme serves a greater structural purpose in recorded song than it does in poetry meant for the page. Rhyme marks the breaks in the lyric much the way that a line break does for the reader of poetry; it generates associations between words and linguistic structures that a poet might rely on visual means to create in a poem.

This sonic roadmap supplies structure, both of sound and of meaning. "We expect lyrics to behave in a certain way when combined with music," explains the songwriter Jimmy Webb. "For instance, we expect rhymes or near rhymes or even false rhymes to fall in certain precise and predetermined locations." These "precise and predetermined locations" include the ends of lyric lines and other places along the line that are accorded rhythmic stress. For the listener, then, rhyme gives shape, signaling points of transition, completed thoughts, and connections across the lyric. More than any single element of poetics, rhyme sets up a habit of linguistic expectation in the listener. The pleasure rhyme brings is based on the balance of that expectation with variation in a process of repetition and revision.

For song lyricists and poets, rhyme imposes a discipline of craft that inspires rather than curtails creative expression. "Far from a constraint," writes Susan Stewart, "rhyme endows us with certain freedoms—among them: the vernacular, including the locality of the poem itself, released from the standard; the monolingual in dialogue with the multilingual; sound opened up by vision, and sound released from meaning entirely; expectation released into surprise; and pattern drawn from the oblivion of time. Rhyme is perfect, imperfect, total, and partial at once." Rhyme's liberating potential can tether sound and meaning tightly to one another or unloose them in an orgy of sound play. Matched with voice and song, rhyme realizes potential that it only hints at on the page. "Rhyming, while being a limitation, has also an element of magic to it," writes Sting. "It is essentially a shamanic art, and to follow its winding path is to reenter that realm that is halfway between sleep and waking, where the mysterious imperative of the unconscious can reveal itself on the page." To understand why rhyme means so much to song lyrics, it helps to begin with the mind and body and end with the imagination.

PATTERN AND RHYME

Just as the body responds to rhythm, the mind responds to rhyme. The brain's predictive capacity filters out things that we can anticipate and rewards us with dopamine when we discover something out of place. In other words, we are pattern-seeking animals that delight in the surprise of a break in those patterns. Rhyme satisfies this cognitive reward system. "We may expect a rhyme sound, but in a good poem we enjoy the unexpected, perhaps farfetched, move, and the unexpected word, that lead us to the right rhyme," writes the literary critic Brian Boyd. Boyd's idea of the "right" rhyme is key. "It is not so much necessary that rhyming be conspicuously clever," explains the songwriter Gene Lees, "although clever rhyming is an attractive and often charming effect, as that it be good rhyming: solid, correct, and executed in such a way that it has a feeling of the natural, the improvisatory, the unpremeditated." In pop songs, the expression of rhyme ranges from the showy to the workmanlike to the unobtrusive and even to the nonexistent.

Consider this simplistic but serviceable rhyme from the Beatles: "Love, love me *do*/You know I love *you*." As Ben Blatt pointed out in early 2014 on Slate.com, *do*/*you* is the most prevalent rhyme pairing among songs appearing on *Billboard*'s Year End Hot 100 chart between 1960 and 2013. The twenty most popular rhymes over that same period are, in order: *do*/*you*; *be*/*me*; *me*/*see*; *true*/*you*; *baby*/__ *me*; *go*/*know*; *through*/*you*; *around*/*down*; *night*/*right*; *mind*/*time*; *to*/*you*; *mine*/*time*; *day*/*way*; *free*/*me*; *away*/*day*; *say*/*way*; *away*/*say*; *too*/*you*; *be*/*see*; *gone*/*on*. Among the twenty rhyme pairs on the list, twelve are full (or perfect) rhymes and the remainder are what is variously termed half, slant, or false rhymes. Sixteen of the pairs involve only single-syllable words.

Given the nature of lyric address, particularly in love songs, it should come as no surprise that "you" and "me" are among the most common words in search of rhymes. It is a cruel twist of linguistic fate that pop music—a music preoccupied with the theme of love—must contend with the fact that English offers only four full rhymes for "love": "above," "dove," "glove," and "shove." In the face of that expressive paucity, songwriters have devised a number of strategies. Many, of course, expand the rhyme palate to include slant rhymes. Others avoid rhyming the word "love"—or even using it—altogether, expressing the intensity of love's emotions by other means. Still others embrace the limitations of love's full rhymes and devise creative ways to turn a phrase. It stands to reason that when the point of view and themes of a song are familiar, the rhymes will be as well. The inverse might also be true: Find a song with unusual themes and it might just present some unusual rhymes as well. Queen, who Blatt points out makes a practice of seeking unusual rhyme pairs, rhymes "poor family" with "monstrosity" on their operatic hit "Bohemian Rhapsody."

Uniqueness alone, however, does not guarantee a great rhyme. Some song lyrics render familiarity a virtue. There's something deeply comforting in having one's expectations satisfied. Graham Parsons's "Return of the Grievous Angel," a duet with Emmylou Harris, is a remarkable song with mostly unremarkable rhymes. The song's final lines illustrate the power of the prosaic one often finds in the rhymes of song lyrics:

And I remembered something you once told me
And I'll be damned if it did not come true
Twenty thousand roads I went down, down, down
And they all led me straight back home to you

Right before our eyes and ears is what Blatt tells us is the fourth most common rhyme pair from the *Billboard* Hot 100 charts—"true" and "you." It's here for a reason, though, one that communicates conflict, comfort, and resolution—an entire relationship captured in a single rhyme pair.

What differentiates a clever rhyme from a stale one is the balance between expectation and surprise. There's a communal context to it as well: a rhyme pair might be fresh and surprising at its moment of conception but grow stale from overuse, just as often happens with similes and metaphors. A rhyme may be richly emotive in one lyric and simply wooden or trite in another.

Placement also often dictates the form a rhyme takes. Not all word sounds are created equal, especially when it comes to end rhymes. "Do you know Keith Richards' theory of songwriting?" Billy Joel asks.

He has this theory and I subscribe to it—it's called vowel movements. When you write certain combinations of notes, certain chords, the rhyme and the sound of the words that came before it have to have a certain sound to it. Like if I wrote a song like, "I love you just the way you ARE." It's a good way to end that phrase. ARE. You can't say "da da da da da FRED." FRED wouldn't have flown. So that vowel sound, "ah(r)," is soft. So Keith says when they write their songs, that's what they do. They just go "ah, ee, oh," what sounds right, and then they figure out what word it's gonna be. I do that a lot. Just the way you are. Zanzibar. I like that "ah(r)" thing.

Leave it to Keith Richards to make a scatological pun out of his rhyme theory. A quick glance at the Rolling Stones' biggest hits suggests that Jagger and Richards put the theory into frequent practice. "Sympathy for the Devil" offers up open vowel rhymes like *name/game* and *taste/waste*. A later hit, "Mixed Emotions," contains languorous rhymes like *coat/throat* and *going/fro-ing*. Richards's vowel movement theory is in keeping with the practice of Tin Pan Alley lyricists, who also sought out long vowel sounds for rhymes at the ends of lines.

Though end rhymes are an expectation in pop, they are by no means an immutable law. Singers and songwriters sometimes work together to affirm while resisting these end rhyme expectations. A rare and remarkable instance of this occurs when a rhyming couplet includes another unrhymed word at the end of the second line. The second verse of Kacey Musgraves's "Back on the Map," for instance, begins like this:

> Something steady, something *good*
> It's probably closer than I thought it *could* be

Just as soon as the couplet "good" and "could" registers in our ear, the lyric subverts that sonic resolution by insisting on the semantic closure that the phrase's meaning demands. Looking only at the words on the page, one might think that what we have here is a rhyming couplet with a sharp enjambment—that "be" should fall on the next line. Listening to the recorded song, though, leaves no room for debate: the melodic phrase demands that "could be" belong on the same line, embedded in the same musical space that the line before it inhabits. Why would a songwriter wish to mess up a perfectly good rhyming couplet? The answer lies in the desire to balance expectation with novelty. These orphan-word rhymes set the unrhymed word in relief, calling attention to its meaning in thought, sound, and feeling. This practice finds powerful expression in the chorus to Adele's "Hello."

> Hello from the outside
> At least I can say that I've tried
> To tell you I'm sorry for breaking your *heart*
> But it don't matter; it clearly doesn't tear you *apart* anymore

Whereas Musgraves's appended word is required to complete the syntactical meaning of the couplet, Adele's couplet is complete in itself. The added word transforms a thought that already seems whole. Adele's realization that the hurt she caused her estranged lover no longer tears him apart *anymore* admits that it once did, and that his recovery from the pain closes all possibility of finding their love again. "Anymore" might be the single most heartbreaking word in the song; Adele's singing charges it with all the regret and loss of the lyric as a whole. It's no surprise that both Musgraves's and Adele's examples come from songs about lost love; these acts of rhyme disruption underscore the unsettled nature of the relationships the lyrics describe. The form fits the function of the rhyme.

Pop songs are often calculating in the ways that they play on the listener's expectations of rhyme. The mind quickly acculturates to rhyme patterns, especially when it comes to full, single-syllabic end rhymes. Lyricists use their knowledge of this habituation to achieve a number of effects: conjuring a mood of imbalance or dis-ease through complicating or withholding the expected rhyme; intensifying the emotion of the end rhyme by augmenting it with internal rhymes; or, in rare cases, leading the mind to a particular rhyme word even though the word actually in the lyric is something entirely different. I call these last rhymes "ghost rhymes," because the rhyming word our mind fills in hovers unexpressed over the word we hear.

Ghost rhymes often serve a comic purpose. At the 2003 ESPY Awards, the actor and singer Jamie Foxx performed a silly slow jam for the tennis player Serena Williams called "Can I Be Your Tennis Ball?" that telegraphs a risqué rhyme only to correct it in time to meet the scrutiny of basic cable: "Do it slow or do it fast/Can I fit inside your . . . bag." The implied slant rhyme (*fast/ass*) set beside the assonance of the lyric as performed (*fast/bag*) creates an impish, if easy, punch line. It invites just enough shock to prompt a few laughs. Ghost rhyme often follows what Peter McGraw and Joel Warner describe in their study of comedy, *The Humor Code*, as a "benign violation." By this theory, "humor only occurs when something seems wrong, unsettling or threatening (i.e., a violation), but simultaneously seems okay, acceptable, or safe (i.e., benign)." In the case of the ghost rhyme, the stated rhyme word provides benign cover for the ghost-rhyme word that would otherwise be experienced as a violation of taste and decorum.

Not every ghost rhyme serves a comic purpose; sometimes songwriters harness its power and appeal to achieve a more sobering effect. A good example of this is the Killers' "Mr. Brightside," where the entire payoff of the lyric relies on rhyming sleight of hand. The song describes a man witnessing a romantic assignation between an ex-girlfriend whom he hasn't gotten over and her new lover. The band's front man, Brandon Flowers, sings these lines in the pre-chorus:

> Now I'm falling asleep and she's calling a cab
> While he's having a smoke and she's taking a drag
> Now they're going to bed and my stomach is sick
> And it's all in my head but she's touching his . . . chest

The first two lines establish a rhyme expectation, with slanting end rhymes (*cab/drag*). The next two lines embed rhyme, introducing a perfect internal rhyme that is picked up in the fourth line (*bed/head*), further underscoring the expectation of a perfect end rhyme to go with "sick." It takes little imagination to figure out what rhyme word might fit the circumstance; the lyric coyly evades it by substituting the word we hear in our head ("dick") with a PG analog ("chest") that not only doesn't rhyme, but actively disrupts the rhyme pattern. The music shifts here as well, setting the lyric even more dramatically in relief. Why do this? One obvious reason is that it offers a clever way for the band to make a radio-friendly song that still slyly communicates its sexualized intentions. It also externalizes the singer's internal dilemma as he struggles with the fact that his imagination is conjuring images that might well be false ("and it's all in my head"). In other words, the song aptly displays what the singer actually sees and what he imagines in the deep corners of his jealousy. The rhyme pattern also creates a vital point of aesthetic interest in the song, one that plays upon the fundamental lyric practice of repetition with a difference. And finally, it implicates the listener in the taboo; after all, we are the ones supplying the naughty word, not the band.

The history of ghost rhyme in popular song stretches back in the American context at least to Tin Pan Alley. Cole Porter, for instance, writes the following lines in "I've Come to Wife It Wealthily in Padua":

> If she scream like a teething brat,
> If she scratch like a tiger cat,
> If she fight like a raging boar,
> I have oft stuck a pig before.

After the *brat/cat* rhyme, the mind is inclined to complete the rhyme for the word at the end of the next line, "boar," and what comes most easily? It must be "whore." Porter disdains that easy rhyme for another, but in keeping with his assiduous craft he simply finds another word that rhymes ("before") instead of subverting the rhyme entirely as the Killers would later do.

A direct descendant of the Broadway stage musical, Disney's recent animated megahit *Frozen* also employs the ghost-rhyming technique. Josh Gad's character of Olaf, the snowman, has a big musical number, "In Summer," that includes the following ghost rhyme that plays up Olaf's ignorance of his fate should he find himself under the sun: "Winter's a good time to stay in and cuddle,/But put me in summer and I'll be a . . . happy snowman!" Olaf's unknowing evasion of the obvious rhyme of "puddle" with "cuddle" underscores his obliviousness. It's a knowing nod from the songwriters, Kristen

Anderson-Lopez and Robert Lopez, aimed not at the core demographic of four-year-olds, but at older children and adults who will be in on the dramatic irony.

This ghost-rhyming technique may have been exploited most effectively, though, in the thrash metal band Anthrax's "I'm the Man." "I'm the Man" is a raucous fusion of ear-sheering guitars and rapid-fire, rap-inspired wordplay. The band started playing it live in 1986 before recording a studio version in 1987, making it among the earliest rap-rock hybrids ever released, alongside Aerosmith and Run-D.M.C.'s "Walk This Way" (1986) and the Beastie Boys' debut album, *Licensed to Ill* (1986). The song is structured on a series of playful verses, each ending with a conscious error or euphemistic substitution that invites a ghost rhyme. Here's an example:

> For a heavy metal band, rap's a different way
> We like to be different and not cliché
> They say rap and metal can never mix
> Well, all of them can suck our . . . sexual organ in the lower
> abdominal area!

In the style of groups like Run-D.M.C., the Anthrax guys trade bars, with drummer Charlie Benante gleefully flubbing the rhyme in the last line only to face quick correction from his bandmates: "No, man, it's 'dicks'!" The song is a series of these silly, self-deprecating gestures that entertain the audience both because they balance anticipation of and surprise in the rhyme's disruption and because they reject the atmosphere of effortless cool that real rap rhymes often inspire. "Although we were really serious about our love for rap, the song is a total joke," recalls Anthrax's rhythm guitarist Scott Ian in his memoir, which takes its title from this very song. "I'm the Man" apotheosizes the ghost rhyme, rendering this strategy of studied imperfection the very form of its art.

Songwriters often respond to the exhaustion of full rhyme by consciously choosing imperfection. There's something unsettling but appealing in the lack of rhyme resolution in the following couplet from Bob Dylan's "Thunder on the Mountain": "I'm gonna raise me an army, some tough sons of bitches / I recruit my army from the orphanages." Technically, this is a mosaic slant rhyme— mosaic in that Dylan rhymes multiple words ("sons of bitches") with a single four-syllable word ("orphanages"), and slant in that "sons of bitches" and "orphanages" do not make a perfect rhyme. In the slippage between the rhyme, however, Dylan wrests interest and energy. "Staying in the unconscious frame of mind, you can pull yourself out and throw up two rhymes first and work back," Dylan told the music historian Paul Zollo. "You get the rhymes first and work it back and then see if you can make it make sense in another kind of way. You can still stay in the unconscious frame of mind to pull it off, which is the state of mind you have to be in anyway."

In his 2015 memoir, Elvis Costello recalls engaging in an impromptu rhyme battle of sorts with Dylan in 2011. Dylan started off by pulling from his pocket a narrow scroll of paper on which he had written a new lyric. Costello remembers the language Dylan read as being strange and remarkable. Not to be outdone, Costello recited a new lyric of his own from memory, ending in this downright Dylanesque multisyllabic rhyming couplet: "Eyes going in and out of focus/Mild and bitter from tuberculosis." "I saw that rhyme register in Bob's eyes like a glancing glove and I thought, *Okay, I got one shot in, I'd better not push my luck*," Costello writes.

In the minds of some songwriters, the techniques Dylan and Costello employ are cheating. A significant number of songwriters, particularly Broadway lyricists, espouse the view that anything less than a full rhyme is an abdication of the songwriter's solemn duty. "All rhymes, even the farthest afield of the near ones (*home/dope*), draw attention to the rhymed word; if you don't want it to be spotlighted, you'd better not rhyme it," Stephen Sondheim writes. "A perfect rhyme snaps the word, and with it the thought, vigorously into place, rendering it easily intelligible; a near rhyme blurs it." Here Sondheim connects clarity and cognition; the rhyme is no mere adornment, but the vessel through which the song communicates most clearly and most evocatively.

On the opposite side of the argument are those who claim that adhering to perfect rhymes is too restrictive, both of sound and of meaning. "I've gotten to where I just don't give a damn anymore," Tom Petty says. "Because I'd rather just deal with what I want to say, as exactly as I want to say it, and I don't want to compromise it for a rhyme. Sometimes, though, if you don't rhyme it, it don't feel good. So, it is the great thorn in the songwriter's side that you've got to pretty much rhyme what you're gonna sing. So that's part of the trick, getting that rhyme to say what you want." Petty's "American Girl" includes only one perfect rhyme pair in the entire song ("alright" and "all night"), but one must listen closely to notice, and once noticed, one hardly cares. What's communicated instead is the song's restless energy and its plainspoken eloquence, embodied in the final lines of the second verse: "God, it's so painful/Something that's so close/And still so far out of reach."

The craft of rhyming is in no small measure, as Petty explains it, the craft of "getting the rhyme to say what you want." For this reason, rhyme dictionaries are many songwriters' constant companions. They aren't a way of cheating, but of surveying the field of possibilities. "Instead of always making the music responsible for a feeling of resolution or irresolution at the end of a section, why not add a further possibility: let the music resolve, but let the rhyme feel a little incomplete, like tide/life or friend/wind," writes Pattison. "It could give the songwriter a whole new set of possibilities—more musical flexibility and more lyrical flexibility. Or, let both the music and the rhyme feel incomplete. Add to the musical emotion. Or, let them both slam the door shut. It's all about prosody: creating musical and lyrical structures that support (indeed, create) your emotional intent."

Sometimes a studied tension between music and lyric is precisely what the songwriter seeks. Leonard Cohen's exalting and exalted "Hallelujah," a modern-day hymn of faith and love and sex, presents the seemingly intractable challenge of identifying rhymes for the song's multisyllabic title. Cohen finds a sly solution, rhyming "hallelujah" across multiple verses with "do you," "overthrew you," "I knew you," "what's it to you," "who outdrew you," and "come to fool you." "They are really false rhymes," Cohen admits, "but they are close enough that the ear is not violated." How close the rhymes are also relies on the choice the singer makes in pronunciation. On both Cohen's original studio recording of the song from 1984's *Various Positions* and Jeff Buckley's famous 1994 cover recording, the singers emphasize rhyme's proximity by pronouncing the phrases as "do ya," "overthrew ya," and so forth. The casual and colloquial voicing underscores rhyme and also introduces a sardonic note, in keeping with the tone of Cohen's overall performance but in contrast with Buckley's sincere and soaring rendition. Years later on his haunting recording from 2009's *Live in London*, Cohen takes a different vocal path: carefully, almost defiantly, enunciating "you" throughout. It's as if he's winking at the audience, letting us know that he'll no longer capitulate to rhyme's small tyranny.

Sufjan Stevens's "Decatur, Round of Applause for Your Step-Mother!" is also a study in rhyme's capacity to express emotional intent by leaving a little irresolution and mystery. The song revels in sound first, playing with the rhyming potential of the word "Decatur" and the way it resists full rhyme. Stevens embraces this kind of multisyllabic rhyme, often termed mosaic rhyme, which Lord Byron used to such great comic effect in canto I, stanza 22 of *Don Juan* with the triple rhyme "But O ye lords of ladies intellectual,/

Inform us truly, have they not henpecked you all?" While Dylan and Cohen largely subvert the comic impulse of the method, Stevens exults in it. Over the course of the song he rhymes "Decatur" with "hate her," "take her," "alligator," "operator," "aviator," "great debater," "emancipator," "congratulate her," and "anticipate her." This cluster of words, also a cluster of sounds, defines the song's playful character even before we hear the whimsical music. "'Decatur' was more fun to sing because of those half-funny half-rhymes ('aviator'?!)," the music critic Jessica Hopper wrote in the *Village Voice*. By embracing the rhyme limitations of an unusual proper noun, Stevens harnesses craft for the purposes of his art.

Rhyme for rhyme's sake can be a cul-de-sac, a cold display of cleverness and craft that actually diminishes the song. "You can rhyme to a fault," argues Jackson Browne. "Often when I don't know where I'm going in a song I begin rhyming. Then I think, 'Come on, cut it out. These sounds rhyme but what does it mean? Talk about something real.'" Talking about something real in a song often means getting a rhyme to say what you want through a certain degree of dilation, breaking the rules of perfect rhyme in favor of capturing a particular grain of meaning. The country legend Loretta Lynn describes the process of composing the lyrics to her best-known song, "Coal Miner's Daughter," as a struggle with rhyme:

> It started "Well, I was borned a coal miner's daughter . . ." which was nothing but the truth. And I went on from there. I made up the melody at the same time, line by line, like I always do. It started out as a bluegrass thing, 'cause that's the way I was raised, with the guitar and the banjo just following along. Really, the way you hear it on the record is the way I imagined it.
>
> I had a little trouble with the rhymes. I had to match up words like "holler" and "daughter" and "water." But after it was all done, the rhymes weren't so important.

Perhaps the rhymes were no longer so important because they no longer announced themselves as rhymes. By bending to the vernacular of Lynn's speech and the grain of her voice, the language comes across with little of the artifice that rhyme often entails. Instead, one hears the conviction, self-revelation, and confession at the heart of Lynn's autobiographical song.

At the opposite extreme are instances when the rhymes themselves dictate their own terms. These are forced rhymes, where the conditions of a lyric lead naturally to a particular rhyme pairing—usually a stale one—and the lyricist appears helpless to resist it. Forced rhymes can cheapen a song's content. "Just because it rhymes doesn't mean it's the right line," says John Rich of the country duo Big & Rich. "Too many times a rhyme short-circuits the process of digging deeper into a lyric and saying something that really matters." The Christian singer-songwriter Amy Grant agrees: "So sometimes writing a song is not a matter of just hammering yourself in the head until you complete the rhyme scheme. A lot of times, it's a matter of walking away from it for ten or fifteen minutes, and waiting for the next line to present itself. And it will eventually, if it's something you really want to say."

It would probably be amusing to spend the remainder of the chapter listing forced rhymes in bad songs, but it's more instructive to look at forced rhyme in a good song. Consider the 2003 Grammy winner for Song of the Year, Jesse Harris's "Don't Know Why," recorded by Norah Jones. The song consists of a series of rhymed couplets, with the important exception of the first verse, which reads:

> I waited 'til I saw the sun
> I don't know why I didn't come
> I left you by the house of fun
> I don't know why I didn't come

One hears the contrast between the repetition of an entire refrain ("I don't know why I didn't come") in the second, fourth, and fifth lines, and the perfect *sun/fun* rhyme in lines one and three. The rhyme, however, comes across as too perfect, given that it has no obvious meaning. Though "saw the sun" is clear and concrete, "house of fun" is opaque. Is it an awkward circumlocution for "funhouse"? If so, how does that situate the scene? Was Harris insistent on the opening line and simply seeking a way to resolve it in a perfect rhyme? Nothing in the remainder of the lyric illuminates the meaning of the reference. Fortunately, the recording's incantatory melody and Jones's mellifluous voice make up for any lyric obscurity born of forced rhyme.

Forced rhymes would seem anathema to good songwriting. Some songs, however, elevate forced rhyme to a conscious aesthetic. Macklemore's 2015 hit "Downtown" is an old-school affair, with stripped down, funky cowbell percussion and guest appearances from rap legends Grandmaster Caz, Melle Mel, and Kool Moe Dee. This old-school aesthetic and comic tone inform

Macklemore's rhyme practice as well, which is marked by lots of full rhymes and a conscious embrace of rhyme's constraints.

Two lines demonstrate how Macklemore artfully resolves a rhyme difficulty by capitulating to sound over sense. For the rhyme play to be understood, it is important to know that Pend Oreille, pronounced *pond-eray*, is a lake in northern Idaho, near where Macklemore recorded much of the album on which this track appears. The lines read: "I take her to *Pend Oreille* and I *water skate*/I mean, *water ski*, ollie ollie *oxen free*." Here internal rhymes satisfy our rhyme expectations. For the lines to work, Macklemore must conceive a rhyme to fit "Pend Oreille," one that makes both sonic and semantic sense. It would make semantic sense for him to say "water ski," something he could conceivably have done on the lake. Instead, he decides to bend to the sonic demands of the rhyme with the nonsensical but successfully slant-rhyming "water skate." Keeping with the mildly absurdist tone of the song, he offers a correction in the next line and uses the phrase he wanted to use in the first place, "water ski," which he then parlays into another forced rhyme—the full rhyming "oxen free," a throwaway phrase. Plenty of things rhyme with "ski," most obviously "me," but the left-field choice Macklemore makes serves the song better than a more logical rhyming word would. Forced rhyme works here because it underscores the comic tone of the song in a way that more natural rhymes would not.

A rote grammarian would be quick to criticize the obvious and hackneyed rhymes in so many pop songs. But why do these rhymes rarely bother the rest of us? More than that, such rhymes often function as an aesthetic virtue, a vessel for profound thought and feeling as expressed in the music of the song. Think about Arlo Guthrie singing these lines:

> Coming into *Los Angeles*
> Bringing in a *couple of keys*
> Don't touch my bags *if you please*
> Mister Customs Man

Forced or not, the run of rhymes—"Los Angeles," "couple of keys," "if you please"—has a playful insouciance that fits the tone and subject of the song. The rhymes are carefully crafted; Guthrie deranges the pronunciation of "Los Angeles" (Loss Angel-eeze) to fit it to the rhyme sounds that follow. Elsewhere, I've termed this technique "transformative rhyme," where an artist takes words that only partially rhyme or don't rhyme at all and alters the pronunciation of one of them to fashion a perfect rhyme with the other. A famous example comes on Harold Arlen and E. Y. Harburg's "If I Only Had a Brain" from the soundtrack to the 1939 film classic *The Wizard of Oz* when the Scarecrow sings "I'd unravel any riddle/For any individ-le." More recently, Kanye West employed the same technique on "Gold Digger" when he rhymes "Serena" and "Trina" with "Jeena-fa" (as in Jennifer Lopez). Both of these rhyme gambits work because they extend the spirit of their respective songs. Transformative rhymes are most effective when the listener gets the sense that the performer and songwriter are in on the joke. When that awareness is in doubt, the rhyme can seem forced or downright cringeworthy, as it does on the R&B singer Blu Cantrell's "Hit Em Up Style (Oops!)," which inexplicably rhymes "Mia" with "shopping spree-ya." Sometimes forced rhymes are just, well, forced.

RHYTHM AND RHYME

Rhyme serves an important function for rhythm, though this function is far from straightforward. The analogy that some draw is to imagine rhymes as traffic signs: A perfect couplet is a stop sign; a slant rhyme feels like a yield; a series of rhymes in the middle and at the end of lines and the speed limit suddenly increases with the hastening of lyric pace; a sudden dearth of rhymes and you've entered a school zone. "Rhyme is the best way to control a lyric's FLOW. Nothing can match rhyme's power in this area. Not phrase length. Not rhythm," argues Pat Pattison. Not everyone agrees. Susan Stewart usefully points to the complications that rhyme introduces to a poem; the same holds for a lyric:

> Rhyme is in this sense always a showcase for the arbitrary nature of the sign and limits our efforts to dominate meaning; rhyming draws us beyond ourselves with its potential for aural pleasure, which, when one is trying to concentrate on univocal meaning and syntactical sequence, can be something like aural pain. Here is the basis of the tension between rhyme and syntax, a tension at the heart of the modernist rejection of rhyme. This disparity is also the reason why syntax motivated by the requirements of rhyme will seem unnatural. Rhyme punctuates and concentrates, it does not flow.

In most respects, Stewart and Pattison are saying the same thing: that rhyme governs the pace of a lyric, from acceleration all the way to a dead stop. While Pattison emphasizes the lyric momentum rhyme generates, Stewart calls attention to the rhythmic cul-de-sacs and the "aural pain" that they often occasion. The tension among unrestrained rhythmic flow; unfettered syntactical expression; and the musical, temporal, and ideational influence of rhyme makes for a complicated interplay of competing forces. The results can be striking and powerful, or chaotic and enervating.

Some of the best examples of this tension between rhythm and rhyme come from rap, with its sheer rhyme density. Consider Lauryn Hill's virtuosic third verse from "Final Hour," a master class in rhyme's many uses. Hill knits a tapestry of patterned sounds made up of full and slant rhymes, both single-syllable and multisyllabic, that overlap with no audible sign of the seams of their construction.

> Now I be breaking bread, sipping Manischewitz *wine*
> Pay no *mind*, party like it's nineteen-ninety-*nine*
> But when it come **down** to **ground** beef like *Palestine*
> Say your *rhyme*, let's see if that get you out your *bind*
> Now I'ma get the **mozzarella** like a **Rockefeller**, still be
> In the Church of **Lalibela**, singing hymns **a cappella**
> Whether posed in **Mirabella** in *couture—or*
> Collecting residuals from off *The Score*
> I'm making *sure* I'm with the Hundred-*Forty-Four*
> I been here *before*, this ain't a battle, this is *war*
> Word to **Boonie**, I make Salaat like a **Sunni**
> Get diplomatic **immunity** in every ghetto **community**
> Had the **opportunity**, went from Hood*shock* to 'hood-**chic**
> But it ain't what you *cop*, it's about what you **keep**
> And even if there are **leaks**, you can't capsize this *ship*
> 'Cause I baptize my *lips* every time I take *sips*

On lines five through seven, where Ms. Hill introduces a dizzying series of multisyllabic rhyming words, she accelerates her rhythm to accommodate the extra syllables. In this case, the rhymes as well as their frequency dictate the pace and tone of the lyric delivery. Hill calls attention to this dramatic pace shift by injecting an extended pause before returning to the more measured flow of the next few lines. The easy delivery doesn't last long; by lines twelve and thirteen the multisyllabics have returned, as has her frantic flow. All of these calculations and adjustments are done on the fly, with a sense of spontaneity that belies the conscious craft at work in rhythm and rhyme conjoined.

Does rhyme serve a distinct set of functions in rap that it does not serve in other genres, such as country or rock or reggae? How might we distinguish rap's use of rhyme from what we're likely to find in metrical poetry? "I hate most contemporary rhyming poetry," the poet Kyle Dargan once told me. "If somebody gives me a poem and I see that it rhymes, I just hand it back to them without comment. But I don't have that same response when it comes to rap. Why is that?" Lucky for me, Dargan answered his own question. The reason, he argues, is the rhythmic variety rap most often confers on the performance. The distance between the beginning of the line and the end rhyme is a space in which a great deal of poetic energy and interest can come to life. "On 'Jigga What, Jigga Who,' Jay Z starts with three trochees, then comes in with three dactyls, then a final spondee: '*Y'all* cats *wan'* act *loco?* / *Hit* 'em with *numerous shots* with the *four-four*,'" Dargan observes. "There's just so damn much rhythmic variety that when we get to the end rhyme it's a welcome regularity—it's a way of grounding us in the familiar and giving license to the rhythm to do its thing."

One rhyme practice that distinguishes rap from other genres is rhyme that follows an aural structure. This offers the welcome points of familiarity that Dargan describes. Lil Wayne may be the greatest exemplar of this rhyming practice. His rhymes exhibit free-associative flexibility, fit through accent rather than perfect structure, and often appear in places other than at the end of the line. After all, when a rhyme is never written down, the difference between internal and end rhymes ceases to carry the same importance as it does for the songwriter working on the page or the poet writing for the reader. To the extent that Lil Wayne's rhymes follow conventional patterns, it is due to the organizing function of the musical bar, which binds his lyrics in the space that a line inhabits in sound. On "6 Foot 7 Foot" he opens with a series of loose rhymes on the same sound:

> Excuse my *charisma*, vodka with a *spritzer*
> Swagger down pat, call my shit *Patricia*
> Young Money *militia* and I am the *commissioner*
> You no wan start Weezy cause the "F" is for *finisher*

The rhymes—full and slant—fly by so fast that it soon becomes unclear which rhyme marks the end of the line and which falls in the middle. Weezy's performance, charged with the idiosyncrasies of his intonation and pronunciation, also elides the difference between full and slant rhymes. The fact that Lil Wayne never writes his lyrics down no doubt critically influences his rhyme style. In this space of sound, the studied rigors of the Tin Pan Alley line seem beside the point.

Another practice popularized by certain rap traditions, but not invented by them, is the oft-frowned-upon act of "rhyming" a word with itself. I use "rhyme" in quotation marks because rhyming in this manner does not constitute a rhyme but an identity. An identity can serve some of the functions usually expected of a rhyme, such as calling attention to a word or establishing patterned repetition, but it does so without the attendant surprise that comes with the unexpected coupling of words at a remove from one another. "An identity makes the word clear, but blunts the line's snap because the accented sound is not a fresh one," observes Stephen Sondheim. He adds that identities are also "death to wit." Certainly identities are often a sign of creative resignation, an exhaustion of inspiration that leads literally to duplication. At other times, they generate an intentional effect, from the incantatory to the numbing to the replicatory. Identities can also be an effective vehicle for emotional expression, be it in circling around the same concept or fixating on feelings of extreme emotion.

The unlikely pair of lyrics that follows illustrates the creative use of identities.

> Got to pay your dues if you wanna sing the blues,
> And you know it don't come *easy*.
> You don't have to shout or leap about,
> You can even play them *easy*.
> (Ringo Starr, "It Don't Come Easy")

> Sat it on them *twenty-two*s, birds go for *twenty-two*
> Lil mama super thick, she say she *twenty-two*
> She seen them *twenty-two*s, we in room two-*twenty-two*
> (Rick Ross, "Hustlin'")

In the first instance, Ringo Starr presents identity as part of a quatrain structure that satisfies the listener's desire for rhyme with the perfect internal rhyme in the first line ("dues" and "blues"), which frees "easy" to do a subtler kind of structural work—and liberates Starr from conjuring some awkward perfect rhyme to go with "easy." The repetition of the word also underscores the song's title, therefore contributing on the level of meaning as well.

The next example, from the Miami rapper Rick Ross, displays a relentless patterning of identity across the verse. Ross repeats some version of "twenty-two" five times in three lines. This repetition calls attention to shifting meaning of the identity in different contexts. In the first use, "twenty-two" refers to twenty-two-inch rims on his car; in the second, to the $22,000 he earns for selling a bird (a kilo of cocaine) wholesale; the third use is the age of the young woman he meets, noteworthy because she has reached the age of majority; the next usage is ambiguous, but seems to reference the rims on his damn car again, which supposedly impress the young woman; and the final use refers to the last two digits of his hotel room, where we imagine that he and the young woman have now retired. These shifting denotations of the same word stretch the meaning of the verse and code Ross's language while displaying his lyrical virtuosity. "Look at how I can use the same words and yet set off new meanings in your head," the lyric announces.

If identity lies in the middle of the rhyme spectrum and perfect rhyme marks a far extreme, then the absence of rhyme entirely marks the other extreme. The conscious act of not rhyming is now unremarkable in literary poetry, where rhyme has long since receded from the aesthetic forefront. However, in song rhyme is still an expectation, if not quite a requirement, of lyric expression. I have already talked about subtler subversions of this expectation, from the unsettling of sound in slant rhyme, to the disruption of placement through internal rhymes, to the profusion of rhyme in everything from regular patterns to seemingly disordered repetition. A few songs forgo rhyme entirely. Sometimes these songs call attention to rhyme's omission, but usually the listener does not even take notice. George and Ira Gershwin's classic "I Got Rhythm" forgoes rhyme in its first verse. In an art in which full rhymes are the rule, how could such subversion escape attention? The answer lies in the ways that these lyrics compensate for the absence of rhyme through other devices of language and sound that satisfy the same desires for repetition and difference. Here are the lyrics:

> I got rhythm
> I got music
> I got my man
> Who could ask for anything more?

> I got daisies
> In green pastures
> I got my man
> Who could ask for anything more?

In the place where rhyme should be, Gershwin introduces several other rhetorical patterns. First, he uses anaphora (kin to epistrophe, it is the repetition of a word or phrase at the beginning of successive clauses), beginning five of the eight lines with the same words, "I got." Next, he employs identity on the level of the line, with the repetition of an entire syntactical unit: "Who could ask for anything more?" He also creates a moment of generative tension between the lyric line and the syntactic unit by enjambing the phrase between lines five and six ("I got daisies/In green pastures"). Finally, the repeated melodic line sets off a percussive pattern that, combined with the vocalist's syncopated delivery, creates a measure of the repetition with a difference that one craves in rhyme. These rhetorical effects combine to cover for the absence of rhyme.

Sometimes rhyme's absence maps onto mood, when the unsettling feeling born of missing something without quite knowing what underscores the emotion of music and lyric. One such example is the lovely ballad "Separate Lives," written by Stephen Bishop and popularized in a 1985 power-ballad duet by Phil Collins and Marilyn Martin. This is a song about disconnection, loss, and longing. Whether listening through the dated overproduction of the Collins/Martin version to catch the beauty of the song itself, or listening to Bishop's own stripped-down acoustic rendition, which has aged far better, "Separate Lives" communicates vulnerability in its lyrics and melody all at once.

As the Gershwin example does, "Separate Lives" compensates for the rhymes it denies us. The absence of definitive rhyme in favor of more subtle assonance underscores the conversational and confessional quality of the lyric. Bishop's version, with its spare acoustic guitar accompaniment, does not provide a foundational rhythm; Bishop strums his chords only when he sings, pausing between lines as if to steel himself for the confession to come. Perhaps the song succeeds in obviating listeners' expectations of resolution in rhyme precisely because it promises so little resolution in any other facet of the song either. Though carefully crafted, "Separate Lives" sounds like spontaneous expression of uncomposed vulnerability.

"Separate Lives" stages a moment of intimacy between the two figures in the song, the lover and the lost beloved, a point of fleeting connection that only underscores the growing distance between them. It's hard to imagine the song generating the same depth of feeling had it followed instead a more conventional structure of end rhymes. Rhyme's absence here serves the song. Even in absentia, though, rhyme still announces its importance to the lyrics. All the energy required to compensate for the loss testifies to the function and value of rhyme in the poetry of pop.

Chapter Six

Figurative Language

I fell for you like a child. Like a child, you whisper softly to me. Like a bridge over troubled water, I will lay me down. Like a bird on a wire, like a drunk in a midnight choir, I have tried in my way to be free. Free as a bird. My heart is like an open highway. Like a drifter, I was born to walk alone. Walk like an Egyptian. Like a virgin. Like a complete unknown. Like a rolling stone.

Songs often speak in simile. Similes, among dozens of other rhetorical figures and forms, are capable of making language memorable, emotive, and strange. As some of the examples above illustrate, however, they can also make lyrics sound predictable and stale. Effective or not, figurative language is a means of unsettling expression, be it through figures of speech that augment, ornament, or otherwise alter everyday language, or through rhetorical forms that fashion patterns of structure and sound. The Romantic poet Percy Bysshe Shelley writes in his *Defence of Poetry* that poetry "awakens and enlarges the mind itself by rendering it the receptacle of a thousand unapprehended combinations of thought. Poetry lifts the veil from the hidden beauty of the world, and makes familiar objects be as if they were not familiar." By lifting what Shelley calls "the veil of familiarity" from the world, poetry renders the familiar unfamiliar, newly charged with wonder and mystery. Rhetorical figures and forms are perhaps the poet's most potent tools for awakening and enlarging the mind. They are the same for the songwriter.

The two preceding chapters grappled with the ways that words shift shape under the enchantment of rhythm and the sonic identity and difference that happens in rhyme. Rhythm and rhyme, most acutely felt in performance, underpin the reason that song lyrics distinguish themselves from most language that we encounter throughout the day. But another strangeness resides primarily in the language of song lyrics itself rather than in how that language sounds when sung. Rhetorical figures like similes and metaphors, and even patterns of language like anaphora and epistrophe, are usually matters of meaning first and only secondarily of sound. They encourage us to imagine one thing as another, or to identify patterns and breaks in patterns, or to reconcile opposing ideas. Figures and forms are the originary space of thought in songs. They may lack the emotive directness of rhythm and rhyme, but they might just mark the closest point of contact between the minds of songwriters and the minds of their listeners.

Song lyrics shine a light on figurative language more so than does common speech, though both are festooned with figures and forms. The language of the lyrics often aims to adorn and to refine whatever nonverbal impulse the song implies. Song lyrics sometimes complicate as well, generating tension by unsettling the emotive inclinations of the music. Yes, song lyrics are sometimes clichéd and trite; clichéd and trite ideas are often just calcified figures of speech. But song lyrics also aspire to novelty and freshness, to rendering the familiar unfamiliar. Because of these and other reasons, song lyrics comprise perhaps the broadest, most accessible body of language upon which to catalog, to explore, and to celebrate the emotive and imaginative potential of rhetorical figures and forms.

Figurative language is so common in pop music that one could pick any week on the *Billboard* Hot 100 chart and find songs that display simile and metaphor as well as a range of more exotic figures and forms. Take the week of December 13, 2003, when the following songs sat atop the singles chart:

1. OutKast, "Hey Ya!"
2. Ludacris, "Stand Up"
3. OutKast feat. Sleepy Brown, "The Way You Move"
4. Kelis, "Milkshake"
5. Beyoncé feat. Sean Paul, "Baby Boy"
6. Chingy feat. Ludacris and Snoop Dogg, "Holidae In"
7. 3 Doors Down, "Here without You"
8. Baby Bash feat. Frankie J, "Suga Suga"
9. R. Kelly, "Step in the Name of Love"
10. Jagged Edge, "Walked Outta Heaven"

Okay, maybe I didn't select this date at random. After all, "Hey Ya!" might contain the most memorable pop-music simile of the new millennium: "Shake it like a Polaroid picture." The evocative quality of the figure was in no way diminished by the Polaroid company's press release urging their dramatically shrinking customer base not to follow André 3000's advice: "Rapid movement during development can cause portions of the film to separate prematurely." Though I sought out "Hey Ya!," I couldn't have guessed what the other songs on the chart that week had in store in the hunt for figures and forms. Kelis's "Milkshake" centers on a provocative, if imprecise, extended metaphor. "My milkshake brings all the boys to the yard," Kelis boasts. The seductive spirit of the statement is clear even if the letter of it is not. On "Suga Suga" Baby Bash and Frankie J use a common figurative ploy when they charge the "suga" in question with a not-so-subtle ambiguity: it's either a woman or weed. Rounding out the top ten is Jagged Edge's "Walked Outta Heaven," which threatens a simile in the first verse only to retreat from it: "The night's as black as . . . black as it's ever been." Whether we read that line as a runaway train of thought or as a spark of plainspoken inspiration is a matter of taste, I suppose.

Just to be fair, consider another week, this time truly at random—September 6, 1969:

1. Rolling Stones, "Honky Tonk Women"
2. Johnny Cash, "A Boy Named Sue"
3. The Archies, "Sugar Sugar"
4. Creedence Clearwater Revival, "Green River"
5. Youngbloods, "Get Together"
6. Jackie DeShannon, "Put a Little Love in Your Heart"
7. Bob Dylan, "Lay Lady Lay"
8. Three Dog Night, "Easy to Be Hard"
9. Neil Diamond, "Sweet Caroline"
10. Tom Jones, "I'll Never Fall in Love Again"

On "Honky Tonk Women," the Rolling Stones deploy the exotic figure of zeugma (more on that later). Dylan invites his lover to lay across his "big brass bed" in "Lay Lady Lay" and shades the experience in the abstract promise that "whatever colors you have in your mind/I'll show them to you and you'll see them shine." Johnny Cash's sly cover of children's poet Shel Silverstein's "A Boy Named Sue" invokes simile to describe the narrator's tussle with the father who gave him a girl's name: "He kicked like a mule and he bit like a crocodile." Perhaps the strangest entry on the list is "Sugar Sugar," by the comic-book characters come to life, the Archies. Unlike Baby Bash and Frankie J's "Suga Suga" from thirty-five years later, this song makes its metaphoric meaning clear from the opening chorus:

> Sugar. Ah, honey, honey
> You are my candy girl
> And you've got me wanting you
> Honey. Ah, sugar, sugar
> You are my candy girl
> And you've got me wanting you

Sweetness with a hint of seduction: Though the metaphor of the beloved as a "candy girl" might lack imagination, it is more than serviceable here. The lyric structures itself in two parts, each of three lines, that work on the principle of repetition with a difference: "sugar" and "honey" take each other's places in lines one and four, while the other lines repeat. Choose any week on the *Billboard* charts—start with the week that you're reading this book—and you'll find examples of what pop songs ask figurative language to do.

FIGURES AND FORMS DEFINED

Rhetorical figures and forms adorn, derange, and organize. They range from patterns of sound, like alliteration, to patterns of thought, like metaphor and metonymy. Some of these figures and forms in songs are nearly invisible, while others call attention to themselves as clever or confusing. Though pop figures and forms generally seek novelty, they tend to do so within the territory of the familiar. An effective figure discovers new things on common ground, even if the newness is only in the point of view or in a subtle reshaping of sound.

One way to group pop's rhetorical tropes is to decide what kind of work they do in the lyric. Figures work primarily in the realm of thought, while forms work primarily in the realm of language and its arrangement. We might usefully divide these two larger categories into smaller ones based on specific functions. Rhetorical figures include tropes that transfer meaning from one thing to another (simile and metaphor, for instance), tropes that exchange meaning between one thing and another (chiasmus), and tropes that transform meaning entirely (antanaclasis). Rhetorical forms impose order (anaphora and epanodos), fashion more idiosyncratic patterns (repetitio), and combine both thought and language into one.

The goal of this chapter is not, however, simply to provide a taxonomy of rhetorical figures and forms as they appear in pop songs. It is not even primarily to explain the songwriter's craft; plenty of books provide step-by-step instructions for building a better metaphor for your song lyric. Rather, my goal is to help explain why certain words or phrases from song lyrics end up lodged in our heads or tattooed on our bodies. Through the alchemy of music and the craft of lyric, the dross of common or even trite ideas becomes the gold and the platinum of great pop songs. A lover bemoaning a lost love becomes "a fat house cat/Nursing my sore blunt tongue" in Iron & Wine's

"Flightless Bird, American Mouth." For the country singer Kacey Musgraves, love "plays you like a fiddle, shakes you like a rattle / Takes away your gun and sends you into battle." Rhetorical figures can transform even run-of-the-mill heartache into a subject of wonder.

Beyond taxonomy, this chapter asks a more basic question about the rhetorical construction of pop songs: Why do pop songs take the shapes that they take? Songs, after all, are the art of emotion, which is to say that they are also the art of rhetoric. Songs make the familiar unfamiliar, transforming common themes into language that, when set to song, excites the senses.

Figurative language is so prevalent in everyday speech and in the language of song lyrics that it's necessary to bracket off what this chapter is not about. This chapter is not about incidental or accidental figures of speech, words or phrases that the song intends as direct expression even if there is a figure lurking within it. If, as Ralph Waldo Emerson observed, all language is "fossil poetry," then one can undoubtedly find figures of speech at work in every lyric. When Oasis's Noel Gallagher asks, "Where were you when we were getting high?" on "Champagne Supernova," "getting high" is a figure of speech since those involved are almost certainly seated or recumbent while enjoying their elevating substance of choice. The meaning is plain, though the metaphor remains. In this instance, the figure of speech exists as shorthand, a well-worn phrase to describe a particular activity. Metaphor here is a matter of convenience, or even indifference, to the lyricist.

The figures and forms of song lyrics that hold the most interest are the products of lyric craft. When I was a graduate student, my teacher Helen Vendler challenged me and my classmates to find within poems what she termed their "salient oddities," those qualities of language that present an enigma, that hold themselves out as indispensable even as they escape full understanding. Listening to song lyrics, the figures and forms that attach themselves most firmly to my consciousness satisfy this same dual aim. They are salient oddities—of language and thought, shape and feeling—and the goal is not so much to resolve them as it is to metabolize them into one's own experience.

What happens when singers and songwriters consciously design figures of speech in order to do something with language and to the listener? Their aim may be to jar a listener's consciousness in tension with the music, or it may mean leaving the figure lurking below the surface of the sound, to be discovered only later in quiet recollection of the lyrics or in close study of them on the page. In such cases, the figure is an instrument of utility and of aesthetics. The figure makes an idea beautiful, ugly, or strange.

THE POWER OF THE STRANGE

Attaching words to things is a figurative act. Most words or phrases, however, become so expected in the language that their figurative strangeness is no longer apparent. We're bombarded every day by esoteric forms that classical rhetoricians came up with names to codify. When a CNN anchor remarks that "the White House announced today that it is seeking to normalize relations with the nation of Cuba," that anchor is employing the rhetorical figure of metonymy by using a building (the White House) to stand in for a government or a person (the president of the United States). There's nothing remarkable about hearing this, though, because we've normalized our own cognitive relation to a figure of speech that would have us believe that a white house can speak.

The first thing to say about artful and striking rhetorical figures and forms is that they are somehow strange. When it comes to similes and metaphors, the best of them tend to find a sweet spot between the conventional and the quirky. "The world is a vampire / Sent to drain," Billy Corgan sings in the arresting metaphor that begins Smashing Pumpkins' "Bullet with Butterfly Wings." That metaphor demands an attendant image. If a figure of speech is too strange, then it will baffle comprehension. If it is too expected, then it will have little impact and may not register as a metaphor at all. When Simon LeBon of Duran Duran sings that he's "hungry like the wolf," it is not a particularly evocative simile because "hungry" is pretty much the first thing one thinks of when it comes to wolves. Certainly, the rhetorical figure does its work by transferring the quality of hunger from animal to man, and from sustenance to passion, but the mind hardly bothers conjuring an image to accompany it.

Compare that simile to the far stranger, and thus more evocative, simile from Bruce Springsteen's "Born in the U.S.A.," where he describes the life of a character who "end[s] up like a dog that's been beat too much." It's hard not to conjure a mental image of the animal, cowed and quivering, chained in the yard, quick to snarl at a passerby but too broken to bark for long. The assumption behind the simile is strange as well; a dog being beaten "too much" suggests that it's possible to beat a dog just enough. The power, too, comes in the casual colloquialism of the grammatically incorrect "been beat too much." The simile sits seamlessly in the verse as a whole:

> Born down in a dead man's town
> The first kick I took is when I hit the ground
> End up like a dog that's been beat too much
> 'til you spend half your life just to cover it up

Springsteen's simile says a simple thing in a powerful way. It tells a common story through uncommon language, opening up a new avenue of emotional connection for the listener. Like Wendy from "Born to Run," like the people from "Darkness at the Edge of Town" with "lives on the line where dreams are found and lost," prosperity for this speaker is always just around the corner but destined never to arrive. Time moves much too fast. Literalizing the figure of speech of "spend[ing] half your life just to cover it up" is particularly tragic for someone who doesn't have that time to spare. Little of that complexity comes through, though, in a paraphrase: *I was born in a town with high unemployment where I never learned the resilience to face setbacks; instead, I simply disguised my weaknesses—to others and even to myself.* Told this way, the story is clichéd. What makes Springsteen's lyrics original and specific is the way he renders the familiar story unfamiliar through figurative language.

In comparison, Duran Duran's "Hungry Like the Wolf" extends its figure of speech to the point of attenuation: "I'm on the hunt, I'm after you," "mouth is alive with juices like wine," and "I howl and I whine, I'm after you." Attenuation isn't a strong enough word for what happens to this already prosaic simile when belabored in the lyric. The difference between what Springsteen does and what Duran Duran does is a matter of craft: In the first instance, the simile functions as an instrument of character development and emotive shading; in the second, it is a lyrical cudgel. Both do their jobs well. One could make the argument that Duran Duran does its job better given how clear its comparison is when set beside the dark and challenging lyric of "Born in the U.S.A.," which is often mistaken as an anthem of unreconstructed American patriotism, a song to play at firework displays. Without a doubt, Springsteen's lyric is more compelling on the page. The Duran Duran lyric, however, silly simile and all, is no less an instance of figurative language put to good use in the service of its song.

These disparate lyrics demonstrate another distinction worth making about figures and forms in popular song. It is the difference between using figures and forms to render the subject something to be puzzled over ("Born in the U.S.A.") and using them to render the subject something readily apparent ("Hungry Like the Wolf"). Both of these, when done well, give birth to meaning, but with dramatically different emotional and cognitive rewards.

The first approach, using a rhetorical figure like the simile to create a moment in the lyric that demands contemplation, is common to the practice of poetry for the page. In her brief and beautiful "The Fisherman's Wife," Amy Lowell crafts a poem whose emotive power radiates from an artful simile:

> When I am alone,
> The wind in the pine-trees
> Is like the shuffling of waves
> Upon the wooden sides of a boat.

In four lines, Lowell conjures a person, place, and atmosphere—the lone speaker surrounded by pine trees blown by the breeze—then layers atop this scene a simile that brings to life another place and atmosphere. This palimpsest demands that we reconcile, in meaning and feeling, the figurative valence with the literal lines. "The Fisherman's Wife," like Springsteen's "Born in the U.S.A.," is a call in search of a response from anyone who reads or hears the words.

In contrast to such subtle and strange layering, rhetorical figures at times express themselves by rendering meaning as transparent as possible, even to the point of obscuring the function of the figure itself. Lyrics such as these aim not to inspire thought through an unexpected or unusual connection, but to provide unobtrusive words to hold the melody or to demonstrate the lyricist's virtuosity in exhausting a simile's range of applications.

"Hungry Like a Wolf" certainly qualifies as such a simile, as does Bob Seger's "Like a Rock," a workmanlike example of pop lyricism that employs simile without any sense of indirection or guile. The chorus is a good illustration:

> Like a rock, I was strong as I could be
> Like a rock, nothin ever got to me
> Like a rock, I was something to see
> Like a rock

Strong, insensate, imposing: These are the transitive qualities the song takes from rock and lends to the singer. The song announces its conceit in its very title. The function therefore of the simile is not to surprise, but to satiate expectation as fully as possible by putting the familiar comparison to work in a number of ways. The plain meaning of the lyrics redirects attention to other elements of the song. The figure of speech doesn't tax the listener's cognitive capacity, leaving more energy to direct to the grain of Seger's voice and the story of his remembered youth.

What are similes doing when they aren't being clever, puzzling, or profound? If we understand that the traditional function of the simile is, in the words of *The Princeton Encyclopedia of Poetry and Poetics*, "to reveal an unexpected likeness between two seemingly disparate things," then what are we to think in those many instances when the comparisons being made in the lyrics to pop songs are anything but unexpected? Popular music is festooned with rhetorical figures—similes and metaphors in particular—that the lyrics leave unfulfilled, unresolved. Pat Benatar's "Love Is a Battlefield" repeats its titular metaphor six times during the chorus of the song, but little else in the lyric builds on its meaning. "Love is like a bomb," Def Leppard's Joe Elliott announces in the first lines of "Pour Some Sugar on Me." How so? Is it dangerous? Does it explode? We'll never know.

A more compelling and more fully realized figurative comparison for love is the Magnetic Fields' "Love Is Like a Bottle of Gin." Though it announces its simile in the title, it does not explicitly state the figurative comparison in the song lyric until the final lines. A listener without the benefit of liner notes, therefore, will arrive inductively at the figurative formulation as it reveals itself over the course of the song's six straight verses. The pairing of love and gin forges an unexpected likeness between disparate things, connected through affinities of action and feeling:

> It makes you blind, it does you in
> It makes you think you're pretty tough
> It makes you prone to crime and sin
> It makes you say things off the cuff

Delivered in Stephin Merritt's deadpan baritone, the arch humor and knowingness of the lines resound. By the end of the song we are invested in the comparison as if it were our own, congratulating ourselves on its cleverness. Merritt, however, resists the facility of his own figure by taking a striking turn in the closing lines: "Love is like a bottle of gin / But a bottle of gin is not like love." At once, the lyric asserts its figurative terms and denies their reciprocity. A listener delighted by the conceit of love as intoxicating, uninhibited, and free must come to terms with the night-side of the connection: Sitting alone at a bar getting drunk off cheap gin looks nothing like love.

"Love Is Like a Bottle of Gin" presents love in language both challenging and invigorating. Love language like this, though, is the exception. The English language rarely gets lazier than it does when it's dealing with love. Whether describing bliss or heartache, love is usually voiced in a conscripted vocabulary. In aiming to describe love's irresistible and dangerous appeal, songs as distanced from one another in time and temperament as the Smiths' "The Hand That Rocks the Cradle," Janet Jackson's "That's the Way Love Goes," Kiss's "Young and Wasted," and Shawn Mendes's "Stitches" have exercised the stock phrase "like a moth to a flame." What once might have sounded novel now sounds plain.

In the matter of heartbreak, a common figure of speech is to say that the loss of love "cuts like a knife." This is certainly serviceable, given that the knife is a unifunctional tool for cutting. We imagine, therefore, that the emotion must cut good and deep. As a simile for the pain of lost love, however, it fails the test of "unexpected likeness." In fact, it now amounts to a cliché, which is to say that its figurative power is all but exhausted. So then why use the phrase at all? What can it still do for a song if it isn't contributing to the figurative power and emotional evocation of the lyric? Perhaps one uses the familiar figure because it is so close at hand. Perhaps, too, the songwriter recognizes the virtue of the familiar. Perhaps we should just ask Bryan Adams.

Adams named an entire album *Cuts Like a Knife*. The titular song uses the phrase in the chorus. His explanation for why he and his songwriting partner settled on the canned phrase is revealing: it was the product of improvised sound, of something like scatting, brought into the form of language. "I think that I'm one of the world's best mumblers, I can mumble some of the best lyrics, but putting them together is another story," Adams recalls. "The best example was when we wrote 'Cuts Like A Knife,' which was just literally a mumble. We looked at each other, rolled the tape back, and it sounded like 'cuts like a knife,' so we started singing that." It's unsurprising that Adams's mumbling would coalesce into a cliché rather than gibberish or some unusual expression. It offers not only a familiar phrase, but one upon which to organize a familiar pop emotion and theme: the response to lost love. I quote the chorus here with part of a verse that precedes it for context:

> I took it all for granted
> But how was I to know
> That you'd be letting go?
>
> Now it cuts like a knife
> But it feels so right
> It cuts like a knife
> But it feels so right

The story the song tells is familiar: *I messed up, now you're gone and I'm painfully regretting it.* What's unexpected, however, is what comes after the simile—"But it feels so right." It's a small but significant adjustment that gives greater specificity to what otherwise is a secondhand emotion. There's truth here: pain and regret being both unwanted and desired. "It feels so right," a phrase, conventional in its own right, more familiar for other phases of a love affair, is out of place here in a way that creates dissonance. In essence, Adams rubs two clichés together and generates some lyric heat.

The same phrase crops up in Tom Bahler's lovelorn ballad "She's Out of My Life," the last song on Michael Jackson's *Off the Wall*. On an album of irresistibly danceable club hits, the song stands out for both its tempo and its tone. Like Bryan Adams's "Cuts Like a Knife," "She's Out of My Life" situates itself in that conventional position of the singer at the end of a love affair. Also like the Adams's lyric, Jackson's performance of Bahler's lyric evinces emotional ambivalence. "I don't know whether to laugh or cry/I don't know whether to live or die/And it cuts like a knife/She's out of my life," Jackson sings in the first verse. The swelling strings and maudlin melody make the song's choice with more decisiveness than does the lyric alone; this is a crying song. Indeed, Jackson delivers the last lines with a quavering voice that finally gives way to tears:

> And she's out of my life
> She's out of my life
> Damned indecision and cursed pride
> Kept my love for her locked deep inside
> And it cuts like a knife
> She's out of my life

Jackson's voice breaks first on "knife," then nearly shatters as he attempts to sing the final line—the last word, "life," comes out like a puff of air. The fact that the last two lines form a couplet, ending on a perfect rhyme, would seem to suggest resolution and finality, but the way Jackson performs the lyrics complicates that conclusion. It's theatrical, a kind of spectacle that endows the song with a depth of feeling that the lyrics only suggest. In his memoir, Jackson recalls, "I got too wrapped up in 'She's Out of My Life.' . . . I cried at the end of a take, because the words suddenly had such a strong effect on me." Little about the words themselves would seem to carry so much feeling; but they are effective vessels for the emotion Jackson brings to them precisely because they are so conventional, so adoptable, so adaptable.

Often song lyrics extend a concrete figure only to complicate it. On T. Rex's "Bang a Gong (Get It On)" we encounter a solid simile in the first line of the second verse—"Well, you're built like a car"—only to find it strangely, wonderfully confounded in the line that follows—"You got a hub cap diamond star halo"—then brought right back to the concrete in the third line: "You're built like a car—Oh, yeah." Either way of using simile—presenting an image that announces itself from the outset, or crafting one that confounds and demands unpacking—is equally the product of the poetic craft. One method is more familiar from lyric poetry and one from advertising or fable; both at their best exemplify the effective function of rhetorical figures and forms in pop lyrics.

SAYING ONE THING, MEANING ANOTHER: SIMILE AND METAPHOR

Similes and metaphors are both figurative comparisons. Though their effects and shading may differ, they function through the same cognitive process. As Robert J. Fogelin describes it, following a long tradition of figurative theory stretching back to Aristotle, "They present a comparison with a transparent incongruity (oddness) that admits of resolution." Similes and metaphors require the mind to solve a puzzle, to span the distance between a subject and a figurative referent, and, in doing so, to experience the sensation of novelty becoming affinity. Fogelin further distinguishes what he terms metaphors of wit, which introduce, then resolve, incongruities, and metaphors as models, which impose "a system of relations from one domain to another." The former often, though not always, express themselves in comedy. As a rhetorical category, then, similes and metaphors can be illuminating as well as obfuscating, commonplace, and remarkable. As parts of songs, they can recede into sound or they can leap out and demand attention that might even detract from the listening experience.

The basic structure of the simile is this: A is like B, with A being the tenor (the subject of description—a person, object, state of being, or concept), and B being the vehicle (the image that lends its qualities to the tenor), to employ the terms conceived long ago by I. A. Richards. In its simplest expression, both tenor and vehicle are nouns: "O my Luve's [tenor] like a red, red rose [vehicle]," as Robert Burns wrote back in 1794. Or "My love [tenor] is like Wo [vehicle]" as Mya sang back in 2003. Similes function by inviting us to find qualities in the referent that are applicable to the subject. In its most straightforward iteration, then, a simile presents a puzzle for the mind to solve. "And it seems to me you lived your life like a candle in the wind," Elton John sings in Bernie Taupin's lyric. The lyric leaves for listeners the task of articulating the comparison: a candle in the wind is susceptible to being snuffed out, like a life cut short. We attach to the subject (the "you" of either Marilyn Monroe or Princess Diana) the referent's quality of vulnerability and ephemerality. Though the simile here has become so commonplace as to register almost as literal expression, it nonetheless amply illustrates the way that similes often work in song lyrics.

One would be hard pressed to find a simpler set of similes than those in Katy Perry's "Firework" (2010), which she composed with the songwriting Svengali Ester Dean as well as the producers StarGate and Sandy Vee. "Firework" exemplifies the way that figurative language can hide in plain sight. The very concept of the song is figurative, as the firework stands in for the hidden self brought to light, and every section of the song, from verse to chorus to bridge and back, is structured around similes and metaphors. When read on the page, the clunkiness of the opening lines exposes itself in a way that it doesn't when cloaked in Perry's climbing melodic arc and stylized phrasing: "Do you ever feel like a plastic bag/Drifting through the wind, wanting to start again?" It's so bad it's almost good. Or try this: "Do you ever feel already buried deep/Six feet under, scream, but no one seems to hear a thing?" What a horrifying image. But Perry's delivery betrays little of the alarm that attends actually conjuring a mental picture of the experience the lines describe. Instead, we simply feel the low simmer of the music, leading to the boiling over of the chorus as Perry pushes to the edge of her vocal range, enacting the explosive spectacle promised in the song's title. The figurative language at play in "Firework" is hardly what one remembers from the song, though it is indispensable to its meaning and feeling. The images are functional, if at times awkward, imprecise, and just plain batty; nonetheless, they propel the song forward in ways that it's hard not to admire.

Often figurative comparisons complete their own puzzle, resolving their incongruities even as they introduce them. On the hair metal band Whitesnake's "Here I Go Again," David Coverdale sings "like a drifter, I was born to walk alone." In this instance, the simile makes explicit the terms of its connection, dimming but not extinguishing the other associations the simile invites—the drifter as aimless, rootless, impoverished. The pleasure of the figure does not come from the mental stimulation of completing a puzzle, but from the vicarious pleasure of seeing someone else, in this case the lyricist/singer, solve the puzzle for us.

Although, as in "Firework," similes may be notably clunky, metaphors are to blame for some of the greatest abuses of pop music. "Indisputably, the effect of crowing images in a lyric can play havoc with a song, giving it a weird effect, like glossolalia," writes Alexander Theroux. An ill-judged use of metaphors may make us feel as though the singer is speaking in tongues and communicating little. Sometimes metaphor can usurp a song's content and become an exercise in form rather than working through form to move listeners. In analyzing the function of metaphor in his song "Only Flame in Town," Elvis Costello observes that the profusion of metaphor in the lyrics risks overtaking the recording. "By the middle of the second verse . . . you start to think, 'Oh god, that's a good one,' 'Aw, that one's a bit dodgy!'" Costello argues that he put metaphor to better use in "Indoor Fireworks": "When you say, 'I'll build a bonfire of my dreams and burn a broken effigy of me and you,' the fact that it extends the fire metaphor is completely secondary to the emotion." The metaphor serves the song. "Effective metaphor suits the context in which it occurs," write Cleanth Brooks and Robert Penn Warren in their classic study of poetics. "Moreover, an effective metaphor pays its own way—that is, it justifies itself by making a real contribution to the writer's total expression."

Sometimes we have to dig a little to unearth an effective metaphor. Nirvana's "Smells Like Teen Spirit" is often disparaged as song lyric even as it is celebrated as recorded song. Kurt Cobain's words, when they can be discerned from the noise of the instruments washing over and under them, are often cryptic and even contradictory. "Just seeing Kurt write the lyrics to a song five minutes before he first sings them, you just kind of find it a little bit hard to believe that the song has a lot to say about something," Nirvana's drummer, Dave Grohl, told Kurt St. Thomas during a 1992 interview just as Nirvana was cresting to superstardom. "You need syllables to fill up this space or you need something that rhymes." Cobain's journals, however, tell another story, revealing craft and construction that challenge romantic notions of lyrics dashed off in minutes. They show him honing his language, starting with sounds and scraps of image and moving to meaning. "To know oh no I told a secret word" becomes "to know oh no a dirty word," which becomes "Oh no I know a dirty word" on the next page and "Uh oh oh no a dirty word" on the one after that.

Perhaps the most puzzling lyric section, reproduced verbatim from the journals, comes at the end of the chorus with this series of seeming abstractions:

> A mulatto. An albino.
> A mosquito. My libido.

In this sequence of three implied metaphors following an unstated "I am . . ." and a final assertion of first-person possession (*my* libido), Cobain generates mystery. He does so by choosing words that many of his listeners will comprehend only vaguely or mishear entirely, both because of the urgency and occasional incoherence of his singing and because the words themselves are unusual, and even more unusual when grouped together. Sure, they all loosely rhyme with one another. Each has three syllables. The first two have a natural association (both have to do with skin color); the last two do not readily connect, either with what comes before or with each other. As a consequence, the mind moves to find some underlying order, something that coheres the sequence. In 1960 the writer Archibald MacLeish asked, "But what meaning *can* there be in this collision of images which do not collide?" Whether there's meaning or not in Nirvana's collision of images that do not collide, the automatic search for coherence nonetheless generates energy and mystery for the song.

Given this energy, it makes sense to attend to the connections and connotations that this strange group of words sets off. "Mulatto" and "albino" call to mind racial identities and skin tones, determined in the first case by the activation of melanin and in the second case by the absence of melanin in the skin, hair, and eyes. A mosquito sucks blood, feeds on it. And the sexual libido, particularly of a teen (who might apply a few swipes of Teen Spirit deodorant in the morning), acts out as a hunger, a necessity to feed and to suck. Are the connections abstract? Of course they are. But that abstraction, even to the point of obscurity, engenders unease that matches the urgency of Cobain's singing and the stridency of the music's driving rhythms and aching guitars.

Most metaphors in popular music, however, tend more to the explicit than to the abstract. Consider Bruno Mars's 2010 hit "Grenade" from his debut album, *Doo-Wops & Hooligans*. The chorus, structured around images of self-sacrifice, enumerates the many ways he "would die for you, baby/But you won't do the same." He would catch a grenade, throw his hand on a blade, jump in front of a train, and take a bullet through the brain. The mind has little time to rest on any one image. In an interview with *GQ*, the journalist Chris Heath asked Mars to reflect on the effects of his figurative language in song, from an "extended metaphor that aligns religion and a vagina" to other potentially blasphemous forays. "If you think it's blasphemous," Mars responds, "then obviously you don't know that it's poetry. You can pick apart all of my songs. A bullet through your brain, man? That's not politically correct. . . . You're not listening to it right if you're picking it apart like that. You know? I can't overthink everything I wrote or worry about that kind of stuff. Hopefully people should know. There's no blasphemy. Or insult to any religion. It's just fucking poetry, whether you believe me or not."

"It's just fucking poetry" is an apt slogan for the poetry of pop—one part profane, one part profound in its call to take things lightly, to allow for pop's sense of play and creative mischief. The phrase is also a reminder of the everyday nature of pop's poetics. If it's just fucking poetry, then it has to be accessible rather than restrictive, aiming to please rather than seeking to confound. It's poetry for the people, focused on emotive impact rather than solely on the more measured effects of deep contemplation. "Poetry begins in trivial metaphors, pretty metaphors, 'grace' metaphors, and goes on to the profoundest thinking that we have," the poet Robert Frost remarked in 1931. "Poetry provides," he continued, "the one permissible way of saying one thing and meaning another." Over the past forty years, no other genre of popular lyric has done more to explore this figurative imperative than the language of rap.

Rap lyrics are a useful way into the more esoteric varieties and applications of figurative language in song lyrics across all genres. Rap revels in simile and puns and a host of rare figures and forms, some of which haven't been in common currency since Cicero. On "One More Chance" Biggie employs kenning, a trope that exchanges a word or proper name for a compound poetic phrase, when he boasts that he's the "mic-ripper, girl-stripper, the Henny-sipper." Jean Grae does the same thing on "Hater's Anthem" when she dubs herself "the cancer-toker, the Mad Hatter, the Jabberwocky of rap." Rap privileges this kind of wordplay for its own sake in a way that other genres rarely do. In fact, some rap songs find coherence not in narrative or in the development of theme or emotion, but in displays of wit and rhetorical mastery. In this regard, rap extends a tradition of poetry as play; public displays of linguistic invention were common in ancient Greece, not to mention in many of the oral traditions of the non-Western world.

One such example of this linguistic invention is actually rap's *reinvention* of the simile. This reinvention is a consequence both of necessity and of method: necessity, because rap uses simile so much that broadening the range of the figure is essential; and method, because rap is often an extemporized form that celebrates the aural, and simile is the most readily accessible figure in extemporized language. Simile needs the least forethought and can stand alone as a phrase. The variations on the conventional simile found in rap work on the principles of elision, substitution, and expansion. This greater descriptive range does not mean better lyrics. Rather, it speaks to a set of formal practices and audience expectations native to the genre. It is the test that the genre sets for itself in gauging an artist's virtuosity.

A notable example of the way rap reworks similes is what I call the associative simile, where the figurative connection falls in the corona of association that surrounds a word rather than directly on the word itself. By traditional measure, associative similes are imprecise or flawed comparisons, but if we dilate our understanding of what a simile can do, we open up a range of expressive possibilities. Associative similes are largely born of the oral tradition and best understood when heard aloud. Take, for instance, this phrase from Kanye West: "I'm so appalled, Spalding ball." The logical connection here is a result of the assonance that connects the short *a* in "appalled" with the short *a*'s in "Spalding" and "ball." Semantically, this implied simile is opaque: "I'm as appalled as a Spalding basketball" is nonsensical. The sense instead derives from the sound, where the vehicle and the tenor are connected through assonance. Simply putting this through the simile formula is not enough.

A striking case of rap's weirding of figurative language began in 2007 when Big Sean, a then little-known MC on Kanye West's G.O.O.D. music label, released a song called "Supa Dupa Lemonade" in which he employed an unusual rhetorical figure, a kind of truncated simile:

> Bank account got me feeling well . . . Fargo
> Balling 'til I get a mil' a check . . . Darko

In these lines and in the ones that follow ("Cause I just black out in the booth . . . charcoal" is perhaps the simplest) Big Sean pauses where listeners expect a "like" to be. Add the "like" back in and these are punning similes of the kind one regularly finds in rap: "I black out in the booth like charcoal," because charcoal is black. "The large amount of money in my bank account has me feeling well like [Wells] Fargo," the bank. "I'm balling [putting in work on craft] until I get a million dollars per check like [former professional basketball player] Darko [Milicic]," because Milicic likely cashed a few such checks and because his first name works great for the double meaning. Only the charcoal figure approaches the criteria of a traditional simile, where the vehicle (charcoal) transfers some quality of its identity to the tenor (the "I" who's blacking out in the booth). The other figures are forged first in sound rather than in sense; as associative similes, they make their figurative connection by landing somewhere in the corona of meaning that surrounds the term rather than connecting directly to the term itself.

Kanye would go on to popularize Big Sean's practice, even giving it a name, "hashtag rap," for the Twitter hashtags that were just starting to dominate social media. Though this hashtag figure would achieve saturation in rap during the first decade of the twenty-first century, its reach is much wider than that. Glancing back across pop lyric history, one finds earlier instances of the same practice. Def Leppard's 1987 hit "Pour Some Sugar on Me," for instance, contains the following: "You got the peaches, I got the cream/Sweet to taste . . . saccharine." Though rap didn't invent it, the hashtag style would become a rap fad, cropping up in numerous lyrics by Drake, Lil Wayne, Nicki Minaj, Ludacris, Juelz Santana, and many others. By 2010, Drake was already pronouncing the style's death. "Well, that flow has been killed by so many rappers. And, I never want to use that flow again in life," he said.

Hashtag rap's popularity has faded, though it has since settled into a more humble but still significant place in rap's figurative repertoire. Macklemore put it to use on 2015's "Downtown," when he rhymes in the song's final lines: "There's layers to this shit, player . . . tiramisu/Let my coattail drag, but I ain't tearing my suit." A simile here would have been labored; with the hashtag, it feels off the cuff. He underscores the figure with a playfully virtuosic mosaic rhyme ("tiramisu"/"tearing my suit"). Here hashtag rap offers a modulation on the traditional punning simile and becomes a way of punctuating a phrase, setting it in sharp relief that would be blunted if the line included "like" or "as."

Given the shifting currents of slang and rap's pop culture points of reference, similes in rap often have a short shelf life. Because artists regularly draw figures from the cultural present, the further removed we are from the moment of composition, the more obscure the figure can become. Rap fosters a sense of spontaneity and immediacy that makes it impactful but also fleeting. Rap lyrics are no more disposable than lyrics from other genres, but they often contain language with a certain manufactured obsolescence—lyrics designed to degrade. Take 1997's "All about the Benjamins," in which Puff Daddy raps "Trying to get my hands on some Grants like Horace." To understand the line the listener must realize that President Ulysses S. Grant is on the fifty-dollar bill and that there was a professional basketball player named Horace Grant, well known in the 1990s for his championship runs with Michael Jordan's Chicago Bulls though not so readily recognized now that he is retired.

A similar challenge besets OutKast's Big Boi when he rhymes on "Two Dope Boyz (in a Cadillac)" that "like Tony Rich nobody knows why," a reference to the largely forgotten R&B act the Tony Rich Project, OutKast's labelmate at the time on LaFace Records, and its 1996 *Billboard* number-two hit "Nobody Knows." Such similes, common in rap, have short half-lives; as the reference ages, it renders the simile essentially unintelligible. Ask Big Boi, however, and he likely won't care. He flipped a clever line. It served its purpose as a display of craft and of subtle cross-promotion, and he probably held no pretentions of sustaining its meaning beyond the moment. One can still enjoy the song, of course, without getting the reference, but it is a distinctive quality of rap that it often sacrifices such lines on the altar of the now.

One more example of rap's renovation of simile may be instructive: the inverted simile. I call it an inverted simile because instead of, as conventional similes do, using an unexpected comparison to characterize a commonplace emotion or state of being (say, the way Wordsworth captures the state of lonely wandering as that of "a cloud / That floats on high o'er vales and hills"), it instead invokes a commonplace comparison to mask an unexpected revelation. The obvious word pairing conceals a coded figurative twist. On 2016's "With Them," for instance, Young Thug boasts, "I got so much jewelry, baby, I got so much water this shit like a mini-lake." The figurative comparison here is banal: something like "I got as much water as a small lake." That's lame enough to get you laughed out of just about any rap cypher. The spark of interest, though, emanates from the figurative valance of "water" here, which he hints at with his earlier reference to jewelry. Appre-

ciating the figurative function of the line requires some small work of de-
duction: What is water in a solid state? Ice. Rappers long ago dubbed their
near-flawless VVS diamonds ice. So Young Thug is trying out new slang at
a figurative remove from the old, then putting it to work in a line at once
straightforward and surprising.

METONYMY, SYNECDOCHE, AND OTHER METAPHORIC FIGURES

A number of other rhetorical tropes follow the logic of metaphor: artful ex-
pression through indirection. Metonymy and synecdoche are common in song
lyrics, just as they are in everyday spoken and written communication. Me-
tonymy uses a quality of a thing to describe the thing itself, while synecdo-
che uses a part of something to describe the whole. Metonymy is calling a
businessman a "suit" because businessmen often wear suits. Synecdoche is
calling a theater "the stage" because the stage is a part of the theater. The
taxonomic distinctions are less important than understanding the work these
figures do in language. In the poetry of pop, figures of substitution serve sev-
eral purposes. They add variety and adornment to typical expression, they
engage the listener in discrete interpretive acts, and they add texture to the
song's diction by contributing to larger patterns in the language. Tropes of
substitution may be obtrusive, when they are cryptic or even incomprehensi-
ble, or they may be incidental, when they go unnoticed.

Most instances of metonymy in song lyrics are similar to those in every-
day conversation, which is to say they are easily metabolized as direct ex-
pression rather than recognized as figurative. Consider the opening lines
from Bob Marley's "Redemption Song": "Old pirates, yes, they rob I/Sold I
to the merchant ships." The meaning is clear: Pirates stole me away and sold
me to slave merchants. The strangeness of pirates selling the animate "I"
to the inanimate "merchant ships" hardly has time to register. Metonymy's
transparency here lets the real strangeness and emotional impact of the line
register fully with the listener: the act of enslaving other human beings that
the song laments.

Often, however, the lyricist employs metonymy for the explicit purpose
of announcing the strangeness of language. The Long Beach rapper O. T.
Genasis scored a viral hit in late 2014 with his drug paean "CoCo," which
features the following emphatic boast: "Baking soda! I got baking soda!"
That might seem a strange thing to brag about, until you realize that baking

soda is a metonym. Not only is baking soda a staple of the American pantry, it is also one of the essential ingredients for producing crack cocaine, the others being distilled water, isopropyl alcohol, and cocaine. For those unfamiliar with the rites of cooking crack, the statement must seem quirky and absurd. In the context of the song, it is part of a patchwork of subterfuge, employing the rhetoric of an underground criminal enterprise for an aboveground audience's titillation and entertainment. Though many listeners may understand the metonymic reference, its artful indirection nonetheless generates a certain playful energy. Whether you know what Genasis means or not, it's funny to hear him shouting "I got baking soda!" The silliness of the line exercises a necessary leavening influence in a song that, by virtue of its booming beat and aggressive vocal delivery, might smack too much of menace.

Another rhetorical figure that practices indirection is euphemism, one of the most common strategies for handling potentially explicit expression in pop music. Euphemism resolves the tension between cursing and the restrictions against doing so in public through the minced oath. Minced oaths are a means of linguistic misdirection whereby explicit terms are rendered less objectionable through erasure, substitution, mispronunciation, or misspelling. Examples abound. Growing up in Salt Lake City in the 1980s, I was surrounded by children exclaiming "Ah, fudge!" and "For the love of Betsy!" as if I were living in an episode of the late-1950s sitcom *Leave It to Beaver*. Minced oaths underscore the deep magic imbedded in the lost explicit words and phrases, the power that history and taboo can impart to a handful of phonemes.

In popular music, minced oaths are widely evident in emended versions of explicit songs and in artists' conscious curtailing of language, either out of personal conviction or commercial calculation. A great example is CeeLo Green's surprise 2010 hit "Fuck You," which built its momentum on YouTube with a simple and striking video that displayed the song's lyrics—curse word and all—against a shifting colored background. Only later did the song build radio airplay, now as the neutered "Forget You." The song's power and appeal come from the bold juxtaposition of the unfiltered profanity and the throwback doo-wop harmonies, rendering the song sweet and satisfying.

Euphemism sometimes builds up around words that are not inherently taboo, and for motivations that have nothing to do with blunting the offense of the language. Hip-hop is, unsurprisingly, a hotbed for such expressions, which become the product of a look-ma-no-hands linguistic playfulness that prizes novelty and cleverness. Take the Golden Age hip-hop term "5000," a way of saying goodbye. It began, simply enough, with the declaration of "I'm out," meaning "I'm leaving." That became "outie," which sounds like Audi, which made a car called the Audi 5000, which led to some simply saying "5000." The Newark rap group EPMD is perhaps best known for using the phrase on their series of "Jane" songs from the early 1990s, uttering the words "Peace, I'm Audi 5000." The rapper Trinidad James resurrected the slang on his 2012 song "One More Molly."

If we go back to the original phrase, "I'm out," we can trace another strain. If you said "I'm out" you meant that you were leaving, which meant that you were about to disappear, which makes you no longer visible like a ghost. Casper is a ghost (a friendly one, at that), hence "I'm Casper," as Punchline rhymes on A Tribe Called Quest's "Rock Rock Y'All." Alternatively, *Ghost* is the title of a popular 1990 movie starring Patrick Swayze, hence the phrase "I'm Swayze." Method Man uses the phrase on his solo hit "Bring the Pain," the comic Andy Samberg memorably resurrects it in 2005 on the *Saturday Night Live* rap parody "Lazy Sunday," and Trinidad James, that connoisseur of vintage rhetorical figures, puts it to use on 2012's "Female$ Welcomed." If you said "I'm Audi," "I'm Casper," or "I'm Swayze" among hip-hop heads in the 1990s they would have known exactly what you meant; it would sound almost like direct speech. If you said the same phrases twenty years later, as Trinidad James does, then the figures will have recaptured some of their original strangeness for a generation far removed from Audi 5000s, which stopped being manufactured under that name in 1988; Casper the Friendly Ghost, whose animated television show is no longer in syndication; and the hirsute heartthrob Swayze, who died in 2009.

Rap is not the only genre that plays this linguistic game of indirection. In American popular music, we can trace this practice back at least to the early decades of the twentieth century, with Tin Pan Alley lyricists and blues singers whose favored mode was the double entendre, a rhetorical means of securing plausible deniability when saying something naughty.

On November 9, 1938, the Broadway musical *Leave It to Me!*, featuring music and lyrics by Cole Porter, premiered at the Imperial Theater. It became a critical and commercial hit, in large part because of Porter's songs. The day after the premiere, everyone was talking about Broadway ingénue Mary Martin's second-act performance of "My Heart Belongs to Daddy," a playful number charged with double entendre. The *New York Times* theater critic Brooks Atkinson wrote that its "mock innocence makes 'My Heart

Belongs to Daddy' the bawdy ballad of the season." Martin was proclaimed the new queen of musical comedy, and Porter's reputation grew even larger.

The premise of the song is simple: A young woman declares her love for an old millionaire while deflecting the sexual attentions of young suitors. Porter finds ribald rhymes like these to suit the nearly unrhymable word "daddy":

> If I invite
> A boy, some night,
> To dine on my fine finnan haddie,
> I just adore
> His asking for more,
> But my heart belongs to Daddy.

The sex is always there, at a plausibly deniable distance from the words, thus implicating the listener in making the erotic meaning along with Porter. Finnan haddie is a cold-smoked Scottish fish, but given the on-stage strip-tease it would have been difficult for the audience to understand the term only on its surface. Later in the verse, Porter's lyrics become less disguised, moving toward a more overtly sexual statement:

> 'Cause my Daddy, he treats me so well.
> He treats it and treats it,
> And then he repeats it,
> Yes, Daddy, he treats it so well.

Porter underscores the carnality of the description through a simple shift in pronouns, from "me" ("he treats me so well") to "it" ("he treats it so well"). "My Heart Belongs to Daddy" epitomized the vestigial Victorian sensibilities of late Depression-era American popular culture, drawn toward sex but demurring when it came to speaking its name.

At the same time, another form of American popular music was thriving. Delta blues had an equal interest in sex and a similar poetic penchant for the double entendre, though it embraced the physical geometry of desire far more explicitly.

Among the migrants who carried Delta blues from the South to the North was Lucille Bogan, a Mississippi-born singer who made her way to New York City and started recording vaudeville songs for Okeh Records in the early 1920s. With Ma Rainey and Bessie Smith, Bogan would soon be recognized as one of the Queens of the Blues. What differentiates Bogan from the others, however, is the explicit language of her lyrics. Where Smith's greatest hits include her renditions of "Downhearted Blues," "The St. Louis Blues," and "Careless Love," all standards, Bogan's catalog veers toward ribald original compositions.

Bogan's most notorious song is the salacious "Shave 'Em Dry," recorded on March 5, 1935. Bogan's lyric is almost dangerously direct, even by today's standards:

> I got nipples on my titties
> Big as the end of my thumb
> I got somethin' between my legs'll
> Make a dead man come
> Oh, daddy
> Baby, won't you shave 'em dry?
> Want you to grind me, baby
> Grind me until I cry
>
> Say, I fucked all night
> And all the night before, baby
> And I feel just like I wanna
> Fuck some more
> Oh, great God, daddy
> Grind me, honey, and shave me dry
> And when you hear me holler, baby
> Want you to shave it dry

Dispensing with euphemism, Bogan sings an unabashed anthem of a woman's sexual desire. At the center of Bogan's lyric is double entendre: "Shave 'em dry" refers on its surface to the act of a man shaving his face without the benefit of water and shaving cream; when employed as metaphor, it means sex without lubrication. On the level of the line, Bogan employs a range of other images to intensify her tone of sexual urgency. From the image of the opening lines ("Big as the end of my thumb") to the vivid boast of her sexual potency ("I got somethin' between my legs'll/Make a dead man come"), these lyrics bring to life a voice that is rendered audible by Bogan's powerful vocal instrument. As the poet Charles Simic observes of Bogan and other artists who court the profane, "There is poetry in some of that smut." Not just poetry—the explicit nature of "Shave 'Em Dry"'s language and description attests to Bogan's surprising linguistic liberation.

Classical Greek rhetoricians would have identified double entendre as the rhetorical figure known as cacemphaton, or a "scurrilous jest or lewd allusion." It is a dual-meaning phrase where one meaning is innocent and literal, and the other is explicit and veiled. So what do we make of something like "Shave 'Em Dry," where the double entendre is surrounded by the explicit expression it is putatively designed to mask? We can resolve this paradox of modesty beside immodest expression when we consider that double entendre is not so much about obscuring but about underscoring through indirection. "The sexual double entendres that drove so many blues lyrics did not hide the blue content from white ears," observes the musicologist Karl Hagstrom Miller. "The folk song collector Guy Johnson admitted in 1927, 'It is doubtful if any group ever has carried its ordinary vulgarities over into respectable song life so completely and successfully as the American Negro. And the ease with which the Negro has put this thing over leads one to suspect that the white man, too, enjoys seeing "the other meaning."' . . . Thinly veiled lyrics enabled attentive white listeners to imagine themselves in on the joke, to take part in the social transgression of talking about sex in public."

Mixing double entendre with explicit language makes the double entendre show itself as a method of adornment and emphasis rather than concealment. Double entendre, in other words, does not create a coded communication for a group of initiates as much as it calls attention to the brash playfulness of the performer. In crafting a rhetorical figure around the sexual act, the sex invariably becomes more palpable than it might have been through clinical or colloquial description alone. Neither "to have intercourse" (the clinical) nor "to fuck" (the colloquial) has quite the same impact as "to shave 'em dry."

THE RHETORIC OF REPETITION

Rhetorical tropes play games with the meanings of words. Rhetorical schemes play games with their arrangement. This, of course, is too absolute a distinction; tropes sometimes rely on patterned arrangement, as in zeugma, and schemes often inflect or even transform the meanings of the words they rearrange, as in repetition, which frequently results in underscoring difference. The distinction, however, is worth retaining. Tropes are primarily invested in the cognitive and the semantic; schemes, in the organizational and aural. Recognizing the kinds of figures at work is the first step in sorting out why and how they work so well.

The simplest, most direct rhetorical methods apparent in songs are schemes, and the simplest and most apparent schemes are those of repetition. Repetition can function on the level of the syllable, as with alliteration, assonance, and consonance; on the level of the word; and on the level of the phrase. It can range from the seemingly haphazard repetition of a single word to the more strictly patterned repetition of words and phrases at particular places along the line, as with anaphora and epistrophe.

"Helplessly Hoping," a beautiful song written by Stephen Stills for Crosby, Stills & Nash, underscores its lilting melody and rich harmonies in its alliterative play in the verses: "Helplessly hoping her harlequin hovers nearby" and "Wordlessly watching, he waits by the window and wonders." Alliteration is the organizing principle of the song. This alliteration is not only playful, like the tongue-twisting "Peter Piper picked a peck of pickled peppers." Instead, it is purposive in its move from adverb to gerund to some specific action. Stills reinforces the connections among initial consonant sounds by having them all fall on rhythmically stressed syllables as well: "*Word*lessly *watch*ing, he *waits* by the *win*dow and *won*ders." What keeps this alliterative and rhythmic effect from becoming gimmicky is the allusive weight of the lyric's subject: the challenge of loving another human being.

Repetition's native domain in pop songs is the chorus, which often serves as a point of stasis from which the verses depart and then return. The shifting relation of each verse to the chorus refreshes the repeated language, staving off monotony and inviting the listener's reinterpretation of the now-familiar words. Roberta Flack turned "Killing Me Softly with His Song," a song originally recorded by the folk singer Lori Lieberman, into a Grammy-winning hit in part by recasting the lyrics to feature the chorus. Whereas Lieberman begins her recording with a verse, Flack's recording begins with the chorus—"Strumming my pain with his fingers/Singing my life with his words/Killing me softly with his song." This not only drops the listener into the song in medias res, it also foregrounds the striking language of the title. Flack repeats the chorus after each of the three verses narrating the singer's encounter with this seductive performer. After the final verse, Flack repeats the chorus three times, for a total of six times in the song. What prevents monotony is the way the song's structure demands that listeners forge new relations to the repeated words, based on either the new narrative point of entry inspired by the verse, the new emotive point prompted by the music and Flack's singing, or both.

Though the chorus is the natural domain of repetition, one finds instances in which the chorus changes over the course of the song in ways both big and small. Sometimes the difference might be the shift of a single word from the first chorus to the second and to third, as in Jimi Hendrix's "The Wind Cries Mary," which moves in growing urgency from "whispers" to "cries" to "screams." Other times, it might be a wholesale reinvention of the language, as in the famous instance of Jimmy Buffett's "Margaritaville" where the shift in the final line of the chorus sketches the arc of the speaker's dawning awareness of culpability: from "But I know it's nobody's fault" to "But I think it could be my fault" to "But I know it's my own damn fault."

Repetition finds its way outside the chorus as well, often doing the work of the chorus in songs that defy conventional verse-chorus structures. Joy Division's "Insight" rejects a chorus but nonetheless satisfies listeners' desire for repetition on the levels of rhyme, rhythm, and phrase. Each section of the song has at least one element of lyric repetition internal to itself and one that connects it to some other part of the song. For instance, in the third of the four lyric sections, the group's singer and songwriter, Ian Curtis, delivers the following lines:

> Reflects a moment in time
> A special moment in time
> Yeah, we wasted our time
> We didn't really have time

From "a moment in time" to "a special moment in time" to "our time" and finally just to "time," the transmuting of the phrase inspires a sense of balance and development. That repetition serves the same structural and aesthetic purpose as a chorus would have, underscoring the dual impulses of stasis and transformation. This reimagining of repetition beyond the chorus became a hallmark of Curtis's compositions for Joy Division. "He played with the structure of the lyrics but without ever losing what it was about the song that makes it strong," recalls Joy Division's bassist, Peter Hook. "You don't listen to it and think, Ah, what an interesting lyrical structure. But it's all in the song. His love of art was showing here. The way he wanted to slightly subvert the normal conventions of rock and pop."

Linguistic repetition is naturally allied with music, which itself almost always relies on repetition. Repeat a word often enough and it looses itself from its semantic moorings and becomes just a sound. This cognitive effect, known as semantic satiation, helps explain why we have a far greater tolerance for repetition in song than we do when we encounter it in speech or in prose. Songwriters must be cognizant, however, of how much repetition their listeners will endure. When asked to analyze Stevie Nicks's songwriting, her bandmate in Fleetwood Mac and onetime romantic partner, Lindsay Buckingham, called attention to her sense for melodic repetition. "She can do repetitive phrases, but it's just how she does it and where she stops doing it, and where she makes a little changeup and how I seem to be able to move sections across that, change what's going on beneath it," he says. When to stop repetition or change it up, be it in melody, rhythm, or language, is an expression of the songwriter's art.

Repetition might be the defining quality of pop songs, both musically and lyrically, but there's a difference between repetition and redundancy. "Redundancy in popular music, which should not be confused with repetition, is not only one of its most glaring faults but to my mind is almost always less a problem of haste than haplessness," writes Alexander Theroux. "It is invariably the result of some poor dweeb sitting down and trying to 'fill' a line for rhythm the way old linotypists used slugs of lead, and often with much the same result." Who's to say, though, when repetition falls into redundancy? Certainly, we have a higher tolerance for repeated words and phrases when they change slightly from iteration to iteration. A singer may alter them in performance, or a word might shift here or there. Not all repetition is created equal.

Find a transcription of just about any pop song and you'll likely find a level of repetition that verges on the redundant, excessive, or absurd when untethered from its performance. A friend of mine posted the concluding lyrics to the Beatles' "Hey Jude" on his social media accounts, eighteen identical lines of "Nah nah nah nah nah nah nah, nah nah nah nah, hey Jude." On the page it looks like some kind of Dadaist experiment; on record, it sounds sensible enough. Staying with the Beatles, one finds numerous instances in which repetition emerges as a fundamental form of their art. Their first *Billboard* number-one hit was 1964's "I Want to Hold Your Hand," in which they repeat the title phrase eleven times in two and a half minutes. And that's just the most obvious repetition. Perhaps a more sonically and semantically powerful instance of repetition comes in the bridge:

> And when I touch you I feel happy inside
> It's such a feeling that my love
> I can't hide, I can't hide, I can't hide

On a semantic level, the repetition makes no sense; it contributes no new information. However, that's not to say that the repetition communicates no new meaning. To find that meaning, one would do well both to look and to listen. The repetition here opens up a pathway to the metalinguistic: that is, to language not as fixed definition but as living meaning in the context of culture. Metalinguistically, the repetition communicates intensified feeling, an amplification the Beatles underscored by harmonizing that steps up in pitch with each repetition. By the end they nearly scream the final word. This song promises on its surface a rather tame kind of love, a grade-school fantasy. But in the bridge, a new kind of passion builds—first with the somewhat scandalous mention of touching, and then with the strange circumlocution that follows it—*"It's such a feeling [touching you] that my love I can't hide"*—a glancing euphemism for sexual arousal.

The Beatles employ a similar lyric ploy on "Please Please Me." One can certainly hear John Lennon's lyric as a plea that a girl "choose" him over another guy. If we expect the same innocence as we listen, we hear "Please please me like I please you" as a man begging his lover to treat him with the same kindness and thoughtfulness with which he treats her—*please, please, please!* Moving from innocence to experience, though, the double entendre is unmistakable. Sexual inferences here are not much of a semantic leap, though it's not one that many of the song's longing listeners likely took, at least not on the conscious level. On the level of emotion and excitement, however, repetition makes meaning all its own.

Repetition's capacity to create meaning can change how we listen. "This shift, effected by repetition, away from what is directly captured by words and toward what is revealed by the structure, prosody, rhythm, and tempo of the utterance of the words, is essentially a shift toward a musical way of listening," writes Elizabeth Hellmuth Margulis. "The act of repetition highlights that there is more to be understood than what the words literally convey, drawing attention to these other qualities." This is not to suggest that behind every lyric repetition lurks some coded meaning left there by the lyricist for us to find. Often, this new register of meaning does not take explicit shape but provides a less definite emotive influence or the puzzle-solving pleasure of finding patterns.

Consider the rhetorical figure of zeugma, by which a word applies in two or more divergent contexts. Historically, writers have tended to deploy this figure for comic effect, as when Charles Dickens observes in *The Pickwick Papers* that "Miss Bolo . . . went straight home in a flood of tears and a sedan-

chair." Songwriters often have used the figure without the same comic in-
tentions, though sometimes still with the same comic effect, as when Alanis
Morissette sings with loving conviction, "You held your breath and the door
for me." It's hard not to chuckle at that line because it retains the comic
formula of applying the same verb ("held") in both a figurative ("held your
breath") and a literal ("held the door") sense. On Blondie's "Look Good in
Blue," Debbie Harry sings, "If it's all right with you / I could give you some
head and shoulders to lie on." Harry dials back some of the cringeworthy
crassness of the line in her phrasing, which stitches "head and shoulders"
tightly together rather than accentuating the zeugma by closing the phrase
at "head" before uttering "and shoulders" with a knowing wink. These in-
stances do not seem comic, exactly, only playful and, in the case of Blondie,
consciously coy.

It is unlikely that Bob Dylan had comedy on his mind when he composed
this zeugma in "Queen Jane Approximately": "Now when all the clowns that
you have commissioned / Have died in battle or in vain." Dylan's lyric comes off
as clever, not comic. The tone is wistful and a little bit admiring, even in his
pain. As with Morissette's somewhat clumsy lines, Dylan's lyric employs a
verb in both literal ("died in battle") and figurative ("died in vain") senses. The
difference, however, rests in the emotive intensity of the image and its imme-
diate juxtaposition; with grander stakes comes graver meaning.

In his compelling short article "In Praise of the Rolling Stones and Their
Zeugmoids," the language writer and lexicographer Ben Zimmer points out
the subtle but striking modifications of the zeugma in several lyrics by the
Rolling Stones. Citing the Stanford linguist Arnold Zwicky, Zimmer offers
the term "zeugmoid" to describe a rhetorical figure in which the use of the
verb in two instances is explicit rather than simply implied. On "Honky Tonk
Women," for instance, Mick Jagger sings, "She blew my nose and then she
blew my mind." It would seem that we have the literal use of the verb ("blew
my nose") as well as the figurative ("blew my mind"). On closer inspection
the first instance also appears to be figurative: "Blew my nose" is not meant
to suggest that his lover offered him a Kleenex, but that she passed him a
mirror with a rolled-up bill and a few generous rails. Jagger also undercuts
the Dickensian comedy of the figure by actually expressing the phrase in full
the second time around, mellowing some of the absurdity. When zeugma in-
vites our minds to fill in the missing part of the phrase, that little bit of
extra cognitive effort sets the literal and the figurative expressions apart
from one another in a way that each phrase discretely expressed does not.

So when Jagger sings it, he sounds cool, maybe a little offhand and mildly boastful, not funny.

Perhaps the most well-turned instance of a zeugmoid might be from "I Can't Make You Love Me," composed by the country songwriters Mike Reid and Allen Shamblin. Over the years the song has been covered by Prince, George Michael, Bon Iver, Adele, and many others, but the definitive version remains the first, the 1991 recording by the blues rock legend Bonnie Raitt. The lyric takes the form of a lament, a distillation of the emotion felt when love only remains on one side. The opening couplet shows the power of measured repetition, the apotheosis of zeugma in pop: "Turn down the lights, turn down the bed / Turn down these voices inside my head." Here we have three distinct uses of a common phrase, three variations that unfurl in natural, unforced communication of isolation and longing. The couplet begins with two literal uses—extinguish the lights and pull back the covers of the bed—then opens into the figurative—dampen the voices of regret in the mind of the speaker/singer. "'I Can't Make You Love Me' is no picnic," Raitt told NPR *Weekend Edition*'s Scott Simon. "I love that song; so does the audience. So it's almost a sacred moment when you share that, that depth of pain with your audience. Because they get really quiet, and I have to summon . . . some other place in order to honor that space." Those opening lines help raise the song to the level of ritual, a ritual born in part of repetition.

Structured repetition carries rhetorical force through its calibration of sound and meaning. Anadiplosis is a rhetorical scheme whereby the last word or phrase from one line (or one sentence or one syntactical unit) is repeated at the beginning of the next. The most cited example of this doesn't come from Shakespeare, but from *Star Wars*, in Yoda's lines: "Fear leads to anger. Anger leads to hate. Hate leads to suffering." Though this is clearly a figurative expression based on the arrangement of words rather than on the transformation of their meanings, it exercises influence on thought through its clear, forceful, and memorable sequencing of emotional states. This is not a subtle figure; like zeugma, it calls attention to its artificiality as part of its purpose. In doing so, it also leaves some trace of the mind that fashioned it. In song lyrics, anadiplosis may hardly register, or it may be so overbearing and overdetermined that it obscures both meaning and feeling in the song.

In the former category is Foo Fighters' "In Your Honor," where the two verses each begin with anadiplosis: "Can you hear me, hear me screaming?" and "Can you feel me, feel me breathing?" The repetition of the phrase adds emphasis without departing entirely from the register of everyday speech.

Underscoring this mirror-image repetition is the chorus, which employs the allied rhetorical schemes of antimetabole, by which words are repeated in successive clauses, in reverse grammatical order ("Mine is yours and yours is mine") and of antithesis, by which words or ideas are juxtaposed, often in parallel structure ("I would die tonight/For you to feel alive"). The overall effect of the lyric is equipoise, underscored by the repetition in the simple melodic line, the repeated guitar figure, and the general tone of sonic stasis.

In the latter category, where anadiplosis creates an ostentatious extreme, is "Glad You Came" from the British boy band the Wanted. The refrain is structured entirely on anadiplosis:

> Turn the lights out now
> Now I'll take you by the hand
> Hand you another drink
> Drink it if you can
> Can you spend a little time?
> Time is slipping away
> Away from us so stay
> Stay with me I can make
> Make you glad you came

These lines read like the spawn of a classical rhetorician and, well, someone who writes disposable pop songs for British boy bands. Though well executed, the lyric comes across as overdetermined. In sacrificing most end rhymes in the name of this exotic rhetorical pattern, the song withholds the comforting expectation and fulfillment that patterned rhyme enacts. In performance, the effect is like stuttering. The recording of the song rounds out some of the sharp edges of the form, though it still announces itself as artificial—and slightly stalkerish given what the singer is asking of the young woman.

In the American context, the concept of repetition with a difference is at the center of musical culture. From blues to jazz to rock to rap, artists have forged musical structures and linguistic forms that strike a balance between expectation and surprise. Of course, that balance can tip too far in one direction or another. There's an art to knowing how much variation the ear will want to entertain. On the Traveling Wilburys' 1989 song "End of the Line," George Harrison, Jeff Lynne, and Roy Orbison take turns singing versions of the chorus while Tom Petty sings the verses. Each turn of the chorus has four lines beginning with the same phrase, an exercise in anaphora: "Well, it's all right . . ." The repetition here underscores the chugging boxcar rhythm, creating a sense of forward motion even as the song circles back on itself. One wonders, though, if a fifth line opening in the same fashion might have pushed the repetition too far, diminishing its propulsive effect.

Some of the most effective and affecting instances of repetition in song lyrics are counterbalanced by difference. The Red Hot Chili Peppers' naked song of addiction, "Under the Bridge," builds to an emotional climax under-girded by the play of repetition and difference:

> Under the bridge downtown
> Is where I drew some blood
> Under the bridge downtown
> I could not get enough
> Under the bridge downtown
> Forgot about my love
> Under the bridge downtown
> I gave my life away

Haunting choral voices perform the bridge, with lead singer and song-writer Anthony Kiedis accenting the lines that follow the repeated phrase "Under the bridge downtown." Recalling the composition of the song, during a time of deep addiction, Kiedis writes in his memoir that he "started free-styling some poetry in my car and putting the words to a melody and sang all the way down the freeway. When I got home, I got out my notebook and wrote the whole thing down in a song structure, even though it was meant to be a poem to deal with my own anguish." The vestiges of the poetic remain, in the anthropomorphized city, in the tone of confessional address, and in the closing lyric passage with the near-Biblical repetition calling attention to the interstices. What stands out, both in lyric and performance, is the vulnerability and pain. When the song begins, Kiedis's voice is close to the microphone, a note of whispered intimacy powerfully manifested in the sound and feel of the recording. In the close, even claustrophobic sonic space the song creates, the repetitions in the lyrics are inescapable; they leave no choice but to engage with the song's emotion, or to turn it off.

Epistrophe, the repetition of a word or phrase at the end of successive lines, is less common than anaphora in pop music, perhaps out of the imperative for rhyme variety at the ends of lines. Nonetheless, one finds instances of its use. John Mellencamp's "Small Town" uses the title phrase as effective epistrophe, balanced with enough variation to refresh the lyric and keep it from slipping into monotony:

> Well, I was born in a small town
> And I live in a small town
> Probably die in a small town
> Oh, those small communities
>
> All my friends are so small town
> My parents live in the same small town
> My job is so small town
> Provides little opportunity

Though the phrase "small communities" feels a bit forced, its cross-lyric connection in multisyllabic slant rhyme with "opportunity" and Mellencamp's huffy delivery save it. The rhyme creates a point of interest and of useful divergence from the pleasurable repetition of "small town." Further staving off redundancy is the melodic variety that subtly shifts the emphasis in each successive return to the repeated phrase. In the second section, two of the instances of "small town" (the first and third lines) are used not as geographic location but as a way of naming an attitude or worldview. The second line, too, introduces novelty by slightly nudging the rhythm of the line, augmenting the phrase as "same small town" and charging it with syllabic stress. Though repetitive, the lyric is never redundant.

Often song lyrics display more than just one scheme of repetition. A great example of this is the Beatles' "All You Need Is Love," which begins with the harmonizing repetition of the word "love," then leads into anaphora ("Nothing you can . . ."), then shifting to the chorus, which entwines two repetition schemes:

> All you need is love
> All you need is love
> All you need is love, love
> Love is all you need

After repeating the first line three times, they repeat the last word ("love") in a higher key, then use it as the first word of the last line, which is itself a rhetorical inversion of the repeated phrase. The effect is chiasmus, a playful self-reflexivity. But they're far from done. After running through the cycle once again, the song ends with the phrase "Love is all you need" repeated call-and-response fashion between solo voice and chorus for nearly a minute—an interminable time in a three-and-a-half-minute song. Whether it's the psychedelic mood, the Summer of Love vibe, the cheeky "She loves you yeah, yeah, yeah" lyric allusion that crops up just when things are on the verge of becoming too predictable, or the accrued credit for genius the Beatles had built up by this point, or whether it's the mantric quality of the music itself, somehow this excessive repetition is not just endurable but pleasurable. The phrase becomes a collection of words, then syllables, then phonemes, then finally a kind of music of its own, deracinated from its denotation, but comfortably, beautifully at home.

Part

III

Chapter Seven

Voice

R od Stewart has a weird voice. An early reviewer characterized it as "hoarse and insistent," which seems about right. Whether singing a pop ballad, an up-tempo dance tune, or a standard of the American songbook, Stewart's voice makes the familiar unfamiliar. The commonplace and the classic alike are deranged in the root sense of the word—causing disarray or disorder—by the force and character of his voice.

No one can really try to sing like Rod Stewart, at least not without resorting to parody. There's something indeterminate about his voice—a certain androgyny and a quality of sound that suggests it's close to fraying. It seems to bear the evidence of damage, perhaps a physical manifestation of a psychic pain. But here it is, after decades of singing, sounding pretty much the same as it always has.

Hear Stewart's voice on a 1930s torch song from his *Great American Songbook* series, then hear it belting out the hook to the rapper A$AP Rocky's 2015 banger "Everyday." On "Everyday," Stewart's vocals sound so fresh that one could be forgiven for not realizing that they are actually sampled from his 1972 recording on Python Lee Jackson's "In a Broken Dream." Stewart's sampled voice serves as a potent aural seasoning, used sparingly and in conjunction with other vocal flavors—A$AP himself, and the R&B singer Miguel, who delivers his own sweetened version of Stewart's hook, "Every day I spend my time / Drinking wine, feeling fine." Stewart's voice is the coolest thing on a cool song.

In Stewart's solo work, one necessarily consumes his voice in large quantities, with resulting dyspepsia for some. In small doses and large, what draws audiences to his performance is that there simply isn't another voice that sounds quite like his, simply not another singer who interprets and delivers a song the way that he does. "I was blessed with distinctiveness," Stewart explains in his memoir. "The voice had its own character, and it was a character—as I knew from taking it onstage so much—that spoke directly to people." This last point is key: the distinctiveness, the weirdness, somehow speaks to people more directly and intensely than a conventionally beautiful voice might speak to them.

Pop music demands a voice, whether singing well or ill, or perhaps not singing at all but speaking or chanting or rapping to a beat. Since the advent of the *Billboard* Hot 100 chart in 1958 only thirteen instrumental songs have reached the number-one spot, the last Jan Hammer's "Miami Vice Theme" in 1985. This predominance of the voice in pop music speaks to listeners' lust for language, as well as to the longing for human connection that the voice promises.

Singing is not speech. Singing requires heightened attention to pronunciation, phrasing, rhythm, pitch, timbre, breath control, and any number of other minute calibrations of vocal expression. Speaking shares a good many of these habits, but the singing voice's defining difference is that it is primarily driven from without rather than from within.

A singer needs a song.

In this regard, singing is a subordinate art. A voice in song needs lyrics, melody, and music to define the parameters of its expression. "Melodies form a marriage with the words," country legend Waylon Jennings observes. "They'll tell you where they want to go, and you can always change them. . . . Your melody goes where the words take you. I depend on a lyric to give me a melody, and a good lyric will pull the melody out of you." Singing, therefore, is also an act of invention. More often than not we hear the singer, not the song.

Many pop song lyrics function primarily as a vehicle for voice, with the voice acting as the lead melodic and percussive instrument whose value rests in sound more than in sense. In fact, the sound often is sense; it communicates musical and emotional meaning. The discernible tone and cadence of a singing or rapping voice, combined with a few easily remembered words and phrases, are the stuff of a great deal of pop music. This is particularly the case in dance music, where the lyric must often simply stay out of the way of the groove. The biggest hit of 2013 was Daft Punk's "Get Lucky," a superb piece of pop with an indelible, though certainly not mind-expanding, lyric:

> She's up all night to sun
> I'm up all night to get some
> We're up all night for good fun
> We're up all night to get lucky

The words here work like drum fills, the repeated *u* vowel-sound acting as a bodily bass drum. End rhyme in the first three lines establishes a pattern that the fourth line disrupts. In a compelling sonic departure, the disyllabic "lucky" follows the sequence of single syllables: "sun," "some," and "fun." Repetition is key, with the phrase "up all night" recurring across all four lines, gaining emphasis and amplification with each return.

The meaning of the lyrics to "Get Lucky" is readily apparent and not particularly compelling on its own, but the sound is something else. Pharrell Williams, who sings lead, suggested as much when he told *Rolling Stone* that after doing his first take, Daft Punk told him to "sing it again, again, again." "Then I did four or five more takes," he recalls; "they picked what they liked, then I sang each of those parts over and over." Singers usually do multiple takes, yet the obsessive attention to the subtleties of Williams's delivery suggests Daft Punk's conscious awareness of his voice working as an instrument, not as a singer delivering a singular interpretation of a lyric.

The mythic ideal of the singer going into the recording booth and delivering an indelible performance is rarely the reality of contemporary recording practice. Most of today's pop vocal recordings are a producer and a sound engineer's composite of several or even dozens of different takes stitched together, sometimes syllable by syllable, into a seamless composite master track. In an extreme example, Christina Aguilera's 2006 track "Here to Stay" was "comped from a hundred different takes," according to the song's sound engineer (and co-writer) Ben Allen. "She nailed every single one," he recalls, "but she wants to comp it until she's in love with it. There's nothing less valid about that." Voice—in whole, in parts, or in the new wholes that the parts make—offers an occasion to explore the confluence of language and sound, music and meaning.

Even more than rhyme, rhythm, or figurative language, voice exposes the limitations of a lyric-driven critical perspective. There is no effective notation to capture vocal performance on the page. Voice demands an account of song attentive to performance, to words in motion rather than at rest. Nonetheless, for the study of singing there is still value in suspending the lyric on the page and creating the fallacy of a fixed form. The text provides a baseline from which to consider just how voice charges language: We can gauge the difference between words and music temporarily at rest and those same words and music in dynamic motion.

The most common form of words in motion, of course, is speech. Speech opens up boundless variations of tone and texture, of pace and pronunciation, that make written language inscrutable by comparison. Singing further enriches language by elevating common speech to the pattern of ritual, with rhythm, pitch, tone, timbre, and the other qualities of voice leaving language at once familiar and strange. When words become sound, then song, they acquire the capacity to make meaning and undo meaning, to communicate feelings, and to evoke responses that the words left alone on the page don't suggest.

For the singer, the challenge begins with something simple on its face, but complex in practice. How do you pronounce words when singing a particular series of notes? A singing voice might dilate the vowels in a lyric line to dozens of times their usual duration. Pitches shift elastically, beyond the bounds of a word's conventional pronunciation. On "Sweet Child o' Mine," for instance, Axl Rose sings the following lines: "Her hair reminds me of a warm, safe place where as a child I'd hide / And pray for the thunder and the rain to quietly pass me by." On the page, the missed rhyme (*hide/by*) rings out; the assonance of the *i*-sound only accentuates this imperfection. In performance, though, Rose introduces a small melodic embellishment to each word—*hi-eee-iiide* and *bi-eee-eye*—that joins them in euphony.

For the listener, the challenge of encountering language in song is this: How do you understand words expressed in performance as compared to how you understand them when read alone, voiced only in your head? Hearing voices means coming in contact with others, either directly or at a distance. Even disembodied voices, the ones talking through cellphones or singing through speakers, are endowed with bone and muscle and skin and features, if only of our mind's devising. We ascribe so much to a singing voice without conscious awareness that, right or wrong, we hear gender, age, race, and even place.

This chapter concerns what happens to song lyrics once singers breathe life into them in recorded performance. It considers voice in popular music as an instrument, an extension of the body, and an intimation of identity. In previous chapters, our attention has been directed to the language of lyrics on the page: the patterns of rhythm and rhyme, and structures of figurative language that become clearer when temporarily suspended in print. The critical approach here will be just the opposite—to take songs as more or less settled documents, and see what happens when voices enchant them, derange them, or otherwise inhabit them through performance.

No fewer than half a dozen fields of knowledge can lay claim to understanding voice. Biologists attend to the physical process whereby human beings generate sounds from the larynx, using a complex choreography of muscle, tendon, palate, tongue, and tissue. Linguists classify the many ways that voices shape human expression, marking differences of pronunciation, accent, place, and time. Musicologists consider the voice in motion in song, describing the aesthetics and ornamentations and ritualized phrasings that extend human expression beyond mere communication to art. Literary scholars explore how voices manifest themselves in written texts, understanding voice as a metaphor for character and affect. Voice, of course, is all of these things, sometimes all at once, and in this chapter I draw on many of these approaches to tell the story of how voice creates, inhabits, and transforms song.

The history of pop music since the advent of rock and roll is the history of the voice's primacy over the lyric. Song lyrics are often seen as disposable syllables in the service of singing. When lyrics are the subject of close attention, it is often for the purposes of ridicule, scorn, or censure. Even in periods in which the lyric has been elevated above the record—the era, for instance, of singer-songwriter troubadours of the 1960s and 1970s—it was always a countercultural impulse to the general understanding of song lyrics as pragmatic and disposable language, words with utility. The most common critique of transcribed lyrics is that they're living only half a life. They've been robbed of their vitality, their sonic character. All of this can be true. But there's also a small, special knowledge that songs reveal only to those who attend to their language temporarily removed from their performance. Understanding exactly what a voice does in song can usefully begin with the song in silence, alone as lyric on the page.

The long-standing tradition of celebrating the voice over the lyric unnecessarily obscures the language of song. However, elevating lyrics above their performance is equally distorting. Rather than creating a canon of pop lyrics so that Steven Tyler can sit with Shakespeare, we might instead cultivate a more careful and nuanced analysis of the many ways that lyric and voice relate to one another. This relationship is far more complicated and far richer than simply a matter of the voice dominating the lyric. Sometimes voices do, indeed, obscure language; sometimes they enshrine it. Sometimes any words really will do, and sometimes songs require the right words in the right order for the right singer. Sometimes the most important creative act, the most important composition, occurs after the lyric is already written. These matters are conditioned by genre, by individual artists' sensibilities, and by particular songs over time.

THE BODY AS INSTRUMENT

Above all, the voice is physical. The voice is produced by the orchestration of the lungs, the vocal folds, the larynx, and the vagus nerve. The National Center for Voice and Speech, based at the University of Utah, explains it this way: "The respiratory system (lungs, diaphragm, and abdominal muscles), laryngeal mechanism (vocal folds, laryngeal cartilages, muscles and nerves) and the supraglottic tract (the spaces above the vocal folds, including the back of your throat, mouth, nasal passages and sinus cavities) all work to produce" the sound of the voice. The sounds the voice makes, from a whisper to a scream and everything in between, are products of this same process. Singing demands far more from the constitutive elements than normal speech, engaging the supraglottic tract to achieve greater resonance, calling on the respiratory system to reach greater volume.

The first quality that a listener encounters in a voice is its timbre. Timbre, as the neurologist Oliver Sacks explains it, "is the particular quality or acoustic richness of a sound produced by an instrument or a voice, independent of its pitch or loudness. . . . The timbre of a sound is influenced by all sorts of factors, including the frequencies of harmonics or overtones and the onset, rise, and decay of acoustic waveforms." Timbre is the primary means by which we distinguish a woman's voice from a man's voice, or Justin Bieber's voice from Barry White's voice. It is also the way we distinguish the same note as played on a trombone as opposed to on a flute or a piano.

From one angle, the voice is the most common instrument in all recorded music. From another, the voice is the body rendered audible. "The emission of song is, in and of itself, the acoustic exhibition of embodiment," argues the musicologist Marco Beghelli. "It is not a sound that comes from a mechanical instrument; rather, it is produced by the very body of the singer, the corporeal flux that emerges from the most hidden cavities, and which determines its particular 'grain' . . . not a generic timbre, codified in advance by technical instruments, but rather a peculiar, elusive, highly individualized, acoustic image of a specific embodiment." Voice is action, orchestrating the body to express sound and meaning. "The voice is our most primordial and valuable instrument," observes the music writer Amanda Petrusich, "and we respond to it more fully, in both spiritual and physiological ways, than almost any other organic sound." The voice holds a privileged place as an instrument both of body and of spirit.

When Roland Barthes famously theorized about the "grain of the voice," his attention was directed at the way that speech, in the form of song, is made flesh. He exalts those voices that bear in language the vestiges of their physical making, a grounding and gravity of that language in the body of the singer. "The 'grain' of the voice is not—or is not merely—its timbre; the *significance* it opens cannot better be defined, indeed, than by the very friction between the music and something else, which something else is the particular language (and nowise the message)," Barthes writes. For Barthes, language asserts its importance to the character of singing in the shape of consonants and vowels as performed rather than in denotation. "The song must speak, must *write*," he continues. "The 'grain,'" he concludes, "is the body in the voice as it sings, the hand as it writes, the limb as it performs."

The pleasure generated by the voice is categorically different from the pleasure of instrumental sound. "In the vocal exercise, lungs, throat, mouth, tongue, and ears all take pleasure," writes the theorist Adriana Cavarero. "This happens, especially in the child, but also again in the adult." "When I sing," Grace Jones explains, "I have to be aware from second to second—of the breathing, the note that has just gone, the note that is coming." One can hear this physical dynamic even on the studio recordings of many singers. Listen, for instance, to Celine Dion and one is always aware of her lungs filling with air or expelling it. Dion's performance is meant to overwhelm her audience, something she underscores by the fact that it appears even to be overwhelming her as she sings.

If its fallibility is any measure, then the voice is certainly an extension of the body. The voice can break and it can wear; it can also be strengthened and trained. "Singing is such an organic process: no amps, no instruments, just flesh and muscle and psyche," explains rocker Pat Benatar. The voice is a frail instrument, subject to scarring, rupture, and attrition over time. Like any musical instrument, it functions through vibration at different frequencies to create sound, but the voice is unique in its embodiment of the performer. As a consequence, voice inhabits the same territory of sublimity and imperfection that marks all things human.

Although the voice is an instrument, unlike a guitar or a saxophone, it is entirely a product of the body. Live performance requires that you actually hear yourself performing rather than relying simply on the placement of fingers on strings and frets, or on black and white keys. Juliana Hatfield remarks on this challenge of voice in live performance with loud guitars, bass, and drums drowning her out. "My voice wasn't a naturally loud instrument and often the ancient, grime-encrusted vocal monitors in front of my feet didn't have the power to boost my voice above the din of the drums and amps," she writes. "Earplugs made my voice louder in my head, while blocking out some of the harshness of the other noises." Part of these singers' descriptions of their craft sounds as if they are speaking of an instrument; part, of their bodies. The voice is both.

The connection between voice and musical instrument is important to jazz music, where instrumentalists often learn the lyrics to the songs they are playing—particularly ballads—so as better to communicate clear emotion in their performance. Musical notes supply only sound; much of the meaning and the feeling resides in the language and the story in the lyrics. Saxophonists like Lester Young and trumpet players like Miles Davis talk about singing through their instruments, their horns becoming modulators for their singing voice. This practical analogy works the other way as well, with jazz singers drawing inspiration from instrumentalists in the ways that they approach a song. Quincy Jones observes that both Sarah Vaughn and Ella Fitzgerald "thought like a horn and sang like a horn. Lyrics were almost secondary to both of them." In reflecting on the cultural milieu of 1960s New York, Bob Dylan recalls listening to John Coltrane, Miles Davis, and Thelonious Monk and integrating certain aspects of their performance styles into his singing. "What they had that I picked up on in my singing—I can hardly even call myself a singer—was a sense of phrasing and dynamics," he says.

Billie Holiday, however, resisted the common assertion that her craft as a singer could be conflated with that of her musical accompanists. "A singer is not like a saxophone," Holiday writes in her autobiography, *Lady Sings the Blues.*

> If you don't sound right, you can't go out and get some new reeds, split them just right. A singer is only a voice, and a voice is completely dependent on the body God gave you. When you walk out there and open your mouth, you never know what's going to happen. I'm not supposed to get a toothache, I'm not supposed to get nervous; I can't throw up or get sick to my stomach; I'm not supposed to get the flu or have a sore throat. I'm supposed to go out there and look pretty and sing good and smile and I'd just better. Why? Because I'm Billie Holiday and I've been in trouble.

Finally, language is what distinguishes the voice from other musical instruments. The singing voice expresses itself through words, and even when it is scatting nonsense syllables, those syllables bend toward linguistic expression. No matter how voicelike the tone of Wynton Marsalis's muted trumpet on his haunting "The Seductress," we never ascribe speech to it. No matter how trumpet-like the tone of Ella Fitzgerald scatting on "One Note Samba," we always understand it as saying something meaningful, even if that meaning is just beyond our grasp. Nonetheless, to borrow the theorist Mladen Dolar's phrase, singing can be "bad communication." As Dolar understands it, singing "brings the voice energetically to the forefront, on purpose, at the expense of meaning." Just because singing announces itself as meaning doesn't make that meaning clear.

Bad communication or not, the singing voice never stops communicating, even when singing moves beyond semantic expression. Most of us can conjure the urgency and energy of Kurt Cobain's voice singing "Smells Like Teen Spirit," but only obsessives and literature professors know all the lyrics. Depending on how you listen, the lyrics can be either essential or beside the point. "Onstage it was amazing to see how much emotional power came from the depths of his body—a gravelly stream of vocal sound," Kim Gordon of Sonic Youth recalls of hearing Cobain sing. "It wasn't screaming, or shrieking, or even punk vitriol, although that's what it sounded like the most. There were also quiet parts, low, moan-ish, when you'd half believe Kurt's voice was hoarse, and then he'd throw himself on the drum set, which in his anger and frustration he seemed to want to annihilate."

Pop in general—and rock in particular—has made a habit of consciously subverting the classical ideal of a consistency of beauty in tone. In its place, observes the musicologist Walter Everett, "many rock vocalists reach out to their audience largely through the physicality of their singing, the degree to which the sounds of their voice suggest in the listener, at least unconsciously, just what their oral cavity is experiencing." The voice under stress, the voice in pain or in extreme emotional states, has become an increasingly prevalent feature of contemporary pop music.

Often in music seemingly raw and untrained expressions are consequences of craft. Some vocalists are known for their signature ad libs; think of the soul/rap continuum of male artists that runs from Sam Cooke ("Whoa-oh-oh!") to James Brown ("Yeow!") to Michael Jackson ("Uh!") to Biggie Smalls ("Uhhh!") to Rick Ross ("Ugh!") to Pusha T ("Yuugh!"). "A lot of people don't understand about the hollering I do," Brown wrote in his memoir. "A man once came up to me in a hotel lobby and said, 'So you're James

Brown. You make a million dollars, and all you do is scream and holler.' 'Yes,' I said, very quiet, 'but I scream and holler on key.'"

It seems wrong to call these vocal styles untrained given how much labor can go into the appearance of spontaneity and struggle. Nonetheless, the vocalists who came to define the latter half of the twentieth century in popular music and inspire the styles that predominate today cultivated a conscious nonchalance and DIY vocal aesthetic. Bob Dylan and Janis Joplin define one stylistic mode. On "Song for Bob Dylan," David Bowie aptly described Dylan as having "a voice like sand and glue." Even pop divas boasting a four-octave range like Whitney Houston, Christina Aguilera, and Ariana Grande were not so much trained in the conservatory as they were in the church or in the recording booth or on Nickelodeon.

Judgments about voice are almost always colored by context—the dictates of a particular genre, or the aesthetics of an audience. It is foolish to propose some universal principle for measuring a great voice; it's equally erroneous to accept the cop-out that all judgments about voice are subjective. The aesthetic measure of voice may be contextual, but it's certainly not solely subjective. In fact, measurable qualities of voice provide starting points for evaluating vocal quality. From there, one mounts arguments using the less quantifiable but nonetheless imperative elements that a gifted voice can conjure.

SINGING AS SONGWRITING

Early in his career, the pioneering label executive Clive Davis vowed "to sign more artists who had performing and vocal skills but just didn't write, to do A&R in the most fundamental meaning of the term: matching artists with repertoire, getting back to that nearly lost, but exciting and fulfilling, part of the record-making process." When he made this decision in 1974, he was going against the new normal of the album-oriented rock era, when singer-songwriters were the ideal. Davis's move marked an atavistic turn to artists who make many songs their own without having made the song itself. Over his long career, Davis signed many singers who gained fame singing other people's songs, from Taylor Dayne to Luther Vandross to Whitney Houston to Kelly Clarkson. Their singing, too, is a kind of songwriting.

Singing in pop is a generative practice. The voice does not merely reproduce a series of notes and words, it embodies a lyric and re-creates it through departures from the lyric as written that reveal the unexpected in the songs just as they are. A great voice is a claim to ownership all its own. Without abrogating the rights of others, it asserts a primary position in the public's imagination. Though the radical poet and teacher Abel Meeropol wrote "Strange Fruit"—first as a poem published in the Marxist publication *New Masses*, and then as a song lyric—no one could reasonably dispute that it is anything other than a Billie Holiday song. As the literary critic Emily Lordi observes in her study of black women singers, *Black Resonance*, "authorship also resides in inventive execution." Holiday and other commanding singers are creative agents, rewriting the songs they sing through tones and inflections, even through the intake of breath.

Claiming that singing is songwriting acknowledges that much of what we value in the language and the sound of musical recordings is a product of vocalists' interpretive choices. My goal is not to confer some legitimizing authority on singers by calling them writers; rather, it is to underscore the authority and influence their voices carry, even in matters like lyric composition. Regardless of the extent of their generative acts of voice, however, singers are not writers—except, of course, when they *are* writers, taking a hand in the creation of language on the page and its rebirth as recorded sound.

Some people are uncomfortable with the idea of singers as songwriters in those instances when the singers don't actually compose word or melody. There is greater authenticity or emotive power, many believe, when performers sing their own songs. "I'd say material is 80 percent of a singer's career," observes the country singer Loretta Lynn. "You can have a great voice, but you'd also better have a new song that fits your style. And the best way is to write the songs yourself." Tom Petty puts it even more succinctly: "If you're gonna sing the song, it's good to write the words yourself, so you can believe it and get behind it." Lynn's and Petty's statements reflect a substantial belief that true singers are also writers.

It comes down to this: Does the singer serve the song, or does the song serve the singer? "We judge pre-rock singing by how perfectly the lyric is served. That's the standard Frank Sinatra exemplifies," writes the novelist Jonathan Lethem. "We judge popular vocals since 1956 by what the singer unearths that the song itself never quite could." Lethem is being polemical and schematic here, but his claim is instructive. The former understanding of singers in service of the song presents vocalists as craftspeople; the latter understanding of singers as those who find something deep and heretofore hidden in the song presents vocalists as artists.

This division privileges the lyric above all. However, in his landmark study of the blues, *Stomping the Blues*, the novelist and essayist Albert Murray makes the important observation that for blues listeners and performers the lyrics themselves were often of secondary importance. We can extend Murray's claims to an entire tradition of popular music that would follow the blues—from rock to R&B and beyond:

> The truth is that when a singer likes the tune he is likely to proceed as if any words will do. Moreover much goes to show that only a very few of the millions of devoted admirers of Ma Rainey, Bessie Smith, Jimmy Rushing, and Big Joe Turner, for instance, can actually understand more than half the words of their lyrics as sung, not to mention the idiomatic imagery and references. Perhaps many respond to what they wish to think is being said rather than to the statement the composer wrote, but even so the chances are that most of their goose pimples and all of their finger snapping and foot tapping are produced by the sound far more often than by the meanings of the words.

For much of the history of pop music it does seem as if "any words would do." Some of the great moments in pop vocal performance happen when the singer bends or even breaks the bonds between language and meaning. The blues stand as the wellspring of a tradition of vocal practice in the United States that privileges feeling over form and that uses sound to clarify sense. Writing to Murray in a 1957 letter, Ralph Ellison extolled the blues singer's capacity to meet or even to exceed the expressive range of poetry. "Bessie Smith singing a good blues may deal with experience as profoundly as [T. S.] Eliot, with the eloquence of the Eliotic poetry being expressed in her voice and phrasing," Ellison wrote. "Human anguish is human anguish, love love." Ellison did not intend poetry as metaphor here, but rather as a matter of practice—the formal exercise of the singer's craft and its capacity to achieve expressive eloquence and directness. "The blues bears witness to the strangeness of each individual's fate," writes the poet Charles Simic. "It begins wordlessly in a moan, a stamp of the foot, a sigh, a hum, and then seeks words for that something or other that has no name in any language and for which all poetry and music seek an approximation." Like the blues, the language of much popular lyric is a record of this search for feeling—sometimes apparent in sounds seeking sense, sometimes in more ordered language, but always expressed through the voice.

Great singers, and even poor singers, engage in work analogous to poetic composition. They co-create the lyric. Their emphasis and inflection, their tonal shading, their orientation to the beat all account for a critical act of composition that deranges and transforms the lyric as written. In an 1871 letter to his publisher, then sixteen-year-old poet Arthur Rimbaud boldly proclaimed that "the Poet makes himself a seer by a long, gigantic and rational derangement of all the senses." So many singers follow the same practice, studiously deranging their senses, and through their senses, the song. "As a singer you impose your melodies," explains Mick Jagger, "and I would impose my melodies over Keith [Richards]'s chord structures. So even though I wasn't a *player*, I would help shape the melody, 'cause I was singing it." Lyrics drive the topline melody in most pop songs, and the singer gives voice to the lyrics. The difference between lyrics on the page and lyrics in performance is one between lyrics at rest and lyrics in motion.

Singers compose in rehearsal and on the fly. The ways that they change the songs they sing are obvious to the ear, rarely apparent to the eye. Frank Sinatra and Billie Holiday weren't songwriters; they never composed a thing. But no one could seriously suggest that they didn't shape the songs they sang. "So enormously powerful were Sinatra's interpretations of songs that even now, looking at the sheet music, I find it impossible to disassociate the printed notes from my memory of his singing," writes Alec Wilder in his classic study, *American Popular Song*. As interpreters rather than composers, Sinatra, Holiday, and other great singers performed a creative act every bit as significant as that of the lyricist.

Indeed, one could expand the matter of authorship beyond songwriters and singers to producers, engineers, and the host of other individuals who contribute to the production of a musical recording. The Beatles had George Martin. Bob Dylan had Daniel Lanois. Radiohead has Nigel Godrich. Managers, producers, businesspeople, and creative minds are part of pop's voice. "The multiple authorship that characterizes popular music production goes a great deal further than the collectivity of band composition," argues the musicologist Nicholas Cook; "it extends to the highly segmented process in which the roles of song-writers, arrangers, and artists are complemented by those of sound engineers, producers, and A&R personnel." Producers can celebrate or bury the voice depending on the choices they make in the mix. For his part, the producer Dave Stewart sees his task as enshrining the voice and its particular capacity for emotive expression. "People want to hear and feel the emotion in the human voice, and for me that's the most important thing to get right," he observes. "There came a point in music when you could have forty-eight tracks, then seventy-two tracks or so, and just create a giant wall of music. . . . I believed in following the voice on its journey." Under the influence of producers and other individuals with the power to shape the music, authorship in pop music is complicated, attesting to the exigencies of both art and commerce.

For the purposes of the poetry of pop, it is useful to remember that the titular author—the songwriter cum poet—is far from the only hand involved in making the music. It falls to us as active listeners to attend to the multiple means by which a song is composed, recontextualized, and reimagined. Nor should songs be conflated with their recordings, or with instances of their live performance. "Songs are more abstract entities than their recordings and they are not produced technologically any more than are poems; they can be recorded, arranged and performed in multiple ways and yet be the same song," writes the philosopher John Andrew Fisher. A song, in other words, lives many lives, constituting a multitude of distinct aesthetic manifestations. These divergent iterations are expressed most palpably through the exercise of a great singing voice.

THE PHONEBOOK TEST

It's often said that Elvis Presley could sing the phonebook and leave the audience enraptured. So could Frank Sinatra, Etta James, Luther Vandross, B. B. King, Kurt Cobain, Donna Summer, Johnny Cash, and a host of others. The idea behind this—call it the Phonebook Test—is that some singers are so lavishly gifted or so charismatic that they can take lifeless lyrics and make them unforgettable. Of course, conferring the phonebook mantle on a singer is a subjective judgment, phrased as hyperbole. Nonetheless, the saying persists as a way of enshrining certain voices over and above the language of the lyrics they sing. Great voices trump language, the argument goes, though not everyone agrees. "People often say that a great singer can sing the phone book and people would buy it," writes Clive Davis in his memoir. "To me, that's completely wrong. The better the singer, the more critical it is that the songs are challenging enough to showcase his or her talents at their absolute best."

Sometimes bad lyrics happen to good singers. Sometimes bad lyrics even happen to good songs. It's no special feat to pick out song lyrics that are silly, saccharine, or cringeworthy. Rather than deriding these lyrics, why not use them as the starting point for a richer line of inquiry? Specifically, why not try to figure out what transpires to render these lyrics tolerable, and even memorable and meaningful, when delivered by a great voice in performance?

Aretha Franklin is a prime candidate for the Phonebook Test and for Davis's counter-theory. One imagines that she would be able to pass any vocal test you sent her way. "No one has been able to 'keep up' with her," observes the English critic Barney Hoskyns. "Her lines tend to be clean and straight rather than arabesque or melismatic, and what stands out more than anything are the sudden, high, almost indignant phrases you hear. . . . The mercurial intelligence of her timing, her compression of phrases within the minutest gaps, is astonishing, and yet it is this intelligence which—running rings round us as it does—can so often lose us."

Give Franklin a silly song, the argument goes, and her interpretive vocal genius will save it. And, indeed, Franklin, like many other vaunted vocalists, at times seems to put her talent willfully to the test. Over the course of her long career, she has recorded many classic songs, from "Rock Steady" and "You're All I Need to Get By" to "Respect." Franklin's catalog also includes songs that, save for her vocal performance, are defiantly forgettable. In 1985 Franklin released *Who's Zoomin' Who?*, her thirty-first studio album. Its lead single was "Freeway of Love," a propulsive pop number accentuated by a Clarence Clemons sax solo. "The strongest cut on the album," Franklin wrote of the song in her memoir, "was between my voice and an absolutely upbeat and hot track hooked up by [producer] Narada [Michael Walden]." Even a singer of Franklin's incomparable gifts seems hard-pressed selling the song's opening lyric: "Knew you'd be a vision in white / How'd you get your pants so tight?"

One response to these bad lyrics might be to diminish the importance of the words in the song entirely. Ignore the tight white pants! However, another way to think about silly pop lyrics is to consider what it takes for lyrics to call attention to themselves in most pop songs. Music creates a linguistic space in which language that might come across as excessive in everyday speech can become comfortable in performance. If someone came up to you and shouted "Ob-la-di, Ob-la-da, life goes on, Oh / La-la-la-la life goes on," you'd think she was nuts. But if you passed the same person singing the words instead, you likely wouldn't give a second glance. It takes something special for a lyric to call attention to itself as language.

Often excesses are deliberate, designed to account for the context of their delivery. Lyrics are strange or silly or sonically extreme so as better to pierce our consciousness. Silly lyrics, after all, are often the most fun to sing. Think of the fun people had in stretching out the "ooo" when singing "I've got the moves like Jagger" with Adam Levine. Words that might come across as meaningless on the page can be deeply affecting when given voice and melody.

Song lyrics are asked to accomplish a range of tasks. Sometimes they are primarily intended to carry a melody; other times they wish to call attention to themselves; and other times they work to highlight an attitude, an emotion, or a story. Each of these aims requires a different set of aesthetic tools. Take the lyric from "Freeway of Love" quoted earlier. The lines by themselves are a little silly, but the work those lines do in the song is sublime. They underscore the power of a forty-three-year-old black woman singing about desire and turning the tables on a culture that often objectifies and catcalls women for what they wear. Franklin's playful objectification of the male in her gaze underscores the song's celebration of freedom, both amorous and otherwise.

Pulling the music away from a lyric and laughing at the lyric for being banal or bland is about the same as pulling the sugar out before making a batch of cookies and then complaining that the cookies just aren't sweet enough. Without the key ingredient, the recipe's bound to fail. And just as too little of something will ruin the mix, too much will do the same. Make the lyrics too mellifluous or too ponderous and the final product can sometimes prove worse for the effort. It makes sense to view lyrics at work in vocal performance, in the context of their silent service to other aesthetic aims.

THE VOICE AT WORK: SPEECH, RAP, AND SONG

The voice does three things with song lyrics: It sings them, it raps them, and it speaks them. We know these when we hear them. However, there are no bright-line distinctions separating them. The three partake of common practices; they blend into one another, with artists often marrying multiple modes to make music with their mouths. Consequently, by analyzing how vocal artists use song, rap, and speech we gain a clearer understanding of how they achieve their emotive and semantic effects. What makes a particular vocal performance so affecting, or so maudlin? Why do people associate rap with aggression and falsetto singing with romance? Do certain styles of vocal performance lend themselves to particular expressive and thematic ends?

Speech and song involve different hemispheres of the brain; speech is left-brain dominant, and song is right-brain dominant. However, speech and song are also defined by extrinsic perception. Studies have demonstrated that certain spoken phrases, when repeated multiple times, will take on the quality of song for listeners. These speech-to-song illusions are an important part of the story of voice because they attest to the liminal spaces across vocal expression. Most of us, though, upon hearing a lyric, decide instantaneously whether it is spoken, rapped, or sung. This judgment involves multivalent calculations that rely on our experience with language and take place on a level beyond conscious awareness.

Some singers play with these assumptions to fashion expressions that call attention to themselves. Even entire genres may favor modes of performance that evade ready categorization. "In singing styles, such as folk and pop, where the intelligibility of the words and their expression can be particularly important, a more flexible approach to voice production is needed than can be achieved in classical singing styles," argues Alan H. D. Watson, an anatomist and neuroscientist specializing in musical performance physiology. "This depends on a technique that is more akin to speech and which would make it difficult to sing at high volume." Frank Sinatra, for instance, sometimes approaches direct speech in his conversational singing style. "There was a tenderness to his voice, a purity and ease of phrasing," recalls Willie Nelson of first hearing Sinatra on the radio. "When he sang the popular songs of the day, I marveled at the natural way he told the story." What Nelson hears as natural is in large part Sinatra's proximity to speech in his singing.

When multiple vocal registers express themselves singly in a song, the results can be both a pleasing listening experience and a study in the range and capacity of voice. Method Man and Mary J. Blige's "I'll Be There for You/You're All I Need" begins with Method Man speaking in a barely decipherable mumble, which gives way to Blige singing ad libs and the chorus (drawn from Marvin Gaye's "You're All I Need"), before opening up to Method Man's rapped verse. The song's appeal relies on the equipoise between the sharp edges of Method Man's rapped syllables and the suppleness of Blige's church-inflected melodies, all framed by snatches of direct speech.

Fetty Wap's "Trap Queen," a breakout hit of 2015, underscores the similarities among speech, rap, and song while ultimately proving their singularities. Speech bookends the song, with Fetty Wap calling out his crew name ("1738!") in the beginning and Fetty Wap's business associate, Nitt Da Gritt, making loud proclamations ("You hear my boy . . . soundin' like a zillion bucks!") at the end. In between, the recording blurs the boundaries between singing and rapping so much that it confuses categories. The fact that so many listeners experience the song as either singing or rapping testifies to the ways Fetty Wap effectively conflates the two. Wikipedia, for instance, categorizes the song as "hip hop" and "trap," both rap descriptors. By contrast, the music website Pigeons & Planes ran an article titled "Fetty Wap Is Not a Rapper." The writer, Justin Charity, states that "Trap Queen" features "no rap at all."

Though too absolute, Charity's article offers a useful corrective; "Trap Queen" includes an instrumental track that one associates with rap, though Fetty Wap's vocal style on most of the recording behaves as singing. In the opening verse he bends the lyrics into a discernible melodic shape, extending the vowels at the ends of lines in a manner characteristic of singing, even as he end-stops his lines like a rapper. The podcast *Switched On Pop* points out that Fetty Wap repeats a C-major triad throughout much of the song, making micro-adjustments to his melodic and rhythmic patterns along the way while staying faithful to the overall melodic contour. If this sounds something less than singing to some ears, it might be because no sustained melody ever emerges, only this patterned repetition of the same melodic fragment.

By the time the chorus to "Trap Queen" arrives, however, Fetty Wap is certainly singing. Over major chord harmony, Fetty Wap sings a minor chord melody that is downright expressive when compared to the truncated melodic line of the first verse. When he returns for the second verse, he is rapping—chopping the end words rather than extending them as he does in singing, underscoring the finality of the end rhyme. Listen to the first verse against the second without the chorus in between and the difference is obvious: Fetty Wap is singing on the first verse and rapping on the second. Gone with the second verse is the lilting embellishment on the rhyme words at the end of lines and the extenuation of vowel sounds. More important, gone are the tonal shifts that shape the melody. In their place is the characteristic rhythmic approach to language commonly associated with rap.

Speaking, rapping, and singing are discrete but interrelated expressions of voice. But what does one do with the spaces in between? When executed crisply and with purpose, shifts among the registers of voice in song provide sonic interest and help to underscore different motives of meaning and emotion. "A technique heard frequently since Hoppy Jones of the Ink Spots made it effective in the 1930s," explains Walter Everett, "is for a singer to drop the vocalizing and shift to the spoken word for an introspective later verse or bridge, as if speaking from the heart, reaching the audience with inner thoughts in a more direct way than an 'artificial' melody is able to do." Moving to the spoken word temporarily untethers the song's vocal utterance from the music, a union instantiated in singing. In moving from song to speech and back to song on numbers like "My Prayer" and "If I Didn't Care," the Ink Spots craft moments of sonic and emotive difference, achieving effects that song or speech alone could not. Though their "talking choruses" sound quaint today, they provided a model upon which later artists would craft more subtle effects using vocal contrast.

Decades after the Ink Spots, the rapper and singer Drake began cultivating his transitions from rap to song and back to rap. Dionne Osborne, Drake's vocal coach, reveals how she encouraged him to move more purposefully within and between his vocal modes. "I mean, singing is just exaggerated speech. You're sustaining the tones; you're holding the notes longer," she explains. "So I tried to get him to do that more with rap, connecting his flow. It's like writing in cursive. The technical term is *legato*. It's a better use for the air when you're singing and makes for a better sound overall." Drake's approach, both to singing and to rapping, is now far more attentive to matching his vocal pitch to the instrumentals. He has come to appreciate the voice as instrument.

Performance close to speech generally endows a lyric with a more direct appeal to language. It also inspires a discombobulating experience of the everyday and the strange when matched with the artful techniques of song. Though some consider Gil Scott-Heron's "The Revolution Will Not Be Televised" a harbinger of rap, it more closely approximates the cadenced speech of preaching or political oratory, with its absence of rhythmic regularity and timbral shape. Scott-Heron's lyrics behave more like prose than like the rhythmically patterned poetry of rap. Though jazz-inflected music plays in the background as Scott-Heron vocalizes, his lyrics are not delivered *in time* to a beat as we would expect of rap. Scott-Heron is exhorting, he's preaching, he's "rapping" in the colloquial sense of street-corner banter, but he isn't rapping as we know it today. The clarity of a vocal performance like "The Revolution Will Not Be Televised" underscores its emphatic political and social critique in a vocal style akin to speech. But its small differences from speech—Scott-Heron's irregular patterns of inflection against the texture of the song's jazz accompaniment—make his message memorable.

Moving from a crossover between rap and speech to a crossover between rap and singing, some artists graft elements of rap cadence to music that otherwise settles comfortably into familiar generic tropes. Anthony Kiedis of the Red Hot Chili Peppers developed a vocal style that transposes certain rap techniques to a new generic and sonic context in punk rock. In the early 1980s Kiedis saw Grandmaster Flash and the Furious Five in concert and was particularly taken with the rap style of Melle Mel, who essentially drafted the blueprint for rapping to a beat. "It was mind-blowing," Kiedis recalls. "I subconsciously vowed I would somehow create that type of energy to entertain others. I didn't have a clue how to write a song or sing, but I thought I could probably figure out how to tell a story in rhythm." This conception of vocal performance as telling a story in rhythm provided Kiedis with both an expression of style and a means of disguising his own vocal limitations. "When [Grandmaster Flash and the Furious Five's] 'The Message' became the hottest thing that summer," Kiedis reveals in his memoir, "it started dawning on me that you don't have to be Al Green or have an incredible Freddie Mercury voice to have a place in the world of music. Rhyming and developing a character were another way to do it."

The vocal style Kiedis practices on songs like "Give It Away" and "Can't Stop" is not quite singing, not quite rapping, but something in between. The similarities to rap extend to the structures of the songs themselves. As in most rap songs, the verses on "Can't Stop" are sixteen bars in length. The song is dominated by rhymed couplets, often of multisyllabic pairs (*shindig/win big*, for instance, and *penetration/generation*). The most arresting moments on "Can't Stop" come in the transitional passages from verse to chorus, where Kiedis shifts from his stylized rap delivery to his natural singing voice. These transitions call attention to Kiedis's two distinct vocal practices. Equally important are the qualities that cohere the performance. The choruses are decidedly sung and follow a rhythmic logic that undergirds the languorous, lilting melody.

Kiedis's cadence on the verses is unmistakably inspired by rap, but his effusive, singsong delivery shows that rapping can approach a kind of singing. Indeed, the song relies on listeners' recognition of Kiedis's vocalizing as something other than rap. No self-respecting rapper in 2002, in the era of Eminem, would ever be caught kicking such an old school flow. However, it works for the Chili Peppers both because of their decidedly rock 'n' roll reputation and because of the defiant confidence with which Kiedis unifies the recording's disparate parts. When Kiedis moves from the sung chorus of "Can't Stop" back to its rapped verse, the shift charges the song with the immediacy and insistence of the rhythm. Kiedis told *Spin* magazine that the song is one of the few examples in the Chili Peppers' catalog in which he wrote lyrics to a rhythm pattern rather than devising the rhythm pattern from the lyrics. The performance, both rhythmically and expressively, captures the spirit of the effusive rapping styles of old-school rap artists like Melle Mel and Kool Moe Dee even as it presents itself as something new, something in between.

For all their possible connections, though, speaking is not rapping and rapping is not singing. Each inhabits a distinct point along an expressive continuum. The differences among them manifest themselves in pitch, tone, rhythm, and pronunciation. Rap shares with speech its indefinite pitch, whereas singing relies on a patterning of definite pitch along a scale to comprise melody. When Jay Z raps "99 Problems," there's simply too much variation in his vocal delivery to assign definite pitches to his words. As a consequence, his flow emulates the conversational quality of speech even as other features of his vocal performance, such as end rhyme or patterns of vocal stress, depart sharply from conventional speech practices. By contrast, when Sam Smith sings "Stay with Me," his voice journeys up and down the scale from definite pitch to definite pitch, creating the melody. Few of the distinguishing qualities of speech remain.

This isn't to suggest that nothing is going on when it comes to the pitch of the rapping voice; pitch is an essential feature of pronunciation, and rappers often order pitches in ways that conventional speech does not even if they don't precisely sing. This becomes apparent when rap vocals are transported to a new sonic context. "When I first tried to synch up one of my favorite rapper's a cappellas with my own music," explains the composer Chilly Gonzales, "I was unpleasantly surprised at the results: sometimes the (hidden) pitch choice of the rapper clashed in a bad way with the chords in my song. That's when I realized that rap isn't talking at all; it just plays on the illusion of conversational, confessional intimacy."

All raps carry "hidden pitch" with more or less reliability. Though never hitting a diatonic key, Lil Wayne hovers between the frequency space of E and F for the entirety of the first verse of his 2008 hit "A Milli." His voice retains a certain intervallic integrity even as it eludes the certainty of a given pitch. By patterning the frequency and timbre of his performance in such a restrictive pitch space, however, Lil Wayne sacrifices the conversational quality that Gonzales ascribes to rap. Instead, the first verse of "A Milli" sounds like chant, like ritual. As Lil Wayne moves into the second and third verse, his performance looses itself from its pitch restriction and the vocal performance takes on a more effusive and conversational quality, even engaging in the pitch-shifting modulation that underscores the line "what's a goon to a goblin."

Rap differs from speech in its clear, if hidden, pitch; rap is also unlike singing in that its pitch is not generally a defining quality of its sound. Rapping relies on patterns of frequency that do not privilege pitch precision but instead suggest broader melodic shapes and tendencies. A rapped lyric can maintain integrity with the shape of its pitch without precisely hitting targeted frequencies. For the listener, perhaps the underlying difference between singing and rapping is that the former depends on implicit identification of pitch and the latter on more liberal outlines of melodic space.

Tone also helps differentiate speech from song. Vocal tones are roughly divided between two registers: the head voice and the chest voice. The head voice resonates through the upper sinus cavities, producing the light and bright vocal tone we associate with soprano and falsetto singing. The chest voice is more deeply resonant, resulting in the richer and thicker sounds that accord with tenor and contralto singing as well as with speech. For most singers the head voice is a voice under pressure; the chest voice, the voice at relative ease. Both can be effective and affecting means of vocal expression in song, but the chest voice more closely approximates the physical dynamics of speech.

In analyzing the distinctive power of Aretha Franklin's voice, Emily Lordi observes that "Franklin's singing stays unusually close to speech registers—closer than singers with a less extensive chest voice range, who must shift into their head voices to reach the notes she reaches, and certainly closer than soprano and falsetto singers, who work primarily in their upper range. Her contralto singing thus produces a curious form of what we might call audio-sympathy: we are at home speaking in this range, but very few people can sing in it (well or otherwise)." When Franklin sings in her chest voice, our comfort with it derives in part from her vocal tone's proximity to speech. By contrast, her forays into her upper-register head voice mark her singing as removed from everyday utterance. So the head voice distinguishes itself as the domain of song, whereas the chest voice is the territory in which speech, rap, and song most often meet.

As for rhythm, casual speech does not usually follow recognizable patterns of rhythmic stress, although it does rely on rhythm and even melody in keeping with the context of spoken expression. Rap's flow depends on rhythmic patterning. Singing does as well, albeit in a looser manner. Rap requires a continuous flow; speech does not. And singing enlists rhythm primarily in service of melody. "Song has repetition built into it—of rhythms, melodic motifs—and this repetition gives song an element of predictability that speech lacks," Daniel J. Levitin writes. By contrast, speech is heterometric, with variability and idiosyncrasy defining its rhythmic contours. Certainly speech is capable of crafting moments of rhythmic patterning—in Sunday sermons, for instance, or in political oratory—but we ascribe musicality to those speech acts, differentiating them from everyday speech, marking them somehow as ritual.

Finally, speech, rap, and song follow divergent practices when it comes to pronouncing words. Just because you can utter a given word or sentence in speech does not mean you can do the same when singing or rapping. Pronouncing words in song is a craft. "I would listen and breathe from my diaphragm," recalls Melissa Etheridge of her apprenticeship as a singer, "and I became aware of how to pronounce words while singing." The defining difference between pronouncing words in speech and in song is the phrasing of vowels. "When you sing," explains the songwriter Gene Lees, "it is the vowels that carry the tone, and, basically, the pitch. The consonants are produced not by the vocal cords but by the mouth. The tongue, teeth, nose, velum, lips, and what is called the alveolar ridge—that's the ridge behind your upper front teeth that you keep touching with the tip of the tongue when you say *tut-tut-tut*—merely articulate the vowels. When you sustain a note, it is the vowel that you hold." One of the most remarkable examples of a singer enchanting a single word in a song is what Whitney Houston does with the word "free" in her classic 1991 rendition of "The Star-Spangled Banner" before Super Bowl XXV. In a short essay published in the *New Yorker* in 2016, the writer Cinque Henderson describes the lyric moment as follows:

> As Houston's voice approached the high note on the word "free," she slowed for suspense and for air, then rang the E-flat above middle C like a bell. With the extra room [her longtime bandleader and arranger Rickey] Minor had given her, she held on to the note for three counts (the traditional score affords "free" only a single count, but [Marvin] Gaye had also lengthened it, whether Houston explicitly remembered that or not). And then, in the split-second relay circuit of choices that we know as instinct, Houston leapt off the back of that E and sent her voice vaulting even higher, dragging out the word "free" with a two-note flourish she invented in the recording booth, just as the measure was about to close. It had the sensation of a frighteningly tight line being pulled even tighter.

Because it ends in a vowel, Houston could hold the word "free" for three counts in a way that she couldn't, for instance, hold its synonyms "independent" or "sovereign." Singing dilates vowels in a way that speech and rap rarely do. A singing voice might expand the vowels in a lyric line to many times their usual duration. This is such a familiar quality of singing that the casual listener never stops to realize how prevalent and foundational the practice of dilating vowel sounds is. Think about the Five Stairsteps singing "Oooooh-ooooh chi-i-ild, things are gonna get e-e-asie-e-er/Oooooh-ooooh chi-i-ild, things'll get bri-i-ighte-er."

Vowels serve a particular function at the ends of musical phrases where one traditionally finds end rhyme. Most consonants truncate a phrase—you can't sustain the word "trapped" or the word "cut"—but vowel sounds allow the melodic charge of pitch and tone, and the play of qualities like melisma. Therefore, song lyrics underscore the vital distinction between closed rhymes and open rhymes. "It is a mark of skill in a lyricist when he uses a lot of open rhymes on long notes at the ends of musical phrases," writes Gene Lees, advocating a staunch position that few contemporary songwriters assiduously hold. On the chorus of "Cupid," Sam Cooke plays with open-ended rhymes, alternating between sustaining the vowel sounds and introducing a curlicue of melisma. I've mapped the different ways he sings the first two lines in his first two passes through the chorus:

> Cupid, draw back your boooow
> And let your arrow go-*oh*
>
> Cupid, draw back your bow-*oh*
> And let your arrow go-*oh*

The change in the first line to melisma in keeping with the second is a subtle difference, underscoring the song's development and the singer's building emotional insistence. This kind of extenuation of syllables would be strange to hear in rap, and stranger still in speech. It's necessary, beautiful, and comforting in song.

In rap, vowels dilate to a limited extent, but essentially approximate the duration of vowel sounds in speech. The result is more words per bar, and more words in general, than in singing. Consonants, with their inherent percussive capacities, are equally if not more highly prized in rap than are vowels. Rap's denser expressive space emphasizes direct communication in a way that singing does not, although moderated by stylized effects like repetition and syncopation. "My raps don't have melodies," Jay Z boasts on "D.O.A. (Death of Auto-Tune)," his 2009 open letter in rhyme to all the rappers trying to be singers. What we hear as a more singerly style in rap—say, 50 Cent on "Many Men" from 2003 or Young Thug on "Constantly Hating" from 2015—is mostly predicated on the MC's pointed fluctuations in vocal pitch rather than on dilation of vowel sounds common to singing.

Listen to Arrested Development's "Tennessee" from 1992, perhaps the most important song in rap's melodic flow tradition, and what you'll hear is the rapper Speech shaping makeshift melodies through unexpected modulations in pitch. "I just wanted to come up with something unique, and I had just started to discover rhyming and putting it into more of a melodic style," Speech recalls. "I had never heard it in hip-hop, really, especially for the whole song. . . . I saw a whole new opportunity to add more emotion to what I was saying when I started to put more melody to it, and so 'Tennessee' was one of the first songs that I did that." Few rappers, though, make such pitch modulations the defining feature of their flows. And fewer still regularly employ the vowel dilation common to singing. A famous exception was 2Pac, whose flow drew as much from African American oratorical traditions, both sacred and secular, as it did from singing. On "Dear Mama," for instance, he extenuates vowels to draw out their emotive potential: "And even as a crack *fieeeeend*, mama / You always was a black *queeeeeen*, mama." He exploits the elasticity of the vowels, emphasizing both the musicality and the slant rhyme in "fiend" and "queen" in a way that underscores the pain and poignancy in the couplet. For all of 2Pac's importance to rap's tradition, though, this central feature of his flow has not been widely adopted.

Instrumental context also helps condition the mode of vocal performance. There's a reason why most rap is in 4/4 time. Common measure fashions a sonic bed upon which the MC can deliver lyrics. The same often holds for singers. Listen to Patti Smith and one hears a kind of performative freedom made possible through the instrumentation. The musicologist Allan F. Moore observes that the music on her classic album *Horses* is "a 'bed of sound' upon which Smith performs and in which the words are free to lose the markers of lyric, rhyme and syllabic consistency, in favour of a looser relation more akin to prose forms: less poem as analogy, then, and more short story, novel, letter, confession, manifesto. Even some of the basic rules of lyric can be broken." When basic rules of lyric and performance are broken, new possibilities emerge, often in the interstices between speech, rap, and singing. The challenge of vocal performance is compounded, of course, when two or more voices come together in song.

SINGING TOGETHER

Whether it is rhythm and blues quartets and quintets defining a sound that would soon be characterized—and caricatured—as doo-wop, the spooky timbre of the Louvin Brothers, the contrapuntal interplay of Simon & Garfunkel, the unearthly precision of the Everly Brothers, the weird and immaculate sound of the Beach Boys, the pan-gender splendor of Peter, Paul & Mary, the sounds of these and dozens of other groups constitute new voices unto themselves.

Voices singing in harmony become their own individuated vocal fingerprint, every bit as recognizable as a great solo voice. "Certain pairings of singers are essentially two instruments pulling together to create one resonance," the critic Ben Ratliff observes. But how does this union of sound and sensibility come about? The answer lies as much in intuition as it does in the science of singing. The group harmony one encounters in genres as farflung as street-corner vocal quartets and bluegrass gatherings fashions a thick sonic texture balanced at its extremes by a rich, resonant bass and a piercing falsetto. There's magic in this particular combination, one whose power may be difficult to put into words, though the evidence is sometimes apparent to the eye as much as to the ear. In one remarkable example of this literalization of vocal harmony's power, Alphonso Feemster of the Washington, D.C.–based Four Bars of Rhythm, a vocal quartet that recorded from the mid-1950s through the 1960s, recalls the following:

> One night we were rehearsing with the Four Bars and we were in my mother's kitchen. . . . So we was rehearsing on a song, and so we hit this harmony note and my mother had some china on the shelf and it shattered. And it amazed me. I said, "We must of been right on." . . . But she didn't mind, you know, 'cause she knew what we were doing. We just sang, and harmony began to take hold of me. 'Cause it was so beautiful; you're really singing it right, you know.

Singing it right—right enough to break your mama's good china—is a condition to which many groups aspire. Graham Nash recalls the moment that he first harmonized with David Crosby and Stephen Stills as a near-spiritual awakening. At a Laurel Canyon party, Nash overheard Stills and Crosby harmonizing together and decided he would join in. "As Stephen launched into the intro again," Nash recalls, "I casually made my way over, standing to his left, and when they hit the opening line—I'm there. I had my breath down, the phrasing, the tuning. I put my harmony above Stephen, and off we sailed. You are livvvv-ing a reality/I left years ago and it quite nearly killed me. In the lonnnng run . . . What a sound! We were locked in, tight as a drum. Flawless three-part harmony. It sounded so soft and beautiful, so incredible that a minute or so into the song we collapsed in laughter." The joy they must have felt this first time singing together is still audible in the studio recording of "You Don't Have to Cry," which would appear on the trio's self-titled 1969 debut. "Something magical had happened, and we all knew it," Nash concludes. "When you sing with two or three people and you get it right—when the whole becomes greater than the sum of its parts—everything kind of lifts a couple feet off the ground. The three of us were levitating, all right. The vibe was so high, it was hard to touch down."

Eventually, they did touch down. Time and excess stole something from each singer, most notably from David Crosby, who struggled for years with a drug addiction that ravaged his vocal instrument. Recalling a reunion tour years later, Nash sadly reports that Crosby's "voice was rough, husky; our harmonies were strained. I couldn't vibe him out, I couldn't anticipate him anymore. The communication between us had stopped." Their group's harmony, which once had been an easy, evanescent thing, had disappeared as quickly and as mysteriously as it first emerged.

Not all voices singing the same song are singing together. Some groups aspire to a conscious discord or even ugliness, a jangling tension born of voices singing in antagonistic cooperation. In her 2015 memoir, Carrie Brownstein recalls the singing style she cultivated with Corin Tucker in their group Sleater-Kinney. "It was a conversation we were having: she had her perspective and I had mine," Brownstein explains. "We would get to the chorus, and intuitively you'd think this is the time for us to all sing together, that there should be a cohesion, but instead we would split apart. It was almost an anti-chorus. We weren't trying to form a solidarity with anyone but ourselves. Could you sing along to Sleater-Kinney? . . . As a listener you have to decide what to follow in the song, which vocal, which guitar."

Listening across Sleater-Kinney's discography, one experiences the distance and tension between the lead vocals not as a flaw but as a beguiling, unsettling aesthetic force. "We didn't want to sing harmonies," Brownstein recalls. "Our songs weren't pretty, nor was our style of singing. It sounded scarier to not sing together, rarely allowing the listener to settle into the music. Everything inside the songs was constantly on the verge of breaking apart—Corin's voice, the narrative, the guitars, so few moments provided any respite at all." Threatening disintegration while somehow retaining sonic integrity, Brownstein's and Tucker's voices stake out a space in sound at a far distance from the close vocal harmonies of Crosby, Stills & Nash. That distance, however, is at least as much the product of an affirmative aesthetic choice as it is one of accident. Sometimes a little ugliness can be beautiful, too. If two or three voices singing together makes for such drama, imagine the chaos and clangor that could result from a few dozen celebrity voices all singing on a seven-minute song.

It is perhaps pop's greatest experiment in voice: Gather nearly four dozen of the most prominent singers in popular music from across all genres to perform a single song for a charitable cause. The song was 1985's "We Are the World," recorded by a pickup choir of stars that would go by the name of USA for Africa. "We Are the World," written by Lionel Richie and Michael Jackson, produced and conducted by Quincy Jones, and performed by Bob Dylan, Willie Nelson, Cyndi Lauper, Bruce Springsteen, Steve Perry, Ray Charles, Stevie Wonder, and others among the who's who of 1980s pop music, set a new standard for celebrity philanthropy. The song raised $60 million for African famine relief and was instrumental in leveraging an additional $800 million in aid from the U.S. government. By that measure alone it was a resounding success.

"We Are the World" also proved to be a commercial success as a single, reaching number one on the *Billboard* Hot 100 chart and selling an estimated 20 million copies around the globe. Another enduring legacy of the song is what it reveals about the nature of voice in popular music. The very act of coordinating so many stars and so many styles is a marvel. Together, the producers and performers took what was potentially another maudlin pop song and rescued it by the integrity of their cause, and also by the unexpectedness and occasional weirdness of the recorded song.

The music and lyrics are serviceable: earnest verses cast in a simple but affecting melody, a rousing and singable chorus, in some ways timeless though still time-bound, with synthesized horns and tinkling keys. At times, the lyrics veer toward cliché ("life, the greatest gift of all," "love is all we need"), but the performance renders them emotionally effective and, at times, even evocative. The song consists of only two verses, a chorus, and a bridge, but it packs in twenty-one vocal solos, not to mention harmonies and ad libs. This distinctive blend of vocal styles enacts the fact that pop music is a capacious form that encompasses a diversity of styles and rejects the idea of limitation. The song simultaneously represents the sublimation of the star culture and its apotheosis; its success relies on a balance of familiarity and surprise, point and counterpoint. "We Are the World" uses voice in all its permutations: as heroic solo instrument, as harmonizing duo and trio, as improvisational tool, and as chorus.

In working with such a disparate group of voices, the producers employed several strategies. Jones recalls in his memoir that he made it a point to record the choral parts first. "I worried," he notes, "that if they had already sung their solo parts they might just leave or something like that." In the final version of the song, the choir doesn't arrive until the end, near the six-minute mark. It's a rich sound, albeit hardly distinguishable from any other group of competent singers under steady direction.

The next strategy the producers employed was to create solo moments for as many singers as possible, and to make those moments play to each singer's vocal strengths. Coproducer Tom Bahler gathered copies of all of the artists' records and listened to find the range that would best suit each of them. In the recorded arrangement of voices, one hears the producers' craft as much as that of the individual singers. Indeed, the most striking thing about the song more than three decades after its release is the often incongruous juxtapositions of voices and styles. One hears the playfulness, humor, and ingenuity at work in shading the song's emotive tones through particular voices in harmony and tension. "The truth is, everyone was given special treatment," recalls Kenny Rogers. "Thanks to the vocal arrangers . . . the parts were given out not on the basis of how big of a star you were but according to who sounded best on each particular part of the song. I didn't hear one person complain about what they were singing or when they sang." Some of the voices working together are natural, as when Michael Jackson and Diana Ross share the first chorus. Who would imagine, though, that Paul Simon and Stevie Wonder would be so suited to harmonize together? Without Wonder, Simon's voice here is staid and small. Without Simon's, Wonder's is overwrought.

The two songwriters feature prominently. Richie sings the song's opening line, and Jackson sings the bridge as well as the first part of the chorus solo before Ross joins him. Jackson and Ross's rendition of the chorus is restrained, true to the song's melody as composed. It has the continuity of two kindred voices, singing alone and in harmony. By the time the chorus comes around again, however, it has been atomized into lyric fragments that highlight the distinctive styles of the singers. Springsteen comes into the chorus growling, followed by Kenny Loggins's keening tenor; then Journey's Steve Perry emotes, and the chorus ends with Daryl Hall singing the song like it's "Method of Modern Love."

As Stephen Holden observed in the *New York Times*, "The vocal solos on 'We Are the World' have been artfully interwoven to emphasize the individuality of each singer. . . . Recorded against a solemn mantric drone that recalls the mood of George Harrison's 'My Sweet Lord,' the voices are layered in a way so as to create a sense of continuous surprise and emotional buildup." "We Are the World" is a study in voice, a virtuosic feat of performance and production that somehow keeps in tenuous balance a patchwork collection of styles.

When one considers the diversity of pop voices assembled for "We Are the World," it is possible to discern patterns, though certainly not a model of the perfect pop voice. Great voices are not always a matter of technical excellence and flawless execution. Sometimes they are the product of tone or timbral quality, a signature vibrato, rubato, or something that under other circumstances might be seen as a flaw. "Even today my voice is hard to categorize," Ray Charles observed. "You can't call it a tenor 'cause it ain't high enough; you can't call it a baritone 'cause it ain't low enough. If there's such a thing as a true lead singer, that's me."

In 1963 the impresario rock producer Phil Spector was in search of a voice. His production style, which would come to be known as the Wall of Sound, relied on layering sonic textures—different timbres and shadings of instrument and voice. Over the course of his career, he put that Wall of Sound to work with gifted singers, from Bill Medley's baritone on the Righteous Brothers' "You've Lost That Loving Feeling" to Tina Turner's harnessed power on "River Deep, Mountain High." But it might well have been the less obviously remarkable voice of Veronica Bennett, soon to become Ronnie Spector, that would help Spector reach his sonic apogee. In 1964 *Presenting the Fabulous Ronettes Featuring Veronica* included a two-minute-and-forty-second piece of pop perfection called "Be My Baby." In her memoir, Ronnie Spector relates the moment of vocal discovery in compelling detail:

> He knew from the first second he heard me that my voice was exactly what he needed to fill in the center of this enormous sound. Phil

had been trying to construct this giant wall of sound ever since he got started in the record business, and when he heard me, he knew my voice was the final brick. I was always surprised at how much Phil used me when he had singers like Fanita James and Darlene Love around. When I'd hear them singing with those great big gospel voices, I'd start to wonder what was so special about my little voice. But I have to give Phil credit. He loved the way I sang, and he knew exactly what to do with my voice. He knew my range. He knew my pitch. He even knew which words sounded best coming out of my mouth. He knew that "Be My Baby" was a perfect song for me, so he constructed the whole record around my voice from the ground up.

Ronnie Spector's "little voice" cuts through the sonic atmosphere of the recording, adding clarity to what might otherwise slip into fuzziness. Her voice inhabits the sizable space of the song's sonic middle. The chorus of anonymous background singers seems at an almost unfathomable distance from Ronnie Spector's lead. In her voice sensuality and vulnerability commingle with a tensile strength. And just when you start to figure things out, the song is over.

Listening across the contemporary pop landscape and pop music's past, one can discern broad patterns in the voices that predominate. In addition to the virtuosos, pop audiences seem to be drawn to voices at the extremes. "I've spent my life listening to singers and realizing which ones could sing really well and are *still* lousy," writes Steven Tyler. "It has nothing to do with perfect pitch or music lessons. Thousands of people sing great, with well-trained voices. The ones that have character in their voices are rare. Fucked-up voices with a ton of character—that's my idea of a great voice."

The human voice at the far end of its register; the vocal instrument under stress; vocal chords vibrating in an unconventional way; voices modulated through technology; voices joining together in harmony or dissonance: These are just some of the ways that pop music has taken voices to the extremes. High voices like the dizzying whistle-tone reach of Mariah Carey, low voices like the basso profundo depths of Barry White or Johnny Cash, screeching voices like AC/DC's Brian Johnson or Guns N' Roses' Axl Rose, the feline strangeness of Eartha Kitt. These voices, as different as they are, share a common distance from pop's norm. Every generation has its vocal standards, voices that are appealing though not necessarily distinctive. But the signature voices of any era are usually the weird ones.

WEIRD VOICES

Consider the case of Joanna Newsom, the indie-folk singer and harpist whose voice prompts such strong visceral responses that it would seem more is at stake than her singing. In 2010 *Vanity Fair* published an article provocatively titled "The Virile Man's Guide to Liking Joanna Newsom." The article was staged as a debate between the journalist Bill Bradley, who thinks that Newsom sings "like a teething infant," and the design-magazine editor, "manly man," and avowed Newsom fan Andrew Wagner. Though Wagner is putatively there to defend Newsom's voice and music—and to give other men license to listen—the article soon devolves into a series of sardonic jibes against Newsom from both sides. "What's with that voice?" Bradley asks. "I've heard the voice described as everything from a 'dying cat' to a 'prepubescent teen whining about the mall,'" Wagner responds. "Both seem apt descriptors. . . . But it is different. It is unique. And in my book, that's worth something." Finally, Wagner's defense of Newsom is that she's weird, and that weird sounds interesting. It's hard to imagine a similar article, playfully intended or not, being written about a male singer—say, the equally strange Tom Waits. This particular brand of dismissal and derision is reserved for women's voices whose "shrillness" and "caterwauling" provide no easy defense.

Listening to others listening to Newsom's voice, one encounters an unresolvable tension: To some ears her voice is precious and affected, to others it is mystical and ethereal. Her voice is in part conditioned by her song craft, its stylized registers of diction, its imbedded rhythms and rhymes drawn from as far back as medieval times. Her voice is also an audible record of a body in pain and recovery, bearing scars of the injury that prompted her 2009 surgery to remove vocal nodules threatening to silence her singing for good. Her voice is equally an instrument in evolution, the product of conscious craft and cultivated control that one can hear in progress from her earliest recordings to now. Newsom herself is perhaps her own best critic. "When I listen back to those first EP's, I'm like, well, that voice does sound fucking crazy," she remarks. "There is no way around it. But I know exactly what space I was in. I was so sure that I didn't know how to sing that I was just going balls out. I was like: I am going to sing my heart out, as crazy as it sounds, and I'm not going to care because there's no hope of sounding anything like what people consider beautiful. I sure as hell wasn't affecting anything. I mean, the institution of singing is inherently an affectation!"

Maybe the best way to write about Newsom's voice is not to describe its sound at all, but rather to chart its history and record its effects on us. Try writing about Newsom's voice without using adjectives and adverbs. Try writing about it without comparing it to another sound or another singer only to resort to using adjectives and adverbs again to mark the difference.

What happens when we confront Newsom's voice on its own terms? On "The Book of Right-On" from Newsom's 2004 full-length debut, *The Milk-Eyed Mender*, Newsom's voice pushes to the forefront of the song, separating itself from the minimalist accompaniment of her plucked harp strings. Newsom's enunciation leaves no avenue for listeners to evade the lyrics' strangeness and indeterminacy: "I killed my dinner with karate/Kick 'em in the face, taste the body." What's weird about these lines isn't so much the voice as what the voice elects to utter. Elsewhere, Newsom's singing plays along with her playful language. She luxuriates in alliteration with a rapper's sense of wordplay: "My fighting fame is fabled/And fortune finds me fit and able." In rhyme, Newsom's voice subverts the simplicity of a particular pairing; "And you do say that you do pray" becomes "And you do say, oh-oh, that you do puh-ray." This voice is in control of itself and also in control of the singer's song craft. Like it or not, it's a voice one can't help but hear.

Weird voices are born, as in the case of Rod Stewart or Newsom, whose voice has launched a thousand think pieces and Reddit rants. They may also be consciously cultivated, as with singers who stretch their upper register into falsetto (like Prince) or those who harmonize with others to produce a voice that is both theirs and someone else's (like the Mamas and the Papas). Weird voices may also be produced, as is the case with artists who use talk boxes, vocoders, Auto-Tune, and other production tools to make their voices sound strange (like T-Pain and Daft Punk and Peter Frampton and even Neil Young, who used the vocoder liberally on his 1982 album, *Trans*). In many of these cases, both the natural and cultured varieties of weird voices achieve a capacity for expression that matches or exceeds that of some of the most gifted singers alive.

This expressive capacity was not always able to reach listeners. When the voices of professional singers first started entering homes through the phonograph and the radio, singers were bombastic shouters. They had to be. Recording technology forced singers to shout to have their voice clearly heard. Add to that the vocal training many of these singers had in vaudeville or on Broadway, and it stands to reason that projection and amplification would be the defining qualities of the voice. With the advent of more-sensitive recording technology, it became possible for singers to modulate. The result was that one could hear on record a greater sense of dynamics in a performance, a greater emotionality, and often a greater intimacy. "Performers adapted to this new technology," explains David Byrne in his book *How Music Works*. "The microphones that recorded singers changed the way they sang and the way their instruments were played. . . . Chet Baker even sang in a whisper, as did João Gilberto, and millions followed. To a listener, these guys are whispering like a lover, right into your ear, getting completely inside your head. Music had never been experienced that way before. Needless to say, without microphones this intimacy wouldn't have been heard at all." In modern production, the choice of microphone is no small matter, with artists and sound engineers favoring particular models and compressors to achieve desired vocal effects.

With the modernization of the recording studio, the distance between the voice in live performance and the recorded voice began to grow. Techniques like overdubbing, multitracking, and punching in enabled artists to duet with themselves, construct a vocal recording that the demands of human breath would not allow in live performance, or stitch a song together from dozens of different takes. The singer-songwriter Shawn Colvin recalls her early studio sessions in which she would work with her producer to assemble a vocal from multiple micro-sonic parts. "I would sometimes comp the vocal, not line by line, not even word by word, but syllable by syllable," she reveals. "Today I would rather chew tinfoil than go to that trouble. If you really can sing, there isn't the need for that kind of microscopic attention, but back then, forget it. I was a total control freak about the singing."

Some see this kind of recording studio work as a bit too Frankenstein's monster. "Recording technology had advanced to the point where studio trickery could enhance a mediocre voice," writes country star Shania Twain. "Just multitracking the lead vocal can lend heft to an otherwise thin set of pipes. An even bigger breakthrough, if you want to call it that, has been the advent of Auto-Tune, an audio pitch corrector that absolves artists of having to sing on key. Too sharp? Too flat? No problem! If you ask me, it seems a bit like cheating."

Cheating or not, studio technology can craft a powerful performance that could not be achieved otherwise. Sam Smith's "Stay with Me" seems straightforward enough; we hear a remarkable lead singer, and a gospel choir coming in on the chorus. The choir, however, is comprised entirely of Smith's own voice layered over itself. The soul singer D'Angelo's self-harmonizing achieves a sublime state that can't quite be replicated in concert. Sasha Frere-Jones, reviewing D'Angelo's 2014 album, *Black Messiah*, in the *New Yorker*, observed in a potent parenthetical: "(D'Angelo harmonizing with himself is one of the most acute pleasures available.)"

Self-harmonizing is often born of necessity, be it practical or aesthetic. John Fogerty recalls that during the 1968 recording session for Creedence Clearwater Revival's "Proud Mary," he couldn't get the band to harmonize the way he wanted on the chorus. "The 'Rollin', rollin', rollin' on the river' has to explode. You don't just go 'Rollin', rollin', rollin': it's 'RRRROllin', RRRROllin', RRRROllin'.' You're slurring up to the note real quick, and your vocal energy happens all at once. You have to explode," he recalls. After multiple takes, the band just couldn't achieve that explosive harmonic effect, so Fogerty sent the rest of the guys out to get a bite to eat while he overdubbed all the vocal parts himself. Listening to the original studio recording now, it's hard to imagine the chorus sounding otherwise. The self-harmonizing adds texture to Fogerty's unmistakable voice, the sandpaper sweetness of his tone and timbre. And it does explode. Because the vocal tones we hear are made of the same elemental stuff, we experience the harmonizing less as a coming together than as a bursting apart—a beautiful atomization of a singular voice.

Modern recording technology supports the idea that recordings can achieve perfection. For instance, Auto-Tune's developers touted its capacity to bring voices closer to a generic ideal. Pitch correction would eliminate flaws, revealing the true nature of the performance and its emotional expression. Though this makes good sense from a technical perspective, it misunderstands the impetus of art. It wasn't long before creative producers and artists put Auto-Tune to work in a way that its developers never intended, using it to bend the voice toward stylized imperfection. As is now well known, the producers of Cher's 1998 career-reviving hit "Believe" used Auto-Tune with the threshold turned to zero to produce a vocal quality that captures the mechanized appeal of the vocoder without denaturing the voice as completely as vocoders do. The warbling, digitized extremes of the voice blend with the more familiar register of the natural voice to birth a hybridized sound. Over the next several years, this conscious misuse of Auto-Tune could be heard on a few tracks here and there, mostly in the realm of the emerging genre of electronic dance music.

Auto-Tune would find its greatest expositor in a rapper turned singer from Tallahassee, Florida. T-Pain is a capable singer, something he displayed during an unassisted vocal performance at the NPR Tiny Desk Concert in 2012 and in an impressive rendition of "The Star-Spangled Banner" before a Dodgers game in 2015. But his true calling is in understanding how to use the technical loophole of Auto-Tune as an instrument for the voice. Whereas many would simply apply the Auto-Tune settings after the singer had recorded the song, T-Pain's innovation was in actually singing directly in Auto-Tune, wresting yet more artistic autonomy from the whims of the pitch correction software. Singing in Auto-Tune allowed T-Pain more precise control of his voice. The resulting sound lent unexpected poignancy to subject matter as seemingly vapid as being in love with a stripper or flirting with a bartender who "made us drinks, to drink / We drunk 'em, got drunk."

As a technique for vocal manipulation, Auto-Tune is only as good as the artist using it. Jay Z's "D.O.A. (Death of Auto-Tune)" called out those pretenders, but did little to detract later adopters. The most eager of these emerged from so-called urban music, which is to say black music. But it is instructive to consider also what happens when Auto-Tune takes root, if fleetingly, in other genres. Imogen Heap, a vaunted experimentalist, makes use of it, as does Justin Vernon of Bon Iver on a song called "Woods," which would inspire Kanye West's "Lost in the World." On *808s & Heartbreak* West embraced Auto-Tune in part because he knew that he was not a professional singer, and in part because he knew that he could manipulate the digital tools to make his voice deeply affecting. Though Kanye's efforts through Auto-Tune inspired some of his worst reviews upon the album's release, the album has since settled into a place of critical esteem because the weirding of his voice helped him to achieve musical and emotive effects that his natural voice could never achieve on its own.

On 2013's *Yeezus* Kanye returns to Auto-Tune for one of the album's finest tracks, "Blood on the Leaves." Writing for *The Talkhouse*, Lou Reed calls attention to the vocal play at work on the recording: "The juxtaposition of vocal tones on 'Blood on the Leaves' is incredible—that pitched-up sample of Nina Simone singing 'Strange Fruit' doing a call-and-response with Kanye's very relaxed Autotuned voice. That is fascinating, aurally, nothing short of spectacular. And holy shit, it's so gorgeous rhythmically, where sometimes the vocal parts are matched and sometimes they clash." Kanye uses Auto-Tune again on 2016's *The Life of Pablo*, scattering it throughout the album as a kind of sonic seasoning.

Perhaps the apotheosis of Auto-Tune, though, has come through the work of the Atlanta-based rapper Future. Future's approach to the technology departs from that of both Kanye and T-Pain in that he does not use it primarily to enhance specific melodic shapes in singing. "I don't think Future gets the technology very well. I don't think he understands how it actually works," T-Pain said during a 2013 interview. "I think he's thinking that you just turn it on, and then it just happens." Indeed, one hears a certain leveling of affect in most of Future's work, a laconic sound akin to the state of mind brought on by the codeine, Ativan, and Xanax that Future so often references in his lyrics. Whereas T-Pain and Kanye both use Auto-Tune as a tool for singing, Future uses it decidedly as a tool for rapping. He uses it, in other words, to underscore his voice as an instrument of percussion, using the warbling effects brought on by his Auto-Tune manipulation to fashion moments of striking emotional vulnerability—not in spite of the robotic nature of his voice but because of it. "Future's voice is often likened to an android, but his music is too messy and bloody and soulful for that," writes the scholar and critic Jack Hamilton. Instead, Hamilton continues, Future "take[s] the post-human and make[s] it human."

This humanizing quality is audible throughout Future's masterful third studio album, 2015's *DS2*. On the final verse of "Fuck Up Some Commas," for instance, Future delivers a barrage of stuttered syllables that settle into longer phrases of greater semantic sense in subsequent bars. The section of the song highlights Future's divergence from T-Pain and others whose approach to Auto-Tune relies on its capacity to adorn extended vocal passages of melisma and other shifts in tone that allow the technology to work in the spaces between the notes—the greater the distance, the more striking the effect. By contrast, Future collapses that distance and instead generally confines his voice to a tight tonal space, punctuated sparingly but affectingly by vocal leaps that ensure his listener is always aware that a cry or moan can sometimes cut through the haze.

Modified voices often leverage their strangeness to achieve striking emotional effects. Consider Daft Punk's *Random Access Memories*, which includes the song "Game of Love." The lead vocal is so compressed and modified that one might think that it would be an inapposite vessel for communicating profound feeling. Do robots have feelings too? In fact, the aridity of the vocal clarifies the emotional meaning of the song, pushing the high notes of pain past the normal register of the human voice and making the song's feeling legible. The computerized voice finds an unexpected and direct point of entry into a romantic situation and a romantic lyric that might have come across as clichéd if delivered by even the most sublime natural voice.

This same capacity for emotional connection is apparent in Roger Troutman's work as Zapp & Roger. "Computer Love" demonstrates that there is something powerful in juxtaposing the soulful natural voice of a singer in the raw with the augmented tones and superhuman vocal range that the vocoder can conjure. Working back and forth, an otherwise paint-by-numbers lyric becomes something irresistible, sexy, quirky, and strange. "In the beginning there was feedback: the machines speaking on their own, answering their supposed masters with shrieks of misalliance," writes Lester Bangs in his essay on the German electronic music innovators Kraftwerk, the first group to popularize the vocoder. "Gradually the humans learned to control the feedback, or thought they did, and the next step was the introduction of more highly refined forms of distortion and artificial sound, in the form of the synthesizer, which the human beings sought also to control," Bangs continues. "In the music of Kraftwerk, and bands like them present and to come, we see at last the fitting culmination of this revolution, as the machines not merely overpower and play the human beings but absorb them, until the scientist and his technology, having developed a higher consciousness of its own, are one and the same." These vocal effects can serve a range of aims. "We used computer-altered vocals more and more," recalls George Clinton of Parliament's trailblazing forays into sonic manipulation of voice, "throwing in shit that no one else was doing in pop records. At one point you can hear me, in a squeaky voice, call someone a fat motherfucker."

Voices are sometimes rendered weird by circumstance, too. Because voice is body, it is physically vulnerable. Whether ravaged by drink and drugs, strained through overuse or improper technique, or eroded by age or injury, pop voices testify to the enduring power of imperfect vocal instruments. The soul legend Curtis Mayfield once admitted that he had a "soft, little voice." At its peak in the 1970s, Mayfield's voice was a cool and controlled instrument, capable of capturing great intimacy and subtle power. On "Pusherman" he edges his natural tenor into a falsetto register that communicates the sly and even sinister seduction of the character he is portraying.

Now hear his voice a quarter century later, as he recorded his final album, 1997's *New World Order*, lying flat, the only position that allowed his lungs enough breath to sing after he was rendered paraplegic by a 1990 stage accident. Imagine Mayfield, a gifted guitarist whose voice and instrument would often entwine, rendered incapable of playing and reduced to parsing out lyrics in labored fragments. Writing on the Poetry Foundation's *Harriet* blog, the poet and critic Fred Moten observed that "Curtis Mayfield recorded

New World Order flat on his back, phrase by phrase, crumb by crumb, singing in the absence of his voice, his guitar, which was in his hands, which he couldn't move. You have to know all that to really understand how deep certain shit is: 'Now is always the right time / To put something positive in your mind' or 'If there's ever something bad you don't wanna see / Just keep on walkin' and let it be.'" Mayfield's voice on these late recordings carries only some of the resonance and clarity of his 1960s and 1970s classics like "People Get Ready" and "Move On Up." The high falsetto is gone. Instead, one hears his aspirations reaching past the limits of his vocal instrument, creating beauty in limitation.

Ozzy Osbourne suffered his own crisis of voice, brought on not by accident but by overindulgence; as he plainly put it, "the coke was fucking up my voice, good and proper." In a mock-medical account from his memoir, he describes the physical effects his cocaine use had on his vocal instrument.

> When you're taking heavy-duty amounts of cocaine, this white gunk starts to trickle down the back of your throat, and you find yourself doing that phlegm-clearing thing all the time—like a sniff, but deeper and gunkier. And that puts a lot of stress on that little titty thing that hangs down at the back of your throat—the epiglottis, or the "clack," as I've always called it. Anyway, I was taking so much coke that I was clearing away the phlegm every couple of minutes, until eventually I tore my clack in half. I was lying in bed at the time in the Sunset Marquis hotel, and I just felt it flop down inside the back of my throat. It was horrific. Then the fucking thing swelled up to the size of a golf ball. I thought: Right, this is it—I'm gonna die now.

Ozzy's voice healed, though his physician did have to cut out his "clack." As different as they are, Mayfield's and Osbourne's respective vocal challenges, brought on by crises of the body, attest to the resilience and capacity of voices under pressure, voices that find a way to continue even if they never quite recover.

HEARING RACE, HEARING GENDER

Voices communicate a great deal about singers—or, perhaps more precisely, listeners impute a great deal about singers based on their voices. We make assumptions about gender, race, age, and place of origin on little more than the evidence of a few bars. "There is no voice without a body," writes Mladen

Dolar, "but yet again this relation is full of pitfalls: it seems that the voice pertains to the wrong body, or doesn't fit the body at all, or disjoints the body from which it emanates." What's more compelling than assigning race, therefore, is examining the pitfalls: the moments of confusion and complexity surrounding voice and the body from which it derives and the ways that voice generally outstrips our analytical capacities to categorize it, generating moments of surprise, reversal, and discovery.

I play a game in my undergraduate courses that I call Black, White, or Prince? The premise is simple: I play half a dozen snippets of songs and have students vote by show of hands whether the person singing is black, white, or, well, Prince. I might start by playing thirty seconds from a well-known artist for whom coding a racial identity will be easy—say, Taylor Swift singing "Blank Space." If I'm in a devious mood, I might select a well-known artist whose racial identity and the racialized assumptions about the style of their singing differ—say, Adele at her most melismatic and soul-inspired. In both cases, almost all the students will vote for white, but they'll be voting on their familiarity with the artist's image, not by the evidence of their ears.

Then the challenge really begins. I'll dig deeper into the pop songbook to decrease the chance that the students will be familiar with the singers and the songs. I might play the Ink Spots, with their clipped articulation and close harmonies that don't accord with stereotypically black performance practices. Or I might play the white soul singer Bobby Caldwell's classic "What You Won't Do for Love" followed by a song by Charley Pride, the great African American country singer. The students soon see that racial categorization of singing voices has more to do with expectations of genre than it does with the actual identities of the singers. The exercise culminates in a discussion of Prince, who refutes essentialist theories of race through his chameleonic musical style as well as through his proudly black yet multiracial self.

The exercise is, of course, reductive; it consciously traffics in stereotype. It is, in other words, problematic with a purpose: to mirror our culture's limited vocabulary of racialized labels so as to show how they fail to account for the reality of racial diversity, multiracial identity, and the mutability of voice. (I could imagine doing another such exercise focused on the illegibility of gender in voice—call it Male, Female, or Prince?) I want my students to draw on their assumptions about genre and the racialization of voice. Ultimately, though, I want them to acknowledge and to interrogate those assumptions.

The inspiration for my exercise comes from "blindfold" tests for instrumental jazz music. Starting in the 1950s the jazz music critic Leonard Feather wrote a column for *Down Beat Magazine* in which he conducted blindfold tests with famous musicians. The trumpeter Roy Eldridge, an African American, defiantly asserted that he could always distinguish a black musician from a white one—and these were instrumentalists, not vocalists. Feather dropped the needle onto the record without revealing anything about the tune and asked Eldridge a simple question: "Is the artist black or white?" More than half the time, Eldridge was wrong. Most of us want legibility when it comes to the race and gender of the voice we hear. Uncertainty is unnerving. When it comes to voice, though, race and gender are often far from clear.

In this moment when society at large is finally beginning to catch up to the reality that race is a social construct with little grounding in biology, one must nonetheless guard against the false assumption that race should not remain a part of our social and cultural discourse. When it comes to the everyday experience of most Americans, race is a very real thing tethered to phenotypic markers as well as to cultural styles and practices. It is also grounded in voice. "The historical concept that black people sang one way and white people sang in a fundamentally different way emerged out of the shift from minstrel authenticity to folkloric authenticity that defined the musical color line. The sonic evidence suggests a much more complicated story," writes Karl Hagstrom Miller in *Segregating Sound*.

This more-complicated story takes us back and forth across the color line, and to the many spaces in between. It underscores Ralph Ellison's claim that in the United States the melting pot has already melted when it comes to culture: "It is here," Ellison writes, "on the level of culture, that the diverse elements of our various backgrounds, our heterogeneous pasts, have indeed come together, 'melted' and undergone metamorphosis. It is here, if we would but recognize it, that elements of the many available tastes, traditions, ways of life, and values that make up the total culture have been ceaselessly appropriated and made their own—consciously, unselfconsciously, or imperialistically—by groups and individuals to whose own backgrounds and traditions they are historically alien." Notwithstanding the purity or impurity of the motivation, the cultural impulse to adapt and to appropriate is inherent to the American cultural milieu.

Singing voices make the matter of adaptation and appropriation audible. When Creedence Clearwater Revival emerged on the music scene in the 1960s, most listeners assumed they were a southern group and, though not black, certainly influenced by African American music. The group's name, their lyric themes, most explicitly rendered in songs like "Born on the Bayou," and their downhome musical style all evoke the South. Most of all, though, it was John Fogerty's voice that signaled something about region and, perhaps, also something about race. As it turned out, Fogerty and his band—which included his brother, Tom, along with Stu Cook and Doug Clifford—were California boys.

In his memoir Fogerty traces his southern vocal sound and lyric themes not to his direct experience but to an affinity of sound and style. "People would listen to my songs and ask, 'Where does this come from?' I had trouble explaining that," Fogerty writes. "I hadn't been to Mississippi when I wrote 'Proud Mary,' nor had I been to Louisiana when I wrote 'Born on the Bayou.' Somehow it all just seemed familiar to me. Still does." Certainly, Fogerty was listening to southern artists, particularly black blues artists. He was reading southern Gothic fiction. The southern landscape offered a more evocative space for his imagination than did the surroundings of his central California birthplace. It's one thing for an individual artist to seek out this freedom of imaginative movement, this expressive range found in voice. It's quite another, though, for an audience to experience that voice as authentic—even more authentically characteristic of a place and a people than the people who actually reside in the place itself. Fogerty's goal was something more particular and more humble than attempting to be something he was not; Fogerty's goal was expressive freedom. Its by-product in audience perception, though, is where complications occur.

The fact that Fogerty was appropriating the sound of a region more than a race might explain why he avoided some of the controversy that has surrounded white artists affecting black sounds. The conscious crafting of Steven Tyler's voice over the course of Aerosmith's early albums offers a useful model for considering the racial appropriation that some hear at play in many artists today. Tyler found his voice somewhere between Aerosmith's first and third albums. By then, they had already recorded one of the band's best-known songs, "Dream On." But something strange and inexplicable happened around 1973 or 1974. The Steven Tyler we now know was born. Of course, someone named "Steven Tyler" is credited as the lead singer on Aerosmith's first three albums, but it wasn't Steven Tyler. It couldn't be. The voice is too pretty, too perfect, and at the same time too plain. It has little of the rasp and growl and howl and break that are the defining qualities of the voice we would come to know on "Walk This Way" and "Love in an Elevator."

"Yes, I changed my voice when we did the final vocals," Tyler reveals, thinking back on his early recordings. "I didn't like my voice, the way it sounded. I was insecure, but nobody told me not to do it. I thought I didn't sound right on tape. To me, it sounded like a neutered or *castrato* voice and I wanted to sound a little bit black because I was from Yonkers and back then James Brown and Sly Stone were the only ones saying anything in music, so I put that shit on. . . . I used this voice for 'One Way Street' and all of that stuff except 'Dream On.' 'Dream On' is the real me."

The band's guitarist, Joe Perry, reflects on those early sessions and on Tyler's vocal affect. "His insecurity was forcing him into a different persona. He overdid it and, compared to his natural singing voice, his voice on the record sounded affected." Tyler would finally admit as much; he was affecting— or trying to affect (I don't really hear it)—blackness in his voice. According to Tyler, "I used an exaggerated black-speak voice on all the tracks except 'Dream On.' I thought it was really cool. The only problem was, nobody knew it was me. 'Ah say-ng lak dis' because I didn't like my voice and it was early on and I wanted to put on a little. To this day, some people still come up to me and ask, 'Who's that singin' on the first album?' I was into James Brown and Sly Stone and just wanted to sound more R&B."

Such racial masking comes into play with other vocal artists. Does Iggy Azalea sound like a black American woman from the South or does she sound like the white Australian woman she is awkwardly affecting the tone and cadence of certain black American women, from the South and the North, who have rapped before her? What matters more—the fact that she's making her voice something other than it is or the fact that she's bad at rapping? "I just want her to stop doing that crazy voice," the Brooklyn-based MC Jean Grae told *Playboy* in 2015. "I have no problem saying this: I feel like it's really fucking offensive. I'm offended. Is that what I'm supposed to sound like? What are you doing? I call it 'verbal blackface.'"

For her part, Iggy Azalea defended her right to self-fashioning. "I think it's really important we all feel free to explore or feel passionate about what-ever u wish. Be as complex and multidimensional and interesting as you possibly can," she tweeted in early 2015 in response to criticisms about her "verbal blackface" from two other black women artists, the rapper Eve and the R&B singer Jill Scott. Azalea was even more to the point speaking to *Complex* two years earlier. "I don't think the voice makes me fake," she said. "It makes me an artist. Voice is my medium. I should have creative rein to do whatever the fuck I want with it."

Most of the debates about Iggy Azalea have centered on the subject of cultural appropriation. But what about the question of cultural *impersonation*? In his defining essay on cultural masking, "Authenticity, or The Lessons of Little Tree," Henry Louis Gates Jr. observes that rendering race and culture in art is always a learned practice, an exercise of craft rather than a simple expression of self. "So it is not just a matter of the outsider boning up while the genuine article just writes what he or she knows. . . . The distasteful truth is that like it or not, all writers are 'cultural impersonators,'" Gates writes. This holds even more powerfully in singers, where listeners encounter performers in the physical instrument of the singing voice, the stylistic markers of musical genre, and the content of the lyrics. The mastery of vocal style is always an act of artifice; it's only a matter of how great a distance singers must bridge and how effective their impersonations are in achieving the style.

When Justin Timberlake left the boy band *NSYNC to go solo, he chose to make R&B. The Timberlake of the frosted tips and choreographed group dance steps seemed ill fitted for a new identity as a modern-day soul man. His Memphis roots, his early introduction to the music of soul singers like Al Green, and his mastery of soul forms tell a more complex truth. Of course, we notice that he is white—and that matters. What matters as well is the humility and respect with which he engages with a historically black genre. Timberlake collaborated closely with the hip-hop and R&B production duo the Neptunes on his 2002 solo debut, *Justified*, then with Timbaland on 2006's *FutureSex/LoveSounds* and 2013's *The 20/20 Experience*. All three albums were very much of their moments, drawing heavily from the popular currents of black American music, and distinctly Timberlake in their savvy self-awareness and sly humor. One doesn't so much get the sense that he's a white man trying to sing black as much as he is a white man finding his own way to celebrate the legacy of black music.

Timberlake's whiteness takes on another significance, though, when his music is packaged and sold for profit. How much of his albums' massive success could be accounted for by the fact that he was giving white listeners the music and style they wanted without asking them to cross the color line? African American critics sounded the alarm in 2013 when, for the first time in the history of the *Billboard* Hot 100 chart, not a single black lead artist reached the number-one spot. During this time, however, many voices that might be coded as black, through style or texture, enjoyed commercial success. Could it be, as Marc Lamont Hill claimed, that "white people are the only ones selling black music"?

A more measured response might question economic practices that reward white "impersonators" of black voices. "There's a sonic preference for blackness—the sounds of blackness—but there's a visual preference for whiteness in our culture, and a human preference for whiteness," argues Princeton professor Imani Perry. "So there's always going to be an advantage for white artists who are able to occupy the spaces of black sound. I think that's something that goes to audiences, but also to record companies, which recognize how deeply racist or racially preferentialist our society is and are trying to make money exploiting that. So for me what becomes incumbent upon the artist is acknowledgement . . . but also increasing opportunities for those whose cultural forms they borrow or are influenced by." Following Perry's formulation, the businesses that profit from the tastes of audiences that long for black sound without black people are primarily responsible for the inequities in our musical culture. At the same time, it is also contingent upon those white artists who benefit from the disparities to cultivate consciousness and create opportunities for black artists whom the system does not reward.

How is Timberlake supposed to acknowledge his debt other than by doing what he does: by making music that wears its influences with pride, by employing talented black artists and producers, and by taking the traditions seriously enough to excel at them? One quickly runs up against the absurdity, as well as the impossibility, of enforcing racialized boundaries of voice. Consider Prince again, the pint-sized powerhouse with a complex racial lineage. Though he is far-ranging in his styles and his fusions of genres, he is generally associated with black music. Enforcing racial orthodoxy in our reception of voice demands a dangerous purity, one that the realities of pop performance vociferously resist. Much of this extends, as well, to matters of gender.

It's the fourth season of NBC's popular singing contest, *The Voice*, and a young African American singer takes the stage during the blind auditions to perform a song made famous by Whitney Houston. Several aspiring divas have done the same over the course of the show's run. In this case the singer is a man. The contestant begins to sing "Saving All My Love for You" in a crystal-clear falsetto. Only the studio audience and the viewing public can see the young man as he sings. The judges' backs are turned so that they will evaluate the artist on voice alone. Their chairs will spin around only if they push their buttons to invite the singer onto their teams.

Perhaps because, as a television viewer, I see this voice come out of the male singer's body, the vocal register, although high, seems unmistakably masculine to me. The judges, however, seem perplexed, not turning their chairs though the voice is thrilling, nearly flawless. Finally, the only woman on the judging panel, the Colombian pop star Shakira, turns her chair and evinces no surprise to find that it is a man singing in falsetto. The song comes to a close with the other judges exchanging glances, hands hovering over their buzzers, but never turning their chairs. What kept them from buzzing in? It surely wasn't the quality of performance; far inferior singers had already been selected. It must have been the difficulty the male judges had envisioning a singer to match the androgyny in the vocal timbre and tone of the voice.

After the singer is finished, all the chairs turn toward him and the three male judges—Adam Levine, Usher, and Blake Shelton—appear genuinely shocked to discover that the singer is a young man. "I wish I knew you were a guy!" Levine implores. Then, affecting a deep baritone, Usher says, "You should at least have thrown in a 'This is for you, girl!'" After the singer leaves the stage, Usher, still shaking his head, says to Shakira: "You'll be able to do things with him that defy gravity because of how high he can go. And women go crazy for a guy with a falsetto."

We could spend a long time unpacking the inborn and acculturated biases and expectations wrapped up in this brief exchange. But to focus on the voice, what's important is this: Male falsetto has never been as simple as guys trying to sound like girls. Indeed, a male singing falsetto rarely sounds like a woman at all. As Walter Everett puts it, "Falsetto itself represents another manner of tonal inconsistency, as it strips away the lower tones from a vocal product, leaving only the highest remnants. Somewhat like a flute because it's almost a pure tone with few harmonics—and never attaining that head-tone ring produced by the perfectly focused lock of overtones sought by the operatic singer—the very high and exceedingly light falsetto voice is created by the complete relaxation of one of the two main sets of voice-related muscles." Falsetto relies on taking something away from the voice (the richness of overtones), and giving something back (the effort and strain that it enacts, even if the voice comes easy to the singer).

Falsetto embodies a sense of play with the possibilities of the human voice. It's doing something unexpected. Falsetto can communicate queerness, as with the disco singer Sylvester, or a certain swaggering heterosexuality, as with Al Green, or something else entirely, as with Prince. There's a power, too, that comes with a voice singing just beyond its comfortable capacity, reaching in a way that reveals the labor involved. Sometimes a singer with a limited vocal range can achieve emotive effects by virtue of the agon that a weak voice communicates when reaching beyond its limits. "In the kinesthetic sensorium," writes Timothy E. Scheurer in his study of American musical performance, "the high-pitched note for which the jazz trumpeter or bluegrass singer has exchanged his soul moves us toward a point at the center of experience, a point without dimensions and therefore out of time that organizes attention and sharply resolves the will." Voices pushing at the boundaries of their range bring them closer to us, closer to our own drive-time efforts. Falsetto therefore shows the fallibility of the voice, a fallibility that's always there, even with great voices.

Of course, not all falsetto is created equal. Mick Jagger's straining shouts at the end of "Sympathy for the Devil" are far removed from Prince's perfectly controlled falsetto tone throughout "If I Was Your Girlfriend." Jagger is pushing beyond his range, and the tensions and imperfections one hears in his voice are a conscious stylization befitting the close of a song sung in the voice of Satan. All the music around him is fraying as his voice frays, giving way to chaos and confusion. By contrast, Prince's voiced seduction is limpid, effortless. One can imagine him singing like this forever.

The voice at play across the spectrum of gendered sounds is a source of fascination. Janet Jackson's "Love Will Never Do (Without You)," for instance, was an act of vocal reinvention. As she had done seven years earlier with *Control*, Jackson was looking to reboot her career and redefine herself as an artist. In 1987, that meant differentiating herself from her family and from the transcendent sound of her far more famous older brother Michael. With "Love Will Never Do (Without You)," Janet embraced her sexuality and strength. Along with the Herb Ritz–directed video, which showed her cavorting on the beach with then-unknown Djimon Honsu and Antonio Sabado Jr., the sound, grounded in image, called attention to her curves and the sensuality of her movement.

"Love Will Never Do" is most striking, though, for its play with voice. It is essentially a duet between Jackson and herself. She sings the first verse an octave lower than her natural singing voice, then raises her voice an octave to the upper register that we are more accustomed to hearing on songs like "The Pleasure Principle" and, later, "Escapade."

What's striking about this performance is that it demonstrates a sonic range for which Jackson is not known. The verse acts as a kind of sonic drag, with Jackson approximating the sound of male tenor crooners of the moment like Ralph Tresvant, Bobby Brown, or even her brother Michael. As a young fan, I was fooled, thinking that the first voice was a man. It reminds me of what Stevie Wonder does on "You Are the Sunshine of My Life" when Jim Gilstrap sings the first two lines of the song, Lani Groves sings the next two lines, then Wonder takes over for the remainder of the song, bending gender and embracing vocal androgyny. It is as if we are hearing the disaggregation and the reaggregation of the parts of Wonder's voice—the high, the low, the wonder of it all.

THE ENDS OF VOICE

Voices moan and scream and cry and laugh and emit any number of sounds that do not follow a clear semantic logic and can't be readily described as speaking, rapping, or singing. These, too, are expressions of the voice, and even when not using words the voice bends toward meaning. "What singles out the voice against the vast ocean of sounds and noises, what defines the voice as special among the infinite array of acoustic phenomena, is its inner relationship with meaning," writes Mladen Dolar. "The voice is something which points toward meaning, it is as if there is an arrow in it which raises the expectation of meaning, the voice is an opening toward meaning." In song, this connection is amplified. "In human song the voice carries speech," Adriana Cavarero explains. "Even when it renders speech incomprehensible or breaks down its syllabic texture, the voice still carries speech and recognizes in it its essential destination." Whereas in speech the voice serves essentially as a conduit for meaning, the voice in song calls attention to the voice itself, the voice as sound beyond sense even as it acts in the service of sense.

Pop music has long been a fertile territory for the scream, the moan, the ad-libbed utterance. "When I heard Janis Joplin at first I thought she was screaming, and then I realized that she was emoting, using her voice in a different way than anyone had. I started to zero in on where those melodies were coming from," observes the singer-songwriter LP, whose compositions for Rihanna and Christina Aguilera balance mainstream appeal with her distinctive sensibilities. Screams can communicate meaning powerfully, particularly on the level of feeling.

This communicability of language in song can be put to the test. One afternoon in the spring of 2015, I was teaching my graduate seminar on the poetics of American song lyrics. A trio of students was presenting that day on the subject of voice in song. The group began by playing Diamanda Galas's arresting and unnerving 1988 live rendition of "Swing Low, Sweet Chariot." They played the three-minute song without introduction or comment. Galas's series of searing extended tones—part song, part scream—render the words and melody nearly unrecognizable. Played at high volume in a closed seminar room on the top floor of the campus library, the performance seemed out of place, even forbidden. Watching the faces of the other students circled around the seminar table, I could see nervous smiles, shock, repulsion, and even anger. When the song came to a close and the group opened discussion, hands flew in the air to express discombobulation.

"Why? What is this?" one student asked.

"This is so annoying," another said.

After hearing the comments, the presenters filled in the song's context, explaining that it was part of a performance Galas gave to commemorate the death of her brother from AIDS; that she was performing a song freighted with meaning in the context of another suffering group, the African American slaves from whom the song originates, to communicate a present-day suffering; that Galas is a vocal performance artist whose work often pushes against the perceived constraints of song and sound, language and form. I could see that some students were gaining at least an intellectual appreciation for the song, but most remained defiant in their feelings of distaste. What was Galas doing? Why would she imagine that an audience would want to hear this?

Galas's rendition of "Swing Low, Sweet Chariot" is the perfect place to close our reassessment of the voice as sound, even beyond sense. For Galas, the discomfort her voice causes is just the point. "When I sing a note, I need to know where it is in my skull, my sternum and my diaphragm," she explains. "My performance is catharsis." In the case of this performance, the words are there, though shrouded in sonic and semantic distortion. Galas underscores Cavarero's assertion that the singing voice, no matter how distorted, recognizes speech as its essential destination.

One need not go to the avant-garde to find instances of vocal expression that distends the expected shape of communication. Such expressions exist across the musical spectrum and often find a place comfortably on the *Billboard* charts. At the height of their popularity in the 1980s, the rock band

Heart, fronted by sisters Ann and Nancy Wilson, scored their biggest hit with the multiplatinum-selling single "Alone." "Alone" is the quintessential 1980s power ballad, written by the songwriting duo of Tom Kelly and Billy Steinberg, who were responsible for other era-defining ballads like Cyndi Lauper's "True Colors" and the Bangles' "Eternal Flame."

"Alone" is a platform for heightened emotion, and Ann Wilson gets everything one can imagine out of the words, from her plaintive rendering of "How can I get you alone?" to her controlled delivery of the opening lines of the first verse. The song is a study in vocal and emotional dynamics, punctuated not in words but in an ad-libbed scream. Ann Wilson recalls that when recording the vocal, her producer, Ron Nevison, "asked me to delay a moment before singing the chorus after the second verse, and to ad-lib. I wasn't sure what to sing, so I let out a scream. It ended up being exactly the primal emotion the song needed to make it rock. I'd been singing Led Zeppelin songs for years, and now I had my own Robert Plant moment on record." The scream lasts four seconds, breaking out of the sonic atmosphere of the drums and sliding easily into the clearly enunciated language of the chorus. It is voice as instrument and body, as sense and feeling. The sound is strange, uncomfortable, and utterly familiar to anyone who's experienced lost love.

Diamanda Galas and Ann Wilson are separated by vast distances of style and aesthetic, but they are unified in their use of the voice to stretch and even to break its bonds with language in the service of emotion. "For some," Grace Slick muses, song is "the purest form of expression, for others a brief passing delight, but it exists like no other art form in every culture, in all languages, giving voice to anyone who wants to sing. And when we sing together, everyone becomes perfect for a while. But only for a while."

The end of voice might be this: the loss of voice, or rather relinquishing voice's primary motive of semantic expression in favor of its primordial communication of feeling that has no need for speech.

Chapter Eight

O ne evening in the summer of 1965, James Brown, the future Godfather of Soul, dropped by Arthur Smith's studio in Charlotte, North Carolina, on his way to a show. He had one hour to record and one song to sing, "Papa's Got a Brand New Bag." A crash of horns, a lilting guitar riff, a bubbling bass line, and the thirty-two-year-old Brown's raspy vocals came together to define the sound that Brown would continue perfecting for more than forty years. "My music—and most music—changed with 'Papa's Got a Brand New Bag,'" Brown wrote years later, and it's hard to say he's wrong. Call it soul. Call it funk. Call it the birth of one of the dominant styles of American popular music.

Something else marks this moment, a detail known only to the few in the room during the session until it was finally made public in 1991 with the release of Brown's career retrospective boxed set, *Star Time*. While recording the song's single take, just before the opening horn hit, Brown hollers out these four words: "This is a hit!"

Brown was right. "Papa's Got a Brand New Bag" ruled the R&B charts for eight consecutive weeks, and it reached number eight on the *Billboard* Hot 100, alongside Sonny & Cher's "I Got You Babe" and Petula Clark's "Downtown." The song, Brown's first top-ten pop hit, endures; *Rolling Stone* magazine ranks it number 72 on its 2004 list of the 500 greatest songs of all time, and it maintains its place in the pop cultural firmament through hip-hop samples, from Kool Moe Dee's "How Ya Like Me Now" to Tyga's "Make It Work," and even through an appearance on *The Simpsons*. "His dances, his language, his music, his style, his pioneering funk, his manner of speaking are stamped into the American consciousness," the novelist and musician James McBride writes of Brown. Though Brown was certainly famous before "Papa's Got a Brand New Bag," the song helped make him legend.

But how did Brown know it would hit? Though a successful performer on the segregated chitlin' circuit, Brown had no record of mainstream popular success at that point upon which to base such certainty. Was it something about the rhythm, the syncopated play of voice, horns, guitar, bass, and drums? "I was hearing everything, even the guitars, like they were drums," Brown reveals. "On playbacks, when I saw the speakers jumping, vibrating a certain way, I knew that was it: deliverance." Perhaps Brown's prescience was simply a lucky accident of his famously outsized ego. Maybe every time in his mind, if not out of his mouth, he'd vow that he was about to record a hit. Or maybe it had to do with that mysterious quality that encompasses lyrics, music, image, and more: the matter of style.

Style is an individual's artistic fingerprint, comprised of certain habits of performance, composition, or both. Style can describe anything from a performer's tonal quality, such as Beyoncé's vibrato or the "voice" of Eddie Van Halen's guitar, to patterns of performance nearly synonymous with genre, such as the "style" of prog rock or of trap music. "Style, of course, is everything in popular music. One wants to be in style, but one also wants to be a little ahead of the style. Ideally, one wants to create one's own style," observed Mike Stoller, the songwriter who, with his partner Jerry Lieber, helped define the style of early rock and roll by writing songs for Elvis and many others. As Stoller's description suggests, style involves both imitation and individuation, both process and product.

Stripped to its essence, style is the patterning of forms that come to define an artist, genre, or time period. Repeated elements forge an identifiable style that others can emulate, if not always replicate. Apprentice artists rely on style's legibility to master their craft and, ultimately, to forge their own identities. Appropriation and adaptation also lead to new styles, although occasionally at the expense of the original artists. In the hypercompetitive marketplace of culture, squabbles over stylistic ownership are frequent and fierce.

In the realm of craft, style is more straightforward. With sound, style includes vocal effects like falsetto or group harmony, production practices like multitracking or Auto-Tune, and myriad other elements. With lyric, style includes diction, distinctive rhyme patterns, the frequency of enjambment, the nature of imagery, and so on. Add the paramusical elements of style that affect an audience's reception of an artist—styles of dress, lifestyle, and image—and you get a sense of how multivalent style can be.

Elsewhere I've written that style is the sum of rules and creativity. I still believe this holds true, though I would add that style in pop music is never simply the result of the artist's hermetic creative process. Style is a social category as well as an aesthetic category. It is conditioned and often complicated by commerce and audience. As a consequence, style is a fluid designation that means different things at different times to different people and may mean different things at any one time as well.

Style is the primary means through which listeners experience the poetics of pop. Rarely do we listen for an isolated rhythm pattern, a particular instance of rhyme, a single simile, or even the voice alone. We experience all of these elements in aggregate, as an experience in sound. Style gives that experience a name and helps navigate the vast array of recorded music to help you find other sounds that may appeal to you as well. Studying style, therefore, is also studying those networks of connection that reside beyond any one song or any one listener, but instead define communities.

STYLE, GENRE, AND FORMAT

Style is not genre, though people often use the terms interchangeably. Genre defines a space of the given; style goes over and above the given to distinguish individual talents and sensibilities. "Genre" is a term of codification; it is a functional generalization. Though no one term can apply equally across a host of recordings, genre helps make some semblance of order out of the chaos. In contrast, "style" aspires to specificity. Even when style makes broad claims, it tethers them to small insights and small patterns that cohere the elements of a broad category.

"Style is a replication of patterning, whether in human behavior or in the artifacts produced by human behavior, that results from a series of choices made within some set of constraints," explains the composer and philosopher Leonard B. Meyer in his oft-cited formulation from "Toward a Theory of Style." Thinking of patterning within constraint driven by conscious choice is a good way of understanding how artists forge pop-musical styles. "A musical style is a finite array of interdependent melodic, rhythmic, harmonic, timbral, textural, and formal relationships and processes," explains the anthropologist Steven Feld. "When these are internalized as learned habits, listeners (including performers and composers) are able to perceive and understand a composition in the style as an intricate network of implicative relationships, or to experience the work as a complex of felt probabilities." Style, therefore, is also relational; it is not a fixed point but is always renegotiating its connection to new stylistic interventions.

Genre is defined by a number of qualities: sonic, visual, social, and commercial. These include but are not limited to the approach to vocalizing, the type and quality of instrumentation, recording and production practices, the audience's identity and expectations, and the relation a genre builds with other genres and with the broader field of popular music. Bluegrass is a genre: When one hears the word one assumes a particular kind of instrumentation (fiddle, banjo, guitar, and mandolin), certain conventions of voice (a distinctive regional accent and prominent vocal harmonies), and a certain place in the vinyl stacks of the record store. Bluegrass as a genre also includes individual style: Bill Monroe's keening tenor shares the genre with Alison Krauss' sweet soprano. For the musicologist Fabian Holt, genre is "a constellation of styles connected by a sense of tradition." This definition fuses the individual sensibilities of artists in a historicized collective of both artists and listeners, distinguishing it from shifting market-based codifications.

Finally, genre is an ahistoric reordering of the story of popular music, a way of arranging and often sanitizing the mixed and mixed-up history of music. In the United States, things are particularly complicated. "American popular music, born out of slavery and the African diaspora, out of minstrelsy and racial appropriation, was recoded in the twentieth century, outside of pop itself, as a set of genres with noble lineages and a mostly clean slate," writes Eric Weisbard. Collapsing the genres back together might be messy, but would also be truer to the history of sonic culture. Again, one is reminded of what Ralph Ellison once observed, that when it comes to culture in America "the melting pot has already melted."

The concept of musical genre is bound up with race in another way as well. Most scholars and other critically thinking people understand that genre, like race, is a fiction, an imposition on the freewheeling nature of individual styles and sounds. At the same time, as with the term "race," the term "genre" is still the common currency of everyday speech. We talk of country and rock and R&B and rap and pop as if they are clearly codified, rather than open and fluid categories. Genre is a fiction, but it is a functional fiction, one that we are not likely to relinquish anytime soon. In fact, genre categories are rapidly expanding. iTunes identifies roughly twenty genres, or twenty-six if one counts the other categories iTunes includes under genre, like "New Artists" and "Essentials." Spotify identifies thirty-two "genres and moods," and their full genre list includes 1,371 entries, from 2-step to zydeco. By the time this book is published, they'll have likely expanded beyond that.

Any analysis of style and genre in pop music must concern itself with concepts beyond the limits of the song itself. "Genre is always collective, musically and socially (a person can have his or her own style, but not genre)," Holt observes. "Conventions and expectations are established through acts of repetition performed by a group of people, and the process of genre formation is in turn often accompanied by the formation of new social collectivities." Genre is relational, both a means of social cohesion and a language of commerce. Even the idea of style, individuated and personal, is never isolated. But as we consider style and genre in the poetry of pop, it is useful temporarily to isolate them from social connections, from what Holt terms "the totality of social space." The goal is not to pretend that these matters don't exist, but to understand better how style and genre imprint themselves in lyric and sound. With that in mind, and accepting the caveat that any piece of music is likely to diverge from the neat definitions imposed on it, it is useful to begin by exploring certain identifiable styles that map roughly onto genre.

Sensing that terms like style and genre are founded on Jell-O, the radio industry—still a powerful commercial force in this era of music streaming—developed the language of format. A format, according to the sociologist Gabriel Rossman, is "radio's version of what organizational theory calls a core strategy. Formats structure radio station behavior in every way. Formats determine a demographic and psychographic target audience." As radio formats have proliferated, they have also become more clearly subdivided. "A radio field structured by format may be particularly inhospitable to music that breaks with extant genre conventions," writes Rossman.

Formats are nonetheless permeable, their integrity far from sacrosanct. On a particular week in early 2014, for instance, John Legend's "All of Me" was in heavy rotation across six different radio formats, from "Urban" to "Adult Contemporary." This kind of cross-format creep is often the case with big pop hits. Reflecting on her format-defying music, Shania Twain writes the following: "The fact that the album was categorized in pop, pop rock, and country pop was my dream: to be an international recording artist, recognized as an artist not of any specific genre, but just appreciated as an artist by all lovers of music. To not be confined meant more to me than the chart numbers, sales figures, and awards."

Radio programmers might talk about formats. The rest of us tend to talk about music. My friend Aaron, a father of two in his thirties, was surprised in a parking lot when he heard the familiar strains of Guns N' Roses' 1987 hit "Welcome to the Jungle" booming out of a teenager's car. The teen parked next to Aaron, who was unbuckling his two children from their car seats. "What do you call this type of music?" Aaron asked him, curious to find out how the kid would classify the same music that was booming out of Aaron's car when he was a teen. "Classic rock, I guess," the teen said, as he was walking away. Then he turned back and looked at Aaron with a pointed gaze. "But also *my* music."

Learning that Guns N' Roses is now classic rock probably came as a shock to Aaron. There's something even more revealing in the story: how readily the teenager took ownership over music recorded before he was born. "My music" is the most variegated conception of genre, but also probably the most practical. "Everyone has a taste biography, a narrative of shifting preferences," writes Carl Wilson. Most of us cobble together an eclectic blend of sounds that may have little in common except the fact that we like them. This was the principle behind iTunes' early 2000s innovation of the shuffle function, which allowed listeners to experience an automated mix of music drawn from their own iTunes libraries. The results, always unexpected, could be incongruous and, at times, inspired. That eclecticism runs counter to the governing philosophy behind more recent curatorial innovations, which are intended to tailor song selections to our particular tastes and to eliminate the rough transitions shuffle gave us. From the sophisticated algorithms behind Pandora to less personalized engines that attempt to match music to our moods, recent innovations in music technology follow a philosophy of similarity rather than surprise.

Neither random shuffle nor curated selection quite captures the experience common to music listeners for most of the twentieth century: buying, borrowing, or bootlegging. At times I wax nostalgic for the days when I was subject to other people's tastes, be it in the limited number of recordings my friends and I owned and shared or in the soft tyranny of commercial radio and music television programming.

When I was in college in the 1990s I often struck up friendships with the following question: What kind of music do you like? The same question was often asked of me. I understood it as an invitation, but also a gentle interrogation. Certain responses would be a welcome sign; others, a warning. Many of my relationships, both filial and romantic, started here. Most often, the answer would come back as some version of this: "I listen to everything but country." Sometimes, too, it would be "I listen to everything but rap," though the people with whom I was speaking were usually too polite or too calculating to say that to a young black man with a big pair of headphones draped around his neck, the sounds of Biggie or 2Pac or A Tribe Called Quest seeping out.

What kind of music do you like? It's a question with big implications. David Byrne reminds us that music "can make us physically well, or horribly ill. It does so many things to us that one can't simply say, as many do, 'Oh, I love all kinds of music.' Really? But some forms of music are diametrically opposed to one another! You can't love them *all*. Not all the time, anyway." I don't ask the question anymore, maybe because I know that the responses I get often have little to do with music. They have far more to do with image. It's no coincidence that the two forms of music people most often say they avoid—country and rap—are also the most seemingly segregated musical genres when it comes to race. In the introduction to *Hidden in the Mix*, the first collection of scholarly essays to address the African American presence in country music, the gender studies scholar Diane Pecknold argues that the public perception of country music as a white American idiom not only overlooks the music's African American roots, but equally, the black performers and listeners who have always been a part of the music. Similarly, recall that rap was born out of a multicultural context of black and Latino youth, as well as recent immigrants from the Caribbean meeting and making music in the South Bronx.

Genre often hinges on race, in part because race is a visible marker of difference, unlike region or class. "One reason race has remained so central to genre definitions is that racial crossover destabilizes the very concept of genre, reliant as it often is on homological conceptions of audience cultures," argues Pecknold. The fiction of genre is founded on the presupposition of homogenous communities, even though most of us listen well beyond any generic bounds. Genre and format are unreliable markers of taste. Clarity of a listening community comes at the cost of mismeasuring the individuals who comprise it.

Music platforms at the beginning of the twenty-first century have ardently pursued the goal of identifying what listeners want to hear and when they want to hear it. The technology aimed at discerning this shares something with efforts by online retailers (most prominently Amazon.com) to develop predictive software designed to increase sales. Amazon's methods center on gathering data on consumer purchasing patterns, but musical tastes resist this model. Music taps more directly into human emotion, which is hard to predict; music is also a more multivectored product. A song presents a tougher challenge than a laundry detergent or a big-screen television when it comes to categorizing like with like. A predictive model for music must account for the complexity of the art form and also for the human beings wishing to relate to that art. What's needed is a science of style.

THE SCIENCE OF STYLE

Tim Westergren and Will Glaser set out to define just such a science of style for music. With the Music Genome Project and its commercial arm, Pandora Radio, they undertook a grand experiment of isolating the constitutive parts of every song ever written with the end goal of curating music suited to individual tastes. "We try to break down every dimension of a song to its most basic building blocks—like melody, harmony, rhythm, instrumentation, vocal performance," Westergren explained to the *Wall Street Journal* in 2010.

A panel of trained listeners (Pandora's website calls them "musicologists," but elsewhere explains that the requirement is a four-year college degree in music, not a doctorate) evaluates each song using several hundred criteria. Songs are classified into one of five generic categories, each with an attendant number of "genes" necessary to define the song with clarity. Pop/rock songs have 150 genes, rap songs have 350, jazz songs have approximately 400, and world and classical music have between 300 and 450.

The goal is to make fine distinctions about songs, offering an inductive definition of style based on objective qualities and informed subjective judgments. "[The classifications] essentially cover all of the granular details of melody, harmony, rhythm, form, compositional qualities and lyrics," Westergren explained in an early interview about the project in 2006. "I think of it as the primary colors, the distinct elements [that make up a song]. For example, there are over 30 attributes that describe the voice alone; how much vibrato, range, ornamentation, tone, performance. The sound of any voice, whether it's a Tuvan throat singer or Mariah Carey, we have a basic collection of primary colors that can describe it in one big continuum."

Spending just a half hour on Pandora is proof enough that style and genre do not always overlap. "It's a new kind of radio," Pandora's website touts, "stations that play only music you like." One afternoon I decided to put this proclamation to the test. I typed in "Beck," the artist that Westergren admitted in 2010 posed the greatest challenge for their model. "His musical vocabulary is outside the musical expression. It's different. We don't quite have the elements to capture it. We don't do a very good job with him," Westergren told a reporter. Perhaps they had solved the Beck conundrum in the years since.

After I entered Beck's name, the following note popped up as Pandora began to play Beck's breakthrough hit, "Loser": "To start things off, we'll play a song that exemplifies the musical style of Beck which features electric rock instrumentation, a subtle use of vocal harmony, repetitive melodic phrasing, demanding instrumental part writing and major key tonality." From that sentence alone, it's clear just why Beck presents such a challenge to Pandora. Stylistically, Beck is a nomad. Indeed, much of his music could broadly be described as involving demanding "electric rock instrumentation" and "subtle vocal harmony," often featuring Beck harmonizing with himself. That hardly accounts for his Grammy-winning acoustic offerings, 2014's *Morning Phase* and its stylistic predecessor, 2002's *Sea Change*; or his Prince-inspired sounds on *Midnite Vultures* (1999). There is no way for Pandora to know which Beck I had in mind.

With the second song, it became clear how Pandora would resolve the multigeneric challenge of an eclectic artist like Beck; it would simply choose one Beck and go with it. "From here on out," the next message informed me, "we'll be exploring other songs and artists that have musical qualities similar to Beck. This track, 'Short Skirt/Long Jacket (Live)' by Cake, has similar basic rock song structures, a subtle use of vocal harmony, major key tonality, mixed acoustic and electric instrumentation and electric guitar riffs." What's instructive here, both for the functional practice of Pandora and for understanding the concept of genre, is the way that this second interpretation of my single input of "Beck" differs from the first. The first thing Pandora did when I asked for Beck was to give me a song by Beck himself, a song representing a single point in his stylistic field. The second thing it did was to define a new musical category mapped onto and across traditional categories, the category of "Beck." Pandora constituted this category by combining the stable qualities of Beck's style as well as the more mutable qualities. The songs that followed were by groups that shared significant things with Beck, though not always the same significant things as the song before or after them: the Black Keys' "Everlasting Light," Big Data's "Dangerous," Beck's "Deadweight" (a different Beck from "Loser"), the White Stripes' "We're Going to Be Friends," and Foster the People's "Pumped Up Kicks." Using conventional terms of genre, these artists might variously be tagged as indie rock or garage rock or electronic, or lumped together as "alternative." Thinking of them in relation to Beck, however, makes them legible on the level of style in a way that the definitions of genre or format never allow.

In my listening session I did not make any additional interventions, though Pandora encourages users to refine their category by voting up or down on a given track. My goal was to gain an impressionistic understanding of how a service like Pandora, as well as the Music Genome Project that powers it, brings together the science and the art of style. The results, provisional and imperfect, are nonetheless illuminating. Style lives not only in an artist or in a particular song, but in a system of varied relations, some strong, some weak, and all defining the space where the concepts of genre and individual style alone aren't enough.

Perhaps the signal innovation in the science of style in popular music over the past two decades has been the rise of data analytics. A data-driven approach now dominates the ways sales are counted, the ways tastes are forged, and the ways popular music is made and promoted. This transformation is evident in the *Billboard* Hot 100 chart, which went from tabulating sales figures from record-store owners and number of spins from radio stations through the first thirty years of the charts, to using point-of-sale data and Nielsen reports in the early 1990s, to streaming and downloading data in the early 2000s. This more-sensitive data reveals that listeners are drawn to the same songs, the same sounds. Writing in *The Atlantic*, Derek Thompson reveals that the top 1 percent of artists now account for 77 percent of all revenue. "As labels have gotten more adept at recognizing what's selling, they've been quicker than ever to invest in copycats," Thompson writes. "People I spoke with in the music industry told me they worried that the reliance on data was leading to a 'clustering' of styles and genres, promoting a dispiriting sameness in pop music." Yet despite the commercial clustering apparent in major label releases, this is also a time of widening dissemination of musical styles. Just as the science of style is working to craft individual soundscapes for everyone, it is also defining an increasingly homogenous common ground of pop.

Familiar sounds and clearly identifiable styles aren't necessarily a bad thing. Pop music has always had its consolidators—those who refine the elements of an existing style—and its innovators—those who depart from existing styles to define new sonic and lyric territories. In writing the history of popular music, we tend to emphasize the innovators, privileging those moments when styles shifted rather than when they settled into clear forms. Both types of artists are essential to the proper function of pop and to a rich understanding of style. The consolidators, after all, do more to define the sharp edges of a style in a given moment. Consolidators define the territory in which most of a given era's music, certainly most of that era's hits, fits. Innovators, by contrast, are sometimes slow to find chart success.

In *The Power of Habit*, the Pulitzer Prize–winning *New York Times* staff writer Charles Duhigg profiles the strange case of the rap group OutKast's crossover 2003 hit "Hey Ya!" When label executives tested the song before its release using a new data-driven technology called Hit Song Science, it rated higher than almost any other song before it. But when the song reached radio, it went nowhere. It sounded too different from everything else on the airwaves, too unfamiliar. "People listen to Top 40 because they want to hear their favorite songs or songs that sound just like their favorite songs," Duhigg explains. "When something different comes on, they're offended. They don't want anything unfamiliar." The song became a major hit only after the label worked with commercial radio to program it in between "sticky" songs—those that sounded more familiar to listeners' ears, more in keeping with stylistic and generic expectations. As listeners got used to "Hey Ya!," it acquired some of that stickiness itself, expanding the stylistic range of expectation to contain its eclectic, frenetic sound. For pop audiences, OutKast's "Hey Ya!" was an innovation predicated on the consolidating influence of the songs that surrounded it.

This innovation/consolidation dynamic functions on the level of individual songs, and on the level of genre and style as well. In the mid-1960s and the 1970s, Kool & the Gang consolidated the emergent stylistic fusion of funk, jazz, and R&B. They modeled their band on the Famous Flames, a tight ensemble whose singer was none other than the great innovator James Brown, while also demonstrating their facility with tender R&B ballads in the style of the Commodores. At the height of Kool & the Gang's commercial success, between 1979's disco-funk "Ladies' Night" and 1980's *Billboard* number-one "Celebration" to 1985's R&B ballad "Cherish," they strung together top-forty hits and platinum and gold records.

By the mid-1980s, R&B meant Kool & the Gang. In January 1984 their ballad "Joanna" held the number-one spot on the chart for two weeks. The lyrics are about as straightforward as a love song can be: "Joanna, I love you / You're the one, the one for me." With a strong lead vocal by J. T. Taylor and doo-wop style background vocals, its texture is decidedly R&B love ballad. The first half of 1984's R&B chart followed suit, with bombastic love songs like Patti LaBelle's "If Only You Knew" and Lionel Richie's "Hello" alongside the occasional funk-inflected dance song like Rockwell's "Somebody's Watching Me" (featuring background vocals by Michael Jackson) and Cameo's "She's Strange." Essentially, the sounds were in keeping with the understanding of R&B that Kool & the Gang had been consolidating since the 1960s.

But something happened in the summer of 1984. For eight consecutive weeks starting on June 30, a single song dominated the R&B charts and climbed up to number two on the *Billboard* Hot 100 charts as well. It announced its difference, its radical innovation, with its inscrutable title: "When Doves Cry." The mystery is only intensified in the lyrics, which call equal attention to the verses and the chorus. The song's structure marks a shift in the lyric center of gravity toward the verses, toward their strangeness and indeterminacy rather than their legibility, toward the metaphoric rather than the concrete. It's still a song from a man to a woman, it's still a kind of love entreaty, but rather than the clear protestation of love in Kool & the Gang's "Joanna" and Patti LaBelle's "If Only You Knew," one hears lines like this:

> Dream if you can a courtyard
> An ocean of violets in bloom
> Animals strike curious poses
> They feel the heat
> The heat between me and you

"Me" and "you" are common enough, but the language that precedes them is vivid and metaphoric. Prince conjures a sonic tableau reminiscent of Hieronymus Bosch's *Garden of Earthly Delights*, with lovers in passionate embrace and animals responding in kind. We're quite a distance past "If only you knew/How much I do/Do love you." Innovation, as my friend Paul D. Miller (aka DJ Spooky that Subliminal Kid) defines it, is "when you refuse to accept the world as it is and try to see its potential." If this is true, then Prince's "When Doves Cry" is a dramatic act of pop innovation, born of seeing the potential of blending the standard and the strange.

By 1984, Prince, born Prince Rogers Nelson in Minneapolis, Minnesota, was already on his sixth album. His 1978 debut and 1979 follow-up had produced a couple songs that cracked the charts. Prince's early albums reflected elements of funk, soul, and rock consolidators. They shared something, too, with the burgeoning independent music movement in Minneapolis described by Jon Kirby in his liner notes to the marvelous collection *Purple Snow: Forecasting the Minneapolis Sound*, as "a slick, black, technologically advanced genre fusion." Listening back to Prince's early albums in light of all that we know Prince would become, something seems obvious that might not have been as clear in the moment of his debut: Prince was an innovator.

Yes, his early music resides in much the same space as that of Kool & the Gang—alternatively, funk-inspired jams and lovelorn soul ballads. One hears, though, an iconoclastic difference from the very start. Some of the songs from his early albums are so conventional that they sound as if Prince were trying to be a good soul man, but doing something else in spite of himself. On "Baby," from Prince's debut, *For You*, he rehearses familiar soul conceits like loving a woman but "barely having enough money for two"; he even recycles familiar rhymes—"do" rhymes with "you" rhymes with "two" in predictable pattern.

The song is strange as well, with unexpected chord changes, crashing cymbals, and layered vocals. Part of this strangeness no doubt springs from the fact that Prince was playing all of the instruments and singing all of the vocal parts himself. As Ben Ratliff observes, "When you are playing most of the instruments yourself, a useful awkwardness can set in. It is unlikely that you will be equally good on every instrument. There's no cross-playing and cross-listening; on the other hand, you're not deferring to someone else and don't need to codify your song or teach it to anyone. The result is that all kinds of idiosyncrasies can occur." Prince may well have been shooting to write an album of classic soul ballads and disco dance tracks. Thankfully, he missed the mark.

An artist aiming for convention and missing is often the precondition for innovation. "A lot of pop music has come out of people failing to copy their model and accidentally creating something new," writes Elvis Costello. "The closer you get to your ideal, the less original you sound." So many new styles are born of failure. Keith Richards failed to play his guitar quite like his idol Chuck Berry, and Mick Jagger failed to sing quite like James Brown, but in missing their marks they defined something new with the Rolling Stones. Only Prince knew if he understood his early albums as "failures" in this way, as trying and failing to copy the artists he emulated. What is indisputable, now nearly forty years and forty studio albums later, is that one hears in those early Prince albums the seeds of an original sound.

As I've argued, though, pop doesn't only require the cutting edge. In fact, the majority of the music that we hear and that we genuinely enjoy is not marked by its novelty but by its fealty to convention. Originality isn't everything in pop music. Most artists at least begin by modeling themselves on the familiar, because the creative process usually begins with emulation. The mind craves familiarity. Most record labels want it, because they want to sell music to all of those listeners who bought similar music from them in the past.

The new science of style confirms the common assumption that listeners want the familiar, but it refines that assumption by suggesting that they want familiarity with just enough difference. Calibrating that balance is an art that remains out of science's reach. With more data comes more clarity about style and taste, but mystery persists. The most successful developers in the music analytics space are the Echo Nest, a company founded by two MIT graduate students and acquired in 2014 by the music streaming service Spotify. The Echo Nest has developed a "music intelligence platform" analyzing some 37 million songs—nearly forty times the number of songs charted by Pandora's Music Genome Project. They have made a portion of this data available to tech developers and academics, meaning that their analytics can power everything from iPhone and Android apps to academic research studies.

Noah Askin, a professor of organizational behavior at INSEAD in Fontainebleau, France, is leading one of these early Echo Nest–powered studies, attempting to understand better how a song becomes a *Billboard* hit. In a December 2015 TEDx talk, he distilled some of his preliminary findings. They seem to confirm what Duhigg observed about OutKast's "Hey Ya!": that a big hit must sound familiar *and* different. "We actually found that the songs that do best on the charts are not those that sound the most similar, but those that are actually optimally differentiated," Askin observes. "That is, of the 25,000 songs that have appeared on the *Billboard* charts since their inception in 1958 until the middle of 2013, the songs that do the best and stay on the charts longest are those that sound similar to what else is going on at the time, *but not too similar*." This tension between the familiar and the fresh is the essence of the hit. No matter our efforts to explicate its stylistic attributes, something about the pop hit remains ineffable. Perhaps the best approach to the mystery of pop's seductive style lies not in analytics, but in looking to one of the basic building blocks of pop songs: the words themselves.

POP DICTION

In the summer of 2015, Musixmatch.com posted an article titled "The Largest Vocabulary in Music," an analysis of the vocabularies of popular musicians' song lyrics. The article drew its inspiration from "The Largest Vocabulary in Hip Hop," posted in late 2014, which compared the vocabulary in rap lyrics to the vocabulary in William Shakespeare's plays and Herman Melville's *Moby-Dick*. "The Largest Vocabulary in Music" looked across the pop landscape and analyzed artists' song lyric data to find the total number of unique words each artist used; the lyric density, or the total number of words used in each artist's one hundred densest songs; and the new word interval, or the average number of words separating words not used in the artists' earlier songs.

This study took as its subject group ninety-three of the ninety-nine bestselling artists from all genres, from the hard rock of Guns N' Roses to the smooth jazz of Kenny G. (Copyright permission could not be secured from the missing six.) The results were striking. Four of the top five artists were from hip-hop: Eminem, Jay Z, 2Pac, and Kanye West. Bob Dylan, classified as "folk," rounded out the top five. The only other hip-hop entry, the Black Eyed Peas, came in at number six. What all of the top artists share—Dylan included—is an urge to extenuate the lyric line. The majority of artists inhabited a narrow space in the middle, with nearly half falling within just 400 words of the average. As one might imagine, multilingual artists fared well, with four placing in the top eleven.

The list has its limitations. The compiler, a graduate student in sound and music computing named Varun Jewalikar, admits that "The Largest Vocabulary in Music" is "meant to be a study, not an academic research paper." Certainly, methodological holes and tenuous inferences abound. Do the lyrics used for the study adhere to uniform transcription practices? If they don't, then the same word might be counted multiple times. Is it fair to ascribe the vocabulary ranking to the performer rather than to the songwriters? Given that some of the performers write all of their lyrics, some write some of their lyrics, some write none of their lyrics, and for some the matter is uncertain, it seems problematic to pass the rankings off as the possessions of the performers alone. What about the fact that the list narrows its field to artists with the highest album sales? That seems a dubious means of seeking the largest vocabulary in music given the fact that mainstream music often follows a lowest-common-denominator mentality.

It would be easy to discredit the methodology and challenge the conclusions of this study. However, provisional as it is, "The Largest Vocabulary in Music" still presents an opportunity to glean insights into the function of language in song lyrics. The report reveals several trends that are at least directionally compelling, although not definitive.

The most obvious trend the study uncovers is the predominance of hip-hop artists at the top of the list. Part of this, as Jewalikar observes in his analysis, can be attributed to the fact that rap generally involves more words per song than other genres. (A few months later, Jewalikar returned with a companion study of lyric vocabularies in eight popular musical genres. Hip-hop was far and away number one with an average of 478 words per song and 98 new words per song; heavy metal came in second with 191 words per song and 29 new words per song.) Eminem, who tops the list, also leads the list of words per song with just over a thousand. In an extreme example from him, like 2013's rapid fire "Rap God," Eminem delivers over 1,500 words in around six minutes. His word palate in the song is fairly straightforward, with one- and two-syllable words predominating. From time to time in the verses, though, one finds knots of multisyllabic density born of rhyme. In the final verse he uses "ricocheting," an unusual word in a song lyric, then follows it with a succession of seven multisyllabic rhymes over the next six lines: "devastating," "demonstrating," "levitating," "never fading," "forever waiting," "celebrating," "elevating." The rhyme impetus compels Eminem to devise words that he might not have used in the normal course of expression.

Why do rappers have so many more words per song than other artists? As I discussed in the previous chapter, rappers do not dilate their vowels in the dramatic manner of singers, leaving considerably more space for additional words on a line. The proliferation of different words in rap is also rooted in the fact that rap tends toward the topical, with references to current events, sports figures, entertainers, and other celebrities that further expand the lyric vocabulary. Rap's rhyme imperative also impels diversity of diction, as MCs seek to distinguish themselves with complex patterns of multisyllabic and slant rhymes. Add to that rap's penchant for slang and neologism and it becomes even clearer how the genre might stand out from all others. Rap's dominance of the study's results would have been far greater had the study not limited itself to the biggest-selling artists of all time. Eminem and the other MCs on the list do not have exceptionally expansive vocabularies when compared to their rapping peers. Looking back to "The Largest Vocabulary in Hip Hop," Eminem doesn't even rise to the median. Aesop Rock, who ranks number one on the list, bests Eminem's vocabulary by over 60 percent.

This doesn't mean, as "The Largest Vocabulary in Hip Hop" claims, that rappers have a more impressive vocabulary than Shakespeare. Such a claim misapprehends the vital distinction between linguistic variety and expressive richness. It also doesn't mean that rap lyrics are more sophisticated than the lyrics of the Beatles or Stevie Wonder or Joni Mitchell. What's often said about something else is also true for vocabularies: It's not the size that matters, but what you do with it. This much is indisputable: Rap lyrics employ many words, more than the lyrics of other genres. Rap's expansive vocabulary shifts attention to rap's narrative qualities, underscores rap's conversational affect, and helps explain rap's appeal as a form of political expression.

The study also leads to examining the relation between vocabulary and commercial sales. Jewalikar takes it as a given that "simpler" vocabularies are more commercially viable, and that pop music seeks the lowest common denominator of communication. "No wonder the simplicity of their lyrics breaks the barriers of geography, age, language and they are admired globally," Jewalikar writes. The problem is that Jewalikar is projecting a qualitative interpretation about lyric language based on a purely quantitative measure. He would be on stronger ground had the study included an analysis of the average number of syllables per word, but even this would provide only a one-dimensional picture.

Data alone will not solve the mystery of the enchanting power some song lyrics hold over us. Data won't explain why we're more likely to be moved by Bob Marley (number seventy-eight) singing "Redemption Song" than by the Black Eyed Peas (number six) performing "My Humps," nor will they account for the fact that sometimes a song finds just the right words and puts them in just the right order. And data certainly can't account for how music and vocal performance have a way of charging banal and repetitive words with the power to move us and to make us think. To make bigger claims about complexity, aesthetics, and style we need a perspective that attends not just to isolated words, but to words in relation.

Rather than considering vocabulary in isolation, think about words themselves and their constellations of meaning. Diction, as *The Princeton Encyclopedia of Poetry and Poetics* defines it, is "the words or phrases chosen for a piece of writing." When those words are chosen for song, the writer must consider diction's relation to sound and to instrumentation. John Fogerty once remarked that his best songwriting came down to "finding a great-sounding word to sing and doing some kind of sympathetic guitar part." "I sort of have a little library of phrases and words in my head that I like," says the singer-songwriter Sarah McLachlan. "Like 'murmur.' Never been able to use it yet, but it's a beautiful word. I like words that say so many things." Studying diction invites analysis of individual words like this, as well as of words in relation. Diction, after all, includes all parts of speech, verb tenses, and articles and prepositions, although it focuses attention on words that distinguish the writer's style.

The poetry critic Helen Vendler encourages readers of poetry to consider *registers* of diction, patterns of language that suggest a particular condition, mood, or thematic coherence. Attending not just to the sheer number of words, or the incidence of unique words, but to how the song lyric puts words to work in unison lends a more practical application to the study of language in song lyrics. Looking to registers of diction helps uncover the connections the lyric makes beyond our conscious awareness, even in songs where it seems not that much is going on. Santana and Rob Thomas scored the second biggest hit in *Billboard* history with 1999's "Smooth." A good measure of the song's popularity undoubtedly rests on Santana's soulful guitar playing, but at least some measure resides in the patterns of the Thomas-penned lyrics. The sense of the song is fairly conventional: a paean to an irresistible but unattainable beloved. Much of the linguistic interest, though, comes from the way the lyrics cluster language around a celestial register: "hot," "midday sun," "melt," "cool," "ocean," "moon," "turning," "world," "round and round." Together, these words conjure an image that elevates the everyday theme of a distant lover to the level of myth.

Diction is perhaps the most obvious distinguishing feature of an artist's individual lyric style, as well as the style of a given genre. "Words in all pop genres work as recruiting symbols; their writers draw on a communal language to create a sense of community," Simon Frith observes. "In general terms, the language of lyrics is used to construct pop genres: disco lyrics endlessly invoke us to dance, effectively connoting consumption; country lyrics use plain language, reported speech, and country singers come across as the detached observers of emotional plight; the message of punk lyrics comes simply from the odd words that stick out of the noisy chorus." Through close attention to diction, one can potentially uncover the registers common to individual songs, to an artist's body of work, or to the songbook of an entire genre.

Some contend that the phrase, not the word, is the basic unit of composition in songwriting. The literary critic Mark Booth argues that many popular songs are a patchwork of prefabricated phrases, whereas most poems are fashioned word by word. This is not a deficiency, Booth argues, but a necessary aesthetic adaptation. "Given the relationship of redundancy to information, a songwriter should not have anything really new to say, at least if he expects to say it with the words of the song alone," Booth writes. "A poet on paper has much greater freedom to test the patience and ingenuity of the reader and to stretch his comprehension. He can aspire to enlarge the reader's world of experience and ideas. But a song, hedged by the demands of unity and clarity, must say things that are simplifications, and generally familiar simplifications."

Because listeners can't slow down the flow of language or glance backward to clarify without disrupting the listening experience, a songwriter does well to use familiar constructions so that listeners can make sense of her meaning. In the introduction to his practical tool for songwriters, *The Modern Rhyming Dictionary*, Gene Lees seems to agree. "Take some ordinary, everyday expression, such as 'Guess Who I Saw Today,' and use it as a song title," he advises apprentice songwriters. "The expression may be a catchword of current slang, or one of the older clichés in language, but in the hands of a master lyricist, it can take on startling freshness and originality, yet retain the advantage of general familiarity." This balance between freshness and familiarity in the language of lyric helps explain how so many well-known recordings are often of songs made up of a series of familiar phrases.

Effective song lyrics do not need to vivify language or incite thought or passion, as good poetry usually does. Sometimes the lyrics consciously aspire to cliché. Speaking of her songwriting, Nicki Minaj observes that she has two different approaches: one for writing imagistically rich language to display her rhyming virtuosity and one for writing big pop hits for the global market. "If you don't speak English," she says, "you still know it's a fun song, just from the tone and the cadence." That helps explain the difference between her virtuosic, star-making verse on Kanye West's "Monster" and her biggest global hit to date, "Super Bass," which comes across as staid and saccharine by comparison. "The foreign tongue is first a kind of music before it becomes a language; it is first pregnant with meaning before the meaning is delivered to me," writes the philosopher Don Ihde in reference to the spoken idiom; song lyrics literalize that musical quality found in plain speech in a foreign language.

For Nicki Minaj, the conscious constraint of expressive range and depth is a part of her art. She understands that to write a hit song that crosses divides of genre and geography almost always requires a chorus comprised of words that express themselves in clear terms. "The brilliance of rock lyrics is that they are indistinct enough to hint at everything," writes David Kirby. "No need to get into specifics."

This aesthetics of the obvious is at work in many pop songs. The lyrics of such songs can come across as careless, which they may well be, but often there's a conscious calculation at work. By deploying well-worn phrases, lyrics are so easily absorbed that the song sounds as if it's been around for years even when it has just come out. One of the best examples of this is "All Star" by Smash Mouth. When it hit the charts near the turn of the twenty-first century it became a global hit, in no small part because of its paint-by-numbers chorus, which amounts to little more than a hodgepodge of clichés:

> Hey now, you're an all star, get your game on, go play
> Hey now, you're a rock star, get the show on, get paid
> And all that glitters is gold
> Only shooting stars break the mold

Upbeat. Inspirational. Aspirational. It's all of those things, not in spite of its wooden language but because of it. The first two lines take little deciphering. The third line refutes a common aphorism ("All that glitters is not gold") in favor of a new vision perfect for the apex of the economic prosperity of the tech boom and the housing bubble. The final line of the chorus is a Frankenstein's monster of mixed metaphor that underscores how prefabricated phrases can work efficiently if not elegantly—in this case, for affirmation. No wonder the song has become a staple in sports arenas. In contrast to the chorus, the verses are downright literary—and decidedly unmemorable. Sometimes an effective pop song demands a language of least resistance.

Sometimes, too, songwriters exploit the comforting space of the obvious to craft subtle subversions and strangeness. On her striking 2013 debut, *Same Trailer Different Park*, the country singer-songwriter Kacey Musgraves fashioned a collection of song lyrics both traditional in their attention to bedrock country diction, themes, and storytelling and avant-garde in their figurative constructions. Her songs, most of which were co-written with Nashville veterans Shane McAnally and Josh Osborne, are festooned with fairy tales gone awry and reinvented clichés that somehow sound fresh again. On "It Is What It Is," for instance, Musgraves takes the commonplace expression of the title and enlivens it in the closing lines of the chorus to capture the unaccountable loss of a love affair: "It is what it is/'til it ain't anymore."

Musgraves makes an art of creatively misdirecting clichés and arriving at newly forged aphorisms. On "Step Off," sticks and stones won't break your bones; instead, they "may build a throne/But you'll be up there all alone." In a 2015 interview with the podcast *Switched On Pop*, the *New Yorker*'s Andrew Marantz marveled at Musgraves's capacity to compose a phrase that "sounds like a cliché, then you realize you've never actually heard it before." She does this on "I Miss You," where she tells a lost lover that she's "as happy as half a heart can do." Or hear it on "Biscuits," a song from her 2015 sophomore album, *Pageant Material*, where she admonishes her listeners to "mind your own biscuits and life will be gravy." Musgraves, like many popular songwriters before her, is at her best when cultivating moments of surprise from common speech, making meaning out of what some mistake as meaningless.

"Some of my favorite songs are meaningless," Sting writes, explaining his inspiration for penning the Police's "De Do Do Do, De Da Da Da," a song that stretches the potential of the stock phrase to the extreme. "I was trying to figure out why I liked songs like 'Da Doo Ron Ron' and 'Do Wah Diddy' and 'Tutti-Frutti.' There's a whole list of songs with just garbage as words that seem to be able to communicate something without necessarily meaning anything." Sting here is exposing his own aesthetic biases, but his point is instructive: Many pop songs communicate more than they mean. They do so, as we've explored in this book, through the play of sound and performance.

I don't want to dismiss so easily song lyrics that seem not to mean much of anything. The Crystals' "Da Doo Ron Ron," produced by Phil Spector, employs such a striking economy of language that it reads on the page like an experimental poem; the constriction of diction is stylized, not haphazard. Manfred Mann's "Do Wah Diddy" distills an entire courtship, from first sight to matrimony, into less than two and a half minutes. Little Richard's "Tutti-Frutti" is a sophisticated document—striking and strange, from the first "Bop bopa-a-lu a whop bam boo" to the last. "It's a huge song musically, but it's also a seminal text in American culture, as much as *Uncle Tom's Cabin*, 'Song of Myself,' and the great documents of the Civil Rights era are. In a sense, it's America's Other National Anthem," writes David Kirby. Kirby's going a bit too far here, but the song gave birth to rock and roll as we know it, which gave birth in so many ways to so many of us. Each of these records works as recording and as song; as lyric alone, each offers a compelling, if incomplete, portrait of an aesthetics of the obvious.

Without the prosaic patterns of the past, many of the later innovations of avant-garde and more expressly "poetic" songwriters might not have been possible. "I was using yesterday's records as blueprints, as all pop music is," writes Elvis Costello, one of the most sophisticated and literary songwriters alive. "All the good pop clichés had been written and there hadn't been any new ones for a while. I wanted to take some of the ready-made clichés that Goffin and King or Smokey Robinson would come up with and come up with my own photo-negative versions of them. Almost every song on my first album was an opposite—a diseased version—of another kind of song." Costello locates the genesis of his distinctive songwriting style in the legible styles of songwriting from the past. Costello's first album, 1977's *My Aim Is True*, includes one of his best-known songs, "Alison." "Alison" is about the night side of love—disappointment and disaffection—rather than the bright side often celebrated in Costello's stylistic models. But it is not a complete renunciation of the romantic sensibilities he inherited. "I'm not going to get too sentimental / Like those other sticky Valentines," he sings, even as the feel of the song and the sound of the singing suggest otherwise.

Words also carry the inflections bestowed by the music and the particular performance of a recording. The multiple lives lyrics lead in language and sound help explain how even a constrained linguistic space can dilate to accommodate a range of emotions. Country music is often derided for the narrow scope of its themes: beer, pickup trucks, and parties down by the river. The August 2015 issue of *Billboard* magazine included an interview with seven top Nashville songwriters. When asked for the words they overuse in their lyrics, Jon Nite, who's written for Keith Urban and Miranda Lambert, said, "Right now, I am instructed by my publishers not to use 'truck' or 'whiskey.' The problem is, I drive an F-150 and I live in Bourbon Country." Ross Copperman, who's written for Kenny Chesney and Dierks Bentley, agreed: "We're all trying to stray from the bro thing, you know? So 'truck,' I guess."

Worn-out words, however, can be born again in the space of the song and the style of the singing. For those acculturated to country music, the familiar language of the lyrics can be both comforting and affecting. "Those old country ballads created a space for sentiment that wasn't always allowed at other times," the Texas-born writer Stephen Graham Jones told me. "You could connect to deep emotions, if only in the confines of the cab of your pickup. It allowed those same guys who were so caught up in the pose—the boot-cut jeans, the hat tilted just right, the lip packed full of dip—to feel fully human for a little while." Certain emotional registers consciously shut off in daily life—vulnerability, grief, loving abandon—become accessible in the span of the song. Music and the language of the lyric offer a way into these places and extend the possibility that listeners can carry that feeling into their everyday lives.

It should come as no surprise, then, that country music is also perhaps the most grown-up popular genre, unafraid to come to terms with adult relationships and problems. "There are a lot of people listening to country music who don't have perfect lives, who have the problems we sing about, whether it's wife abuse, drinking, cheating, or whatever," writes Reba Mc-Entire. "If it's a good song and people hear the message—the person in that song fixed his marriage and so can I, or the woman in this song walked out on a man who was beating up on her and so can I—well, you've used your music to make a statement and maybe to offer hope or another way." Singers who sing about beer and pickups as twenty-something upstarts might find themselves exploring a markedly different register as they enter middle age. That doesn't mean that songs about heartache and divorce are necessarily superior to songs about parties down by the lake. It just means that the music can contain a broad range of human experience.

So what's country? "If it sounds country, that's what it is. It's a country song," Kris Kristofferson drawls at the beginning of his live recording of "Me and Bobby McGee." That may be the best definition we can get. No single register of diction can encompass a genre. And no register, however dominant, is necessarily a barrier to emotive expression. Perhaps the best way to come to terms with style as it manifests itself in song is to listen to, and read closely, a handful of particular songs together.

READING STYLE IN THREE SONGS

When we listen to a song we bring preconceptions about what the song should be and an emergent conception of what the song is becoming in the listening. Before we know a song, we may make assumptions about genre ("country songs are about love and heartache, and occasionally about beer, pickup trucks, and dogs") or assumptions based on personal or situational experience ("so and so recommended this album, so it'll probably be like this" or "I'm hearing this song at the gym, which always keeps it locked to the light-rock station, so that's what this song must be"). While listening to a song, the particulars of the song itself either confirm or complicate initial expectations. As the mind identifies patterns, as one becomes more familiar with the song, the potency of surprise dissipates. Dilute it enough and interest wanes. However, there is a sweet spot balanced between these states, where the surprise has mellowed but not lost all potency and the familiarity is comforting rather than cloying.

In *Songbook* the novelist Nick Hornby recapitulates a favorite explanation for how and why we listen repeatedly to the same song. "Dave Eggers has a theory that we play songs over and over, those of us who do, because we have to 'solve' them," Hornby writes, "and it's true that in our early relationship with, and courtship of, a new song, there is a stage which is akin to a sort of emotional puzzlement." Puzzlement is a productive emotion for a critic; indeed, it might be the governing impulse behind some of the greatest criticism. "My books always begin with an unanswered question," my former teacher Helen Vendler once told me. We may apply the same principle of puzzlement even to casual encounters with songs; often it is active when we aren't consciously aware that we are applying it in the first place.

An attentive listener will experience a country song, a rock song, and a rap song in different ways from one another. The kinds of details that demand attention will vary widely, as will the aperture of attention itself. Does the song invite more scrutiny on the gestalt or on the acute level? Do we let the sounds wash over us, or is our ear captured by certain individual words or phrases? Are the lyrics in the foreground, in the background, or do they jump back and forth?

Eminem's songs, for instance, generally foreground the rapping voice with a steady beat below it and maybe some sampled sounds above it. By contrast, Thom Yorke's voice in Radiohead's songs often recedes into the mix, becoming another part of the music. For an audible demonstration of just how much difference the mix can make in our perception of the voice in song, compare the original issue of the Rolling Stones' *Exile on Main Street*, which tends to bury Mick Jagger's voice in the mix, with the "lost" tracks reissued in 2010, which push Jagger into the sonic foreground. These production choices, neither one necessarily better than the other, condition how we apprehend the style of the recorded performance. Some songs announce from the start that they are vehicles for voice, while others understate vocal virtuosity in the name of illuminating the lyrics. Some of these differences track generally with genre, while many vary from singer to singer, from song to song.

Try consciously applying these principles of style to three songs, vastly different from one another in genre, audience, and time period. It's unlikely that you'll be drawn to all three equally; in fact, the more you like one, the less you'll probably like the others. Hearing the three in succession could be considered the kind of cruel trick usually attributed to iTunes' shuffle function. Certainly Pandora would never play these three in sequence. I hope, however, that this little listening experiment will illuminate the unwritten and unspoken habits of listening that govern the way many of us approach style in pop music.

I've selected these three songs not quite at random but close to it: Hank Snow's "The Engineer's Child" (1946), the Dø's "Dust It Off" (2011), and Chance the Rapper featuring Vic Mensa and Twista's "Cocoa Butter Kisses" (2013). My goal was not to select three songs with a tangible point of connection—say, three songs about New York City, or three songs recorded in 1978. Rather, I chose what I judge to be good representations of their respective genres and styles: a country and western ballad, an indie-pop tone study, and a rap posse cut. If anything coheres these three songs it is the fact that none of them could be considered mainstream; Hank Snow predates the *Billboard* Hot 100 charts, the Dø reside somewhere below or beyond it, and Chance the Rapper's song appeared on the then twenty-year-old's breakthrough mixtape. You might not know them all; you might not know a single one. That's fine. The goal is to listen with purpose, marking the distance between your preconceptions and the song itself, noting emerging patterns and structures that define your experience of listening to each song. You'll find each of them on YouTube, and I encourage you to listen to them before reading on.

Hank Snow, "The Engineer's Child" (1946)

The country music pioneer Hank Snow's "The Engineer's Child" is a conventional tune with just enough strangeness to keep it interesting. As a lyric form, it follows the dictates of the traditional ballad. It is narrative-driven and sentimental. Steel guitar dominates the song's instrumentation, aided by a two-bar fiddle solo. The song's chugging rhythm is akin to the train it describes. What stands out most, though, is Snow's voice, baleful and deep. He recounts the story of a husband, a railroad engineer, called away from his wife and ailing infant child. As his train rattles through the darkness toward home, the engineer awaits a sign from the window ("If our baby's dead, just show the red").

What could make a more universal emotive appeal than the thought of a child on the verge of death? It is, of course, a coercive emotion; the song demands and expects a specific response. However, the lyric's narrative structure complicates the song's straightforward sentimentality and adds depth. The lyrics shift point of view from the third-person sympathetic chronicler in the first verse, to the engineer/protagonist in the second verse, and finally to the mother in the third verse. The rudimentary recording technology and the fact that the song speaks directly to us from a period when the survival of a child to adulthood was far from certain work together to saturate the song in sepia tones.

Given this song's strong narrative, on the acute level it demands attention engaged with the events the song describes. On the gestalt level, patterns emerge from the ballad form and the repetition of the chorus. The first time through, the song evokes tension and apprehension. The second time, one finds a modest reassurance and a place for hope.

The Dø's, "Dust It Off" (2011)

The Finnish-French indie-pop duo the Dø's "Dust It Off" begins with an intake of breath that leads to—nothing. A second intake of breath leads to song. A naked piano figure provides the sole sonic setting for the singer, a young woman whose voice is at once vulnerable and enduring. The song offers no anchoring stability of form, no chorus or refrain. What lends it coherence is the repeated vocal pattern, which is looser than a melody but undeniably melodic.

Unlike "The Engineer's Child," "Dust It Off" does not dictate a specific emotional response from the listener. Instead, "Dust It Off" creates a mood, a less determined but still defined space of feeling generated by the nervous energy of the repeated piano figure, the jumps in melody, and Olivia Merhilati's singing voice. Where "The Engineer's Child" insists on its melodramatic narrative, "Dust It Off" deflects narrative logic. The song sets a mood and creates a cognitive space, through the lyrics' abstraction, that is defined without being definite. One gets the feeling that these lyrics portend more meaning than they actually contain. One also gets the feeling that the lyrics were written by a songwriter for whom English is a second language, which might help explain the song's attention to words as sound and feeling. Though not quite nonsense verse, the lyric functions on the same logic; enough of the structures of ideas are in place to leave the impression that the ideas are fully formed, even if they remain elusive to the most focused critical ear. It necessarily shifts listening attention from the acute to the gestalt.

Chance the Rapper Featuring Vic Mensa and Twista, "Cocoa Butter Kisses" (2013)

The third song in our sequence is Chance the Rapper's "Cocoa Butter Kisses," from his 2013 mixtape, *Acid Rap*. The fact that this song appears on a mixtape is significant. As a form the mixtape emphasizes spontaneity and disposability, although recent releases have sounded more like studio albums in their production quality and thematic cohesion. The second point of difference from the previous examples is that this song involves more than one voice. It is what's known in hip-hop as a posse cut, in which a succession of rappers flow over the same beat with more or less attention to a loose theme. The bulk of the song is taken up by the verses, where the theme is far from clear. In fact, each of the three MCs goes in a different thematic direction. The song's coherence isn't in theme, but rather in how each MC flows to the beat. In this regard, the performance is akin to a jazz cutting session, where each soloist tries to outshine the other. One doesn't long for narrative or thematic coherence because the song calls attention instead to micro-patterns: the discrete effects of flow and rhyme, the particular figures of speech and turns of phrase, the isolated lyric references.

"Cocoa Butter Kisses" lends itself to decoding in a way that "The Engineer's Child" does not, given that Snow's song makes its meaning so plain. It also is more satisfying on the level of figurative language than the Dø's "Dust It Off" because its figures inevitably resolve into something either readily apparent or clarified through decoding. The song provides a certain melodic appeal through the sung chorus, serviceably rendered by Chance the Rapper himself in a way that invites singing along without fear of being left behind. Repetition of the chorus anchors the song, holding it together as a whole. The song's gestalt appeal lies in the beat and the clear structure of verse and chorus. The acute appeal, the source of much of the song's interest, resides in discrete displays of lyric virtuosity. For instance, Twista makes a surprising reference to the Higgs boson, a subatomic particle ("And when it come to rapping fast, I'm the Higgs boson").

"Cocoa Butter Kisses" differs in striking ways from "Dust It Off." Neither song provides the concrete narrative of "The Engineer's Child," but the lyrics of "Dust It Off" cohere in a kind of emotive and ideational logic. Where Chance the Rapper's rhymes call acute attention to language, the Dø's lyrics resist comprehension and push toward the gestalt. To put it another way, "Cocoa Butter Kisses" holds together as a series of small parts that are only loosely related, though always relatable. "Dust It Off," in contrast, coheres through the accretion of image and feeling, which makes for a gestalt logic that satisfies a listener's desire for some kind of meaning making by the whole.

How much of these differences are the product of genre and how much they are the product of the artists' individual styles is a question open to discussion. Comparing songs across such vast differences of style is a useful approach to understanding the fixed and the moveable features of their respective forms. Another approach is to consider what happens when one song finds expression across two or more distinctive styles: the cover song.

STYLE AND THE COVER SONG

A cover is a recording of a song by someone other than the original songwriter or performer. Sometimes covers mirror the original recordings down to the singer's vocal inflections. Other times, they take the originals apart and build them back up in a different genre and sonic space. Just how much and what parts of a song must stay the same, though, is open to analysis. Do we hear Patti Smith's "Gloria" as a cover of Them's "Gloria" in spite of the dramatic differences in arrangement and lyrics? What about when the original artist reinterprets his or her own song, making dramatic changes to lyric and melody, as Bob Dylan is wont to do with the songs from his expansive catalog?

For all the possible relations among original recordings and their covers, copyright law keeps the connection relatively close. The law affords anyone the opportunity to cover any song provided they pay the price in advance. Securing the mechanical license for a composition grants the right to record and distribute a cover version of a song in one's own style, provided that it does not substantially change "the basic melody or the fundamental character of the work." What constitutes "the fundamental character," however, is not clearly defined. In practice it has come to mean little or no alteration to the melody and the lyrics. Given all the legal constraints facing those who wish to record a cover, why do so many artists choose to do it anyway? The reasons are many, but we can usefully highlight these:

(1) *To capitalize on something that's already proven to be popular.* In 1955 Little Richard's original composition "Tutti Frutti" reached number seventeen on the *Billboard* charts at the same time that Pat Boone's cover version reached number twelve. In the early days of rock and roll when the single was king, it was common practice for singers to cover songs that had already enjoyed chart success. The cover is commerce.

(2) *To let your audience know something about yourself or your band.* The Rolling Stones' first American release, 1964's *England's Newest Hitmakers*, comprises almost entirely covers of blues and soul tunes by Willie Dixon, Jimmy Reed, Phil Spector, Chuck Berry, Holland/Dozier/Holland, and others. Most of the original artists' recordings were not particularly commercial at the time; the Stones and the other mostly English bands at the cutting edge of the rock revolution made them mainstream by virtue of their cover versions. Their choice of songs expressed their musical influences. "We were almost Jesuits—let's say missionaries. Our whole aim was to turn London on to rhythm and blues and the blues. That was the scope of our whole universe," Keith Richards told Marc Maron in 2015. One need only listen to the covers from their debut album to guess exactly what artists and albums mattered most to the group. By letting their listeners into their record collection, they forged intimacy with them.

(3) *To preserve or to regain something we're losing or have lost.* Jack White has become a one-man preservation society for a body of early blues recordings that the English invasion largely overlooked a few generations before. He's done this through acts of actual musical archivism, best represented by the *Rise and Fall of Paramount Records* series, and also through his carefully curated covers of some of these same old blues tunes. He released a seven-inch cover of bluesman Willie McTell's "Lord Send Me an Angel" in 2000 and a wrathful cover of Sun House's "Death Letter" on *De Stijl*. Covers will lead his listeners back to the original, if only to listen for what White so obviously hears there himself.

(4) *To correct, to complete, or to reimagine a song that on its own seems unresolved.* This might mean, for instance, stripping away the

dated period production qualities that keep listeners of today from hearing the beauty of the song underneath. It might mean conceiving a new conclusion to a song left incomplete. It could mean shifting the gender of the pronouns in the lyrics, or keeping the pronouns the same while changing the gender of the singer. These constitute a radical species of cover because they engage in a dialectical relationship that leaves both the original and the cover transformed.

One could identify an equal number of reasons why listeners seem so drawn to covers. At its most basic level, the cover satisfies the ear's desire for familiarity and difference. It's the same reason that live recordings can be so exciting: we listen both for the fulfillment of sonic expectations and for moments of surprise. Cover songs occasion a sonic palimpsest; we hear the new version over and against the original and take note of the differences. Hearing the cover with knowledge of the original highlights the exertion of the new artist's style and sensibility. We can come to know new artists by their differences and distances from the artists and songs with which we are already familiar.

The French soul singer Ben L'Oncle Soul's recorded body of work consists almost entirely of cover tunes, many of which owe their appeal to his radical displacement in genre, gender, and voice of our inherent expectations of the original song. The White Stripes' "Seven Nation Army" becomes a soul stirrer while still retaining the defining character of the original's vicious guitar riff. The Spice Girls' "Say You'll Be There" reveals its surprising poignancy when stripped of its dated production. Other songs, though, are diminished. Katy Perry's mildly transgressive "I Kissed a Girl" becomes standard issue when sung by a man without changing the gendered pronoun. With covers not everything is better, but something is always changed.

On other occasions, the pleasure to be had from a cover has little to do with the original recording, even to the point of making many forget that there was anything else that came before it. Jimi Hendrix incites a sonic revolution on "All Along the Watchtower" that does the unthinkable of supplanting Bob Dylan's original in many listeners' minds. I've heard even knowledgeable music people talk about "that Whitney Houston song 'I Will Always Love You,'" when it was Dolly Parton who wrote and recorded it years earlier. The sheer virtuosity and bombast of Whitney's version drowns out the small and personal (and equally remarkable) version by Dolly. Countless websites offer lists of covers that are "better than the original." At any given time in our collective cultural moment such judgments may shift toward or away from the original in what the music critic Carl Wilson terms the "Epidemic of Second Thought"—the "cycles of revisionism" that move critical consensus toward innovation and the new (the cover) or toward preservation and the "authentic" (the original). The beauty for individual listeners, though, is that we don't have to choose one over the other.

It's unlikely that Don Henley set out to write songs worthy of covers when he began recording his third post-Eagles album, *The End of the Innocence*, in 1988. The album sold more than 6 million copies and spawned three top-forty singles, each of which would soon become part of the contemporary pop music repertoire. The soul singer India.Arie covered "The Heart of the Matter" on her 2006 album, *Testimony: Vol. 1, Life & Relationship*. More than a dozen artists, from the Ataris to KT Tunstall, have covered "The Boys of Summer." By far the most intriguing case study for covers, though, is the title song. "The End of the Innocence," which Henley wrote with the pianist and singer Bruce Hornsby, was the album's lead single and its most successful, reaching number eight on the pop charts during the summer of 1989. This was the summer of Milli Vanilli and New Kids on the Block, of Paula Abdul and Bobby Brown. It was a summer, in other words, dominated by dance music and love ballads, a summer like so many others.

By contrast, "The End of the Innocence" is about ambivalence. At once, it is a social critique of American empire after eight years of Ronald Reagan, that "tired old man that we elected king." On the other, it is a nostalgic glance back at a simpler place and time. Both lyrically and musically, the song embodies tension. Minor chords of concern in the verses give way to major chords of hope in the chorus. I can recall listening to "The End of the Innocence" at fifteen and getting caught up in the romance of it all. I imagined myself living in the chorus, where I'd invite a young lady to lay her head down on the ground and let her hair fall all around me. Listening to the song today, it is still beautiful, though tarnished a bit by time. The unfaltering ba-bum-crack of the programmed drum machine dates it, as do Hornsby's lovely but overfamiliar piano chords and the jazz great Wayne Shorter's dulcet soprano solo—tastefully played, but rendered guilty by association through sonic proximity to the canned facility of Kenny G's soporific solos.

Indeed, "The End of the Innocence" is a song ready made for smooth jazz, where easy instrumentals wash away the complications of the lyrics. Five years after Henley's single charted, the John Tesh Project recorded the first cover version, suitable for elevator transportation. More striking, though, were Bob Dylan's live concert covers of the song. Dylan stays faithful both to lyric and melody, and his voice, far more abrasive than Henley's honied tenor, tips the song's tone more decidedly toward invective. The most curious cover is by co-writer Hornsby's touring super group, featuring Bonnie Raitt, Shawn Colvin, David Lindley, and Jackson Browne. Performing the song for Jay Leno on *The Tonight Show*, Hornsby saws away on the accordion as the rest divvy up parts to sing, the whole performance somehow adding up to less than the sum of its parts.

Then there's the case of Okkervil River's "The End of the Innocence" cover. In the summer of 2014, a quarter century after the original song's release, the indie folk group included their radical reinterpretation on a free album of covers posted to their website. Okkervil River's frontman and lyricist, Will Sheff, recalls first hearing the song as a child in his father's car as they listened to Casey Kasem's *American Top 40* on Sunday mornings. "Shuffled in with sappy late-'80s cuts like 'From a Distance' and 'Cuts Both Ways,' 'The End of the Innocence' stood out," he wrote in *Rolling Stone* soon after Henley's attorneys issued a cease and desist order to have the cover removed from Okkervil River's website. "Sonically it was just as soggy as those Bette Midler and Gloria Estefan ballads, but there was this deflated masculine middle-aged world-weariness to it that haunted me, although I wouldn't have thought of those exact words at the time."

Henley's objections to Okkervil River's cover went beyond the fact that the band had not secured permission before posting it. Indeed, it is unlikely Henley would have granted that right given his low opinion of what Okkervil River did. "They don't understand the law," Henley told Australia's *Daily Telegraph* in June 2014. "You can't re-write the lyrics to somebody else's songs and record it [*sic*] and put it on the Internet. I'm sorry, but it wasn't an improvement. We were not impressed."

After listening to Okkervil River's cover, it's easy to understand why Henley was upset. Sheff's version is more or less faithful to the original in word and melody through the first verse and into the chorus, announcing its difference only with the home demo quality of its recording, which strips away the layers of the original's production down to voice and acoustic guitar. As a consequence, when Sheff sings the last lines of the first chorus ("This is the end/This is the end of the innocence"), the recording enacts the lyrics; when he sings "end" the song does in fact end, giving way to a silence that seems final until it isn't. By contrast, when Henley's voice pauses between those lines the space is filled with drums, synths, and Hornsby's industrious piano comps.

The real weirding of Okkervil River's cover begins with the next verse, though, where Sheff lyrically disrupts the meaning and the meter of the original. Henley's lovely "O beautiful for spacious skies / Now those skies are threatening" becomes "O beautiful for spacious skies / Turned smogified and threatening." Sheff's neologism is awkward, but purposely so. It shifts the song's registers of diction, which Henley and Hornsby neatly divide between the foreboding language of social critique of the verses and the pastoral language of safe retreat of the chorus. The cover exchanges the original's promise of washing away society's sin and finding respite as the "tall grass waves" with the image of stripping down to the skin and watching as the "tall grass dries."

Sheff repeatedly denies the consolations of Henley's original: the warm nostalgia of the country, the sweet assuredness of Henley's phrasing, the comforting shape of the melody. The first half of the song is still within the bounds of the common cover. Its subtle subversions, however, presage more radical reinventions to come. Sheff closes his cover of the song with an entirely new verse and chorus that he felt more fittingly resolved the song's subject. "'The End of the Innocence' is surprisingly fatalistic and despairing for a pop radio hit, but it seems to back off of that despair at the end," Sheff wrote after being forced to take the song down. "I felt like it would be interesting if the lyrics worked through that feeling of despair and tried to understand it and take it to the limit, as it were." Reflecting a year later on the whole matter of his cover and Henley's response, Sheff told the podcast *Pitch* the following:

[Henley's] song is saying, "I'm an old, irrelevant sack of shit and people like me ruin the world. And the world is fucked now." And then at the end he's kinda like, "Oh, well, as long as you love me we'll go away and it'll be great." And it's like, "No, that's not true! That's not how that song ends." You know what I mean? And so I felt like I wanted to take that song and drive it into the tree instead of drive it off into the sunset. And, I mean, I think it pissed him off for that reason.

In Sheff's alternative conclusion, the place of solace promised by Henley's chorus is gone. While Henley reclines with his lover, Sheff finds that his former hiding place is now just a "place that I rent." When Sheff speaks to his beloved, saying that he sees her head hanging low and hope draining out, he might as well be speaking to Henley's song itself. "This is the end," he sings, echoing Henley's resolution. Then he hits us in the face with "You know it's the end"—a line that denies even the euphony of the original melody, before closing with the same lyric sung in a decidedly different tone than the original: *This is the end of the innocence.* The difference is that Sheff makes us believe it.

One can understand why Okkervil River's cover would have pissed Henley off. It violates the integrity of his composition. Henley's original is a song, after all, about the possibility of escape from worldliness and pain. Sheff denies that recourse, rendering so many of the things that go down easy in the song now labored and pained—Henley's smooth tenor becomes Sheff's world-weary warble, Hornsby's brave block chords become Sheff's spare strums, Henley's lyrical language becomes Sheff's awkward neologisms and strained syntax, Henley's clear contrast between innocence and experience becomes Sheff's muddied reality in which beauty and ugliness intermingle. Of course, we all know which song's vision of the world is closer to the world in which we live. The only question is how much truth one desires from pop songs.

Sheff's cover is in dynamic relation to Henley's original. Henley's song escapes to beauty and nostalgia—of the uncorrupted landscape, of the union of a man and a woman offering up their best defense in love. "The End of the Innocence" joins a long tradition of literature and songs of loss and mourning: the elegy. Sheff rejects the elegiac impulse, asserting instead that Henley's original is finally just another poisoned fairy tale.

Depending on one's aesthetic and sensibility, Okkervil River's version can send you running back to the warm embrace of the original or give you the vocabulary for explaining your rejection of it. Either way, it does no disservice to Henley's original. What it does is occasion a more profound and immediate reflection on the tension that Henley's song concerned itself with in the first place: What is one to do when the world is crumbling all around us? If the song's commitments are true, one wonders why Henley would object to Sheff's extension of their aims. Henley's song even anticipates Sheff's practice when it quotes the famous opening line from "America the Beautiful," one of the anthems of American exceptionalism, only to subvert it. Sheff does on a large scale what Henley does on the small scale in that single line, and unlike Henley's subversion, Sheff's finishes the job—allowing for no comfort in the face of faltering empire.

COPYRIGHT AND THE COVER SONG

For Okkervil River and for a generation of artists weaned on the remixes and samples of hip-hop, the cover song is not an act of imitation and theft, but one of creation. "I feel like it's very native to art, this talking back and forth between generations, between artists, adding your own thing, changing it, spinning it around, undermining the original emotion, building a house entirely out of pieces of other people's houses," Sheff said. On Twitter, he offered the following distillation of principle: "(Honestly I think copyright law is garbage that damages the culture. Some of the best art is built around (loving) theft & defacement.)"

Such "loving theft" is the point where culture meets commerce. The natural state of culture is freedom, including free exchange and free expression. In contrast, commerce entails regulation and restriction. But without commerce, the creative impulse has no way to sustain itself. The relationship between freedom and commerce is crucial in popular music because so many commercial interests are at work and there is so much money to be made. We need to feed our artists; there's no shame in that. At the same time, we do not want to choke the source of their creativity, which is the free range of aesthetic motion and the free exercise of the vernacular process, that hallmark of American culture. "Every pop musician is a thief and a magpie," observes Elvis Costello. "I have an emotional affinity for certain styles, but none of them belong to me." To whom, then, do styles belong? How much of a sound, how much of a style, can be owned? How much are we willing as a society to restrict the process of adaptation and adoption that has always been at the core of musical culture?

"Popular music as an industry is based on intellectual property rights," argues Tara Brabazon. If this is true, then we are living in the golden age of intellectual property and music copyright litigation. This is partly a result of scarcity in the music industry, where rights holders feel compelled to capitalize on whatever they can. It's partly a consequence of the litigious nature of our culture and the readily available access to almost every sound that gets produced. It's also a consequence of the recent success of some litigants, which inspires other artists to file similar lawsuits.

Copyright generally protects melody and lyrics. "The copyright of a musical composition is based on the top-line melody, the specific harmonies that support it, and, in the case of a song or opera, the lyrics. There is no acknowledgement of groove, sound, texture, or arrangement—all of which are features of the recorded music of our era that we listeners have come to savor and identify as integral to an artist's work," David Byrne wrote in 2013. In the swiftly evolving field of music copyright law, a few things are clear: Melody is sacrosanct, as is language. Increasingly, it appears that courts—or at least juries like the one that decided in favor of the Marvin Gaye estate in its dispute with Robin Thicke and Pharrell Williams over "Blurred Lines"— are considering other things open to ownership, even a groove, a feel, or timbre. Rhythms, however, have generally been exempted from copyright, save for in cases of samples like James Brown's "Funky Drummer" beat.

What about a vocal cadence, a quality that structures the shape of a song as much as a melody? What about a groove, or, even more abstract, a sonic feel? Should courts treat these as they do a melody? Should they be protected or considered fair game? These questions underlie a series of events in 2015 that seemed to change the mindset if not the law around the ownership of sound and style. The first occurred when Tom Petty's attorneys secured co-writing credit and royalty sharing from Sam Smith for the resemblance between Smith's Grammy-winning "Stay with Me" from 2014 and Tom Petty's 1989 hit "I Won't Back Down." The second was the suit between Robin Thicke and Pharrell Williams and the Marvin Gaye estate regarding Thicke's 2014 hit "Blurred Lines" and Gaye's "Got to Give It Up" from 1977. Much has been written about these already, with more still to come.

At least as it concerns the poetry of pop, an even more compelling instance of style adaptation never reached litigation. When Mark Ronson and Bruno Mars's ubiquitous hit "Uptown Funk" debuted on commercial radio in November 2014, it sounded like nothing else playing at the time. Although it was distinctive in its pop moment, the song is decidedly imitative. Depending on your perspective, it is either slavishly derivative or cleverly celebratory of a good many styles, artists, and individual songs. One hears a panoply of 1970s and 1980s funk, from the Gap Band to Prince to the Sequence to Roger Troutman's Zapp & Roger. It's in the groove, the guitar licks, the horn hits, the call-and-response between Mars and his background singers. It's even in the video, which looks a lot like an outtake from the Time rocking their set on Prince's *Purple Rain* film. None of these influences is credited. This is fair enough, given that most of these allusions and echoes are either part of a long history of African American oral practice or recontextualized enough to be untraceable to a certain song.

"Uptown Funk" owes a more particular debt, however, one that is acknowledged in the publication rights but that firmly undercuts the song's claims to its own style. That debt is to the bizarre viral rap hit by a larger-than-life character from Atlanta named Trinidad James, called "All Gold Everything." The press linking the two songs has focused exclusively on the way that "Uptown Funk" repurposes the signature refrain from "All Gold Everything": "Don't believe me? Just watch." James repeats the line twelve times; "Uptown Funk" does him five better. The line is memorable, and certainly plays a part in the remarkable success of "Uptown Funk." At four my daughter went through a phase where she would run around the house repeating that line incessantly, and this after hearing it only once. Given the repetition of such a distinctive phrase, it makes sense that Ronson would forestall any claims by offering James a share of royalties.

When I first heard "Uptown Funk" Trinidad James did not cross my mind. What did, however, was the song's strangeness, its anomalous existence in the popular soundscape of 2014, which was dominated by pop country ballads and EDM-inspired everything else. Thinking back, the strangeness did not reside primarily in the canned funk, something that the song performs rather than inhabits. Rather, it was in Mars's stutter-step vocal delivery, broken by unusual elisions, pauses, and antiphonal echoes. Mars is a singer, at times a crooner; here he was locating his voice in the song's groove like he was a percussionist—with sharp hits, percussive riffs, and vocal jabs. He was relating to the rhythm more like a rapper than a singer, through rhythm more than melody. To be sure, the song has a melody, though not one you're likely to whistle while you work. What sets "Uptown Funk" apart is its rhythmic texture in the instrumentation and in the voices as they play off one another.

This brings me back to my earlier question: Can you copyright a cadence? It wasn't long before I decided to listen to Trinidad James's song again, and what I found was that the cadence of "Uptown Funk" is a near replica of James's, sometimes down to the specific words. Look at how each song begins, first "Uptown Funk," then "All Gold Everything." The italics show exact word replications, while the bold print shows identical rhythmic replications.

This hit that ice cold	*This* ain't for no fuck nigga
Michelle Pfeiffer, that white gold	You a real nigga, then fuck with me
This one for them hood girls	*This one for the hood* niggas
Them good girls, straight masterpieces	Hipster bitches that shop at Lenox
Stylin', wilin'	**Dark skinned, light skinned**

More telling, though, are the lines that follow:

I'm too hot **(hot damn)** / For the hoes, **my nigga**
Call the police and the fireman / That's pussy popping at Magic City
I'm too hot (**hot damn**) / Flash strong, **my nigga**
Make a dragon wanna retire, man / Then come match that shit with me
I'm too hot **(hot damn)** / Smoking mid, **my nigga**
Say my name, you know who I am / Then don't pass that shit to me
I'm too hot (hot damn) / This one for my niggas
And my band *'bout that money* **(Break it down)** / And bitches *'bout that money* **(Cash Out)**

James's profane punctuation ("my nigga") becomes the playfully antiquated "hot damn," with the same preceding medial caesura. Further, the sixteenth line of "Uptown Funk" nearly repeats the sixteenth line of "All Gold Everything." It is as if Ronson and Mars put tracing paper over James's lyrics, repeating the structure of the cadence down to the pattern of stressed and unstressed syllables. Why does all of this matter? Well, it speaks to an unacknowledged debt that is, to my reading, even greater than the debt the song owes to the host of funk songs that it references and interpolates. This debt to James poses both an aesthetic and, potentially, a legal question: To whom does the cadence belong? To James for constructing it, as basic and repetitive as that "it" is? To Ronson and Mars for endowing it with a certain melody? Or to no one at all? Perhaps Ronson anticipated the legal question about cadence as well, giving James credit not just for the cribbed catchphrase but for the rhythm of the vocal line as well.

The question of whether vocal cadence can be copyrighted has broad implications for rap, which has been closely scrutinized when it comes to sampling, but which has garnered almost no attention when it comes to the intellectual property of the MC's flow. In the hip-hop community, MCs often talk about other rappers stealing their flows; such theft is looked down upon but hasn't been the subject of litigation in the way that a surreptitious sample has. If rap in particular, and pop music in general, is to be respected and protected, it might be worth considering the degree to which flow can be owned and whether a style can, indeed, be copyrighted.

For us as listeners, though, it's a simpler matter than it is for the artists. We're free to enjoy Mark Ronson and Bruno Mars's "Uptown Funk" and Trinidad James's "All Gold Everything" with knowledge of their connection or in ignorance of it. In both cases, the flow just works. Whatever its debts, "Uptown Funk" captures a style that's also its own.

CROSS-GENRE COVERS

The crooner Paul Anka has been recording covers since he was a teen heart-throb in the late 1950s. He covered the Drifters' "Save the Last Dance for Me" in 1963 and Frank Sinatra's signature tune "My Way" in 1974. In 2005 he recorded an entire album of pop covers that included a striking rendition of Nirvana's grunge anthem "Smells Like Teen Spirit." Anka's version brings more swing than angst, with big-band accompaniment to go along with his jaunty delivery of the lyrics. There's an element of kitsch at work, but the cover also underscores Anka's unfailing professionalism in arranging and delivering songs as well as the integrity of Nirvana's original. As Anka explains it, "'Smells Like Teen Spirit' works with a swing arrangement because it's poetry and it has a real cool melody to swing to." In an instance like this, the song's displacement from genre and from the defining style of its performance results in revelation rather than stagnation.

Cross-genre covers help define both the genre of the original, the donor song, and the genre of the cover, the recipient song. By seeing what changes— say, how the Gourds fashion a melody for Snoop Dogg's original lyrics on "Gin & Juice"—and what remains, but now calls attention to itself in a way that it doesn't in the original song—say, how the white singer-songwriter Ben Folds retains the word "nigga" in his acoustic cover of Dr. Dre's "Bitches Ain't Shit"—it is possible to isolate some of the defining stylistic features of the original. Like Ben Folds's cover of Dr. Dre, many cross-genre covers are also cross-racial and cross-cultural covers as well, which means that they carry significance that stretches beyond aesthetics and taste.

Fetty Wap's "Trap Queen" is a stylistic hybrid, both singing and rapping, both loopy love song and drug tale. Fetty Wap dubs his style "Ignorant R&B," perhaps for the ways that he takes staple soul elements like extolling a woman's faithfulness and their mutual passion while setting their story in the underworld of drug dealing. The most striking hybridity, though, is the way that "Trap Queen" blends sing-along vocal delivery and mass-appeal electronic instrumentals with thematic and linguistic insularity. You don't need to be conversant in the song's arcane language—cooking pies, bandos, and the titular site of the trap—to comprehend the song's meaning. The fact that the song remained in the *Billboard* Hot 100 top ten for months testifies to its crossover appeal, even as it has retained its legitimacy in the narrower realm of hip-hop and R&B.

However, the mainstream saturation of "Trap Queen" does not prepare one for the cover by the twee English crooner Ed Sheeran. During a visit to *The Tonight Show*, Sheeran recorded a version of the song backstage with the house band, the Roots. Sheeran frequently integrates rap covers into his live shows, creating a conscious dissonance that lends some needed edge to his sensitive sound, and some welcome melody to the songs he covers. In this instance, Sheeran accentuates the nascent melodic qualities in Fetty Wap's hybrid rapping-singing vocal delivery, committing to the limited but potent melodic possibilities of the original song. The more profound transformation occurs with the lyrics, which change by staying entirely the same. The difference is, when Sheeran speaks of cooking pies with his beloved, one wonders whether they'll be apple or cherry.

Sheeran's cover, like the best pop-music covers, calls attention to what is distinctively appealing about the original while it underscores the stylistic fingerprint of the artist recording the cover. In the distance between original and cover, one can isolate what the new singer brings to the song. In proximity, one sees the elemental qualities of the original composition that survive any stylistic conversion. Sheeran's "Trap Queen" is a new manifestation of the ironic cover, best defined in 1996 by the music critic Jake London. Traditionally, the ironic cover is a product of the cognitive dissonance brought on by a cool band (in London's example, the Replacements) covering a song by a decidedly uncool one (Kiss's "Black Diamond"). The caché of the cool band gives listeners license to enjoy in public the "uncool" music that many of them might already enjoy in private. For its part, the cool band is free to embrace the pleasure of the original—be it out of nostalgia, a genuine appreciation for the song, or both—knowing that they are protected by what London terms "preemptive irony," which "disarm[s] the critic by calling the novelty of his or her enterprise into question before the critic has a chance to call the artist's enterprise into question."

London's formulation fits elegantly with, say, an up-and-coming Run-D.M.C. covering a then lukewarm Aerosmith's "Walk This Way" in 1986, or Okkervil River covering George Benson's disco-jazz 1980 hit "Give Me the Night" on their 2013 EP of eighties covers, *Golden Opportunities 3*—the album that also boasted their controversial cover of Don Henley's "The End of the Innocence." But the Fetty Wap–Ed Sheeran exchange is something different. If forced to define them in a binary, then surely Fetty Wap is the cool to Sheeran's uncool. The pattern, then, is reversed. Instead of a cool band resurrecting an uncool song, it's an uncool artist covering a cool song.

The ironic currency of the cover, the reason Sheeran would choose to do "Trap Queen," then, is not centered on critical taste but on something else: on race. Sheeran's act of preemptive irony is not aimed at excusing the *song*, but rather at excusing *himself* and his image of coffee shop, middle-of-the-road pop. "Trap Queen" gives him edge, while showing him to be self-aware enough to be the first to laugh at how unlikely it is for him to sing such a song. The humor comes in the distance between Sheeran's boy-next-door public image (an image, incidentally, that doesn't necessarily square with reality) and the explicit content of Fetty Wap's original. Sheeran's cover also implicitly invites us as listeners to side with him in exoticizing "Trap Queen," in exploiting it as a source of amazement and amusement. It's a racial game that plays into centuries-old black-white cultural binaries. Sheeran's cover relies on notions of black cool and white squareness, black danger and white safety, that have long been part of the American racial imagination.

One final example of this cross-racial cover dynamic will suffice. Early in 2011, the R&B singer Chris Brown released "Look at Me Now," a Diplo and Afrojack–produced club banger featuring the rappers Lil Wayne and Busta Rhymes that peaked at number six on the *Billboard* Hot 100 chart and has earned more than 350 million YouTube views. The song's cultural saturation far exceeds its chart position. But why? In most respects, "Look at Me Now" is a paint-by-numbers hip-hop/R&B recording. Brown delivers his lyrics with unselfconscious bluster; there's nary a hint of self-awareness behind his swagger and his boasts. The song celebrates wealth and sexual prowess. It's less a Chris Brown song than it is a Lil Wayne song, and it is less a Lil Wayne song than it is a Busta Rhymes song. Busta Rhymes delivers the most memorable performance with a rapid-fire display of rap virtuosity. In eighteen bars, he is by turns sinister and playful. His delivery creates the tone, not the words, which flash by in such rapid succession that most escape comprehension.

The longevity and cultural impact of "Look at Me Now" are due in part to the fact that it quickly became an exemplar of an emergent cultural trend: the hipster cover. The hipster cover is one in which a rap or R&B (read: black) song is ironically performed by a white artist or comedian, usually in a performance style that contrasts sharply with the lyric content. Think again of Sheeran's rendition of Fetty Wap's "Trap Queen." In the case of "Look at Me

Now," the cover in question was by the pop duo Karmin, which consists of vocalist Amy Heidemann and instrumentalist/producer Nick Noonan. In the YouTube clip a preening and posing Heidemann delivers all the lyrics to the song verbatim, save for the conspicuous omission of the word "nigga," to the stripped-down accompaniment of Noonan's keyboard. The cover draws its novelty from the obvious contrast between the over-the-top boasts of the lyrics (a kind of black male hip-hop mythos) and the ironic performance. Heidemann regenders the song and recodes it in race and in genre.

Much of the cover's appeal lies in the same qualities that made the original remarkable, namely, the virtuosity of the lyric delivery of the Busta Rhymes verse. Heidemann distinguishes herself as a talented performer in her own right, irrespective of the ironic play and intentions of the song as a whole. She deserves the dust-off-the-shoulder "I'm done" at the end of the verse almost as much as Busta Rhymes does. The Karmin version cuts against the original's tone of self-seriousness even as it celebrates the original's rapid-fire percussive vocalization. In fact, Karmin's cover might make the Chris Brown version more palatable by encouraging listeners who know both versions to direct their attention to what makes the song great rather than to what makes it objectionable and even, when combined with Brown's off-the-record transgressions, repulsive. The tone of the cover supplies a leavening self-awareness that the original lacks, while the quality of the cover version's performance reflects the virtuosity of the original. As a result, we don't dismiss the original as we might have had the cover been simply comic, nor do we dismiss the cover as we would have had it been a rote repetition of the original.

Somewhere in the relation between Chris Brown's original and Karmin's cover of "Look at Me Now" is a key to understanding the present disposition of musical culture when it comes to race and style. The past decade has seen cross-genre and cross-racial covers emerge from novelties on the peripheries of music to become a musical force. These covers exist almost entirely in the pop space of the web and are inextricable from their visual evidence of racial difference. They must be seen as well as heard.

Take, for instance, Jimmy Fallon's spoof group the Ragtime Gals' (with guest performer Kevin Spacey) cover of R&B crooner Jason Derulo's "Talk Dirty," complete with barbershop harmonies. Fallon extends a long-standing *Tonight Show* tradition stretching back to the 1950s when host Steve Allen performed a sardonic reading of Gene Vincent's 1956 rockabilly hit "Be-Bop-A-Lula" to polite chuckles from the audience. Both Allen's and Fallon's performances owe their appeal to a series of contrasts and contradictions that their listeners are asked to resolve. In the Derulo original, words like "booty" and the sexual provocation of the line "first class seat on my lap, girl" are unremarkable because they confirm expectations of genre, and perhaps also of gender and race. When shifted out of genre, out of race, and even out of time when delivered a cappella by five white men dressed up in straw hats and 1920s-style suits, the lyrics reveal their comic excess and innate absurdity. *Who says this kind of stuff? This can't be serious.*

But who is the joke on here? Certainly it's on Derulo and others like him who pass off such paltry lyrics with the sweet distraction of style and sound. The joke is also on the cover performers, whom we see as the squares. Unfortunately, this humor reinforces racial paradigms in which the black artist is cool and sexual and transgressive and the white artist is awkward and asexual and safe. These parodies are at once new and familiar: The novelty comes from hearing songs in a new genre, a new style, and a new voice; the familiarity comes from the way these covers reaffirm faulty assumptions about race, gender, and power. In the latter regard, there is something fundamentally conservative and antiprogressive about these covers, in their effect if not always in their intentions.

Scott Bradlee's "Postmodern Jukebox" also revels in the creative discontinuities and discoveries found in the distance between song and performance in cross-genre covers. His YouTube channel includes an ever-expanding catalog of cover versions of pop songs, new and old, recast in genre and time period. Perhaps the best known of these is a haunting and beautiful 2013 clip entitled "Sad Clown with the Golden Voice," a version of Lorde's "Royals" with vocals by Puddles the Clown, an Atlanta-based performance artist and singer with a rich and resonant baritone that contrasts with his white face paint and comic attire.

Bradlee's covers investigate the interplay of genre and sound far more deeply than Fallon's barbershop quartet skits do. This is due in large part to the mixed-race identity of the performers; this isn't a "Hey, look how cute the white boy/girl is by saying dirty words that black people say." Instead, these covers revel in the sonic possibilities inherent in the act of taking a song out of its native performance style and recasting it using the conventions of another style. There's theater to the clips as well, with period costumes, dance steps, and, of course, the sad clown, but the focus is on the sonic appeal. One can listen with pleasure to the audio alone.

I know that I'm betraying my own aesthetic bias in the contrast between these two cover song practices. I do think that one is more sophisticated than the other. That's not to suggest that I don't enjoy the joke of the simpler covers at times as well. Both speak to the present state of pop music; both reveal sometimes hidden desires in sound and style.

Chapter
Nine

The bluesman Willie Dixon believed that songs should arouse empathy through story. "When you're writing a song," he told an interviewer, "you're projecting how somebody else feels. 'How would I feel if that happened to me?' When you're in a position to put things in a poetic form, it creates sweetness, understanding, and emphasis. Some people just get up and recite a poem. I think when you sing it in a blues form you get more attention for it." The communicative power of singing extends beyond the blues, of course, something Dixon must have known well given how many of his songs were covered over the years by artists across many genres, from Aretha Franklin to the Rolling Stones to George Thorogood.

Dixon's "Hoochie Coochie Man," a song first recorded by Muddy Waters in 1954 and covered over the years by everyone from Jimi Hendrix to Dion to the New York Dolls, projects a character of mythic scale. It's a song full of outlandish boasts and sexual bravado, and subtler forms of self-affirmation as well ("But you know I'm him / Everybody knows I'm him") that must have sounded particularly radical coming from the pen of a black man like Dixon and the voice of a black man like Waters in the same year as the landmark *Brown v. Board of Education* decision began dismantling Jim Crow segregation. The song's expression of empathetic connection through language and sound, structured by the songwriter's craft, accounts for its capacity to connect to listeners these many years later.

Sometimes this empathetic connection happens through details, the specificity of setting or character or time. But sometimes the calculated blurring of details engages the listener more fully in the co-construction of meaning and image. "I know from writing lyrics that some details—names, places, locations—are desirable; they anchor the piece in the real world," writes David Byrne. "But so are ambiguities. By letting the listener or viewer fill in the blanks, complete the picture (or piece of music), the work becomes personalized and the audience can adapt it to their own lives and situations. They become more involved with the work, and an intimacy and involvement becomes possible that perfection might have kept at bay." As it is with other literary forms, the goal of the song lyric is to provide just enough detail to invite that mingling of authorial and readerly invention. The goal is to conjure a story.

Songs tell stories. Stories are the primary means through which the mind orders experience and then communicates that experience to others. One of the pop songwriter's jobs is to tell a story in a handful of verses, a practice that emerges from an oral tradition in which songs served the social functions of communal entertainment and collective memory. Though it may be hard to imagine the typical three-and-a-half-minute *Billboard* hit descending from Homeric epics and the fifteenth-century ballad stanza, the epic poem and the ballad comprise part of the narrative heritage of the contemporary pop song. As do all modes of story, ancient and modern, pop music and the poetic forms of their lyrics come together to entertain, to instruct, and to commemorate.

Song narratives share a great deal with written and spoken narratives, but differ in ways that complicate character, setting, time, and the rest of the constitutive elements of a storyworld. Like stories in an oral tradition, we experience songs in real time rather than as written artifacts perused at our leisure. Song stories also differ fundamentally from stories spoken aloud in that the narrative drives of their lyrics work in conjunction with, and sometimes in subservience to, music's melodic, harmonic, and rhythmic impulses.

Understanding how story expresses itself in song, though, begins even before the lyric. Instrumental music, too, tells a story, if we understand it, as Theodor Adorno does Gustav Mahler's orchestral songs, as that which "narrates without narrative." One usually finds in instrumental music the rudiments of plot, which is to say a beginning, a middle, and an end. One finds instrumental voices that interact with one another as if in conflict or communion or conversation. One also finds the emotive push and pull of harmonics and melody and rhythm that stands as a kind of semiotics of sound—a way of making meaning through a language of aural signs. "Like stories, music is said to be central to human ordering, shaping, and meaning-making needs," observe the literary critics Linda and Michael Hutcheon.

Though critics continue to dispute whether the connection between music and narrative is metaphorical or actual, an increasing number of musicologists and narrative scholars argue for a narratology of instrumental music, that is, a means of studying "the logic, principles, and practices of narrative representation," in the words of the literary critic Marie-Laure Ryan. Instrumental music, writes Ryan, "cannot imitate speech, represent thought, narrate actions, or express causal relations." "Its mimetic abilities," she continues "are limited to the imitation of aural phenomena: the gurgling of a brook, the song of birds, or the rumbling of thunder." That being said, instrumental music can inspire listeners' impressions of narrativity, albeit of an indeterminate variety. "Narrative content is something that is read into a composition rather than read from it," Ryan argues. Music carries certain advantages when it comes to narrative, namely, its capacity to conjure emotion and its direct means of expressing time. When fitted with the language of lyrics, song becomes a potent way to tell stories.

A comprehensive understanding of storytelling in human experience must account for stories voiced in songs. Minimally defined, a story is a narrative of events. Narrative, in the words of the literary theorists James Phelan and Peter J. Rabinowitz, "is somebody telling somebody else, on some occasions, and for some purposes, that something happened to someone or something." Narrative is not always a series of ordered events, of course; nor is it always framed as direct communication. Some stories disrupt temporality, as Bob Dylan does on "Tangled Up in Blue" by presenting the past and the present at the same time. Some reject narrative purpose, as Jack White does on the Raconteurs' "Carolina Drama" when he sings these opening lines: "I'm not sure if there's a point to this story / But I'm going to tell it again." Some disguise the intended hearer of the narrator's story, as Townes Van Zandt does on "Pancho and Lefty." Stories like these leave us to find our way through worlds in which the air the characters breathe is composed of different stuff from our own.

Rather than a sequence of events, narrative is an event in itself. It is, in other words, a rhetorical act. To quote Phelan and Rabinowitz again, narrative is "a multidimensional purposive communication from a teller to an audience." This construction of teller and audience, metaphoric as it relates to literature in print, is literal when it comes to recorded songs. Songs invite empathy. "Remember," the producer and performer Nile Rodgers wrote, reflecting on the enduring success of one his collaborators, Madonna, "the artist is telling a story, one that we must believe—the ability to convey feelings is the key to pop, not perfect technique." Emotive connection between teller and audience is story's defining difference in song. Songs are engines of empathy that work through the voice's direct address to listeners and through the "I," "you," and "we" of most lyrics.

Lyric density also shapes story. More words usually mean a greater capacity for narrative expression. We tend to associate rap, country, and folk music with narrative in part because they are densely linguistic. Bruce Springsteen averages 281 words per song; Eminem averages over a thousand. Compare those numbers to the 102 words per song average of the Beatles' *Abbey Road* and it is clear why there might be greater potential for narrative to find a home in the songs of rock troubadours and rap MCs. Conversely, the greater lyric density of these genres might speak to the artists' need to fit their forms to their expressive desires.

Stories take on a range of forms and invent structures that defy conventional chronology. Song lyrics do the same. A taxonomy of storytelling in pop songs includes numerous modes. The most common mode is vaguely narrative; it has a protagonist, the "I" of the singer, and at least one other character, often the beloved "you." I say it is vaguely narrative because it is reliant on feeling rather than incident. It resists paraphrase because it is not centrally concerned with narrative action. Think of Paul McCartney singing "When I find myself in times of struggle / Mother Mary comes to me" on "Let It Be," or Stevie Nicks revealing "Well, I've been afraid of changing / 'Cause I've built my life around you" on Fleetwood Mac's "Landslide," or really the majority of pop songs ever recorded. A far smaller but significant category consists of songs that make narrative a central feature of their form. They satisfy the requirements of setting, character, and action. They are amenable to paraphrase. These are songs like the Temptations' "Papa Was a Rolling Stone," recounting a son's talk with his mother about his wayward father, and Joni Mitchell's "The Last Time I Saw Richard," whose opening line establishes time and setting ("The last time I saw Richard was Detroit in '68"). Most songs relate incidents and feelings; a few enact dramas.

But not all songs tell stories, or at least not a story as we conventionally think of it in our culture, which is to say as something with a beginning, a middle, and an end. Many songs are ambient, emotive. They work through image and feeling. They reject narrative action and refuse to be upfront about their meaning. Lyric obscurity or fuzziness also occludes narrative. Lyrics sometimes clarify, sometimes particularize, and sometimes complicate the narrative and emotive impulses that listeners gather from the music. Storytelling is a social action, though it is not the only social action song enacts. A consonance of feeling, as one finds in genres as far-flung as gospel and death metal, can fulfill the social function of song just as ably as a well-rendered story.

Nonetheless, as Chuck Berry once put it, "a song is written for the story." Whether telling a story or summing up a feeling, song lyrics work with rhythms, melodies, chords, and harmonies to affect a listener's consciousness. The goal of this chapter is to expand the categories of narrative to account for the multimodal stories that songs often tell. It concerns both the songs in which narrative is incidental and those in which it is active in telling stories. We'll begin by considering the ways that all songs are stories in the broadest sense, and end by exploring the specific ways that pop songs create new worlds ready to inhabit.

THE LOW END THEORY

What are pop songs doing when they are only vaguely narrative—which is to say, what are pop songs doing most of the time? Even in rap and country, genres often associated with narrative, most songs aren't primarily about story either. Glance through Jay Z's catalog, and for every "Song Cry," a painful confession of personal failures to a distant lover, you'll find a dozen songs like "Otis," an ode to excess. Even Jay Z's best-known story, which describes a roadside confrontation with a police officer on "99 Problems," only takes up the second verse of a song that is not otherwise narrative. George Jones scored a big hit in 1983 with a simile-driven song called "Tennessee Whiskey"—a song that Chris Stapleton would take all the way to number one on the *Billboard* country charts in 2015—while the B-side, "Almost Persuaded," is the song with the story: a taut three-minute narrative about a married man resisting the allures of a younger woman.

Could it be that pop songs are better off being about nothing more than the joyous clash and clangor of syllables and sounds? "There's a theory that really good rock & roll is all below the waist," Lou Reed told the writer Bill Flanagan. "The theory continues—if I understand it right—that as you introduce any other kind of thought to it, it starts to stutter and become less rock & roll, less danceable, less everything, until it's no fun at all. There is that point of view." Following this theory—I call it, with apologies to A Tribe Called Quest, the Low End Theory—a pop recording should locate its energy below the waist, in the groove, in the sex, in the feet rather than in the head. The emblem for such a theory could be Elvis Presley on *The Ed Sullivan Show*, the camera frame cropping just above the waist, inadvertently emphasizing what was going on down below. It could be Madonna crawling across the stage while performing "Like a Virgin" at the 1984 MTV Video Music Awards or Michael Jackson repeatedly grabbing his crotch during his halftime performance at 1993's Super Bowl. It could be Nicki Minaj twerking and Miley Cyrus trying to twerk. The Low End Theory encompasses a sonic attitude that's all about the bass, no treble, and a cognitive attitude that privileges sound over semantics. Narrative, after all, tends to draw us into the mind, away from the visceral energy and erotic pleasure of the body.

Reed, however, described this theory of popular music in order to refute it. First with the Velvet Underground and later as a solo artist, Reed cultivated a style that demanded listeners' attention, even as it still served the music's below-the-waist imperative. "Then there's *my* point of view," Reed continues, "that says if you do it right you should be able to have everything you had before and—if you want it—you should be able to have these other levels. You can have a plot, you can have a whole mess of things going on for the people who want to hear it. Other people don't have to. But it should still be in there as a rock & roll thing—i.e., not get too wordy, not get bogged down in anything that takes away from the basic fun of a rock record." Reed's use of "record" here instead of "song" reminds us that the dual purposes of pop need not be served in lyric alone.

As song lyric, the Velvet Underground's "I'm Waiting for the Man" demands immense cognitive attention, drawing us entirely above the waist to the top of our heads; it's a song, rich with narrative detail, about copping heroin: the "twenty-six dollars in my hand," the uptown address on 125th and Lexington, the dealer's style of shoes, the scraps of dialogue between the black dealer and the "white boy" junkie. Experiencing the lyric as recorded song, though, shifts the center of aesthetic gravity closer to the waist, or below. The percussive pounding of piano, bass, drums, and electric guitar blends together in singular purpose and in nearly singular sound, rendering the song strangely, seductively danceable despite the starkness of the lyrics.

When Flanagan shared Reed's theory with Sting, Sting responded by describing another theory of pop music that makes room for both extremes. "We're now conditioned to expect nothing of lyrics, to know that as long as they have the semblance of meaning that's enough," Sting said. "And that's the function of abstract art, abstract poetry. You can't really tell what's good and what's bad. I agree with Lou Reed—with some songs it doesn't matter. And there's room for that music. But there's also room for serious, well-thought-out lyrics." The duality between songs in which the meaning of the lyrics doesn't matter and those that offer "serious, well-thought-out lyrics" is schematically useful. However, it fails to account for the fact that many so-called frivolous lyrics are also well thought out, as a vessel for sound, for instance, or as a cue for a particular emotion.

Take Harry Nilsson's "Coconut." It's simple enough, both in lyric and music. Musically, the entire song consists of a single chord and an alternating bass note. Lyrically, it's what some dismissively label a novelty song; in this case, the majority of the lyric comprises a simple recipe for curing an upset stomach: "You put the lime in the coconut, you drink them both up." What makes the song indelible, though, is how Nilsson narrows the vocabulary and calibrates the repetition to fashion a pleasing series of rhythmic echoes, vocal inflections, and sonic textures. The song is playful and funny. Above all, it's good.

Pop demands that we interrogate easy oppositions: silly/serious, simple/complex, above/below the waist. These dichotomies can be useful beginnings, but they demand refinement. Writing about fellow folk legend Woody Guthrie, Pete Seeger cautioned us not to be fooled by the seeming simplicity of Guthrie's music. "His songs are deceptively simple," Seeger writes. "Only after they have become part of your life do you realize how great they are. Any damn fool can get complicated. It takes genius to attain simplicity." We do well to keep Seeger's words in mind. When reading lyrics on the page, there's a natural tendency to privilege those that are outwardly literary: lyrics that are narrative-driven, for instance, or richly textured with figurative language and densely patterned in rhyme and syntax. However, a necessary part of the poetics of pop rests in examining the craft at work in the plainspoken, the minimal, even the underdeveloped. Such lyrics are less likely to make their full worth known on the page; their value becomes apparent when we look at the lyrics while listening to their performance as sound recording.

No one is likely to be favorably impressed when reading the lyrics to Chic's 1979 disco hit "Good Times." The lyrics offer little story to follow, few images to unpack, and not much in the way of rhyme patterns. But the lyrics underlie the song's arresting quality in performance. To return to Reed's theory, "Good Times" clearly qualifies as a below-the-waist song; the funky bass line inaugurated an entire genre of music in hip-hop when the "Good Times" instrumental became the basis of the Sugar Hill Gang's "Rapper's Delight." That said, "Good Times" still invites enough above-the-waist interest to make it a compelling object of critical reflection. Think of the salient oddity of the phrase "clams on a half-shell and roller skates, roller skates." Even the most seemingly vacuous pop lyric likely has at least something to offer on close inspection. Some songs, however, promise far richer rewards. With the expansion of pop's ambitions as a storytelling medium and as a literary form, songwriters have fashioned works of startling scope.

More ambitious songs, however, are not always better songs, just as more ambitious recordings are not always better recordings. Received opinion holds that pop music attends to only a handful of themes, the preeminent of which is love, or love's lesser urges. Ted Gioia writes that "love has been a dominant theme of popular song for at least a thousand years." Some of the greatest song lyrics ever written concern love. Nonetheless, the bias persists that a song about, say, a disgraced prizefighter (Bob Dylan's "Hurricane") is necessarily more sophisticated than a song about a girl meeting a boy (Rihanna's "We Found Love") or a girl meeting a girl (Ani DiFranco's "Shameless").

The turn toward pop songs as a medium of broad expressive range can be marked from one obvious point: the 1960s, with Bob Dylan, and after him, the Beatles. "One of the great legacies of the Beatles was to extend the subject matter of the genre," writes Steve Turner in his account of the Beatles' songwriting, *A Hard Day's Write*. "Fewer than half the songs on *Revolver* were about love. The rest of the songs on this album ranged from taxation to Tibetan Buddhism." This thematic variety is worth noting, but I resist the attendant assumption that this means the recordings are superior because of the lyrics' thematic reach. As a post-Beatles Paul McCartney would sing, "Some people want to fill the world with silly love songs/And what's wrong with that?"

In his own account of the Beatles' songwriting, Dominic Pedler cautions against ascribing an evolutionary arc of refinement when comparing the more straightforward structures and lyric themes of the Beatles' early recordings with their more experimental and thematically diverse later recordings.

But were the songs that originally fuelled Beatlemania really so naïve compared with what came later? Of course, the Beatles matured as songwriters in myriad respects, as would naturally be expected of any artists over the course of a decade of development. But a preoccupation with the group's pioneering recording practices threatens to obscure the extensive array of musical principles evident in their writing as early as their debut album, *Please Please Me*. Similarly, there is the trap of assuming that innocent pop songs, lyrically long on youthful exuberance, must necessarily be short on musical substance. And *vice versa*, that hip themes of counterculture, rebellion, philosophy and cynicism automatically make for 'superior' music.

The trap is that we assume that not only do these lyrics make for superior music, but they also make for superior poetry. My own literary interests are equally piqued by the near-Dada strangeness of a late-career song like "Come Together" and by the spare and moving early-career "This Boy." If we understand poetry not as a matter always of adornment and indirection but, in the words of the poet Audre Lorde, as "a revelatory distillation of experience," then the plainspoken economy of so much song lyric finds a central place in the poetry of pop.

Another approach to pop says that it is, in fact, possible to stray too far from the bread-and-butter lyric themes of love and happiness, love and trouble. Elvis Costello began his career by crafting what he called "diseased versions" of classic pop love songs to arrive at another kind of love song. "I carried on with that for some time," he writes, "until I hit subjects that were too big for pop songs. Despite what some of the *weightier* songwriters of today will tell you, there are some ideas pop songs won't carry effectively. They'll always sound pompous or overreaching. I always tried to stay away from writing about big issues." It's worth recalling, though, that Costello is the singer-songwriter behind "Shipbuilding," a scathing song about England's military-industrial complex. Costello may wish to steer away from "big" issues, but as his own varied body of work demonstrates, pop songs have the capacity to take on any subject.

Some songwriters argue that it is easier to write about the dark than about the light. "Beauty can be very challenging," says Michael Stipe of R.E.M., a group known for brooding and cerebral lyrics. "It can really be challenging. It's so much easier to write about angst and anger and fear and darkness and fucked-up feelings than to write about incredible, intense happiness. Happiness just sounds dorky. We've all experienced it, but it's much harder in a pop song to pull that off. It's much easier to pull off the darker stuff." This attitude may explain why Stipe cringes knowing that one of his biggest hits might be the band's happiest, dorkiest song: "Shiny Happy People."

Could it be, then, that pop music is as limited in its thematic scope and narrative point of view as it seems? Perhaps there are stories that pop should not or cannot tell. "There are five things to write songs about: I'm leaving you. You're leaving me. I want you. You don't want me. I believe in something. Five subjects, and twelve notes. For all that, we musicians do pretty well," Costello elsewhere observes. Constraint, of course, can be generative. A songwriter needs limits, be they formal or thematic, organic or imposed. When those limits cluster around certain subjects and exclude other voices, then it might be time for intervention.

All but the most abstract song lyrics employ some element of storytelling. "The three minute pop song has proved an ideal structuring device for filmic montages to signify the passing of time or an emotional transformation," writes education professor Tara Brabazon. Songs that consciously embrace the forms of narrative—point of view, temporality, climax, and resolution— have a particular impact on consciousness. "When we are being told a story, things change dramatically," writes Leo Widrich in his article on the science of storytelling. "Not only are the language processing parts in our brain activated, but any other area in our brain that we would use when experiencing the events of the story are too."

Neuroscience suggests that our brains do not always differentiate between represented and real experience. Listening to music activates the brain's mirror-neuron system, which, the UCLA researcher Istvan Molnar-Szakacs observes, "allows someone to identify with another by providing an automatic, pre-cognitive mechanism by which to understand their actions by mapping them onto our own neural representations of those actions. In addition, it represents the intention behind those actions." Simply put, listening to music is always a social activity, a communion with the singers and musicians present only in sound. So when we listen to Otis Redding's recording of "(Sittin' on) The Dock of the Bay," we take in Redding's first-person narrative and also somehow watch "the tide roll away" ourselves, feeling the damp weathered boards beneath us and seeing the sun dip below the horizon. The song evokes both linguistic and sensory response. The capacity of songs not simply to describe an imagined experience but also to activate in the listener a sensory and emotional response to that imagined experience has radical implications for how we hear music. We are all active listeners, whether we know it or not. The value, then, of consciously attending to the stories that songs tell is in understanding the songs as objects of critical and aesthetic attention, and in better understanding consciousness.

Gaining a fuller understanding of storytelling in pop songs means unlearning the habit of obsessing over so-called hidden meanings while ignoring surface structures and effects. It means understanding that song lyrics, like lyric poems, resist attempts at paraphrase. It's easy enough to summarize the lyrics to Mac Davis's "In the Ghetto," a song made famous in 1969 by an aging Elvis Presley, desperate for a comeback. *A child is born to an overburdened mother on the South Side of Chicago. From the start, he's fated for a life of desperation and crime, ending in death and mourning.* Lost in the description, though, is the song's exquisite melodrama, generated by Presley's quavering voice atop the sentimental strings, picked guitar, and wailing female backup singers. Lost is the fact that, for all the song's coercive sentimentality, there's something moving in the way that Presley sings the final line: "And his momma cries."

The meaning and power of Presley's recording of "In the Ghetto" reside as much or more in his performance as they reside in Davis's lyrics and music, and as much or more in our experience of hearing the song as they reside in our comprehension of the meaning of its story. This is not to say that the story's social comment is inconsequential, but that whatever consequence it has is in large part a product of Presley's performance of Davis's song. "Works of art need to attract and arouse audiences before they 'mean,'" argues the literary critic Brian Boyd. "Every detail of a work will affect the moment-by-moment attention it receives, but not necessarily a meaning abstracted from the story. Our minds can focus on only a few things at once. To hold an audience, in a world of competing demands on attention, an author [or, in our case, a songwriter and singer] needs to be an inventive intuitive psychologist." We understand the song, and something in the song understands us.

The stories song lyrics tell are not simply imbedded in their meanings. Sometimes stories are deeply intimate testimonies, like Trent Reznor's "Hurt," a song about his heroin addiction that was so painful for him that he was initially averse to the idea of Johnny Cash covering it. At other times, the stories pop songs tell are occasions for lyricist and singer to escape the self and embody imagined personas. Sometimes song lyrics abandon meaning, edging toward nonsense verse and luxuriating instead in the play of syllable and sound. One could even argue that the production and arrangement of pop music, beyond the lyrics, constitute a kind of storytelling, with their attention to pacing, tonal shift, climax, and resolution. Still, the most apparent expression of story in pop music lies in the beginnings, middles, and ends of the lyrics.

BEGINNINGS, MIDDLES, AND ENDS

After publishing his classic novel *Invisible Man* in 1952, Ralph Ellison spent the next forty years of his life, until his death in 1994, laboring over a second novel. Ellison amassed thousands of pages of episodic drafts and notes, but he left no comprehensive table of contents to act as a road map for whoever had the task of piecing together his literary jigsaw puzzle. Along with Ellison's literary executor, John Callahan, I had both the blessing and the burden of editing the disparate drafts of Ellison's novel into a publishable whole, which after more than a decade of labor resulted in *Three Days before the Shooting . . .* , a thousand-page collection of Ellison's narrative sequences. Early in the editorial process, Callahan related a conversation that he had with Ellison's widow, Fanny. Still holding on to the promise that a complete novel was hidden somewhere in the mountains of pages, she said to him, "John, there has to be a beginning, a middle, and an end."

For Ellison's second novel, the integrity of a linear narrative structure was not to be. In place of forward momentum from beginning to middle to end was a series of circles, sometimes intersecting and sometimes isolated. The linear model, however, is well suited to the pop song. "We must accomplish our aims and tell our entire story in a time frame of about three minutes (plus or minus). Every word, every note must count," writes Jimmy Webb. "This means among other things that we are not vouchsafed the luxury that some of our literary cousins have—the meandering and descriptive setting of scene, the leisurely development of a myriad of colorful characters and the exploration of plot in counterpoint throughout a seamless and climactic story line that culminates in every pesky loose end being tied off in a bowline."

Many songs fulfill that move from beginning to middle to end, or, as we might also figure it, the narrative schema of commencement-crisis-resolution. Consider a familiar lyric like the Eagles' "Hotel California." It has a clear beginning ("On a dark desert highway, cool wind in my hair") that situates the listener in narrative perspective and setting. The middle defines a point of crisis through the oblique threat of the feminine antagonist and the host of other men—suitors, fellow sufferers, both?—who reside in this spectral hotel ("And still those voices are calling from far away / Wake you up in the middle of the night just to hear them say"). The narrative's conclusion forestalls resolution, both in the lyrics ("You can check out any time you like, but you can never leave") and in the music, which continues for two more minutes, featuring an iconic guitar solo before fading into silent irresolution.

Most discussions of "Hotel California" center on the potential metaphoric valences of the story rather than on its narrative. Is it a song about an actual place? Perhaps the drug rehabilitation center that members of the Eagles might have visited? Something else? Such lines of questioning are ultimately limited. "Oh, God," Don Henley told *Crawdaddy!* around the time of the song's release, "you can interpret that a million different ways." Then Glenn Frey piped in: "We'll stay off that one. We cannot betray our own poetry." Most fans who want to speculate about "Hotel California" would have likely ignored what the band had to say about it anyway, not necessarily out of defiance but out of desire to maintain the aura of mystery the song so richly conjures. It might therefore be more useful to reflect on what makes a song's story particularly potent as a recording.

One of the most powerful ways that songs invite listeners into the language of their lyrics is through a mystery that demands engagement, if not always resolution. In discussing a poem, Helen Vendler would always ask her students to consider the antecedent scenario—an imaginative conjecture as to what might have preceded the poem's beginning. "In life, things don't simply start up for nothing," points out the narrative theorist Brian Richardson, by which he means that individual lives are always knitted in a complex social fabric that exists before them and continues after them. Though it's easy enough to mark the textual beginning of a poem or the temporal beginning of a song, it is far more challenging—and rewarding—to reflect on their reasons for coming into being.

What do we imagine has happened just before the poem or song lyric commences to provoke this kind of speech? What might have prompted the speaker to break silence and to seek this particular form of expression? Why has the poet or songwriter chosen this point of entry? Why has the singer taken a particular approach to delivering the lyric? Song lyrics often invite these questions. "Busted flat in Baton Rouge, headin' for the trains / Feelin' nearly faded as my jeans" begins Kris Kristofferson's "Me and Bobby Mc-Gee." The mystery surrounding the antecedent scenario helps explain why these opening lines are so striking. We know that the speaker is broke, and we know that he—or, in Janis Joplin's iconic cover, she—is, in the evocative image, "feelin' nearly faded as my jeans." In this case, the questions inspired by the opening lines stimulate the construction of character from the very beginning of the song. In capturing interest the lyrics also capture empathy, which builds investment in the story the song has to tell.

Iggy Pop's "Lust for Life," from 1977, suggests a different kind of antecedent scenario. The song begins like this:

Here comes Johnny Yen again
With the liquor and drugs
And the flesh machine
He's gonna to do another striptease

Narrative tension springs from the juxtaposition of the shock value of its open invocation of liquor and drugs, the opacity of the phrase "flesh machine," the strangeness of the name Johnny Yen, and the implication that all of this is routine ("Here comes Johnny Yen *again*" to do "*another* striptease"). Resolving the mysteries of these lines might lead to the literary source of inspiration, William S. Burroughs's novel *The Ticket That Exploded*, which introduces Johnny Yen, "the Boy-Girl Other Half strip tease God of sexual frustration." One need not follow that particular referential thread, however, to be entranced by the manic energy of Iggy Pop's vocal delivery and these evocative opening lines. Reflecting on antecedent scenario is about asking questions more than it is about settling on answers.

Sometimes a song's invitation to the listener to contemplate the lyric's antecedent scenario is an indispensable part of the song's success. The Talking Heads' "Once in a Lifetime" begins with a direct address to the listener: "And you may find yourself living in a shotgun shack/And you may find yourself in another part of the world/And you may find yourself behind the wheel of a large automobile." The succession of phrases beginning with "and" suggests a beginning in medias res; the structure of anaphora matched with Byrne's speech-song vocal delivery captures the mood of an evangelical sermon. Both Byrne's tone and the direct address of the opening lyric render "Once in a Lifetime" confrontational and compelling.

Finding the middle of a song is less obvious. When it comes to narrative arc, the middle is not always the temporal midpoint in the song. For the purposes of a lyric's structure, the middle might usefully be figured as the pivot point in the narrative action, the high point of tension either on the register of incident or of emotion. Because the middle in this formulation is not a fixed point, it seeks definition and context from what surrounds it. In *Tunesmith* Jimmy Webb outlines the practice of charting the emotional trajectory of a song. "When drafted effectively a lyric will usually begin with a question, puzzle or ambiguity and then build to a revelation or declaration, an emotional payoff or high point," Webb writes. "When a composer sets such a lyric to music it is only logical to assume that one of the primary functions of the tune will be to enhance the emotional dynamic of the lyric (or vice versa if the melody comes first). How does a melody do this? By changing direction effectively." That change of direction often marks the song's climax, which defines itself against the equilibrium of the opening and the resolution of the song's conclusion. Often a sonic shift musically underscores this lyric transition, through the introduction of a bridge or some other change of sonic climate.

A vivid, albeit somewhat schematic, rendering of this kind of climactic middle comes in Idina Menzel's performance of "Let It Go," the ubiquitous signature song from the animated feature *Frozen*. The emotive trajectory of the song builds slowly, with dynamic development from the controlled opening verse to the impassioned end. The climax, both musically and lyrically, comes with the bridge, in which Menzel, voicing the self-exiled Princess Elsa, asserts, "I'm never going back; the past is in my past," before returning triumphantly to the chorus. "Let It Go," like many of the songs on the *Frozen* soundtrack, owes its success to a sense of song craft born of the Broadway tradition. Like Tin Pan Alley songs of decades past, "Let It Go" relies on its structural precision to guide its listeners' emotional responses. The song certainly could not be accused of subtlety, but it effectively illustrates the critical value of attending to the middle of a song's narrative, its emotional center.

The middle can also serve an organizing function on the level of narrative. Shawn Colvin's "Sunny Came Home" illustrates the power of the middle of a song to organize what comes before it and what follows it. In just over four minutes, the song stages an atmospheric drama, portentous and opaque. Roughly speaking, the song tells of a woman's abuse and her arsonous revenge, but it does not follow the explicit tradition of the murder ballad. Instead, the song renders its drama in subtle shifts of language and tone. The pivot point of the song is the bridge, which falls at the middle of the recording (2:16 of 4:23). Before the bridge, the song alternates twice between the apprehensive tone of the verses and the brightness and release of the choruses. The bridge is disconcertingly subdued, both in Colvin's near-whispered vocal delivery and in the stripped-down musical accompaniment that builds to the line "strike a match, go on and do it" that lead into the triumphant return to the chorus. The chorus, and the following section that is musically identical to the chorus but divergent in lyrics, now feels like a release; no longer tempered by the foreboding tone of the verse, the chorus—and with it, we imagine, Sunny—can live unburdened and free.

"Sunny Came Home" closes by reclaiming the song's title. The words "Sunny came home" appear six times in the song, four times before the bridge and twice after it. Each time before the pivot point of the bridge, it is an enjambed phrase ("Sunny came home/to her favorite room," ". . . with a mission," ". . . with a list of names," ". . . with a vengeance"). After the bridge, the phrase becomes a complete declarative sentence unto itself: "Sunny came home." The song's final lyrics underscore the certainty of this resolution, and the fading language echoes the fading music, from "Sunny came home," to "came home," and finally simply to "home." In a song that rejects explicit storytelling and relies on inference, a careful structure around a climactic and cathartic middle point makes the song emotionally legible.

As a discrete node in a song lyric, the end is obvious; it is when the song resigns itself to silence. Songs end in any number of ways, from the fade that suggests the interminability of the music to the natural decay of the last chord struck or the last note sung. Regardless of the sonic means of a song's conclusion, the end is often also an occasion to address questions the lyric leaves unresolved. When the song fades out or when the final note gives way, what avenues of thought demand attention? Tom Petty's "American Girl," for instance, ends in both semantic and emotive irreconcilability: "God, it's so painful when something that's so close/Is still so far out of reach." The statement is at once axiomatic and specific, resigned but not despairing. It is an appeal: to God, but also to the listener. The line makes the song's challenge our own. "I don't think I've ever written [a song] where I knew how it was going to end up," Tom Petty remarked to Paul Zollo. "So the endings sometimes are kind of ambiguous. But I think in song it's got to be. You don't want to nail it down too much. In songwriting, I think the better ones have some element of ambiguity, where it allows the listener to create his own picture. And those are the ones I like." Often lyric and music mark the depth of their emotive and cognitive impression by how much work remains for listeners to do in their wake.

Eminem's "Stan" designs its narrative and emotive payoff to come at the very end of the lyric. This epistolary song consists of three verses written as letters from an obsessed fan who goes from fawning to deranged with each letter that meets with no reply; the fan's final letter narrates the murder of his girlfriend, trapped in the trunk of his car, and his own suicide as he drives off a bridge. The fourth and concluding verse is Eminem's belated letter back to the fan. The final lines of the verse, which are the final lines of the song, offer the narrative turn:

I just don't want you to do some crazy shit
I seen this one shit on the news a couple weeks ago that made me sick
Some dude was drunk and drove his car over a bridge
And had his girlfriend in the trunk, and she was pregnant with his kid
And in the car they found a tape, but they didn't say who it was to
Come to think about it, his name was, it was you . . .
Damn

Lightning strikes as Eminem's final word fades, punctuating the revelation and the dramatic irony of the situation: The audience already knows what the character of the song, "Slim," Eminem's alter ego Slim Shady, finds out. The revelation, in other words, is not for the listener, but for the character Eminem in a song of Eminem's own design, a self-conscious comment on the fraught relationship between celebrities and their fans. The ending provokes vicarious shock and surprise that settle into reflection on obsession and isolation. The recording as a whole is a study in the play of voice across characters. It is also a testament to the power of endings as vehicles for thought and feeling.

Often it is the coordination of beginning (the curiosity over antecedent scenario), middle (the point of climax), and end (the resonance that follows a song's formal resolution) that makes for a classic song. One final example will serve to illustrate all three. George Jones's "He Stopped Loving Her Today" has been called the greatest country song ever written; certainly it showcases the melancholy and melodrama that country sometimes shares with the blues. The song's opening line, "He said, 'I'll love you 'til I die,'" is the beginning of an end: the end of a marriage or a love affair and the beginning of a protracted period of loss and longing. Importantly, Jones is the chronicler of the story rather than the heartbroken man himself, a position that frames the narrative at a third-person remove but nonetheless allows for empathy. "Singing *is* George," Waylon Jennings observed. "He tries to live, breathe, and eat the song while he's singing it, and he's told me that, especially when he's in the studio, his mind goes completely blank but for the focus of the story and the melody in his throat. He imagines the man, or woman, he's singing about and how they might be reacting to every word." That empathy is on display here.

The middle of the song, in terms of its climax and pivot, comes at the 2:17 mark of the 3:17 song when Jones moves from song to speech, narrating the woman's return. "You know, she came to see him one last time," Jones begins, as a female singer's voice wails in the background. Then he breaks through the third-person narrative frame to speak about the situation in the first person: "Oh, we all wondered if she would. And it kept running through my mind, this time he's over her for good." By shifting from song to speech, and then by speaking for himself and for the imagined community that knows this unnamed man, Jones crafts an atmosphere of authenticity and intimacy. The melodrama is now a drama on a human scale, at least for a time.

When Jones's voice returns, singing again, the song has changed once more. The central line of the chorus, "He stopped loving her today," now takes on its full meaning. They'll put a wreath on his door; they'll carry him away. We recall the declaration that opens the song (He said, "I'll love you 'til I die"), and we now know that the man has passed away. As Jones put it simply in his memoir, "The song is about a man who loved a woman so much it killed him when she left." That subject is unremarkable in the annals of popular song. Here, however, the songwriter and singer's orchestration of beginning, middle, and end renovates and renews a familiar melodramatic tale.

HOW WE HEAR NARRATIVE

When a story becomes a lyric, then a song, it fundamentally transforms the listening experience. Memory functions in diametrically opposed ways when the mind confronts a written narrative or one set to song. When processing written words, the mind quickly discards the surface effects of language to capture the information being communicated. When hearing music, the mind hovers over those same surface effects and linguistic patterns, the stuff of rhythm and melody and figurative language. These elements constitute the meaning of the performance even more than the information and incident being communicated. As a result, song lyrics exist in an unusual relationship to memory. They invite reflection on repeated patterns even as they support an unreflective recollection of the whole. This trick of memory helps to explain instances when we might know every line of a song and can sing along, but we never stop to think about what the words actually mean.

In 2013 *Paste* magazine ran a series titled "Secretly Horrifying Song Lyrics" in which writers offered running glosses on well-known lyrics that people rarely interrogate. Examples ran the gamut, from the Human League's "Don't You Want Me" to the Kinks' "Art Lover." The articles are satiric, underscoring a serious point: Our perception of the stories that songs tell can change drastically when we actually pay attention to what the words have to say. Philip Bailey, the onetime lead singer of the R&B group Earth, Wind & Fire, reveals how flabbergasted he is that people still come up to him to say that they got married to "Reasons," a song he co-wrote with Maurice White about one-night stands on the road. Undoubtedly the newlyweds knew each and every word, but "didn't anyone bother to listen to the lyrics?" Perhaps they were only attending to the lyrics of the chorus ("the reasons, reasons that we're here") rather than those of the morally compromised verses. In this case it's a matter of hearing only what they want to hear.

The French philosopher Peter Szendy observes that pop songs often take up residence in the mind in spite of our best efforts to expel them. "Most of the time," he writes, "we do not understand, and do not want to understand, what they are saying, the story they are telling. We listen to them without lending them an ear, welcoming them grudgingly, thinking we must be deaf to worn-out words and washed-out lyrics carried by these manufactured melodic products diffused on such a large scale." For Szendy, our unawareness of, or resistance to, specific meaning is actually a spur to memory. "Yet," he points out, "it is precisely because we do not want to get anything out of musical commodities—upon which we impose censorship unaware of itself—it is for this very reason that they are all the more ready to reemerge when we are least expecting it, without our having called them up or desired them. They come back then, these haunting melodies; they come back in us and in spite of ourselves to speak to us about us. They even make us gain access to ourselves."

A perceived misalignment between melody and lyric may also interfere with listeners' comprehension of a song's story. The country music legend Buck Owens observes that one of his best-known songs, the ballad "Together Again," is often misunderstood precisely because of the tension between melody and lyrics. "The funny thing about 'Together Again' is that it's actually a happy song," he writes, "but since the melody is kind of mournful sounding, most people think it's really sad. That's because they haven't listened to the lyrics. The singer is talking about how his tears have stopped falling and how his lonely nights are over because he's back together with the woman he loves. The guy couldn't be happier—but I put the lyrics to this slow, melancholy melody—and that's what causes folks to misunderstand what the song is really about." Paul Simon does the same on "My Little Town," the Talking Heads do it on "Don't Worry about the Government," and other examples abound in the pop-music catalog. Tension can be generative; such songs demand conscious attention on the part of the listener.

Whether drawing meaning from specific lyrics or from generalized musical patterns, when most of us follow narrative in song on a conscious level we look for something concrete, often incidents in imagined lives. The key word here, however, is "imagined." As our minds and memories absorb narrative and drift between the impressionistic and the precise, we must also bear in mind that the stuff of narrative in song is an artist's or artists' conscious craft. It is not reality. Although genre and style may condition certain habits of narration, and although certain genres may lend themselves to songs of incident and other genres to more abstract songs of feeling, all songs construct illusions.

"Well, songs are just thoughts," Bob Dylan told the interviewer Bill Flanagan when asked about the "literal reality" of his lyrics. "For the moment they stop time. Songs are supposed to be heroic enough to give the illusion of stopping time. With just that thought. To hear a song is to hear someone's thought, no matter what they're describing. If you see something and you think it's important enough to describe, then that's your thought. You only think one thought at a time, so what you come up with is really what you're given. When you sit around and imagine things to do and to write and to think—that's fantasy. I've never been much into that." The British rocker Richard Thompson prefers to think of songs as "mediated reality," rendered through the songwriter's imagination and the musicians' exercises of craft.

These exercises of craft mold narrative. All narratives are stories, but not all stories are narratives. Stories are simply sequences of events that become narration by virtue of their structured telling. A story lives in the air, but a narrative takes more tangible shape, be it a Homeric epic or a graphic novel. "Narration reveals the finite in its fragile uniqueness, and sings its glory," observes Adriana Cavarero. Narration is a crafted thing, though also a delicate art.

Songs, therefore, would seem to be an anomaly: stories without a text. In fact, songs almost always leave an artifact (be it handwritten lyrics, published sheet music, or even just a digital audio file), though we generally experience them in sound. In our era of compressed audio files and streaming services, most of us are almost entirely alienated from the physical manifestation of the song, as vinyl or CD or some other format. This matters because it helps explain how in listening to the story a song has to tell we can lose sight of the craftedness of the tale, its highly wrought artifice through which it conjures a persona, invites empathetic identification, or incites curiosity and close attention.

The contemporary pop song is the site of numerous narrative drives. Jimmy Webb identifies nine categories of songs, conditioned by temporality, tone, and narrative mode. One could come up with even more, but we might usefully classify song narratives into two broad categories. The first category is the tale, or story-song. The second is the study in persona.

THE STORY-SONG

"A song is a short story," writes Willie Nelson. He ought to know. As the writer of more than 2,500 songs over seven decades he has certainly earned the right to make such grand proclamations. But to what extent is Nelson speaking in metaphor and to what extent in fact?

On a literal level, the story-song comes closest to fulfilling Nelson's one-to-one identification of song with story. Story-songs are invested in outward action, as in the Charlie Daniels Band's "The Devil Went Down to Georgia" or Harry Chapin's "Cat's in the Cradle." They resemble what we colloquially understand a story to be: linear narratives that move from beginning to middle to end. To expand Nelson's dictum, song lyrics are never just narratives. Although they harness the emotional power accessible only through story, they do so in a medium with the immediacy of poetry. Pop songs are generally meant to reward their audience richly on first encounter. The best songs balance emotional depth with surface effects.

In a typical story-song, the vehicle for the story is the verse, and the most common form of verse-based story-song is the ballad. Over the course of pop-music history the ballad's popularity has waxed and waned, but it remains a mainstay of country music, which may be why country is often spoken of as a storyteller's genre. One finds a rich catalog of story-songs across country music's history. "Most of our songs told a story," recalls Loretta Lynn. "You could tell me that's the old-fashioned way people had of telling the news, before newspapers and radio. All I know is, most country songs are ballads." The ballads of which Lynn speaks are traditional, story-driven ballads. The songwriter Jimmy Webb traces the lineage: "It is in the Scots, Irish and English ballads and reels transplanted to the Deep South, subtly altered by African and Christian laments, pounding rhythms and 'field hollers,' that the roots of modern American songwriting reside." Webb differentiates the ballad as colloquially invoked to refer to a slow love song from the ballad as traditionally construed as "a story told in song utilizing multiple verses that are musically identical. What would seem to define the 'form' of the ballad is the story that it tells. The song goes on long enough to tell the tale, so that its length and number of verses is dictated by its plot points and can consist of as many verses as are needed to serve the narrative's beginning, middle and end."

The plot-driven ballad is far less prevalent today than it once was in popular music, though it expresses itself vividly in country music. Reflecting on "Lucille," one of the dozens of ballads he recorded, Kenny Rogers observes that it is "a classic example of the story-song." He continues, "First, in these kinds of ballads, you know exactly where you are from the first line. *In a bar in Toledo across from the depot.* Then the song takes you on a journey and drops you off at the end with a powerful feeling." Establishing setting and enacting emotional transformation through a journey grounded in narrative detail and incident are qualities that define the genre of the story-song, both inside and outside the historical frame of the ballad.

Sometimes a balladeer and sometimes a rocker, Bruce Springsteen may be the modern master of the story-song, often producing entire albums that function as song cycles circling around a group of characters, a particular setting, and a particular time. His characters might be born in autobiographical memory, but Springsteen employs his narrative craft to untether them from that specificity without robbing them of their communicative power. "They're all *emotionally* yours," Springsteen says of the characters that populate his songs. "They're part of your emotional life and in that sense, you could say the songs are all yours. In the sense of the detail that you hang the emotions on—that'll vary." Across Springsteen's career, his approach to crafting characters has evolved. "The characters on *Born to Run* were less eccentric and less local than on *Greetings* and *The Wild, the Innocent.* They could have been anybody and everybody," Springsteen writes. "When the screen door slams on 'Thunder Road,' you're not necessarily on the Jersey Shore anymore. You could be anywhere in America. These were the beginnings of the characters whose lives I would trace in my work for the next two decades."

Springsteen is acutely aware of how music and lyric work together to craft narrative. Reflecting on "Tom Joad," Springsteen reveals that "the melodies were uncomplicated, yet played an important role in the storytelling process. The simplicity and plainness, the austere rhythms defined who these characters were and how they expressed themselves." For all our attention to storytelling in song as a narrative technique, it's worth recalling that songs are primarily a sonic expression. "The precision of the storytelling in these types of songs is very important," Springsteen continues. "The correct detail can speak volumes about who your character is, while the wrong one can shred the credibility of your story. When you get the music and the lyrics right in these songs, your voice disappears into the voices of those you've chosen to write about." Attention to incident, and to voice, including the singing voice and the voice of the song's persona, are defining features of Springsteen's craft and the storyteller's craft as a whole. In a passage worth quoting at length, Springsteen reflects on his songwriting as a matter primarily of narrative:

> When I'd write rock music, music with the whole band, it would sometimes start out purely musically, and then I'd find my way to some lyrics. I haven't written like that in a while. In much of my recent writing, the lyrics have preceded the music, though the music is always in the back of my mind. In most of the recent songs, I tell violent stories very quietly. You're hearing characters' thoughts—what they're thinking after all the events that have shaped their situation have transpired. So I try to get that internal sound, like that feeling at night when you're in bed and staring at the ceiling, reflective in some fashion. I wanted the songs to have the kind of intimacy that took you inside yourself and then back out into the world. I'll use music as a way of defining and coloring the characters, conveying the characters' rhythm of speech and pace. The music acts as a very still surface, and the lyrics create a violent emotional life over it, or under it, and I let those elements bang up against each other. Music can seem incidental, but it ends up being very important. It allows you to suggest the passage of time in just a couple of quiet beats. Years can go by in a few bars, whereas a writer will have to come up with a clever way of saying, "And then years went by . . ." Thank God I don't have to do any of that! Songwriting allows you to cheat tremendously. You can present an entire life in a few minutes. And then hopefully, at the end, you reveal something about yourself and your audience and the person in the song. It has a little in common with short-story writing in that it's character-driven. The characters are confronting the questions that everyone is trying to sort out for themselves, their moral issues, the way those issues rear their heads in the outside world.

No matter how naturalistic Springsteen's narratives, it is important to remember that they are, in fact, crafted. Nick Hornby reminds us of this in his inimitable way when he observes, "In Bruce Springsteen songs, you can either stay and rot, or you can escape and burn. That's OK; he's a songwriter, after all, and he needs simple choices like that in his songs. But nobody ever writes about how it is possible to escape and rot—how escapes can go off at half-cock, how you can leave the suburbs for the city but end up living a limp suburban life anyway. That's what happened to me; that's what happens to most people." Songs are not life. They can sometimes present themselves as imagined and organized life, but they are always constructs governed by artists' values and intentions.

It is also important to remember that story-songs are not necessarily complex. "The majority of popular songs express one moment's feeling—a single emotion like desire ('Can't Take My Eyes Off You'), or surprise ('I Can't Believe That You're in Love with Me'), or regret ('Didn't We')," Sheila Davis writes in her classic *The Craft of Lyric Writing.* "Some make a simple statement (or ask a simple question): 'Don't Fence Me In,' 'All I Want for Christmas Is My Two Front Teeth,' or 'What's Love Got to Do with It?' Those 'ideas' are self-evident because the titles tell all. Lyrics with plots may be thought to say something more complex; but well-written story songs also embody a simple idea that can be summarized in a few words." In addition to thinking about songs with a complex, plot-driven architecture, it is also necessary to turn to those driven by feeling and persona.

PERSONA SONGS

Valerie June's music has been variously described as folk, country, blues, gospel, soul, and bluegrass. She is a black female singer-songwriter with a defiantly independent musical vision. It might be best to think of her simply as a storyteller in song. In a revealing interview with National Public Radio, June characterized her songwriting process as a communion with voices. "Usually, it's not my own voice," she said. "It's usually many different voices, and that's always a hard subject to talk about because it kind of sounds crazy, you know, to say, hey, I hear an older black male voice. Sometimes, I hear a younger woman's voice. Sometimes, I hear a child's voice or, you know, there's many, many different voices, either you feel connected to them and you write them down. I try to write down every song that comes to me, and if you just write every song, then you get to the good ones."

June's emphasis on individual voices epitomizes the nature of the persona song, with its interest in the internal lives and drives of characters. Persona accounts for songs that take the explicit shape of dramatic monologues, like the Rolling Stones' "Sympathy for the Devil." Persona also might be understood to include just about every other song that does not privilege narrative action but rather explores the "I" of the singer or the "we" of a relationship. In this regard, at least, there's an element of narrative craft functioning in even those lyrics bereft of outward incident.

Persona is a product of lyric and voice. "The way that a persona becomes clear to a listener is partly, self-evidently, through the lyrics of the track but, perhaps more importantly, by means of the melody through which those lyrics are delivered, and by means of the voice through which the lyrics and melody are articulated," observes the musicologist Allan F. Moore. The voice as persona entwines with the voice as instrument, but the difference is worth exploring. Voice as persona is an act of conjuring consciousness, either a constructed character brought to life by singer and songwriter, or a constructed self that we're meant to associate with the singer. "With each record I've done so far, the narrator of the record has been some version of myself," Joanna Newsom explains to Marc Maron. "It hasn't been a pure, unedited version of myself, but it's been sort of a—you know, the stories, the songs have elements of autobiography, or speaking to my own experience and they are united by some common character, and that character is an exaggerated and/or edited and/or stylized version of myself." This kind of constructed lyric self in song, assembled from autobiography or exaggeration, conscious evasion or pure fancy, invites a relationship with listeners. Sometimes song lyrics in performance aspire to the condition of the human voice overheard. On other occasions, the voice addresses a specific audience directly. On still other occasions, the idea of address is never taken up at all or is beside the point.

When the singer is not the songwriter, finding consonance between lyrics and the performing self is an external process, focused on selection. "From the beginning of my life as a singer I knew immediately whether a song was meant for me," recalls the folk singer Judy Collins. "There are songs I will never sing because they have a phrase I would never speak. Language is so very intimate and vital, and I choose only those songs that reflect the way I might say things." For the singer-songwriter, alignment is primarily an internal process. The country singer Loretta Lynn elevates the connection between the lyrics she writes and performs and the life she leads to a first principle of her craft and a way to expand the expressive range of the country genre. "Most of my songs were from the woman's point of view," she states. "In the old days, country music was directed at the men—truck-driving songs, easy women, cheating songs." A singer telling her own story, even if that story is a reflection of a collective experience, can achieve revolutionary things. "People often say, 'Where do you come up with all of these songs?' Well, I don't come up with them! I've lived them! I tell it like it is," Lynn writes in her memoir.

"Telling it like it is" can be a gesture at authenticity or the thing itself; for the audience, it often doesn't matter. Even autobiography is governed by narrative craft. What Adriana Cavarero terms the "narratable self" is the urge in us all to have our story told, for our lives to become the subject of narration by others. "The narratable self finds its home, not simply in a conscious exercise of remembering, but in the spontaneous narrating structure of memory itself," Cavarero writes. "This is why we have defined the self as *narratable* instead of *narrated*." The narratable self is not a matter of how the mind structures one's past, a process that is always fallible. Rather, the narratable self is a social selfhood, the product of relations with others. "I've always been good at chronicling the many moods of my life, but mostly I have done it through my music," writes Melissa Etheridge. "I tell stories of life, pain, joy, and love in three-minute snippets—little glimpses of who I am or who people perceive me to be." That blend of perception of self and others defines the space of the "I" in popular music.

We encounter the same interpretive challenge when it comes to first-person narration in song lyrics as we do in literature, where we must grapple with the indeterminacy of relation between author and speaker. Is the "I" of Anne Sexton's "Her Kind" necessarily the poet herself? *I have gone out, a possessed witch, / haunting the black air, braver at night.* Most literary critics find this to be an unhelpful question, one that leads away from the poem itself and into the morass of biography. In pop songs, unlocking the identity of the lyric "I" is a nearly irresistible matter; the prying attentions of celebrity-obsessed culture work to strip naked the pop singer's persona in hopes of revealing the person underneath. Add to that the fact that the lyric "I" is audible, that another person is claiming the name right before our ears and sometimes before our eyes, and the confusion and the conflation make sense. Is the "I" of David Byrne's "This Must Be the Place (Naïve Melody)" Byrne himself?

> Home is where I want to be
> Pick me up and turn me round
> I feel numb, born with a weak heart
> I guess I must be having fun

Reading the lyrics, hearing Byrne sing them on the studio recording from the Talking Heads' 1983 album *Speaking in Tongues*, seeing Byrne perform them today live as a certain cast of light shines across the stage, it's easy to conceive dozens of questions more interesting than wondering whether the "I" is in fact he.

That said, the lyric "I" is certainly worthy of discussion. Sometimes the pronoun makes all the difference. In a striking last-minute revision to his classic "Tangled Up in Blue," Bob Dylan went back to the studio to rerecord much of the song in the first person rather than the third person. What was a song at arm's length became palpable through the personal, as Dylan understood that his listeners required the bridge of the personal to access more fully the emotions in the song. He gave his listeners not his narrated self, but a narratable self. "Like many writers who present an autobiographical surface," explains Richard Tillinghast, "Dylan works with the illusion of an actual life—autobiography as a poetic convenience, a resource, a vehicle for communication with an audience. 'I' really *can* be 'another,' and particularly for people who create lyrics and tell stories, the self is no fixed commodity."

For a gifted singer, the "I" need not have any autobiographical connection. "People often think the lyrics you're singing have some special personal significance for you, which often isn't true," Michael Jackson observes. "It is important to reach people, to move them. Sometimes one can do this with the mosaic of the music melody arrangement and lyrics, sometimes it is the intellectual content of the lyrics." The country singer Reba McEntire agrees: "I used to believe that you can't sing songs that contradict your own personal lifestyle. But after a few years of maturing, I found that it's best to find the songs people can relate to—whether you can or not."

The "I" of the pop song contains multitudes. The most revealing autobiographical song lyrics depend on the perception of others. Though Ralph Ellison once observed that "we tell ourselves our individual stories so that we might better understand the collective," Cavarero would counter by warning against the erasure of individuality. "The effect—or, perhaps, the empathetic motive for reciprocal narration—thus risks frustrating that reciprocal appearance of *uniqueness* that qualifies the dynamic of recognition as an ethic," she writes. "To recognize oneself *in* the other is indeed quite different from recognizing the irremediable uniqueness of the other." Though the idea that one should aspire to recognizing the other in the self has become an accepted ideal in many societies, perhaps the preferable goal is to recognize that which is disparate and defining in the other.

What happens when we listen with the conscious ear for that "irremediable uniqueness" of experience and expression in the song? When it comes to confessional song lyrics, the assumption is that they generate their emotional appeal through empathy and vicarious engagement. This, however, is an illusion. The intimate spaces that song lyrics visit are stagings of intimacy. This observation is not meant to take anything away from their power, only to acknowledge the essential exercise of craft on matters closest to the heart. James Taylor is among the first names that come to mind when one thinks of confessional songwriters. Though he admits that his songs come across as often nakedly autobiographical, he troubles the assumption that songwriting can ever be confession. "It departs from being anything like a real representation of what I am," Taylor tells Bill Flanagan. "It seems autobiographical because it is self-referred and it's intimate and some of it is downright confessional. But it also has to rhyme and fit into a musical context. And as the song goes through, various ideas will be set against one another." The songwriter's imperative of form, from rhyme to prosody to diction, means that few songs ever end up as pure confession, even if they begin as such.

Trent Reznor's "Hurt" may be among the most emotionally bare lyrics in contemporary music, but it too is subject to complications of form and performance. "Hurt" was the final track on Nine Inch Nails' 1994 album *The Downward Spiral*. It responds both to circumstances of the persona at the center of the concept album and also autobiographically to Reznor's struggles with heroin addiction. "I hurt myself today to see if I still feel / I focus on the pain, the only thing that's real," Reznor sings over an instrumental track thick with dissonance and distortion. The song might seem like an unlikely candidate for a cover, but eight years later Johnny Cash recorded "Hurt" for his final album, *American IV: The Man Comes Around*, just a year before his death. What began as a six-minute study in pain becomes a distilled three-minute accounting for a life of pain, both suffered and inflicted. Cash's voice is weathered, his pitch at times imprecise, but his masterful phrasing renders the cover at once a testament to Cash's estimable gifts and to the durability and power of Reznor's song.

Reznor's response to Cash's cover, which garnered even more attention due to the striking Mark Romanek–directed video that accompanied it, was ambivalent at best. "It felt invasive," Reznor recalls, years later. "It was my child. It was like I was building a home, and someone else moved into it. When I write a song, I'm only considering myself as the one narrating it. It's my voice. So it did seem very odd at first." Certainly one could never mistake Cash's voice—neither his physical instrument nor the persona he embodies in delivering the lyric—for Reznor's. Reznor eventually came around to appreciating his song's second life, its second voice. "I haven't listened to my version since then. I've been so proud of what they've done with it that I haven't thought that much about it. I'm over my initial shock, and I realize that's what music's all about. I've thrown some things in the pot, and now it's turned into something else. It's a pretty powerful thing."

Sometimes an artist's persona can rise to the level of ego or even identity. Rap is the obvious genre in which this happens, although a few rap artists, like Kanye West and Kendrick Lamar, use all or part of their given names. Of course, even artists using their real names still construct a persona, even multiple personas. "I Love Kanye," Kanye's forty-four-second a cappella celebration of his multitudinous self from 2016's *The Life of Pablo*, anatomizes the construction of a public persona. "See, I invented Kanye, it wasn't any Kanyes/And now I look and look around and there's so many Kanyes," he rhymes, gesturing at his host of imitators, and also at his own complex, compound identity. In addition to the many meanings of Kanye, West also inhabits Yeezy, a nickname that he elevates in song to a full-fledged alter ego. There's a distinction of intensity, though not necessarily of kind, between taking on a stage name—like Katheryn Elizabeth Hudson going by Katy Perry, or Paul Hewson going by Bono, or Declan Patrick McManus going by Elvis Costello—and taking on an alter ego. One need only hear Marilyn Manson (Brian Hugh Warner) talk about it to understand the craftedness of a persona expressed first in song, then on the stage:

Marilyn Manson was the perfect story protagonist for a frustrated writer like myself. He was a character who, because of his contempt for the world around him and, more so, himself, does everything he can to trick people into liking him. And then, once he wins their confidence, he uses it to destroy them. He would have been in a longish short story, about sixty pages. The title would have been "The Payback," and it would have been rejected by seventeen magazines.

Today, it would be in the garage of my parent's house in Florida, faded and mildewed with all the other stories. But it was too good an idea to rot.

Marilyn Manson's name fit perfectly with his dangerous, androgynous persona. He intended to offend. "As a performer, I wanted to be the loudest, most persistent alarm clock I could be, because there didn't seem like any other way to snap society out of its Christianity- and media-induced coma," he recalls. Now, many years later, this character born of a song-lyric persona has subsumed the performer's public self, at least in the public eye. It is nearly impossible to find present-day photographs of Manson without his signature white powder makeup and livid red lip. The song has possessed the body, but in doing so the song often gets overlooked in favor of the extreme image. "A lot of people like to pass me off as a devil worshipper," Manson says. "That could only be true if I considered myself to be the devil, because I tend to be narcissistic and believe in my own strength and my own identity. I find God to be what exists in what you create. I make music. That's coming in touch with God when I write a story, when I come up with a phrase or paint a picture, because that's about creating. Art gives people a reason to be alive."

The story-song and the persona-driven song meet most vividly in a space beyond the recording itself—in the music video. Videos are perhaps the most powerful medium for narrative expression; their relation to pop-song lyrics and recordings illuminates a final part of the life of lyrics as story.

MUSIC VIDEOS AND THE ANTI-NARRATIVE

I was a failed writer of music video treatments. Sometime in 2005 my old college roommate, Justin Francis, now a well-regarded director living in Los Angeles, asked me to try my hand at writing a treatment—a brief narrative and visual script—for a song he had just been sent. "Give it a shot," he told me. "I know you can help me." His confidence in me was encouraging, but when I sat down to write for the song I realized how unfamiliar I was with the conventions of music video narrative. I knew that a treatment was a kind of mini-script, and I knew from watching music videos since I was a child that a video could be anything from an abstract visual piece like Björk's "All Is Full of Love" to a concert clip like Def Leppard's "Pour Some Sugar on Me" to a multi-act narrative like Michael Jackson's "Thriller." I decided that the best approach was to start with the song and let it announce what kind of video it needed to be.

For those of us who grew up in the era of MTV, pop music is a narrative medium because pop music is a visual medium, with music videos rendering even the most abstract song as a story. Music videos act variously in the service of the song's narrative, as a substitute in the absence of a song's clear narrative, and in tension (or even out-and-out defiance) of a song's narrative. Without even knowing it, I already had a narrative vocabulary from which to draw. As a viewer, I'd been training to write music videos for years now. At least that's what I told myself.

The song was "So Sick," by the then little-known R&B singer Ne-Yo. Though Ne-Yo was a new artist, he was a music veteran, having written hit songs for several other performers. This was to be his breakout as a solo artist, so it made the impact of the video all the more vital. Broadly speaking, "So Sick" is a song about love and loss. It begins at the end of the speaker's relationship: "Gotta change my answering machine now that I'm alone." The chorus self-referentially bemoans the love song itself, "And I'm so sick of love songs, so tired of tears." I listened to the song dozens of times: while I walked across the college campus where I was teaching, while I lifted weights at the gym, while I wallowed in my own sense of loss and longing caused by my bicoastal relationship with my then-girlfriend (now my wife). I connected with the song, both lyrically and sonically, with its restrained accompaniment and bittersweet melody.

As I sat down to write my treatment, I approached it from two directions: the narrative and the imagistic. On the narrative level, I keyed in on certain details that established setting, suggested incident, or implied temporality. We know the separated lovers once shared an apartment, we know that it's been months since they were together, we even know the date of their anniversary (July 15) because it's marked on his calendar, and we know that he is listening to the radio and being emotionally torn apart by every love song that reminds him of the love he's lost. I could feel these details coalescing into the rudiments of a narrative. I could even envision setting—a city, perhaps New York—and a time period—the present, with a certain noir-inspired sensibility.

At the same time, I couldn't shake an image when hearing the song: rain against a lighted windowpane. The rain image likely came to me from the music itself, which suggests falling raindrops. And then, of course, there's the old conventionalized association in music of raindrops as teardrops. The image had a more personal source for me; I have a vivid memory of waiting in a parked car outside the grocery store as a child of seven or eight while my mother shopped—it was the 1980s, so a car seemed a perfectly reasonable place to leave a child—and I was watching rain bead up on the windshield and leave a snaking trail as it slid down the glass. I was moved by the moment; I still am, just by the memory of the image. The recollection captures a mood and, in doing so, the essence of a story that does not require a beginning, middle, and end to make meaning.

My first draft of the "So Sick" treatment was an awkward hybrid of the narrative and the imagistic. It began with an image of rain on a windowpane, then became overdetermined narrative as Ne-Yo did the things the lyrics describe—checking his answering machine, erasing the anniversary date on his calendar, adjusting his radio. I cringe now to think how naïve I was in my approach, and at the same time how earnest. I shudder to think that I sent this early draft to my friend, who sent me back some encouraging notes, asking me to "refine" the concept and "strip away" the excess. He wanted more details, but the right kind of details.

I revised, producing a treatment that I thought communicated my sense of the story. My friend, dealing with multiple submissions, submitted my treatment with little adjustment. The job went elsewhere. Hype Williams's video for the song was inexplicably set on a ski slope in Aspen with Ne-Yo wearing a fur-collared coat and glancing pensively out of the windows of a multimillion-dollar house overlooking snow-capped mountains. Though any number of reasons can explain why one director gets a video over another, I knew that my treatment hadn't helped. Looking back, I now understand that my treatment demonstrated a fundamental lack of understanding of the function of the music video in relation to a pop song, and of the very nature of narrative in pop. I made the mistake of aspiring to mimesis, of rendering in image what the lyrics were saying rather than seeking something evocative and visually striking that might accompany and accentuate the music and lyrics together as song. It was all about providing actions, communicating strong ideas in visual terms. I came, too late, to understand the music video treatment more as a sales pitch than a piece of creative prose, as a story told through a visual vocabulary rather than a linguistic one.

My early efforts at writing music video treatments mirrored the early years of music videos as a medium, with the slavish attention to lyric and the idea that the visuals must represent the incidents the song describes. The first videos that appeared on MTV on August 1, 1981, were almost exclusively performance clips (The Buggles' "Video Killed the Radio Star," Rod Stewart's "She Won't Dance with Me," Pat Benatar's "You Better Run"). The exceptions were strange hybrids like REO Speedwagon's "Keep on Loving You," which begins with the lead singer, the prodigiously mulleted Kevin Cronin, on what we imagine is a psychoanalyst's couch speaking about a woman who haunts his memory: "Here's the problem, doctor. It's this new album. I wrote a song about a girl. I made her up! It was only a song, but I can't get her out of my mind. Every time I think of her, I picture her with the other guys—never with me. She's driving me nuts. But she's sooo beautiful."

Cut to said woman, a striking brunette gazing fixedly at the middle distance. The camera pulls back to reveal that her attention is directed at a small television screen where Cronin and the rest of Speedwagon are performing their song. The remainder of the clip cuts between conventional concert footage and shots of the woman, clothed in a white fur coat, with the band members lounging on the couch, inexplicably in formal attire. As the song draws to a close, we return to the room where the woman, now wearing pink lingerie, sits on the couch watching the television with that same fixed gaze, the guys from the band sitting beside her watching as well, though she doesn't acknowledge their presence. She turns off the television and we cut back to Cronin on the couch: "It happens every time I play this song. Where does she come from, doctor? Who is this woman?" And—surprise— the camera pans to reveal that the doctor is the mystery woman herself. "I've absolutely no idea," she says as she lets down her hair. End scene.

Years later, Cronin recalled the experience of the video: "For *Hi Infidelity*, we'd made four videos in one day with Bruce Gowers. They were horrible. 'Keep On Loving You' made us look like even bigger dorks than we were. It starts with me sitting in a psychiatrist's office—a female psychiatrist, because someone figured out that you had to have a hot chick in the video." Even this rudimentary video understood something that I still had to learn: When it comes to narrative, a music video need only have the thinnest relation to the song itself. What matters is the story that music and image tell together on the level of style and feeling.

Music videos are not beholden to the narrative and incident of a song, but they serve many important purposes—even today when music videos now reside online rather than on television. They can help to evoke a mood, like the seductive one-shot clip for D'Angelo's "Untitled (How Does It Feel)." They can satisfy the narrative urge all on their own, like No Doubt's film noir– inspired video for "It's My Life." They can fashion metanarratives with no apparent correlation to the lyrics, like Britney Spears's "Toxic," in which she goes around in a comic-strip world killing men for no particular reason. They can render apparent what is only implicit in the lyric, as is the case with Pearl Jam's "Jeremy" or Aerosmith's "Janie's Got a Gun." Other videos, like the clip for Taylor Swift's "Blank Space," come together at the same time as the song rather than as a retrospective creative act.

Music videos offer a way of approaching storytelling in song lyrics at an angle; as visual media that support narrative, videos underscore the constraints of expressing songs' stories in words alone. Out of those constraints, of course, emerge opportunities. The narratives in songs ask the listener to participate in the construction of image in a way that video forestalls by its rich saturation of visual stimuli. Sometimes the best thing is to turn away from the screen and just play the song. Listening to the stories pop songs tell connects us to the long tradition of storytelling as an oral form—to the power of recitation, memory, and voice.

Conclusion

ow do poets listen to pop songs? Do they hear things that the rest of us don't? Do they count the rhythms of the lines? Do they separate the half from the full rhymes? Do they feel the song more deeply because of their knowledge of the inner workings of syllables and sounds, or does that knowledge get in the way of listening?

How do pop singers read poems? Do they hear music that the rest of us miss? Do they feel compelled to perform, to speak, even to sing? If we read poems the way that singers sing song lyrics, might poems feel less distant than they sometimes do in their inscrutable silence?

Read pop songs like poems. Sing poems like pop songs. Both acts will seem unnatural, perhaps even perverse. Some parts won't fit. But the practice can inspire new clarity and insight. It can offer fresh awareness of the careful craft of a line from a song that you've known half your life—a line that stuck with you, and now you know why. Familiarity and nostalgia play their parts; so too do words arranged in a certain order and sung by a certain voice in a certain way against certain sounds.

Poetry and pop songs, as different as they are, are united in this: They are both equally impractical. Both, in the harsh light of utilitarianism, are utterly useless. Although people reserve a certain respect for poetry, they do so out of reverence for a craft largely out of phase with the time, as one respects a watchmaker or a cobbler for the mastery required to do small things with great skill. In contrast, people disregard or disparage pop songs as disposable cultural confections. But where do we go when our hearts are broken, when we celebrate, when we mourn? Often we turn to pop songs. Lyrics that at other times seem silly or slight or saccharine become necessary. Although we need neither poetry nor pop to live, it's hard to live without them.

The poetic tools of sound, meaning, and feeling are at work in even the most banal pop song, just as they are at work in the most trite ode or sonnet. Yet the poetics of pop songs remains overshadowed by bombastic polemics on whether this or that songwriter should be considered a poet. By focusing on such matters of nomenclature, we overlook an opportunity to engage the tools of poetic analysis to understand and to appreciate one of the most widely disseminated lyric traditions in the world.

As rhythm and rhyme recede from contemporary poetry, pop song lyrics have emerged as the most accessible and exciting body of language to showcase the music of words. In fact, many of the tools of poetic analysis we learn in school, including scanning the rhythm of lyrics, identifying rhyme patterns, and looking for registers of diction, work better on song lyrics than they do on most contemporary poetry.

Poets, songwriters, and critics often draw a bright line between poetry and song lyrics; indeed, there are differences worth preserving for the betterment of both forms. Just because pop song lyrics do not meet the expectations of contemporary poetry, however, doesn't mean that they are somehow a debased form. "I often lament that true songwriting will end up as an arcane folk art, like Appalachian basket weaving or divining water with a stick," observes the singer and songwriter Rosanne Cash. "In dark moments, I suspect that no one really appreciates the beauty of a precisely rhymed couplet, sewn perfectly into a heartrending melody, delivered by an honest voice. I have devoted my entire adult life to the pursuit of that beauty, to discovering the internal rules of each individual song, to revealing the truth, and not the facts, of its subject matter, and to understanding the subtleties of tempo, feeling, and tone." This book has been dedicated to appreciating and analyzing—and appreciating through analyzing—the manifold beauties of language, form, and sound that are unique to pop song craft.

Popular music is in a continual process of renovation and rebirth. If we find less to comment on in the poetics of pop's song lyrics today than we might have in the past, it does not mean that there's nothing there but rather that we must adjust our eyes and our ears so as better to see and to hear the music around us. Much of this poetics resides in performance rather than in the language of the lyric; it rests in vocalists' phrasings and intonations, in the interplay between the lyric as voiced and the music as played, in the decisions of producers and sound engineers. In fact, in most ways pop's poetics is a more complicated affair today than it has ever been.

Studying song lyrics creates a new connection and commitment to the music we love—and perhaps to the music for which we previously did not care. The new pleasure radiates from the cerebral joy of close analysis in the revelation of pattern and form, as well as from the more visceral enjoyment of listening to familiar recordings again, the experience now subtly and silently enriched by new discovery. Accepting song lyrics' identity as poetry gives us the opportunity to direct a different critical gaze at them than our collective habits of listening and music criticism normally use.

Pop songs are far more than the sum of their poetic parts; they always find full expression in sound and performance. Through the poetry of pop, we also come to understand that the work of analysis is enacted through looking at the parts that comprise the whole rather than at the whole all at once. This book has approached the fullness of performance through the specific lens of lyrics, emphasizing the fundamental dynamic between language and sound that gives life to pop music. Given the arguments for denying song lyrics the status of poetry, one better have good reasons to read the poetry of pop anyway. I'll leave you with a few:

Read song lyrics to reconnect with the pleasures of rhythm and rhyme, familiar from childhood and once common in page-born poetry, now largely forgotten.

Read song lyrics to recognize the often-overlooked craft of songwriters and musicians, singers and producers, who work together to create aesthetic artifacts of beauty, power, and cool.

Read song lyrics to illuminate the complex and shifting relationships that lyrics establish with their music and their performance.

Read song lyrics to learn about poetic structures and forms in a user-friendly way, with a familiar body of language.

Read song lyrics to understand what so many people hear in them, whether or not the songs speak to you.

Read song lyrics because even when they comprise only half, or less, of a song, they command attention.

Read song lyrics because they're often more compelling than they need to be to satisfy the performative demands of their songs.

Read song lyrics because you want to write better songs.

Read song lyrics because you want to write better *about* songs.

Read song lyrics because no songs will be harmed in the process; if you love a song before reading the lyrics, you'll love it still.

The poetry of pop is never about lyrics alone. The dance of word and music makes songs act on our imagination and emotions just as the best poems do. As attentive readers, our task is to unlock the mysteries of lyric expression through the poetics of form, as well as through the ineffable qualities of voice and music. This is the poetry of pop.

Appendix

The playlists that follow present recordings and song lyrics to consider as you continue to explore the poetry of pop. They take inspiration from *Ego Trip's Book of Rap Lists* (1999), which took inspiration from Dave Marsh and Kevin Stein's *The Book of Rock Lists* (1981). Both books are driven by a fan's love and loathing of particular artists and songs, as well as a scholar's and fan's attention to detail. Their lists range from the silly to the sublime and concern everything from sound to fashion. The lists presented here focus on the matters of poetics and performance addressed in this book. Unless otherwise noted, all songs are identified with the performers and the specific recordings that made them famous.

I've organized the lists following the book's chapter sequence so that you may peruse them while you read their respective chapters, or save them all to read at the end. Add to the lists yourself, supplementing them with new examples and devising lists of your own. These lists are neither exhaustive nor definitive. They're exploratory. Think of them as a series of trailheads from which to commence self-guided treks through pop's language and sound. Singers and songwriters can use them to find good examples of song craft. Teachers can use them to structure lesson plans. Students can use them to deepen their familiarity with poetry and poetics. Just about anyone can find something surprising in these collections of songs.

CHAPTER ONE: LYRIC AND SONG
Eleven Pop Songs Adapted from Poems (and Two Inspired by Poets)

Pop songs and poems aren't the same—unless they are. The songs listed below borrow their lyrics, entirely or in part, from poems by others. In some instances, lyrics and poetry are identical. In others, the lyrics derive inspiration in more subtle ways. Wilco's "Born Alone," for instance, took shape after lead singer and songwriter Jeff Tweedy browsed through a poetry anthology in search of inspiration. "I wasn't coming up with anything specific," he said, "so I opened up a book of American poetry and randomly turned to the Emily Dickinson pages, no one poem in particular. I took a lot of words, most of them verbs, and put them against words that looked appealing to me from [John Greenleaf] Whittier and other 1800s poetry. It's just looking at the words and writing a little poem trying to use as many of them as possible." Listen to the songs as you look at the lyrics and the poems side by side. What's changed and what's stayed the same? What makes some lyrics more successful than others at bridging the gap between poetry and song?

Song: Judy Collins, "Golden Apples of the Sun" (1962)
Poem: William Butler Yeats, "The Song of Wandering Aengus" (1899)

Song: Iron Maiden, "Rime of the Ancient Mariner" (1984)
Poem: Samuel Taylor Coleridge, "The Rime of the Ancient Mariner" (1798)

Song: Sting, "Sister Moon" (1987)
Poem: William Shakespeare, Sonnet 130 (1609)

Song: Vic Chesnutt, "Stevie Smith" (1990)
Poem: Stevie Smith, "Not Waving but Drowning" (1957)

Song: Sheryl Crow, "All I Wanna Do" (1993)
Poem: Wyn Cooper, "Fun" (1987)

Songs: Richard Buckner, *The Hill* (2000)
Poems: Edgar Lee Masters, *Spoon River Anthology* (1915)

Song: Nickel Creek, "Sweet Afton" (2000)
Poem: Robert Burns, "Sweet Afton" (1791)

Song: Brazilian Girls, "Me Gustas Cuando Callas" (2005)
Poem: Pablo Neruda, "Poema XV" (1924)

Song: Okkervil River, "John Allyn Smith Sails" (2007)
Poet: John Berryman (1914–1972)

Song: Mumford & Sons, "Sigh No More" (2009)
Poem: William Shakespeare, "Sigh No More" from *Much Ado about Nothing* (1598/1600)

Song: Natalie Merchant, "Maggie and Milly and Molly and May" (2010)
Poem: E. E. Cummings, "maggie and milly and molly and may" (1958)

Song: Esperanza Spalding, "Little Fly" (2010)
Poem: William Blake, "The Fly" (1794)

Song: Wilco, "Born Alone" (2011)
Poets: Emily Dickinson, John Greenleaf Whittier, and others.

A Playlist for Poetry Lovers

Brian Buckley and Kate Hunter are the proprietors of Innisfree Poetry Bookstore and Café in Boulder, Colorado, one of only four poetry-focused bookstores in the United States. Visiting the store, you're likely to hear an eclectic mix of music, from Radiohead to Rakim, as you browse the shelves stacked with all manner of poetry, classic and contemporary. I asked Brian to devise a playlist pairing songs with poems, united by theme or form or feeling. What resulted is a celebration of unexpected connections across time and genre. I've used this list to structure a week of study in both my undergraduate and graduate seminars. It helps me to model for students the continuity of experience between music and poetry as exemplified in one person's lifelong love affair with language. "The road to the poetry shop began with the transistor radio that wrapped around the bed pole at the pillow end of my bed," Brian tells me. "Now I open a shop every morning and am surrounded by poetry and music. It's hard to fathom the arc of my life without the artists and songs, the poems and lyrics on this list."

Bob Dylan, "Visions of Johanna" (1966), and Kevin Young, "Hurricane Song" (2015)

Joni Mitchell, "Big Yellow Taxi" (1970), and Jane Kenyon, "Otherwise" (2005)

Stevie Wonder, "Living for the City" (1973), and Philip Levine, "What Work Is" (1991)

The Clash, "Lost in the Supermarket" (1979), and Allen Ginsberg, "A Supermarket in California" (1955)

Bob Marley, "Redemption Song" (1980), and Phillis Wheatley, "On Being Brought from Africa to America" (1773)

U2, "A Sort of Homecoming" (1984), and W. B. Yeats, "The Lake Isle of Innisfree" (1890)

Tracy Chapman, "Fast Car" (1988), and César Vallejo, "Piedra negra sobre una piedra blanca"/"Black Stone Lying on a White Stone" (1939/1971 Robert Bly translation)

Sinéad O'Connor, "Black Boys on Mopeds" (1990), and Langston Hughes, "I Look at the World" (1930)

Neil Young, "Helpless" (1993), and Sinéad Morrissey, "Driving Alone on a Snowy Evening (After Frost)" (2005)

Joseph Arthur, "In the Sun" (2000), and Jimmy Santiago Baca, "What Is Broken Is What God Blesses" (2007)

Some Poets Pick Some Song Lyrics Worth Reading

Poets love pop songs, too. I asked a handful of poets to name a particular song lyric that they believe richly rewards our reading attention. What lyrics capture their ears? Are there particular lyrics that have influenced their styles and informed their own poetic practices? I'll let them tell you.

H. L. Hix picks Bobbie Gentry's "Ode to Billie Joe" (1967). It will surely be the most *uncool* choice in this playlist, and it was long "before my time" (I didn't encounter it until many years after it had disappeared off the charts), but Bobbie Gentry's "Ode to Billie Joe" brilliantly achieves (in a song that is *all* lyrics—the guitar just keeps the rhythm) a poetic value I find powerful: subordination of *event* to *situation*. "Ode to Billie Joe" seems ostensibly about events: the narrator and Billie Joe throwing something off the bridge, Billie Joe jumping off the bridge, and so on. But although those events get named, they are mostly withheld: we don't know what the pair were throwing off the bridge, we don't know why Billie Joe killed himself. What is revealed with utter clarity is the narrator's situation: she is spoken *to* and spoken *about* within the poem, but she herself is never allowed to speak; she is closely monitored (told to wipe her feet, interrogated for not eating, observed and reported on) but not *recognized* at all; she is kept in place by her society, but is afforded no place in her society; kinship relations are enforced on her from without, but the kinship she *feels* is denied her. In Gottlob Frege's terms, "Ode to Billie Joe" obscures reference in order to disclose sense. In Aristotle's terms, "Ode to Billie Joe" inverts the tragic focus on *mythos* for a lyric focus on *ethos*. The narrator makes no explicit criticism of her society, but her implicit critique is devastating. She does not declare her social alienation and erasure, but I feel it all the more strongly for its *not* being declared. Her protest takes the form of lamentation. I experience "Ode to Billie Joe" as a most robust fulfillment of Emily Dickinson's advice to "tell all the truth but tell it slant."

Kyle Dargan picks Marvin Gaye's "Inner City Blues (Makes Me Wanna Holler)" (1971). Anyone who has taken a workshop with me has heard my idea about writing poetry being like building the lightest possible plane that will fly. Sometimes, that is. There is a place for excess, for everything in poetic intent, but, staying with this idea of efficiency and vicious concision, Marvin Gaye and James Nyx's "Inner City Blues (Makes Me Wanna Holler)" has impressed me for a long time by capturing so much depth and nuance with so little. The sense of being caught in an inescapable economic spiral builds over the verses, but let's start with the second: "Inflation, no chance / to increase finance. / Bills pile up sky high. / Send that boy off to die." "Inflation, no chance" is an economics white paper in itself, but the juxtaposition of all four lines makes it possible to see a connection among poverty, loss of economic ground, and the pressures to enlist (and die) in the army. A sparse-sparse, quiet but wrenching verse that creates space for the "holler" to emerge as the chorus.

Evie Shockley picks Joni Mitchell's "Hejira" (1976). Set with an impossible task (pick *one*??), I default to the songwriter who, for me, set the standard of song lyrics as poetry. "Hejira" is not my top Joni Mitchell song for listening, but these are definitely the lyrics I'd most want to *read*. From the gorgeous one-word title (an Arabic word signifying a flight from danger or journey to a more congenial place), we move into the "melancholy" meditation of a woman who travels to escape from "the petty wars / that shell shock love away." She's recovering from a relationship that seems to have been overpowering—relieved to be released back to herself, but at the same time, in withdrawal. The quatrain that moves me perhaps most of all carries forward both her theme of duality and her breathtaking talent for making abstractions tangible through metaphorical images: "In the church they light the candles/And the wax rolls down like tears/There's the hope and the hopelessness/I've witnessed thirty years." There. One image does double duty, daring us to pretend that the fire burning within us is not also burning us, or that we can avoid for long being "suck[ed] . . . back" into connection with others by our need to and for love.

Raza Ali Hasan picks Talking Heads' "Once in a Lifetime" (1980). W. H. Auden reputedly mined the Beatles songbook in his search for new influences for his own work. I am no Auden, but in the poem "British Steel," which is the last poem in my newest poetry collection, *Sorrows of the Warrior Class* (2015), I riff on lines not from the Beatles but from an American band: "*Once in a Lifetime,*/you may find yourself,/pondering how the English," is the first stanza. The line "you may find yourself" appears another three times, and "you may tell yourself," twice. The final stanza goes like this: "You may say to yourself/*Same as it ever was.*/*Same as it ever was.*" Yes, you guessed it, I am talking of Talking Heads' "Once in a Lifetime." The British, as the title of the poem implies, steal in three different ways. In the poem the British are stealing steel-making technology from India. The poet (that's me) is stealing lines from the pop song in order to call the British imperialists. But the truth is I wasn't stealing in order to call the British first-class thieves, but to do something about the long-standing hold this song and its lines have on me. Call it jealousy, not sought-out influence. I stole those Talking Heads lines and used them verbatim in my poetic world—at last making them mine.

Douglas Kearney picks De La Soul's "I Am I Be" (1993). It all comes together on this one—the opening chorus collage of "I am ——; I be ——" statements is the sonic predecessor of A Tribe Called Quest's *Midnight Marauders* cover, but lyrically it sets up a cascading and layered anaphora (which Pos reprises at the head of his first verse and that envoi of a third; and which Dove revises in a kind of phrasal chiasmus as his last line of the second verse). Within the verses themselves, Pos remixes clichés from common English (including "I am an early bird but the feathers are black/so the apples that I catch are usually all worms"); alludes to past examples of people misunderstanding who he is and what he does (". . . to bring the peace,/not in the flower/but the As-salaam Alaik' and the third I am."); and, in one of the song's loveliest moments, says simply: "I cherish the twilight"—a thorn rhyme line (though it's assonant with "maximized" and "right size") that, when voiced, sounds almost like a sigh relieving the density of his flow. Dove, ever underrated, abstracts his imagery to the point that I feel I can turn his words like three-dimensional objects shaped in letterforms and what he's describing. My favorite bars—and I quote this every chance I get to show how dope he is: "I bring the element H-to-the-2/so you owe me what's coming/when I'm raining on your new parade"—of course, H_2O, thus water. But also, H(ip) H(op) and rap's association with water (flow, spit); "raining on your new parade" suggests battling but also De La's place as sly critics of peers from within hip-hop culture. Please. Listen to it right now.

Noah Eli Gordon picks Jawbreaker's "Lurker II: Dark Son of Night" (1995). Although the band's single major label release ultimately failed to garner them the success of their peers like Green Day, and other post-punk acts of the early nineties, there's a near cult-like following for Jawbreaker, due in no small part to Blake Schwarzenbach's emotionally tinged, sonically attuned lyrics. Rather than the story behind domestic failure and dejection, Schwarzenbach condenses into a series of objective correlatives the emotional tenor of events—the core feelings associated with a postmodern Prufrock: "Two room condo, treeless cul-de-sac./A nun's dark habit. All arm, no follow through." Here, that "All arm" also carries with it the homophonic echo of *alarm*, doubling the sense of a fraught relationship that is already over just a few lines later: "Hook up the Sega. Have sex alone." True to his dexterous balance between the sonic and referential potential of words, Schwarzenbach, later in the song, offers another gem of an image in this line about a tree's fallen fruit: "Dead in sunshine, decomposing there." That "Dead in" is also a *dead-end*, as well as something *deadened*. There is between the page and the performance, between the words as written out and the echo each carries when heard aloud, a transformative polysemy, one that, thankfully, keeps Jawbreaker very much alive.

Major Jackson picks the Fugees' "How Many Mics" (1996). "Problem with no man/Before black, I'm first human/Appetite to write like Frederick Douglass with a slave hand." The above excerpt from "How Many Mics," one of the tightest cuts on the Fugees' classic and impactful album *The Score*, has graced and blessed my writing space for nearly twenty years now and served as an example of how allusion and metaphor can harness and expose deeper levels of meaning. Of the talented and distinctive trio members whose cypher-like, improvisatory rhyming skills turned them into household names overnight, Wyclef, Lauryn Hill, and Pras, it is Wyclef who slips this bit of subtle black history onto the album and in one of their most successful tracks. Emcees and poets either live or die by metaphor or allusion. In the best-case scenario, metaphors and allusions create bridges, reaffirming shared knowledge, and tap into a reader or listener's awareness and consciousness, or at worst, they can leave them hanging by their sheer unfamiliarity and novelty. No matter the genre of music, rock, hip-hop, or R&B, I have always gravitated towards those lyricists who reference history, literature, or current events: as a teenager, I thrilled in recognizing that U2's "Sunday Bloody Sunday" was a direct address of the Troubles in Ireland or that the Cure's "Killing an Arab" was a lyric in the persona of Meursault, Albert Camus's protagonist in the novel *The Stranger.* I guess listening to one of my mother's favorite Marvin Gaye albums, *What's Going On,* encouraged me to demand more from song lyrics. It could be said Wyclef built his reputation as a rapper by name-dropping, showcasing his wide range of allusions, and in "How Many Mics," they are plentiful: by the time he has finished his portion of the song, he plays golf with David Sonnenberg; runs through Crown Heights screaming "Mazel tov"; makes deals with Tommy Mottola; wishes to survive like Seal in the song "Crazy"; notices drug fiends dance like John Travolta in the movie *Grease*; and narrates once getting hit by Guinness stout. But it is his reference to the famous slave narrative *The Autobiography of Frederick Douglass* that resonates most with me. I have always felt that hip-hop, like poetry, is a question of liberty attained through literacy, one of creation and maintenance of style that sings an individual's life. To express oneself in words on a page or in a song is one of the highest acts of freedom. As an enslaved descendant of Africans in America, Douglass yearned for freedom, and like many black folk, found learning how to read and write the ticket toward a greater self-awareness and independence. Douglass not only writes himself into freedom but writes himself into existence, inscribes his humanity. That ongoing hunger among black folk, and indeed, in all of us, is reflected in Wyclef's words of immense power, yet said so succinctly and wittily, I might add.

Adrian Matejka picks Radiohead's "Paranoid Android" (1997). "When I am king, you will be first against the wall / With your opinion, which is of no consequence at all." Sometimes, Thom Yorke's lyrics are deeply encoded and need musical gestures to open up for the listener. But other times, as with "Paranoid Android" and many of the songs on *OK Computer,* the lyrics are so tight and generous to their disconnected, pre-Millennium listeners that no musical exposition is necessary. Yorke's false bravado in these lyrics captured my frustrations and insecurities (back then and now) with being housed in our amorphous, digital neighborhoods. And when he lingers on "consequence" so that each of the three syllables become their own musical continent, the contradictions in self-fulfillment and community get cracked wide open.

Julie Carr picks Cake's "Short Skirt / Long Jacket" (2001). John McCrea sings through my car and through my son who is singing along. He's seventeen. This song, he says, is a lesson in negative space. There's that break, that longgggg silence just after the first "longgggg jacket"—it's the Citibank lit up late, the empty moment between swiping your card to unlock the door and the door unlocking. There's the little exhale after the next "long jacket," like the breath between high school and college when you're riding shotgun with your mom but almost done. There's that gap between McCrea's "I want a girl" and the back-up's "hey, ho," "na-na na na na," which is the space between being the boy dreaming a girl and being the woman who once was one. Then there's the empty space at the back of the throat, what we named "flat affect" just when he was born, those Citibank years, those temp years, those liquid years strolling on even flatter Brooklyn streets. And then finally there's that nothing, that rest or that dead space, when the song just cuts right off and the boy is gone.

The Eleven Chapter Illustrations: Leland Chapin's Liner Notes

When first conceiving the book, I knew I wanted some visual accompaniment to the language and the sound of pop music. I approached a friend, the artist Leland Chapin, with the following proposition: listen to a handful of songs from the book and inter-pret them as image. I drew inspiration from an unlikely source: sixteenth-century German woodcuts. The Nuremberg Prints captured the music and the revelry of tavern culture and were intended for everyday people, not just elite art collectors. Leland proved more than up to the task, bringing unexpected insight and a deep sense of soul to his rich illustrations. Below you'll find his notes for all the images that begin the chapters.

Guns N' Roses, "Welcome to the Jungle" (1987). My father is an anthropolo-gist who works with indigenous peoples. I've had many adventures walking with him through rainforests in Panama, Belize, and Colombia. These images sprang to mind when listening to GNR's sonic jungle. I envisioned an intimate concert on a dreamy stage filled with clouds, intended only for the wildest animals.

Joni Mitchell, "Big Yellow Taxi" (1970). Joni warns her listeners to slow down and listen to Mother Nature. It brought to mind family farms and a bygone era in which many of us lived closer to nature—before we paved paradise to put up a parking lot.

Marvin Gaye, "What's Going On" (1971). These lyrics were a call to action then, and they remain so today. I wanted the image to capture Marvin's inner turmoil as well as the outer turmoil that surrounded him then, that surrounds us now.

Jimi Hendrix, "Purple Haze" (1967). Legend holds that the song was not in-tended as a drug allegory, but rather as a chronicle of a vivid dream Hendrix had in which he found himself under the sea, lost in the purple haze of jelly-fish. I wanted to capture that fanciful image.

The Rolling Stones, "(I Can't Get No) Satisfaction" (1965). The Golden Ratio is apparent throughout the universe, from the formation of galaxies to the growth of plants and the structure of the human body. It lent itself quite natu-rally to illustrating the Stones' uncanny longevity.

Stevie Wonder, "Higher Ground" (1973). I always thought of those lyrics like the layers in tiramisu: he arrays the strata of society, illuminating our inter-dependence. I wanted to portray those layers in the image, with Stevie's vi-brant energy radiating from the center.

Jay Z & Kanye West, "No Church in the Wild" (2011). This song conjures im-agery of everything from gods and kings to faceless mobs of protestors. Heavy breathing, animals growling and screeching—it hits your ears in waves. Ex-ploring it visually brought me to a kind of fractured stained glass style of col-lage and drawing.

Aretha Franklin, "Respect" (1967). Aretha is the Queen of Soul. I wanted the illustration to capture her regal bearing as well as her deep spirituality. It might sound funny, but I kept thinking of her as a kind of musical Jedi. What you see is the result.

Amy Winehouse, "Rehab" (2006). This drawing represents the idea of Amy Winehouse as a deeply inventive and original vocalist who felt pressured to become a commodity.

Bob Dylan, "Talkin' New York" (1962). The one-man band: songwriter, poet, and enigma. I first encountered Dylan's music in college. Years later, as an art teacher I analyzed his watercolor paintings with my students. Here, I tried to capture his independence as a young artist.

Prince, "When Doves Cry" (1984). Prince's song has always evoked in my mind the brilliant title of Maya Angelou's first autobiography, *I Know Why the Caged Bird Sings*. Perfectly gender fluid, he was both handsome and beauti-ful. A man of faith and of principle, I tried to make his image as monumental as his legacy.

CHAPTER TWO: READING
Out of the Blue: Ten Songs Supposedly Written in Ten Minutes (or So)

A striking number of songwriters claim to have composed some of their most famous songs in ten minutes. It's almost always ten minutes, not five or seven or fifteen. Maybe this is just an example of artists playing into the mythos of creative genius, the idea of lightning-strike inspiration that's been with us at least since the Enlightenment.

But what if we take these songwriters at their word? What are the mechanics of composing in so little time a classic like Bob Dylan's "Blowin' in the Wind" or Al Green's "Let's Stay Together"? The Welsh theorist Raymond Williams posits about literature that the key to creative practice is "the rare capacity to articulate and to form, to make latencies actual and momentary insights permanent." Perhaps artists are able to write these songs with such speed because they have been writing them all along—not explicitly, but through cultivating their sense for syllables and sounds in the song-writer's craft. It really comes down to what constitutes writing a song—whether we start the stopwatch at the point at which the words begin to take final form or at which the intimations of musical ideas begin coalescing in the mind.

Aerosmith's Steven Tyler explains the whole ten-minute song mystery in his own inimitable way: "When a song comes to you and you write it in ten minutes, you think, There it is. Dropped in our laps like a stork dropping a baby. It was always there. The song. On the inside . . . I just had to get rid of the placental crap that was around it. Because at the end of the day, who really wrote that? If Dylan were here, he would tell you in his laid-back Bobness, 'Well, now where would it come from?' Out of the blue, lines come to you."

Jerry Lieber and Mike Stoller on composing the Coasters' "Yakety Yak" (1958). "'Take out the papers and the trash!' Just like that, I yelled back, 'Or you don't get no spending cash!' The tune just demanded two-part harmony; ten minutes later, 'Yakety Yak' was born."

Bob Dylan, "Blowin' in the Wind" (1963). "I wrote 'Blowin' in the Wind' in ten minutes, just put words to an old spiritual, probably something I learned from Carter Family records. That's the folk tradition. You use what's been handed down."

The Rolling Stones, "(I Can't Get No) Satisfaction" (1965). In its assemblage of the 500 greatest songs of all time, *Rolling Stone* magazine offered the following: "Two decades later, Jagger admitted that 'Satisfaction' was 'my view of the world, my frustration with everything.' Inspired by that riff and the title line, also Richards' idea, Jagger wrote the words—a litany of disgust with 'America, its advertising syndrome, the constant barrage'—in 10 minutes, by the motel pool the day after Richards' dream."

Irving Caesar, "You Can Dance with Any Girl at All" from *No, No, Nanette* (1970). "Vincent [Youmans] and I went home that night and in about ten minutes I wrote 'You Can Dance with Any Girl at All'—I can write very fast when it hits me. Sometimes lousy, sure, but always fast. What the hell, [George] Gershwin and I wrote 'Swanee' [1919] in about eleven minutes flat!"

John Denver, "Annie's Song" (1974). The song came to Denver in 1974 while he was on a ski lift. "In the ten minutes it took to reach the top of the mountain, the song was there. I skied back down, drove home, went up to my office, and learned the song on the guitar," he recalls in his memoir.

ZZ Top, "Tush" (1975). Dusty Hill wrote "Tush" in ten minutes on tour during a soundcheck.

The Clash, "48 Hours" (1977). Mick Jones recalls how he and Joe Strummer composed the song: "We went upstairs and wrote '48 Hours' in about ten minutes flat," Jones recalls. "Joe always called it hacking or tailoring."

Elvis Costello and the Attractions, "Everyday I Write the Book" (1983). Costello was shocked to see this song, which he had "written for a lark in ten minutes," finding success on the *Billboard* charts. It was his first hit in the United States.

Tom Petty and the Heartbreakers, "Southern Accents" (1985). "It's a funny song," Petty told Bill Flanagan. "I didn't think about it when I was writing it. It's one of those that just came in very quickly, almost word for word, in minutes. I remember it was real late and this song came down. I turned on my cassette and just played it on the piano and the lyrics were just off the top of my head."

Young Thug, "Danny Glover" (2013). "I did a song in eight minutes," Young Thug told *Dazed*. "I thought everybody could write songs that fast. But working with a lot of them, they don't. Wayne and Drake, it takes them so long to do a song. I understand why, because they want it to be perfect. But I think I can do a perfect song in ten minutes . . . I did 'Danny Glover' in eight minutes."

CHAPTER THREE: LISTENING
Seven Salient Oddities

The poetry scholar Helen Vendler asks her students to identify salient oddities when reading poems. A salient oddity is some feature of the composition that at once compels attention and defies initial understanding. Identifying such moments often provides a valuable point of critical and conversational departure. With song lyrics and recordings, spotting salient oddities is one way of coming to terms with the mysterious and ineffable qualities in the music. The following examples are drawn from my own listening life. I hope that they'll prompt your own curiosity, too.

The Coasters, "Little Egypt (Ying-Yang)" (1961). The Rock & Roll Hall of Famers Jerry Leiber and Mike Stoller scored a string of hits with the Coasters, most notably "Yakety Yak" in 1958. On the lesser-known "Little Egypt" they pulled out all the lyric and production stops on what Stoller called their "comic playlet," which includes a carnival barker and the sounds of "seven kids" singing "gitchy-gitchy." The "kids," whose high-pitched voices we hear from 2:20 until the song's close, were actually all voiced by Stoller himself. "[Sound engineer] Tommy Dowd slowed the tape down to half speed," he revealed in his joint autobiography with Leiber. "I recorded over the last refrain so, played at normal speed, my voice was an octave higher. I sounded like one of the Chipmunks."

The Beatles, "I Am the Walrus" (1967). "Walrus" is pastiche. Resolved to confound even the most committed overanalyzers, John Lennon set out to layer the recording with so many sounds, so many shards of lyric language, that no one could possibly conceive a coherent reading of the song. The song contains many salient oddities, from the lyric ("Sitting on a cornflake, waiting for the van to come") to the sonic (Lennon's distorted vocal tone, the result of sound engineer Geoff Emerick's suggestion that Lennon use a poor-quality microphone). Lennon later revealed that "I Am the Walrus" was one of his favorite tracks "because it's one of those that has enough little bitties going to keep you interested even a hundred years later." One of those little bitties comes near the recording's end, when strange voices push through the mix. A keen ear will discern lines from Shakespeare's *King Lear*, which were recorded directly from a BBC radio broadcast as Ringo Starr tuned the dial.

Crosby, Stills & Nash, "Marrakesh Express" (1969). David Crosby mumbles something indiscernible at the beginning of the song. It would seem to be gibberish, though it effectively conjures a certain sense of exoticism in a song that marvels at the sights and sounds of an unfamiliar place.

Guns N' Roses, "Paradise City" (1987). A minute and nineteen seconds into the original studio recording of the song a whistle blares out, igniting a blistering guitar riff. It works. It's something that one learns to anticipate after a few listenings. But why does it work?

Oasis, "Wonderwall" (1995). At last count, the group "Noel Gallagher's Cough at the Start of 'Wonderwall'" boasts some 340 followers on Facebook. Undoubtedly, many more of the millions who purchased *(What's the Story) Morning Glory?*, the band's 1995 album on which the song appeared, have paused to puzzle over the small moment as well. On *Morning Glory*, the cough actually comes at the end of the previous track, "Roll with It," though on subsequent compilation albums it appears at the beginning of "Wonderwall" instead. Why does it matter? Because it's just the sort of detail—seemingly casual, offhand—that is likely the result of certain care on someone's part.

Foo Fighters, "Everlong" (1997). What sounds like a telephone conversation—muted, crackling, and mostly incomprehensible—breaks into the song just after the second-to-last pass through the chorus (3:03–3:25). The words, low in the mix, create a pleasing dynamics in a song that spends so much of its time so loud. The whispered words, especially conspicuous for half of the twenty-two-second span when the only supporting instrument is an electric guitar, have confounded attentive listeners since the album's release. Some of the mystery was lifted, however, when the band revealed that lead singer Dave Grohl scrambled three recordings of his voice: reading a love letter, a technical manual, and a story about the father of a studio technician. Of course, listeners are still left to puzzle over the work that section does in the song.

D'Angelo and the Vanguard, "Really Love" (2014). The first voice we hear isn't D'Angelo's but that of an unidentified woman speaking Spanish. Her voice is set low enough in the mix that not all her words are clearly discernible. Enough are clear, though, to spark one's curiosity, and to evoke a sense of her complicating counternarrative to D'Angelo's lithe love lyric. The mystery woman, it turns out, is Gina Figueroa, a Nuyorican artist whom the website remezcla.com tracked down for an interview. "I sat face-to-face with him and recited my spoken word to him," Figueroa recalls. "I told him about our love story. That was like my poem and my story to him." Her spoken contribution adds texture, meaning, and feeling to the Grammy-winning song.

CHAPTER FOUR: RHYTHM
Five Songs with Dummy Lyrics That Became Actual Lyrics

Often songwriters fashion dummy lyrics as rhythmic, syllabic, and melodic placeholders for the finished words of the recorded song. For most songwriters—and certainly for most *Billboard* hit songwriters—it is imperative that the lyrics *sound* right before one troubles about what they mean. A list of songs follows in which all or part of the recorded lyric is retained from the dummy lyrics. Such lyrics provide us with an occasion to explore just how much or how little sense a pop song must make to be appealing. What do the dummy lyrics do, what emotions do they generate, that other words might otherwise fail to achieve?

Irving Caesar, "Tea for Two" (1924)

Paul Anka, "Diana" (1957)

The Crystals, "Da Doo Ron Ron" (1963)

Burt Bacharach, "Raindrops Keep Fallin' on My Head" (1969)

Common, "The Light" (2000)

What the Silence Said: Twenty-Six Pauses in Pop Songs

Silence can say the song has ended, or that it is about to commence. It can signal that something's gone wrong, or that something irrepressible is coming back to life. One of the most memorable chapters in Jennifer Egan's Pulitzer Prize–winning 2010 novel *A Visit from the Goon Squad* consists entirely of a PowerPoint presentation entitled "Great Rock and Roll Pauses" put together by one of her characters, the twelve-year-old Alison Blake. She identifies thirteen songs, from the Zombies' "Time of the Season" to Garbage's "Supervixen," that employ some kind of a pause in the music and the singing. About Jimi Hendrix's "Foxy Lady," she writes: "Another great early pause: 2 seconds long, coming 2:23 seconds into a 3:19-minute-long song. But this one isn't total silence; we can hear Jimi breathing in the background." What's so evocative about this passage, both in and out of the context of the novel, is the manner in which it displays the fundamental spirit of fandom: a joyous obsession over the details.

Inspired by Egan and her character, I offer some additions to Alison's list. In some of these songs, the silence serves as a sonic surprise—catching things up in mid-sequence. In others, it marks a false ending, a makeshift dam that the music soon floods through. I've only included songs that come to rest in complete silence for a second or more. Therefore, I've not listed EMF's "Unbelievable" or Van Halen's "Loss of Control," where the silence is too short; or the famous pause in Whitney Houston's rendition of "I Will Always Love You," where one still hears the decay of the synthesized strings in the space where her voice builds up for its triumphant return. Here are the thirteen songs from Goon Squad followed by thirteen of my own selections.

The Four Tops, "Bernadette" (1967)

Jimi Hendrix, "Foxy Lady" (1967)

The Zombies, "Time of the Season" (1968)

Led Zeppelin, "Good Times, Bad Times" (1969)

The Doobie Brothers, "Long Train Runnin'" (1973)

David Bowie, "Young Americans" (1975)

The Police, "Roxanne" (1978)

George Michael, "Faith" (1987)

NOFX, "Please Play This Song on the Radio" (1992)

Garbage, "Supervixen" (1995)

Semisonic, "Closing Time" (1998)

The Frames, "Mighty Sword" (2001)

An Horse, "Rearrange Beds" (2009)

The Young Rascals, "Good Lovin'" (1966). An extended pause (1:58–2:00) and an emphatic return to song promise that the band is irrepressible. They'll be with you all night, or for two minutes, thirty-one seconds—whichever comes first.

INXS, "Never Tear Us Apart" (1987). The first two times coming out of the chorus, Michael Hutchence's title words give way to silence, at 00:49–00:51 and again at 1:48–1:50.

Roxette, "The Look" (1988). "And I go la la la la la la. . . ." A suffocating silence (3:09–3:11) is relieved by the hook.

Fugazi, "Waiting Room" (1988). Twenty-two seconds in, things go silent for more than three seconds (00:22–00:25.5)—the song seems over as soon as it starts. Soon sound comes rushing back. This gambol sets us up for the surprise of the song's close, where the music stops just as abruptly, but this time never to return.

Ween, "Captain Fantasy" (1991). What sounds like an acoustic demo for the actual song stops playing, the bass lagging behind for a pulse, then the song proper begins after a protracted span of silence (00:19–00:22). With twenty seconds left, the song fades out and the acoustic demo/rehearsal returns to close the song in symmetry.

Lyle Lovett, "I've Been to Memphis" (1992). In this song, silence signals copia—the band's incessant urge to play on. An extended pause (2:35–2:38) opens into a series of jazz-inflected solos, then Lovett returns at 3:11 for another round of singing. Things seem to be wrapping up around the four-minute mark, and we get a two-second pause before the song continues with a piano solo that fades but never resolves into silence again. The band plays on into infinity.

Aerosmith, "Livin' on the Edge" (1993). Steven Tyler tells us he "would rather be hangin on," but the music does not, stopping abruptly on that final word. From 3:26 to 3:30 we get a silence that is not silence, like the echoing white noise of a seashell cupped to the ear, before the bass drum strikes four times, signaling a return to screeching sound.

Nine Inch Nails, "March of the Pigs" (1994). "Now doesn't that make you feel better?" Trent Reznor asks us, his voice trailing off on the last syllable until 1:20, when a piano chord holds on four seconds longer before giving into two seconds of silence (1:24–1:26), which can no longer hold back the explosion of sound that follows it. At 2:32, Reznor returns to the same line, but this time the song gives way to silence for good.

Green Day, "Good Riddance (Time of Your Life)" (1997). We encounter two stops and starts at the very beginning of the track. I suppose this studied imperfection suggests the band's DIY sincerity, a pose more than a fact of life.

The Strokes, "Hard to Explain" (2001). The frenetic jam cuts out just long enough (2:06–2:08) for you to glance down to see if your earbuds got disconnected.

Bright Eyes, "False Advertising" (2002). "Now all anyone's listening for are the mistakes," Conor Oberst sings before silence that seems to give his critics just what they want. At 2:07 a woman's voice breaks in—"Oh, I'm sorry"—to which Oberst replies, "No, it's ok. It's ok." At 2:12, he counts the song back in ("1-2-3-1-2-3"). The break, a planned mistake, compounds the song's irony: it's meant to sound spontaneous and unadorned, but the whole thing is planned and composed.

Queens of the Stone Age, "You Think I Ain't Worth a Dollar, but I Feel Like a Millionaire" (2002). A textbook example of the false ending, going silent from 2:38 to 2:42 of a 3:13 song before the music uncoils itself again in a frenzy of churning bass, guitar, drums, and Nick Oliveri's guttural "uh!" My friend Douglas Kearney prefers their false ending a few tracks later on the same album, on "Song for the Dead," where the band pulls up short from 5:09 to 5:12 before coming back for forty seconds more.

The Distillers, "Drain the Blood" (2003). At 2:02 the background vocals and chugging instrumentation cease, leaving only Brody Dalle singing "I'll make it yours, so here we go" (2:02–2:04). The silence that follows (2:05–2:06) is enough to make us believe the song has ended, but back come voice and instruments at 2:07 with the chorus.

CHAPTER FIVE: RHYME
Fifteen Lyrics That Effectively Rhyme "Moon" with "June"

Since Tin Pan Alley days, the perfect rhyme pair of "moon" and "June" has come to stand for the path of compositional least resistance. In fact, the lyrics written to disparage the rhyme pair as clichéd are now far more familiar than the ones that invoked the rhyme in the first place. The songs below follow another strategy. Each lyric has unlocked some way to employ the rhyme pair in a way that is still invigorating and thoughtful. Sometimes this means embracing the cliché. With others it means imagining the words' relation outside of a rhymed couplet. In still others it means rendering their rhyme relation almost inaudible by enlisting the words in other poetic functions. Together, these lyrics demonstrate that even exhausted rhymes can find a second wind if the song is right.

Creedence Clearwater Revival, "Suzie Q" (1968). From 2:30 to 2:47 the band repeats the words "moon" and "June," though it sounds more like a mantra than a lyric. "I was kind of poking fun at Tin Pan Alley, how they'd use all these simple words that rhymed," the singer and songwriter John Fogerty recalls.

> Now many moons and many Junes
> Have passed since we made land
> > Procol Harum, "A Salty Dog" (1969)

> They fell asleep in the sand underneath the Florida moon
> In June
> Lola counted rainbows; Frankie counted sheep
> > Jimmy Buffett, "Frank and Lola" (1985)

> Sister killed her baby 'cause she couldn't afford to feed it
> And we're sending people to the moon

September my cousin tried reefer for the very first time
Now he's doing horse—it's June
> Prince, "Sign o' the Times" (1987)

Ain't gonna give ya no moon in June
Never see you, it'll be too soon
> Motörhead, "Shut You Down" (1991)

Bye, June
I'm going to the moon
It better be by June
Because I'm going to the moon
> Smashing Pumpkins, "Bye June" (1991)

Ooh, sneaky moon, ooh, sneaky moon
June bug buzzin on the front porch light
> Tanya Tucker, "Sneaky Moon" (1993)

Underlying depression
Have to crawl into my room
Underlying depression
Don't want to know about the moon in June
> Van Morrison, "Underlying Depression" (1995)

Moons in June, I've given up on that stuff
Arms have charms, but I've no hope of falling in love
> The Magnetic Fields, "With Whom to Dance?" (1995)

The piercing, radiant moon
The storming of poor June
> System of a Down, "Spiders" (1998)

Or maybe I should get a farm in southern France
Where the winds are wispy and the villagers dance
And you and I, we'd sleep beneath a moon
Moon in June, and sleep 'til noon
> Lou Reed, "Modern Dance" (2000)

Was he worried we might go too far
Maybe wind up rhyming "moon" and "June"
> Elton John, "Tinderbox" (2006)

It's a man on the moon and fireflies in June
And kids selling lemonade
> Rodney Atkins, "It's America" (2009)

The new June moon shootin on a blue lagoon
Shoo, as DOOM zooms in on a platoon
MF DOOM on J. Dilla, "Sniper Elite" (2009)

So once you've approved and the money shifts
You and your band on the moon June twenty-fifth
Open Mike Eagle, "Jon Lovitz
(Fantasy Booking Yarn)" (2014)

Seven Ghost Rhymes

In a ghost rhyme the songwriter leads the listener to anticipate a particular rhyme word (often an explicit one) only to substitute another word or sound in its place. I call them ghost rhymes because the rhyming word our mind conjures hovers unexpressed over what we actually hear. On her 2010 song "Cherry Red," for instance, the Norwegian rocker Ida Maria threads a ghost rhyme throughout the chorus, repeating it a half dozen times in under three minutes. "I'm gonna wear my cherry red / I'm gonna give you lotsa . . ." She never completes the rhyme as our ear expects it, by turns letting the music fill the space of the unexpressed word, or interjecting the anodyne phrase "room in my bed," or breaking off into a strange spoken interlude. Below you'll find songs that exploit the potentialities of ghost rhyme. Some singers provide a sanitized rhyme alternative to the rhyme the lyrics imply. Others devise some other element of sound to take the rhyme's place.

Every time I sing, you say I'm off key
Why can't you see how much this hurts me?
With your perfect beauty and your perfect pitch
You're a perfect . . . terror
Antonio Carlos Jobim (Lyrics by Gene Lees), "Desafinado
(Off-Key)" (1967)

So, as this rap is winding down
It's plain to see we wear the crown
You know Anthrax is number one
But we don't care, we just wanna have . . . a festival!
Anthrax, "I'm the Man" (1987)

Well, I took my baby uptown
Well, to show her that I had some class
The drink tab, I could not pay
You know, I ended the date with a foot up my . . . [horn squeal]
Royal Crown Revue, "Datin' with No Dough" (1996)

Held you when you were sick; even . . . [drum hit]
Kelis, "Caught out There" (1999)

If you save yourself for marriage you're a bore
If you don't save yourself for marriage you're a horr . . . ible person
> Kacey Musgraves, "Follow Your Arrow" (2013)

I'll be sleeping on the left side of the bed
Open doors for me and you might get some . . . kisses
> Meghan Trainor, "Dear Future Husband" (2015)

I would never go and chat what we talkin about
You the only one I know could fit it all in her . . . Man!
> Drake on DJ Khaled, "For Free" (2016)

Eight Triple (and Two Quadruple) Rhymes

Triple rhymes—that is, rhymes of words with three syllables—are a far more varied practice in song lyrics than in page-born poetry, where they are usually reserved only for light or comic verse. Because song lyrics live primarily in sound, the strangeness and artificiality of triple rhymes on the page are often normalized. To complete such rhymes, poets and songwriters sometimes pair a multisyllabic word with phrases comprised of two or more shorter (often monosyllabic) words, a practice known as mosaic rhyme. In performance, triple rhymes—and the occasional quadruple rhymes, and more—marry rhyme with rhythm, dominating the pattern of the line. As a consequence, the tone of such rhymes can run from the slightly sardonic to the clever to the downright somber. On Rush's "Digital Man," for instance, Neil Peart leads listeners through a series of multisyllabic rhymes that together shape the sound of the song, rhyming "observation" with "conversation," "anesthetic" with "and synthetic," "information" with "adaptation," and more. Below are a few examples of the varied uses of multisyllabic rhymes in pop lyrics.

> On that famous *thoroughfare*
> With their noses *in the air*
> > Irving Berlin, "Puttin' On the
> > Ritz" (1929)

> Funny how my *memory skips*
> While looking over *manuscripts*
> Of unpublished rhyme
> Drinking my vodka and lime
> > Simon & Garfunkel, "Hazy
> > Shade of Winter" (1966)

> So happy *together*
> And how is *the weather*?
> > The Turtles, "Happy Together" (1967)

He starts to *shake and cough*
Just like the old man in
That book by *Nabokov*

> The Police, "Don't Stand So Close to Me" (1980)

You consider me a young *apprentice*
Caught between the Scylla and *Charybdis*

> The Police, "Wrapped around Your Finger" (1983)

Music can be such a *revelation*
Dancing around, you feel the *sweet sensation*

> Madonna, "Into the Groove" (1985)

The landlord says your *rent is late*
He may have to *litigate*

> Bobby McFerrin, "Don't Worry, Be Happy" (1988)

Dead in the middle of Little *Italy*
Little did we know that we riddled two middlemen who didn't do *diddly*

> Big Pun, "Twinz (Deep Cover '98)" (1998)

What are we to Heart *Huckabee*, art fuckery *suddenly*

> Aesop Rock, "None Shall Pass" (2007)

Thought that you were in it for the paper
Never thought I'd take *you serious*
Now I need you, not a moment later
Losing it, I'm so *delirious*

> Justin Bieber, "No Pressure" (2015)

Twenty Songs without Rhyme

When songs don't contain rhyme, it's usually for a reason. Sometimes it is out of specific design—a way, for instance, for songwriters to test their skills by imposing an artificial formal constraint. At such times, the lyricist often devises means of compensating for the loss of rhyme by inventing other kinds of sonic patterns and repetitions to satisfy the ear's desire for rhyme's ordering pleasure. Other times the absence of rhyme is a direct consequence of performance style—the more conversational and stream-of-consciousness the lyric, the less likely it is to display patterned rhyme. We don't miss rhyme as much here because our ears hear the lyrics as something akin to speech. Still other times rhyme is absent because, well, the songs are undisciplined or just aren't very good. Rhyme's absence here is a sign of the lyricist's resignation in the face of the challenge of craft.

Rhyming effectively and naturally is a difficult thing to do. As difficult as rhyming is, though, *not* rhyming while still writing a good song might be the most difficult thing of all. Some of the songs listed below use other forms of repetition to take up the work that rhyme has abandoned. Dashboard Confessional uses a heavy dose of anaphora, repeating "And she" at the beginning of successive lines throughout the song. Songs can also capture a conversational tone, like Tracy Chapman's "Fast Car" or Suzanne Vega's "Tom's Diner," which render the ear less likely to hear the strangeness of rhyme's absence. Many songs employ identity, such as Kate Bush's "Under the Ivy," which includes the lines "Go right to the rose / Go right to the white rose." Others use alliteration. Some songs verge on rhyme, but refuse the comfort of the couplet, like Sonic Youth's subtle subversion in "Skip Tracer" when Kim Gordon sings "L.A. is more confusing now than anywhere I've ever been to / I'm from New York City, breath it out and let it in," the "to" denying our ears an easy end rhyme (been/in). In the fleeting seconds of a 4:28 song that otherwise abjures rhyme, R.E.M.'s Michael Stipe offers these simple, playful rhymes in "Losing My Religion": "Try, cry / Why try?"

John Blackburn, "Moonlight in Vermont" (1944)

Woody Guthrie (with Martin Hoffman), "Deportee (Plane Wreck at Los Gatos)" (1961)

Simon & Garfunkel, "America" (1968)

The Velvet Underground, "Stephanie Says" (1968)

The Beatles, "Across the Universe" (1970)

Suzanne Vega, "Tom's Diner" (1987)

R.E.M., "Losing My Religion" (1991)

Björk, "The Anchor Song" (1993)

Sonic Youth, "Skip Tracer" (1995)

Dar Williams, "The Pointless, Yet Poignant, Crisis of a Co-Ed" (1996)

Ben Folds Five, "Cigarette" (1997)

Kate Bush, "Under the Ivy" (1997)

Radiohead, "Karma Police" (1997)

Tracy Chapman, "Another Sun" (2002)

Kelly Clarkson, "Because of You" (2004)

Rise Against, "The Approaching Curve" (2006)

Radiohead, "Jigsaw Falling into Place" (2007)

Bon Iver, "For Emma" (2008)

PJ Harvey, "In the Dark Places" (2011)

Coheed and Cambria, "You Got Spirit, Kid" (2015)

Six Transformative Rhymes

Transformative rhymes are one response to rhyme's constraint—born of resignation or inspired invention. The singing or rapping voice has the capacity to bend syllables and sounds, making two words sound like rhymes when they actually aren't. I call these transformative rhymes because the performer reshapes the sound of one or more of the words to make them meet in rhyme. Transformative rhymes go further even than standard wrenched rhymes where, for instance, a poet might rhyme "lie" with "poetry" as W. H. Auden does in "In Memory of W. B. Yeats." Rap may be the most familiar domain for such a practice, but it is widespread across genres. Here are a handful of examples in which lyricists respond to rhyme's challenge by breaking words apart and refashioning them to fit their own sense of sound.

> Well, you wanna be loved? Huh. Hey, that's *okay*
> 'Cause it falls in line right with my sexual*i-tay*
> > TLC, "Baby-Baby-Baby" (1992)

> Don't want to be your *mama*
> Just want to make you *come-a*
> > Andre 3000 of OutKast, "Hey Ya!" (2003)

> Good does not come without pain
> Meaning, before it gets better, it's gon get *worse*
> Like my homies on the sick side still dyin over turf
> That don't belong to *urse*, I mean us. . . .
> > Khujo Goodie from OutKast, "Reset" (2003)

> When *they see him*, whips be *European*
> If *you're a ten* chances *you're with him*
> If you're a five you know you riding *with them*
> Sick *with the pen* . . .
> > Jay Z, "La-La-La (Excuse Me Miss Again)" (2003)

> Don't ever fix your lips like *collagen*
> And say something when you gon end up *apologin'*
> > Kanye West, "Can't Tell Me Nothing" (2007)

> I say you the *bestest*, lean in for a *big kiss*
> > Lana del Rey, "Video Games" (2011)

CHAPTER SIX: FIGURATIVE LANGUAGE
Twelve Acts of Alliteration

In the poet's toolbox, alliteration is more ax than scalpel. The repetition of an initial consonant across several words can often lead to hackneyed lyrics. Nonetheless, when done with a certain restraint or conscious abandon it can prove a pleasing means of patterning. Joanna Newsom takes the latter course on "The Book of Right-On," where she embraces alliteration's artifice in a playful run of six: "My fighting fame is fabled / And fortune finds me fit and able." In the instances that follow, the songs harness the small music of consonant repetition, often yoking it with rhythmic stress to create moments of sonic interest.

> And I'd let that lonesome whistle
> Blow my blues away
>> Johnny Cash, "Folsom Prison Blues" (1955)

> The savage soldier sticks his head
> In sand and then complains
>> Bob Dylan, "Gates of Eden" (1965)

> It was the third of June, another sleepy, dusty Delta day
>> Bobbie Gentry, "Ode to Billie Joe" (1967)

> They paved paradise and put up a parking lot
>> Joni Mitchell, "Big Yellow Taxi" (1970)

> Let it be, let it be, let it be, let it be
> Whisper words of wisdom, let it be
>> The Beatles, "Let It Be" (1970)

> The shifting shafts of shining weave the fabric of their dreams
>> Rush, "Jacob's Ladder" (1980)

> And when she shines she really shows you all she can
>> Duran Duran, "Rio" (1982)

> He's got a force field and a flexible plan
> He's got a date with fate in a black sedan
> He plays fast forward just as long as he can
>> Rush, "Digital Man" (1982)

> Picture perfection, pursuing paper with a passion
>> 2Pac, "If I Die 2Nite" (1995)

> Picture perfect, I paint a perfect picture
>> 2Pac, "2 of Amerikaz Most Wanted" (1996)

So I take it for a ride on a sunny summer Sunday afternoon
                The Presidents of the United States of America,
                                        "Mach 5" (1996)

Said I'm so sick of love songs, so sad and slow
                                Ne-Yo, "So Sick" (2006)

Eight Instances of Double Entendre to Satisfy Your Dirty Mind

Double entendre is not simply a matter of a lyric carrying multiple meanings; one of those meanings must be suggestive, usually of a sexual nature. It is not a matter of a clean surface meaning and dirty hidden meaning, either. Double entendre rarely sets out to deceive; rather, like a burlesque show, the artful concealment is part of the titillating appeal. Given that so many pop songs are about sex anyway, it should come as no surprise that they are also about sex when they suggest double meanings. Here are some instances in which the lyric's playful double entendre shines a light on both sexual text and subtext.

I need a little steam-heat on my floor
Maybe I can fix things up so they'll go
What's the matter, hard papa?
Come on and save your mama's soul
                Bessie Smith, "I Need a Little Sugar in My Bowl" (1931)

When everybody's tryin to sleep
I'm somewhere makin my midnight creep
Every mornin the rooster crow
Something tell me I got to go
                        Howlin' Wolf, "Back Door Man" (1961)

Squeeze me, baby, 'til the juice runs down my leg
The way you squeeze my lemon, I'm gonna fall right out of bed, bed, bed,
    be—yeah!
                        Led Zeppelin, "The Lemon Song" (1969)

Last night I tried to tease her
I gave my love a little pinch
She said now stop that jivin
Now whip out your big ten inch
                        Aerosmith, "Big Ten Inch Record" (1975)

Oh my God, here you are
Prettiest thing in life I've ever seen

Close my eyes, what's it like?
What's it like inside your tamborine?

Prince, "Tamborine" (1985)

Let me know when we're getting close
You can slide on out or we can head on down the road

Alan Jackson, "Country Boy" (2008)

Are you brave enough to let me see your peacock?
What you're waiting for, it's time for you to show it off
Don't be a shy kinda guy; I'll bet it's beautiful
(Come on, baby, let me see what you hidin underneath)

Katy Perry, "Peacock" (2010)

It's a stick up, no more makeup
Get that ass on the floor
Ladies, put your lipstick up
Double entendre, double entendre

Flo Rida feat. LooKas and Sage the Gemini,
"Goin' Down for Real (GDFR)" (2015)

Repetition and Difference in the Chorus:
Third Time Breaks Your Heart

The chorus in popular music is usually defined by its constancy. Verses head off in any number of directions, but the chorus brings us back. Some choruses, however, change even as the words stay pretty much the same. They generate their dynamism by the transformation that occurs around them, the new point of entry that the verse takes back into the chorus. In this list, the novelist and diehard country music fan Stephen Graham Jones presents songs that use this technique to elicit strong emotional responses. I'll let Stephen take it from here:

This isn't local only to country, and certainly isn't restricted to just the country I grew up with, but this era of country did seem custom-fitted for songs that use this trick. It's that time-honored shift where a line is gone through twice, more or less innocently, so you think you have the full weight of it. But then that third verse, it wraps that line in a slightly different context—one you should have seen coming, but are happy you didn't, as it allows that release any good punchline does. Except this punch, it's in the heart, or at least in the jar where you keep your tears. And in each of these cases, the songwriter named the song with that line. There's upbeat versions, too, of course—from George Jones's "Corvette Song" to Earl Thomas Conley's "Somewhere between Right and Wrong," and clever examples all across pop, but the Harry Chapin-esque ambush-sentimentality paired with the "ruggedness" of steel-guitar country is apparently some sort of chocolate-and-peanut-butter situation (crunchy shell, soft center?), judging by how far each of these songs got to go. Or, how far they took each of these artists.

Instead of quite chronological, these are ordered more from those needing the least unpacking to those that take the form to its next level. Note too the absence of the Highwaymen from these proceedings: no Kris, no Waylon, no Johnny, no Willie. No Merle, either, and no Roger Miller, no Townes van Zandt. Would this be because this format for a song is closer to pop than "real" country—Conway Twitty is here—or was this just a fad that passed while all these songwriters were either lost in or kicking dope? Again, not sure, but it's fun to think about, and a good playlist to cue up if you're alone in the cab, and have your darkest sunglasses on.

Kathy Mattea, "Where've You Been?" (1989)

John Conlee, "Old School" (1999)

Tim McGraw, "Don't Take the Girl" (1994)

Ricky Van Shelton, "Keep It between the Lines" (1991)

Confederate Railroad, "When You Leave That Way You Can Never Come Back" (1992)

The Oak Ridge Boys, "Come On In (You Did the Best You Could Do)" (1978)

Conway Twitty, "That's My Job" (1987)

George Strait, "Love without End, Amen" (1990)

Collin Raye, "Love, Me" (1991) [The rare *two*-verse configuration]

Sawyer Brown, "The Walk" (1991) [Lots of these are dad songs, yeah]

Martina McBride, "Independence Day" (1993) [Even this one]

Trisha Yearwood, "She's in Love with the Boy" (1991) [Note the change of *person*]

Alan Jackson, "Drive (for Daddy Gene)" (2002) [Note the leap into the subjunctive]

Jamey Johnson, "In Color" (2008)

Eight Similes (Well, One's a Metaphor) Gone Wrong

Similes sometimes give songwriting a bad name. They often occasion cringeworthy comparisons, because they are obvious (see "Like a Rock"), nonsensical (see "Stay Beautiful"), or bizarre (see "Aqualung"). Of course, one suspect simile doesn't doom a song. Witness Chuck Berry's 1958 classic "Johnny B. Goode," a veritable pop magna carta, which describes a country boy who could play a guitar "just like a-ringin' a bell." That's either the worst pop simile ever or the best—there's no in-between. As you'll see from the examples that follow, even similes that seem to go wrong can help the song go right.

Feeling like a dead duck
Spitting out pieces of his broken luck
> Jethro Tull, "Aqualung" (1971)

My mama loves me, she loves me
She get down on her knees and hug me
Oh, she love me like a rock
> Paul Simon, "Loves Me Like a Rock" (1973)

I'm a shooting star leaping through the sky
Like a tiger defying the laws of gravity
I'm a racing car passing by like Lady Godiva
I'm going to go go go. There's no stopping me
> Queen, "Don't Stop Me Now" (1978)

Got shiny diamonds
Like the eyes of a cat in the black and blue
Something is coming for you
> Dio, "Holy Diver" (1983)

Life's an empty picture
When you're living alone
Maybe that's the reason
Every heart needs a home
> Donny Osmond, "Soldier of Love" (1989)

If I could draw a map of a boy
That I would like
Your résumé would shine through like a bright green light
> That Dog, "Ms. Wrong" (1995)

I strap on my guitar just like a .45
I pray each night my aim is true

I'm shooting for the heart a looking in your eyes
Singin the cowboy blues

> Gary Allan, "Cowboy Blues" (1999)

Corey's eyes are like a jungle
He smiles, it's like the radio
He whispers songs into my window
In words that nobody knows

> Taylor Swift, "Stay Beautiful" (2006)

Seven Similes (Well, Three Are Metaphors) Gone Right

Figurative language is not simply about adornment. The most captivating similes in songs appeal to the listener on multiple levels, whether in sound, image, or meaning. Look for the ways that the figurative comparison illuminates some quality of thought or feeling in its subject.

Love is a burning thing
And it makes a fiery ring
Bound by wild desire
I fell into a ring of fire

> Johnny Cash, "Ring of Fire" (1963)

But my words like silent raindrops fell
And echoed in the wells of silence

> Simon & Garfunkel, "The Sound of Silence" (1966)

Oh, you are in my blood like holy wine

> Joni Mitchell, "A Case of You" (1971)

Step out the front door like a ghost into the fog
Where no one notices the contrast of white on white
And in between the moon and you, angels get a better view
Of the crumbling difference between wrong and right

> Counting Crows, "Round Here" (1993)

I'm harder than me tryna park a Dodge
When I'm drunk as fuck, right next to a humongous truck
In a two-car garage

> Eminem, "Forgot about Dre" (1999)

Now I'm a fat house cat
Nursing my sore blunt tongue
Watching the warm poison rats
Curl through the wide fence cracks

> Iron & Wine, "Flightless Bird, American Mouth" (2007)

All of my thoughts of you
Bullets through rotten fruit
Come apart at the seams
Now I know what dying means

The National, "Graceless" (2013)

Six Examples of Antanaclasis

Antanaclasis is a rhetorical figure that works on the principle of the mirror image: repeating a word but shifting its meaning to create a pun based in homonym—two words that sound alike but mean different things. Most often, lyrics that employ antanaclasis are playful and self-consciously clever. They are moments in which the songwriter foregrounds wordplay.

I'm a man of means, by no means
King of the road

Roger Miller, "King of the Road" (1965)

But just because a record has a groove don't make it in the groove

Stevie Wonder, "Sir Duke" (1976)

And, hey, barkeep, what's keeping you?
Keep pouring drinks
For all these palookas
Hey, you know what I thinks?

Tom Waits, "A Sight for Sore Eyes" (1977)

I'm from the murder capital where they murder for capital

Jay Z, "Lucifer" (2003)

I ain't as good as I once was
But I'm as good once as I ever was

Toby Keith, "As Good as I Once Was" (2005)

I'm not a businessman, I'm a business, man

Jay Z on Kanye West's "Diamonds from
Sierra Leone (Remix)" (2005)

CHAPTER SEVEN: VOICE
Some Whispers, Some Screams

The voice is often most compelling at its extremes, the whisper and the scream. A whisper invites intimacy and commands close attention. In sound recording, it is often a stylized effect—something that can't be readily reduplicated in live performance. The scream opens up a connection to the animal in woman and man, to the primal urges and angst. It renders the listener more acutely aware of the body from which the voice emerges. Screams are different from shouts. John Lydon (formerly Johnny Rotten) has been shouting for decades. AC/DC, under the vocal administrations of both Bon Scott and Brian Johnson, made the scream a basic element of their style. Paul McCartney shouts the lyrics on the Beatles' "Twist and Shout"; he doesn't scream until the end (1:33–1:36). Screams can be sensual and scary; they can be downright rock 'n' roll and deeply soulful. You'll find screams in obvious places—in thrash metal, in gospel and R&B, in rock of all types. You'll also find it in unexpected places where the scream builds energy out of the contrasting quiet that surrounds it. Scream's opposite, the whisper, also holds a vital place in pop, though it is less common. Together, whispers and screams mark out a territory of voice that reaches below and beyond language to a register of expression otherwise unattainable.

Whispers

John & Yoko and the Plastic Ono Band, "Happy Xmas (War Is Over)" (1971). Before the music begins, Yoko Ono whispers "Happy Christmas, Kyoko"—Kyoko is her daughter—and John Lennon whispers "Happy Christmas, Julian"—Julian is his son.

The Rolling Stones, "Angie" (1973). Jagger sings "Let me whisper in your ear" and then he does just that between 1:56 and 2:00, repeating Angie's name twice. The whisper is intimate, even invasive. It extends the mood of the recording as a whole, which is closely mic'd and stripped down to acoustic instruments.

The Clash, "Straight to Hell" (1982). After singing the opening two verses, Joe Strummer begins panting into the microphone at 3:53, quickening the pace of his breathing before spitting out "Straight to hell" (4:03–4:04) in a harsh whisper.

The Cure, "Lullaby" (1989). Robert Smith slowly whispers "I spy/Something beginning with an s" (00:13–00:18), luxuriating in the sibilance. We don't hear his voice again until 1:01.

Madonna, "Justify My Love" (1990). Madonna essentially delivers the entire song in an amplified whisper.

Guns N' Roses, "Estranged" (1991). Whispers are not always quiet. In this instance, the whisper is actually louder than the main vocal. Its amplification underscores Axl Rose's desperation at this moment of the lyric on one of Guns N' Roses' longest songs (9:24). Rose sings "Still talking to myself and nobody's home" (2:57–3:03). Then in a stage whisper, he gasps "alone" (3:05).

Michael Jackson, "In the Closet" (1991). Jackson invites one of his famous friends, Princess Stephanie of Monaco, to whisper these lines: "There is something I have to say to you. If you promise, I'll understand. I cannot contain myself when in your presence. I'm so humbled. Touch me. Don't hide our love, woman to man" (00:05–00:28) before producer Teddy Riley's new jack swing track sets in. The princess returns at 2:04–2:19, then Michael whispers back to her at 2:35–2:42. It's all starting to get a little uncomfortable . . . Several more whispered exchanges follow, which I'll let you track for yourself should you so desire.

PJ Harvey, "Down by the Water" (1995). PJ Harvey caps a macabre narrative, in which she sings as a mother who for unknown reasons seems to have drowned her daughter, with eight repetitions of the whispered lines, "Little fish, big fish swimming in the water / Come back here, man. Give me my daughter" (2:03–3:08). These whispers complicate an already ambiguous plot.

Mariah Carey, "Bliss" (1999). Listeners know Carey's voice best when it is high and loud, reaching into the whistle register. She flaunts that here from 0:52 to 1:24, from 2:01 to 2:35, and finally from 2:54 to 4:10. The balance of the song is comfortably in her middle register, much of it pitched as a whisper.

Ying Yang Twins, "Wait (The Whisper Song)" (2005). The Ying Yang Twins, Kaine and D-Roc, rap the entire three-minute track in whispers. Their unsubtle seduction—really sexual provocation—is rendered all the more audible for the whispered tone.

Janet Jackson, "Rock with U" (2008). Whether echoing a sung word or phrase or interjecting another, Janet Jackson's whispers are spoken, slow, and close. She positions many of these whispered words in between lines and consciously in tension with the music's rhythm, lending them an impromptu feel. She whispers "You're so sexy" (3:07–3:08) between two sung lines, and you believe it.

Jason Derulo, "Want to Want Me" (2015). Derulo whispers at the very beginning of the song, when he reminds us of his last name—uttering it like an aural graffiti tag.

Screams

Screamin' Jay Hawkins, "I Put a Spell on You" (1956). This song is a 2:24 master class in all manner of grunting, hollering, wailing, whooping, and, yes, screaming. Cue it up at 1:46, for instance, or at 2:17, and you'll realize how Hawkins earned his moniker.

Little Richard, "Jenny, Jenny" (1957). Richard's signature "whoo" punctuates nearly every other line in this song, which was a top-ten hit from Richard's debut album, though it is now overshadowed by such classics as "Tutti Frutti" and "Long Tall Sally." At the center of the two-minute song he lets out a protracted scream (from 00:53 to 00:56), which melts into a sax solo. A year later, on "Good Golly Miss Molly," Richard reprises the pattern—accenting his vocal delivery with wailing "whoos" and letting out one ecstatic scream near the middle of the song, this time between 1:09 and 1:11, again ushering in an instrumental solo.

James Brown, "I Got You (I Feel Good)" (1964). The song begins with one of the iconic screams in recorded music. You'll hear Brown's scream across his discography, from "Cold Sweat" (1967) to "The Payback" (1974), and you'll hear its influence in the vocal styles of other artists on this list, from Mick Jagger to Michael Jackson, Robert Plant to Steven Tyler.

Wilson Pickett, "Land of 1000 Dances" (1966). Just after Pickett, in unison with his background singers, belts out his now-ubiquitous "Naa na-na-na-naa na-na-na-naa na-na-naa-na-na-naa na-na-na-naa" (00:47–00:53), he lets out a "wow!" that stretches across a full measure (00:54–00:57).

The Doors, "The End" (1967). Jim Morrison was fond of screaming. You can hear him doing it on "Backdoor Man" and "Light My Fire" as well, which, like "The End," are songs from the group's self-titled debut LP. On "The End," Morrison interrupts a protracted, rhythmically spoken riff about a son who tells his father that he wants to kill him to utter the following: "Mother, I want to . . ." (7:25–7:40). His voice trails off and then gives way to screaming, near-indecipherable words at first, then just noise, before resolving in a melodic lilt (7:41–7:47). The song still has four minutes remaining.

The Crazy World of Arthur Brown, "Fire" (1968). "I am the god of hellfire," Arthur Brown proclaims at the top. The rest of the track confirms it, building up to the following sequence: "You're going to burn, burn, burn, burn, burn, burn, burn, burn, burn, burn, . . ." then Brown's cackle from 2:05 to 2:07, then his scream from 2:07 to 2:16. A few final screams close the under-three-minute track, just for good measure.

Janis Joplin with Big Brother and the Holding Company, "Piece of My Heart" (1968). Joplin sings "You know you got it" (3:28–3:30), then follows with an open-mouthed scream ("owww!") from 3:31 to 3:32, that's every bit as iconic as James Brown's.

The Beatles, "Revolution" (1968). The guitar comes out screaming, then a drum hit, then the voice lets out a feral wail from 00:06 to 00:08. "After a first reduction," write Philippe Margotin and Jean-Michel Guesdon in *All the Songs: The Story behind Every Beatles Release*, "John recorded his vocal and right away he double-tracked it and gave the song a screaming introduction."

Rolling Stones, "Gimme Shelter" (1969). This song has plenty of shouting. Mick Jagger shouts his lyrics throughout, and background singer Merry Clayton, whose vocals were a late addition to the track, meets and exceeds Jagger's passion on the chorus. But this list isn't about shouting. The scream comes at

3:01 when Clayton's pitch of emotion makes her voice break on the word "murder"; it's a sheering sound—a piercing, passing, and unmistakable shriek. Even Mick seems to recognize it; you can hear him let out an appreciative "whoo" right after.

The Stooges, "T.V. Eye" (1970). In the song's first eleven seconds one hears four varieties of scream: (1) a throaty "Lord!" (2) a shriek, (3) a yip, and (4) a screamed phrase I can't make out that's really just an occasion to holler. Periodically throughout the song, you hear some more screams, mostly from Iggy Pop. This song also provides a three-second silence, from 3:22 to 3:25, worthy of a place on another list here as well.

The Who, "Won't Get Fooled Again" (1971). Pete Townshend posited that this track "screams defiance at those who feel any cause is better than no cause, that death in a sick society is better than putting up with it, or resigning ourselves to wait for change." Roger Daltrey quite literally screams defiance between 7:45 and 7:48, rending a roughly two-minute instrumental section.

Deep Purple, "Highway Star" (1972). Ian Gillan's nine-second scream (00:26–00:34) opens the track. Over the course of its sonic trajectory, it becomes louder, fuller with additional voices, and higher in pitch, ending as a sinister siren.

Aerosmith, "Dream On" (1973). Steven Tyler, the self-dubbed Demon of Screamin', may have bigger and badder screams than the ones you'll encounter on this classic early track. What makes these stand out, though, is the contrast between the purity of Tyler's natural voice here and the evidence of his emergent screaming style. Listen as his pitch climbs as he repeats "dream on" (3:24–3:33), culminating in a scream that oscillates between high and higher pitches before thinning and eventually fading in exhaustion (3:34–3:40).

Pixies, "Tame" (1989). Black Francis alternatingly whispers and screams throughout this short recording. Though he initially launches his vicious and throaty screams from the word "tame" (1:34–1:35), its repetition and the increasingly raw stress he places on the vowel render his screams less about what he says and more about how he says it (1:37–1:54).

Asphalt Ballet, "Hell's Kitchen" (1991). We hear a good scream right off the top at 00:04–00:11, and lead singer Gary Jeffries's voice always seems on the verge of screaming again.

Nirvana, "Where Did You Sleep Last Night (Unplugged)" (1994). On this unplugged set for MTV, Kurt Cobain is uncharacteristically restrained through the first half of the song, but the pressure is building. Between 3:49 and 3:52 he lets a burst of pressure out in a scream that starts as the word "shiver" but ends in sheer sound beyond words.

Björk, "It's Oh So Quiet" (1995). Björk's unexpected, staccato screams are especially jarring here against the otherwise ordered sonic palate—"Wow! Bam!" (00:49–00:50).

Radiohead, "Climbing Up the Walls" (1997). Thom Yorke closes the track by repeating the line "Climbing up the walls," beginning at 3:42. Against squealing violins, Yorke's high-pitched melody creates an uncanny sonic atmosphere. The word "wall" distorts into tormented screams at 4:01.

Kanye West, "I Am a God" (2013). Recent vintage Kanye likes to scream. Hear him on 2016's "Facts." But his best screams, to my ear, come on *Yeezus*, specifically on "I Am a God." Two screams occur between 2:11 and 2:19, becoming choppy as they fade out and the beat returns, and four occur between 2:51 and 3:19, each of them succeeded by rapid, heavy breathing.

Alabama Shakes, "Don't Wanna Fight" (2015). Lead singer Brittany Howard's voice slides into a scream just as the singing begins, from 00:37 to 00:40. The scream was improvised in the studio on the first take. "I didn't think we'd keep it," Howard recalls. "It's like a velociraptor scream," says drummer Steve Johnson. "When I first heard it, it was kinda shocking."

And a Few Laughs . . .

Laughter in song can signal a number of things: joyful exuberance, or the staging of such; off-the-cuff reaction, or the staging of such; a response to something hysterical, or just plain hysterics. "Laughing into tracks represents momentary authority—one passed from the musician to the listener and shared by both. Laughter is a denial of artiness," writes the critic Ben Ratliff. In several of the songs below, one can hear what Ratliff means. With others, however, the laughter sounds less like a denial of artiness than the thing itself—a conscious construction, a gesture of spontaneity that is actually the product of considerable calculation. Sometimes laughter is as light as it seems, and sometimes it portends something deeper, something darker. As Ralph Ellison reminds us, quoting Charles Baudelaire, "The wise man never laughs but that he trembles." In these songs, one can at times hear the wise man, the wise woman, trembling behind the laughter.

Joe Cuba, "El Pito (I'll Never Go Back to Georgia)" (1965). Neuyorican king of the Boogaloo, Joe Cuba scored a crossover hit with this rowdy dance number. Cuba borrowed the song's signature phrase, "I'll never go back to Georgia," from jazz trumpeter Dizzy Gillespie's "Manteca" (1947), and the anti-racist vow captured black and brown sentiment in both eras even as it knitted perfectly with Cuba's clave rhythm pattern. Raucous laughter breaks out at times throughout the song, celebrating the groove and staving off the blues.

The Velvet Underground, "Temptation inside Your Heart" (1968). Lou Reed giggles at 2:21 and 2:23 of a 2:30 track.

Joni Mitchell, "Big Yellow Taxi" (1970). She laughs from 2:10 to 2:13 of this 2:14 track, laughing at her own play with the chorus where she sings "paved paradise" in falsetto and "put up a parking lot" in bass.

Janis Joplin, "Mercedes Benz" (1971). Hear her famous cackle at the song's end, from 1:41 to 1:43.

The Gap Band, "I Don't Believe You Want to Get Up and Dance (Oops Upside Your Head)" (1979). If you ever want to hear a grown man giggle, listen to this. It's lead singer Charlie Wilson's signature sound, and he unleashes it throughout this song and many others to follow. It became so closely associated with Wilson's style that on 1992's "It's Gonna Be Alright," a duet between then A-list R&B crooner Aaron Hall and a down-but-not-out Wilson, it occasions a joke. The song begins with Hall offering heartfelt reflections over a new jack swing track: "Yo, I finally got a song with my mentor. Yeah, you, Charlie." Wilson lets out one of his hiccupped giggles, then Hall playfully tells him, "Don't do that no more, man." They both laugh.

Ozzy Osbourne, "Crazy Train" (1980). "All aboard," Ozzy hollers, then he guffaws from 00:02 to 00:04. Pitch-shifted laugher from 4:38 to 4:40 brings the song to a close.

Yazoo, "Situation (U.S. 12-Inch Mix)" (1982). You hear a woman's bubbling laughter at the beginning (00:02–00:05), then a bit more to close the track (2:26–2:30).

Michael Jackson, "Thriller" (1982). Vincent Price's iconic eleven-second laugh (5:44–5:55) at the close of his song-ending monologue evokes classic film horror and kitsch in equal measure.

New Order, "Every Little Counts" (1986). This laugh (0:17–0:24) plays like Bernard Sumner's spontaneous reaction to the cringeworthy lyrics he's singing ("I think you are a pig / You should be in a zoo"). He loses it once he reaches "you" and finally gets it together a couple bars later. He almost loses it again at 2:34, but keeps his composure. This song also includes a dramatic pause, from 2:46 to 2:48, that renders it worthy of a list a few pages back.

Metallica, "Master of Puppets" (1986). You need to listen to more than eight minutes of this 8:36 track to hear the laughter, a demonic, distorted laugh at 8:14–8:15, then a tormented chorus of them from 8:17 to 8:27.

Neneh Cherry, "Buffalo Stance" (1989). Cherry, affecting different voices, laughs at her own playfulness from 3:12 to 3:15.

Nicki Minaj, "Anaconda" (2014). Minaj's rollicking cackle runs from 3:08 to 3:11, and then another peal sounds from 3:36 to 3:41.

Ten Recordings That Move between Speaking and Singing

One of the most striking vocal effects a performer can achieve comes in moving between speaking and singing. For certain artists this is a common practice. Barry White, for instance, uses words spoken in his buttery bass-baritone as a method of seduction. Taylor Swift often speaks in her songs as a way of enacting another kind of intimacy, inviting a sense of friendship with her listeners. Of course, the line between speech and song is often blurry. Bob Dylan, Lou Reed, and Johnny Cash all variously collapse the distance between speech and song in their conversational deliveries. By contrast, the songs listed here call attention to the difference between the registers, highlighting sharp sonic ascents from speaking to singing. To illustrate this contrast, consider Edward Sharpe and the Magnetic Zeros' "Home," where the simple melody of the verses blends the shape of singing with the directness of speech, the chorus fully embraces song, and a conversational interlude is simply spoken. The song finds its balance in the blending of these disparate parts. In the list below you'll hear the pre-song patter of B. B. King, the R&B interludes of the Ink Spots and Boyz II Men, the distorted sounds of R.E.M. and Pavement, and more. In each, speech is a distinctive sonic register that opens up new expressive range for the songs.

The Ink Spots, "If I Didn't Care" (1939). "If I didn't care, honey chile, more than words can say," Hoppy Jones begins in his "talking bass" interlude, which runs from 1:38 to 2:17. Moving from Bill Kenny's honied chorus to Jones's plainspoken restatement of the lyrics lends solidity to the song's sweet seduction.

The Supremes, "Love Is Here and Now You're Gone" (1967). Over the chorus, Diana Ross interjects dramatic overdubs—at 00:41–00:48, 1:24–1:30, and 2:05–2:11—that the song's producers make little effort to integrate into the recording. It is as if we can hear someone turning one knob to bring the music down and another to bring Ross's voice up. The result is jarring, but somehow compelling.

The Velvet Underground, "I Found a Reason" (1970). The song derives its rich harmonies from its obvious doo-wop influences. Those same soulful sounds likely inspired Lou Reed's spoken interlude ("Honey, I found a reason to keep livin'"), which runs from 1:43 to 2:18.

The Chi-Lites, "Have You Seen Her" (1971). "Have You Seen Her" is a melodrama of lost love. Lead singer Eugene Record mourns his lover: "Why, oh, why did she have to leave and/Go away? Oh yeah./Oh-oh-oh-oh-oh, I've been used to having someone to lean on/And I'm lost. Baby, I'm lost." Another drama plays out in the voice: the song moves from Record's spoken introduction, delivered in his natural voice, to a falsetto choral section, then to Record's solo falsetto singing. The vocal pattern then mirrors itself, ending with a final spoken section that leads back to singing once more.

Barry White, "Can't Get Enough of Your Love, Babe" (1974). In 2010, *Psychology Today* featured an article on the "Barry White Effect," which posits that "generally speaking, women are attracted to men with deep voices in part because this is an auditory cue linked to testosterone, a hormone that is associated with male phenotypic quality." White himself seems to have known this intuitively. On this song and many others he plays to his vocal strengths by beginning with his seductive speech before leading into equally seductive song.

R.E.M., "Belong" (1991). Michael Stipe speaks every word of the song through distortion; the only singing comes with his strings of melodic "ohs," which serve as a kind of chorus. "The vocal on 'Belong,' I sang that directly into a Walkman," Stipe told *Rolling Stone* in a 1992 interview, explaining how he sought to degrade the quality of his vocal sound. "I don't like the clarity," he continued, "because it doesn't allow me as much latitude to just flail, to just be a melody and let the words, the meaning, flow out."

Boyz II Men, "End of the Road" (1992). The writer Sam Greenspan precedes me in celebrating Boyz II Men's bass voice, Michael McCary, and McCary's spoken interludes. On Greenspan's website, 11points.com, he gathers the "11 Best Deep-Voiced Boyz II Men Monologues," beginning, of course, with the spoken portions of this song. "End of the Road" presents two monologues, a brief one at the beginning of the song (00:07–00:19) and a longer one that marks the song's climax (3:34–4:22). Speech opens a space to particularize the terms of the vulnerability that the singing puts on display.

Pavement, "Conduit for Sale!" (1992). Channeling another talky-song, Fall's "New Face in Hell" (1980), Stephen Malkmus delivers seemingly cut-and-paste lyrics over a lo-fi groove. The blank affect of the spoken verses sits in contrast to the urgency of Malkmus's repeated cries of "I'm tryin'."

Edward Sharpe and the Magnetic Zeros, "Home" (2009). Alex Ebert and Jade Castrinos engage in a playful conversation between 3:14 and 3:48, which is eventually swallowed up by the triumphant chorus.

Taylor Swift, "Blank Space" (2014). Swift has several songs that exploit the expressive capacities of the spoken interlude. Famously, there's her "this sick beat" monologue on "Shake It Off." On "Blank Space," she uses her spoken register more sparingly, but nonetheless affectingly. On the last line of the second verse, she cuts off the lilting melodic line and instead speaks the final line: "'Cause, darling, I'm a nightmare dressed like a daydream" (2:07–2:10). The effect is something akin to what happens when the beat drops out from under a rapper's dopest line—Swift's swaggering coup de grâce.

Adam Bradley's "Black, White, or Prince" Playlist

Below is a list of some of the actual songs that I've played for my students during my Black, White, or Prince game. As you'll recall, it's a quiz in which I ask my students to code by race the singing voices that they hear. After getting a sense of the class's collective opinion through a show of hands, I unmask the performer by projecting a picture on the screen. The goal is to unsettle my students' assumptions about what a "white" or "black" person can sound like while also opening up useful discussions about the singing practices common to certain genres.

The Ink Spots, "My Prayer" (1939) [Black group that students might think "sounds white"]

Charley Pride, "Is Anybody Goin' to San Antone" (1970) [Black country singer who sounds like . . . a black country singer, but the students might be tricked by assumptions of genre]

Teena Marie, "Square Biz" (1981) [White soul singer]

Bobby Caldwell, "What You Won't Do for Love" (1978) [White soul singer]

Prince, "I Wanna Be Your Lover" (1979) [Prince]

Earth, Wind & Fire, "Let's Groove" (1981) [Robot—special bonus round . . .]

CHAPTER EIGHT: STYLE
Twenty-Six Cross-Genre Covers

Cover recordings were the norm in early rock 'n' roll, when it wasn't out of the ordinary for the same song to chart for multiple artists, even during the same week. For listeners, the appeal of the cover is that it simultaneously satisfies our desire for familiarity and for novelty. Hearing a familiar song performed in an unfamiliar way can make for great listening, particularly when that cover also transforms the stylistic context of the original. The examples that follow are compelling for the ways they reinvent the source songs and also for how they provide a means of measuring the stylistic contours of a given artist and even genre.

"All Along the Watchtower," Jimi Hendrix (1968); original by Bob Dylan (1967)

"Piece of My Heart," Janis Joplin with Big Brother and the Holding Company (1968); original by Erma Franklin (1967)

"Walk On By," Isaac Hayes (1969); original by Dionne Warwick (1964)

"Hey Jude," Wilson Pickett (1969); original by the Beatles (1968)

"Black Magic Woman," Santana (1970); original by Fleetwood Mac (1968)

"Proud Mary," Ike & Tina Turner (1971); original by Creedence Clearwater Revival (1969)

"Just the Way You Are" by Barry White (1978); original by Billy Joel (1977)

"Take Me to the River," Talking Heads (1978); original by Al Green (1974)

"Got to Get You into My Life," Earth, Wind & Fire (1978); original by the Beatles (1966)

"Tainted Love," Soft Cell (1981); original by Gloria Jones (1976)

"Higher Ground," Red Hot Chili Peppers (1989); original by Stevie Wonder (1973)

"Downtown Train," Rod Stewart (1990); original by Tom Waits (1985)

"I Will Always Love You," Whitney Houston (1992); original by Dolly Parton (1974)

"Live and Let Die," Guns N' Roses (1991); original by Wings (1973)

"The Man Who Sold the World (Unplugged)," Nirvana (1994); original, "The Man Who Sold the World" by David Bowie (1970)

"Cruisin'," D'Angelo (1995); original by Smokey Robinson (1979)

"Killing Me Softly," The Fugees (1996); original, "Killing Me Softly with His Song" by Lori Lieberman (1972)

"Can't Take My Eyes Off of You," Lauryn Hill (1998); original, "Can't Take My Eyes Off You" by Frankie Valli (1967)

"Feeling Good," Muse (2001); original by Nina Simone (1965)

"I Wanna Be Your Dog," Uncle Tupelo (2002); original by The Stooges (1969)

"Hurt," Johnny Cash (2002); original by Nine Inch Nails (1994)

"Such Great Heights," Iron & Wine (2003); original by the Postal Service (2003)

"Make You Feel My Love," Adele (2008); original by Bob Dylan (1997)

"If I Were a Boy," Reba McIntire (2010); original by Beyoncé (2008)

"Leopard-Skin Pill-Box Hat," Beck (2009); original by Bob Dylan (1966)

"Never Gonna Give You Up," The Black Keys (2010); original, "Never Give You Up" by Jerry Butler (1968)

CHAPTER NINE: STORY
Twenty Epistolary Recordings

The conceit of the letter—open, absconded, and otherwise—has a long literary lineage. Eighteenth-century European novels like Samuel Richardson's *Pamela* (1740) in England and Pierre Choderlos de Laclos's *Les Liaisons dangereuses* (1782) in France employed the epistolary form in defining the terms of the novel as a genre. What remains appealing about the epistolary form for pop-song lyrics today is that it conjures a sense of intimacy and connection between the voices in the work of art and their audience. Whereas a novel or a poem maintains the letter's identity as written document, the song demands another kind of suspension of disbelief: that the letter is also voiced for listening ears.

When a song—or even an entire album—invokes the epistolary form, it usually aims for authenticity, openness, and vulnerability. Often, the letter is also a confession. Sometimes the song-as-letter offers a confession to someone who literally can't hear it, as with "Fire and Rain," which posits the song itself as a physical thing ("I walked out this morning and I wrote down this song/I just can't remember who to send it to"). Sometimes it is a letter to someone whom the narrator knows won't be able to hear it, like 2Pac's "Letter 2 My Unborn." When song lyrics are couched as letters it allows for communication that regular conversation might not, as with Leonard Cohen's "Famous Blue Raincoat" and Dar Williams's "If I Wrote You."

The Beatles, "P.S. I Love You" (1963)

James Taylor, "Fire and Rain" (1970)

Leonard Cohen, "Famous Blue Raincoat" (1971)

Rod Stewart, "You Wear It Well" (1972)

John Prine, "Dear Abby" (1973)

Bill Withers, "I Can't Write Left-Handed" (1973)

Tom Waits, "Christmas Card from a Hooker in Minneapolis" (1978)

Kate Bush, "Babooshka" (1980)

Michelle Shocked, "Anchorage" (1988)

Nas feat. Q-Tip, "One Love" (1994)

Dar Williams, "If I Wrote You" (1997)

Alanis Morissette, "Unsent" (1998)

2Pac, "Letter 2 My Unborn" (2001)

They Might Be Giants, "Renew My Subscription" (2004)

Dropkick Murphys, "Last Letter Home" (2005)

Joell Ortiz feat. Dante Hawkins, "Letter to Obama" (2008)

They Might Be Giants, "My Brother the Ape" (2009)

R. Kelly, *Love Letter* (2010)

Lil Wayne, "Dear Anne (Stan Part 2)" (2011)

Mary Lambert, *Letters Don't Talk* (2012)

Thirteen Dramatic Monologues

In poetry dramatic monologues are sustained first-person utterances in the voice of characters (that is, speakers other than the poet him- or herself, often drawn from history), expressing psychological complexity and intense states of being and feeling. The best-known examples from the literary tradition include Robert Browning's "My Last Duchess" (1842) and "Fra Lippo Lippi" (1855), along with Alfred, Lord Tennyson's "The Lotos-eaters" (1832). Dramatic monologues stand out in the history of song lyric because they enshrine the character above the singer him- or herself. The dramatic monologue places the singer in the role of the bard, inhabiting an experience that the audience is to understand as separate and distinct from the singer's own. The form thrives in folk music and rock music, with Bruce Springsteen—represented here three times—being perhaps the greatest master of the form.

Bob Dylan, "A Hard Rain's A-Gonna Fall" (1963)

Bobby Gentry, "Ode to Billie Joe" (1967)

Tammy Wynette, "D-I-V-O-R-C-E" (1968)

Kenny Rogers and the First Edition, "Ruby, Don't Take Your Love to Town" (1969)

Johnny Cash, "A Boy Named Sue" (1969)

Simon & Garfunkel, "The Boxer" (1970)

The Rolling Stones, "Sister Morphine" (1971)

Bruce Springsteen, "Nebraska" (1982)

Townes Van Zandt, "Sanitarium Blues" (1999)

Immortal Technique, "Dance with the Devil" (2001)

Bruce Springsteen, "Paradise" (2002)

The Decemberists, "The Mariner's Revenge Song" (2005)

Bruce Springsteen, "Matamoros Banks" (2005)

Twelve Songs That Use the Second Person

The first person predominates in popular song. It is the most naturalistic: a voice is communicating to us, so it makes sense that it would claim the "I" in doing so. The second person announces its artifice. The "you" can come across as presumptuous, even domineering. It can be a way of speaking the "I" at a plausibly deniable distance. When handled right, however, as in Bob Dylan's "Ballad of a Thin Man," it is a subtle form of coercion that invites us to participate in the action of the song's story. In songs like this, the first person melts away, and all that exists is the "you" that we might imagine is us. In other songs, the intended "you" is clearly defined, as in Paul Simon's song for his daughter, "Father and Daughter." In other instances, the second-person address works in conjunction with the ever-present first-person voice, explicit or implied, of the singer. In Juvenile's "Ha," for instance, the rapper is speaking decidedly to a specific you—whether a particular person or a class of people or both. Unlike "Ballad of a Thin Man," "Ha" does not extend an invitation for the listener to claim the subject position of the "you." Quite the contrary, we are witnessing an exchange between the first-person voice of the singer and the second-person "you" that the speaker is addressing.

Frank Sinatra, "(Love Is) The Tender Trap" (1955)

Bob Dylan, "Ballad of a Thin Man" (1965)

The Beatles, "For No One" (1966)

Leonard Cohen, "Suzanne" (1967)

Billy Joel, "Captain Jack" (1973)

ABBA, "Dancing Queen" (1976)

Dire Straits, "Sultans of Swing" (1978)

Talking Heads, "Once in a Lifetime" (1980)

U2, "A Sort of Homecoming" (1984)

Juvenile, "Ha" (1998)

Paul Simon, "Father and Daughter" (2006)

The Hold Steady, "You Can Make Him Like You" (2006)

Five Songs (and One Album) That Disrupt Narrative Chronology

The conventional plot arc of beginning, middle, and end describes the majority of story-songs in the popular musical tradition. In such instances, a fixed (or slightly shifting) chorus serves to underscore the dynamic changes enacted in the verses. From time to time, however, songwriters consciously subvert listeners' narrative expectations. This narrative displacement happens when artists embrace the inherent circularity of the typical song form, flashing back or forward, or otherwise reordering chronology. "And oh, my god, look, you've just discovered/The way that one thing can lead to another," the Pet Shop Boys sing on "One Thing Leads to Another," their narrative of a man's demise told in reverse. The songs below all call attention to those nodes of narrative where one thing leads to another. Together, they testify to the restless drive to imagine new ways of telling old stories in song.

Bob Dylan, "All Along the Watchtower" (1967)

Pet Shop Boys, "One Thing Leads to Another" (1993)

Nas, "Rewind" (2001)

Nas, "Blaze a 50" (2002)

The Roots, *Undun* (2011)

SomeKindaWonderful, "Reverse" (2014)

Notes

INTRODUCTION

"If, as now seems" Eric Weisbard, *Listen Again: A Momentary History of Pop Music* (Durham, NC: Duke University Press, 2007), 1–2.

"to encompass just about" Quoted in Carl Wilson, *Let's Talk about Love: Why Other People Have Such Bad Taste* (New York: Bloomsbury Academic, 2014), 171.

CHAPTER ONE: LYRIC AND SONG

"bested only by" "Rihanna's 'Diamonds' Shines Atop Hot 100," by Gary Trust, *Billboard*, http://www.billboard.com/articles/news/474056/rihannas-diamonds-shines-atop-hot-100 (accessed May 11, 2016).

"said to have composed in fourteen minutes" "How a Song Written by Sia Furler Becomes a Hit," by Steve Knopper, *New York Times*, April 21, 2014, http://6thfloor .blogs.nytimes.com/2014/04/21/how-a-song-written-by-sia-furler-becomes-a-hit/?_r=0 (accessed May 11, 2106).

"characterizes as 'insipid'" "Rihanna, Icy Hot and Steely-Strong: Rihanna's Album 'Unapologetic' Makes Most of Her Talent," by Jon Caramanica, *New York Times*, November 20, 2012, http://www.nytimes.com/2012/11/21/arts/music/rihannas-album -unapologetic-makes-most-of-her-talent.html (accessed May 11, 2106).

"I don't exactly know how poetry" Joanna Newsom, interviewed by Marc Maron, *WTF*, Episode 709, May 23, 2016, http://www.wtfpod.com/podcast/episode-709-joanna -newsom (accessed May 24, 2016).

"a piece of writing" "poem, n.," OED Online, September 2015, Oxford University Press, http://0-www.oed.com.libraries.colorado.edu/view/Entry/146514?redirected From=poem (accessed September 12, 2015).

"despite their differences" Lawrence M. Zbikowski, *Conceptualizing Music: Cognitive Structure, Theory, and Analysis* (Oxford: Oxford University Press, 2002), Kindle edition.

"In music, some notes" Daniel J. Levitin, *The World in Six Songs: How the Musical Brain Created Human Nature* (New York: Dutton, 2008), 23.

"noise too is part of meaning" Edward Kamau Brathwaite, *History of the Voice: Development of Nation Language in Anglophone Caribbean Poetry* (London: New Beacon Books, 1984), 17.

"I respect poetry" David Ritz, *Divided Soul: The Life of Marvin Gaye* (New York: McGraw-Hill, 1985), 164.

"Lyrics by definition lack something" Stephen Sondheim, *Finishing the Hat: Collected Lyrics (1954–1981) with Attendant Comments, Principles, Heresies, Grudges, Whines and Anecdotes* (New York: Knopf, 2010), xviii.

"Good song lyrics" Simon Frith, *Performing Rites: Evaluating Popular Music* (Oxford: Oxford University Press, 1998), 181.

"A completed poem" Sheila Davis, *The Craft of Lyric Writing* (Cincinnati, OH: Writer's Digest Books, 1985), 6–7.

"The other half of everything" Glyn Maxwell, *On Poetry* (Cambridge, MA: Harvard University Press, 2013), 13.

"The auditory arts of music" Levitin, *World in Six Songs*, 121–122.

"Music is no luxury" Oliver Sacks, *Musicophilia: Tales of Music and the Brain* (New York: Knopf, 2007), Kindle edition.

"The simple truth" Jimmy Webb, *Tunesmith: Inside the Art of Songwriting* (New York: Hyperion, 1998), 48.

"for having created new poetic" "Press Release," The Nobel Prize for Literature 2016, https://www.nobelprize.org/nobel_prizes/literature/laureates/2016/press.html (accessed October 22, 2016).

"He is a great poet" "Prize Announcement," The Nobel Prize for Literature 2016, https://www.nobelprize.org/nobel_prizes/literature/laureates/2016/announcement .html (accessed October 22, 2016).

"Of all the nonsense" Greil Marcus, *Mystery Train: Images of America in Rock 'n' Roll Music* (New York: Dutton, 1975), 87.

"I like 'Across the Universe'" Peter Herbst, *The Rolling Stone Interviews: Talking with the Legends of Rock & Roll, 1967–1980* (New York: St. Martin's/Rolling Stone Press, 1981), 145.

"could stand without the music" Nora Ephron and Susan Edmiston, "Bob Dylan Interview," in Jonathan Eisen, ed., *The Age of Rock 2: Sights and Sounds of the American Cultural Revolution* (New York: Random House, 1970), 65.

"It ain't the melodies" Bob Dylan, *The Lyrics: 1961–2012*, ed. Christopher Ricks (New York: Simon and Schuster, 2014), ix.

"I don't think that" Bill Flanagan, *Written in My Soul: Conversations with Rock's Great Songwriters* (New York: RosettaBooks, 2010), Kindle edition.

CHAPTER TWO: READING

"Like the novel" Kevin J. H. Dettmar, *Is Rock Dead?* (New York: Routledge, 2006), xvii.

"Unless the reader happens" Quoted in Sondheim, *Finishing the Hat*, xvii.

"in the air" Stephen Dobyns, *Next Word, Better Word: The Craft of Writing Poetry* (New York: Palgrave Macmillan, 2011), 69.

"Back then we didn't know" Peter Hook, *Unknown Pleasures: Inside Joy Division* (New York: It Books, 2013), 172–173.

"As a singer and a writer" Quoted in Flanagan, *Written in My Soul*, Kindle edition.

"You don't really need musical notation" Elvis Costello, *Unfaithful Music & Disappearing Ink* (New York: Blue Rider Press, 2015), 294.

"Song lyrics exist independently" Peter Astor and Keith Negus, "More than a Performance: Song Lyrics and the Practices of Songwriting," in Lee Marshall and Dave Liang, eds., *Popular Music Matters: Essays in Honour of Simon Frith* (Burlington, VT: Ashgate, 2014).

"A record is" Albin Zak, *The Poetics of Rock: Cutting Tracks, Making Records* (Berkeley: University of California Press, 2001), 44.

"Writing about things" Seth S. Horowitz, *The Universal Sense: How Hearing Shapes the Mind* (New York: Bloomsbury, 2012), Introduction, Kindle edition.

"Lyrics are written" Gene Lees, *The Modern Rhyming Dictionary* (New York: Cherry Lane Music, 1989), 29.

"From Stevie Wonder to Steely Dan" "Pharrell Williams Masterclass with Students at NYU Clive Davis Institute," YouTube video, https://www.youtube.com /watch?v=G0u7lXy7pDg (accessed March 18, 2016).

"We all wrote to the same" Paul Anka and David Dalton, *My Way: An Autobiography* (New York: St. Martin's Press, 2014), Kindle edition.

"Once I got the bridge" The-Dream's verified annotation on "Single Ladies (Put a Ring On It)." Genius.com, http://genius.com/5055043 (accessed July 30, 2016).

CHAPTER THREE: LISTENING

"Music has the power to stop time" Ahmir "Questlove" Thompson and Ben Greenman, *Mo' Meta Blues: The World According to Questlove* (New York: Grand Central Publishing, 2013), 272.

"do not pretend their decisions" Bruce Jackson (ed.), *Get Your Ass in the Water and Swim Like Me: African-American Narrative Poetry from the Oral Tradition* (New York: Routledge, 2004), Preface.

"I have often found" Zak, *Poetics of Rock*, 86.

"in existence, power, favour" "ephemeral, adj. and n.," OED Online, March 2016, Oxford University Press, http://0-www.oed.com.libraries.colorado.edu/view/Entry /63199?redirectedFrom=ephemeral (accessed March 31, 2016).

"The best pop songs" Frith, *Performing Rites*, 182.

"Song lyrics can take" Adrian Matejka conversation with author on August 28, 2014.

"My phrasing is peculiar to me" Willie Nelson and David Ritz, *It's a Long Story: My Life* (New York: Little, Brown, 2015), 145.

"imaginative transformation" M. H. Abrams, "Constructing and Deconstructing," in Morris Eaves and Michael Fisher, eds., *Romanticism and Contemporary Criticism* (Ithaca, NY: Cornell University Press, 1986), 167.

"essence or shape" "Gestalt | gestalt, n.," OED Online, March 2016, Oxford University Press, http://0-www.oed.com.libraries.colorado.edu/view/Entry/77951?redirected From=gestalt (accessed March 31, 2016).

"This is the power" Levitin, *World in Six Songs*, 31.

"Heya @Pharrell" Pharrell Williams, Twitter post, February 5, 2014, 2:12 a.m., http://twitter.com/Pharrell.

"Lovin-ughhhhh" MetroLyrics, http://www.metrolyrics.com/loving-you-lyrics-minnie -riperton.html (accessed September 12, 2015).

"The hook can" "You Ask, We Answer: What's a Hook?" by Tom Cole, NPR.org, October 15, 2010, http://www.npr.org/sections/therecord/2010/10/15/130588663/you -ask-we-answer-what-s-a-hook.

"There is not one note" Dave Stewart, *Sweet Dreams Are Made of This: A Life in Music* (New York: New American Library, 2016), 96.

"In a track-and-hook song" John Seabrook, *The Song Machine* (New York: Norton, 2015), 202.

As the pianist "Chilly Gonzales' 'Pop Music Masterclass' featuring Taylor Swift's 'Shake It Off,'" YouTube video, 4:29, posted by "Chilly Gonzales," January 5, 2015, https://www.youtube.com/watch?v=0Wog-34Kbb0.

CHAPTER FOUR: RHYTHM

"If you don't have the sound" Anthony DeCurtis, *In Other Words: Artists Talk about Life and Work* (Winona, MN: Hal Leonard, 2006), Kindle edition.

"nothing but rhythm" Jimi Hendrix and Tony Brown, *Jimi Hendrix "Talking": Jimi Hendrix in His Own Words* (London: Omnibus, 2003), Kindle edition.

"Music is a foreign language" Stephen Sondheim, *Look, I Made a Hat: Collected Lyrics (1981–2011) with Attendant Comments, Amplifications, Dogmas, Harangues, Digressions, Anecdotes and Miscellany* (New York: Knopf, 2011), xvii.

"The control and perception" Jack Perricone, *Melody in Songwriting: Tools and Techniques for Writing Hit Songs* (Boston: Berklee Press, 2000), Kindle edition.

"(that is, like musical notes" Lewis Turco, *The Book of Forms: A Handbook of Poetics* (Hanover, NH: University Press of New England, 2000), 33.

"They are reinforced" Mark W. Booth, *The Experience of Songs* (New Haven, CT: Yale University Press, 1981), 8.

"The em-*pha*-sis is on the wrong" "Searching for Max Martin," *Switched On Pop*, November 20, 2015, http://www.switchedonpop.com/?p=489.

"Just like the rising and falling" Greg Allman, *My Cross to Bear* (New York: William Morrow, 2012), 402.

"relating to a regular repeated pattern" "rhythm, n.," OED Online, September 2015, Oxford University Press, http://0-www.oed.com.libraries.colorado.edu/view/Entry /165403?rskey=frgYD1&result=1&isAdvanced=false (accessed September 12, 2015).

"The word has retained" Derek Attridge, "Rhythm," in *The Princeton Encyclopedia of Poetry and Poetics* (Princeton, NJ: Princeton University Press, 2012), 1195.

"the pattern of movement in time" Harold S. Powers, "Rhythm," in *The Harvard Dictionary of Music*, ed. Don Michael Randel (Cambridge, MA: Harvard University Press, 2003), 723.

"Rhythm in music provides" Levitin, *World in Six Songs*, 50.

"The rhythm section" Walter Everett, *The Foundations of Rock from "Blue Suede Shoes" to "Suite: Judy Blue Eyes"* (Oxford: Oxford University Press, 2009), Kindle edition.

"The fundamental unit" Alex James, *Bit of a Blur* (New York: Sphere Publishing, 2010), Kindle edition.

"There's joy in repetition." Prince, "Joy in Repetition," *Graffiti Bridge* (1990).

"In song and in dance" Friedrich Nietzsche, *Basic Writings of Nietzsche* (New York: Modern Library, 2009), Kindle edition.

"The rhythmic properties" Steven Pinker, *Language, Cognition, and Human Nature: Selected Articles* (Oxford: Oxford University Press, 2013), 239.

"Rhythm turns listeners" Sacks, *Musicophilia*, Kindle edition.

"kinesthetic listening" Charles Keil, "Theory of Participatory Discrepancies: A Progress Report," *Ethnomusicology* 39, no. 1 (1995): 10.

"Across repeated listenings" Elizabeth Hellmuth Margulis, *On Repeat: How Music Plays the Mind* (Oxford: Oxford University Press, 2013), Kindle edition.

"The reason why rhythm" Frith, *Performing Rites*, 143.

"Jazz was originally" "The Devil's Music: 1920s Jazz," PBS, February 2, 2000.

"I think that nothing less" Quoted in Tricia Rose, *The Hip Hop Wars: What We Talk about When We Talk about Hip Hop—and Why It Matters* (New York: Basic Civitas, 2008), 95.

"using and keeping of drums" Quoted in Daniel Cavicchi, *Listening and Longing: Music Lovers in the Age of Barnum* (Middletown, CT: Wesleyan University Press, 2011), Kindle edition.

"Rhythmic content means" Quoted in Robert Pinsky, *Singing School: Learning to Write (and Read) Poetry by Studying with the Masters* (New York: Norton, 2014), 75–76.

"The song is layered" Quoted in Michaeleen Doucleff, "Anatomy of a Dance Hit: Why We Love to Boogie with Pharrell," NPR, May 30, 2014.

"Knowing when not to play" Shelia E. and Wendy Holden, *The Beat of My Own Drum: A Memoir* (New York: Atria, 2014), Kindle edition.

"One can't have rhythm" Everett, *Foundations*, Kindle edition.

"Of course it is fundamentally daffy" Stephen Fry, *The Ode Less Travelled: Unlocking the Poet Within* (London: Hutchinson, 2005), 61.

"When you put words to a melody" S. Davis, *Craft of Lyric Writing*, 214.

"Lyrics are 'married'" Pat Pattison, *Songwriting: Essential Guide to Lyric Form and Structure* (Milwaukee, WI: Hal Leonard, 2007), Kindle edition.

"It seems that the words" Quoted in DeCurtis, *In Other Words*, Kindle edition.

"He didn't have the words" Eric Clapton, *The Autobiography* (New York: Three Rivers Press, 2008), Kindle edition.

"Riding in a car" Peter Ames Carlin, *Paul McCartney: A Life* (New York: Simon and Schuster, 2009), 119.

"They're good" Quoted in Philippe Margotin and Jean-Michel Guesdon, *All The Songs: The Story behind Every Beatles Release* (New York: Hachette Books, 2013), Kindle edition.

"I use nonsense words" Anka and Dalton, *My Way*, 145.

"I'm screaming nonsense vowels" John Fogerty, *Fortunate Son: My Life, My Music* (New York: Little, Brown, 2015), 163.

"a kind of nonsense thing" Quoted in Stephen Bishop, *Songs in the Rough: From "Heartbreak Hotel" to "Higher Love," Rock's Greatest Songs in Rough Draft Form* (New York: St. Martin's Press, 1996), 110.

"I kinda knew I had to" "Phil Collins: *No Jacket Required* Vinyl Icon," by Johnny Black, *Hi-Fi News & Record Review*, April 2011.

"I would listen back" Steven Tyler, *Does the Noise in My Head Bother You? A Rock 'n' Roll Memoir* (New York: Ecco, 2011), Kindle edition.

"Watching him record" Ritz, *Divided Soul*, 181.

"from lines to sentences to paragraphs" Quoted in Jim Fricke and Charlie Ahearn, *Yes Yes Y'all: The Experience Music Project Oral History of Hip-Hop's First Decade* (New York: Da Capo Press, 2002), 79.

"A good MC" Kyle Dargan conversation with author on September 5, 2014.

"So much of his stuff comes" Charles Keil and Steven Feld, *Music Grooves: Essays and Dialogues* (Chicago: University of Chicago Press, 1994), 26.

"Say anything" Patti Smith, *Just Kids* (New York: HarperCollins, 2010), Kindle edition.

"It is a mark of skill" Lees, *Modern Rhyming Dictionary*, 12.

"Performers can color" Sondheim, *Finishing the Hat*, xviii.

"Melody should mirror" Webb, *Tunesmith*, 178.

"In songwriting, uniformity" Webb, *Tunesmith*, 90.

"Composers, on the other hand" S. Davis, *Craft of Lyric Writing*, 216.

"There is nothing about beginning" Webb, *Tunesmith*, 49.

"Now, I've seen him write" Quoted in DeCurtis, *In Other Words*, Kindle edition.

"Melodies are the easiest part" Willie Nelson and Bud Shrake, *Willie: An Autobiography* (New York: Cooper Square Press, 2000), 137.

"I had an affinity for jazz" Gil Scott-Heron, *The Last Holiday: A Memoir* (New York: Grove Press, 2012), 159.

"The metronomic cadences" Webb, *Tunesmith*, 89.

"A song is a magical marriage" Webb, *Tunesmith*, 70.

"Words hold meaning" Margulis, *On Repeat*, Kindle edition.

"Van Morrison is interested" Lester Bangs, *Psychotic Reactions and Carburetor Dung: The Work of a Legendary Critic: Rock 'n' Roll as Literature and Literature as Rock 'n' Roll*, ed. Greil Marcus (New York: Anchor, 2013), 22.

"I get to a point where I" Quoted in DeCurtis, *In Other Words*, Kindle edition.

"You know why they sang it" Tyler, *Does the Noise*, Kindle edition.

"It helps define the meter" http://www.effingham.com/bishop/DonHenley.htm (accessed April 1, 2016).

"excessively polysyllabic words" Nile Rodgers, *Le Freak: An Upside Down Story of Family, Disco, and Destiny* (New York: Spiegel and Grau, 2011), 168–169.

"a reader who silently mouths" David Caplan, *Questions of Possibility: Contemporary Poetry and Poetic Form* (New York: Oxford University Press, 2005), Kindle edition.

"Words are so important to country music" Waylon Jennings, *Waylon: An Autobiography* (Chicago: Chicago Review Press, 2012), Kindle edition.

"Some singers like to work" Quincy Jones, *Q: The Autobiography of Quincy Jones* (New York: Three Rivers Press, 2002), Kindle edition.

"A good singer will often" David Byrne, *How Music Works* (San Francisco: McSweeny's, 2013), 44–45.

"The three masters of rubato" Jerry Wexler, *Rhythm and Blues: A Life in American Music* (New York: Knopf, 2012), 41.

"Even though I was writing a country song" Nelson and Shrake, *Willie*, 140–141.

"I found I could get ahead" Nelson and Shrake, *Willie*, 141.

"There is something perfectly imperfect" Quoted in "The Shazam Effect," by Derek Thompson, *The Atlantic*, December 2014.

"The lurches and hesitations are internalized" Byrne, *How Music Works*, 45.

"Perhaps Redding's most effective tool" Allan F. Moore, *Analyzing Popular Music* (Cambridge: Cambridge University Press, 2003), Kindle edition.

"According to [Catherine] Clément" Adriana Cavarero, *For More Than One Voice: Toward a Philosophy of Vocal Expression* (Stanford, CA: Stanford University Press, 2005), 125–126.

"When I'd sing a lyric" Ronnie Spector and Vince Waldron, *Be My Baby: How I Survived Mascara, Miniskirts, and Madness, or My Life as a Fabulous Ronette* (New York: Harmony Books, 1990), Kindle edition.

CHAPTER FIVE: RHYME

"Seizing a scrap of waste paper" "Dr. Samuel F. Smith Dead," *New York Times*, November 16, 1895, http://query.nytimes.com/mem/archive-free/pdf?_r=1&res=9B 03E6DE1E3DE433A25754C1A9679D94649ED7CF&oref=slogin (accessed August 2, 2016).

"I think that a song should be poetic" Quoted in Loraine Alterman, "The Other Smokey Robinson—Songwriter," *Detroit Free Press*, October 14, 1966.

"a rhyme-drenched era" David Caplan, *Rhyme's Challenge: Hip Hop, Poetry, and Contemporary Rhyming Culture* (Oxford: Oxford University Press, 2014), Kindle edition.

"One discards rhyme" Ezra Pound, *Selected Prose: 1909–1965* (New York: New Directions, 1973), 375.

"And now your kinsfolk" Maxwell, *On Poetry*, 109.

"the repetition of a vowel" Percy G. Adams and Stephen Cushman, "Assonance," in *The Princeton Encyclopedia of Poetry and Poetics*, 94.

"A striking feature of the history" Susan Stewart, "Rhyme and Freedom," quoted in Marjorie Perloff and Craig Dworkin, *The Sound of Poetry, the Poetry of Sound* (Chicago: University of Chicago Press, 2009), Kindle edition.

"Parcheesi" Lyrics from the song "Little Ol' Tune" (1957), as published in Robert Kimball, Barry Day, Miles Kreuger, and Eric Davis, eds., *The Complete Lyrics of Johnny Mercer* (New York: Knopf, 2009), 265.

"We abandoned the trite" Graham Nash, *Wild Tales: A Rock & Roll Life* (New York: Crown Archetype, 2013), Kindle edition.

"Who now, in *your* now" Maxwell, *On Poetry*, 100.

"Rap—so many words" "Rolling Stones Guitarist Keith Richards Calls Metallica and Black Sabbath 'Great Jokes,' Says Rap Is for 'Tone-Deaf People' in Free-Wheeling Interview," by Jim Farber, *New York Daily News*, September 3, 2015.

"How much such recitation" Sacks, *Musicophilia*, Kindle edition.

"I'm not a big believer in rhyme" Quoted in Bill DeMain, *In Their Own Words: Songwriters Talk about the Creative Process* (Westport, CT: Praeger, 2004), Kindle edition.

"I hate the tyranny of rhyme" Quoted in DeMain, *In Their Own Words*, Kindle edition.

"Rhyme is a play with words" Jeffrey Wainwright, *Poetry: The Basics* (New York: Routledge, 2004), 102.

"Songs are made for ears, not eyes" Pat Pattison, *Rhyming Techniques and Strategies* (Boston: Berklee Press, 1991), Kindle edition.

"We expect lyrics to behave" Webb, *Tunesmith*, 94.

"Far from a constraint" Quoted in Perloff and Dworkin, *Sound of Poetry*, Kindle edition.

"Rhyming, while being a limitation" Sting, *Lyrics* (New York: Dial Press, 2007), 154.

"We may expect a rhyme sound" Brian Boyd, *Why Lyrics Last: Evolution, Cognition, and Shakespeare's Sonnets* (Cambridge, MA: Harvard University Press, 2012), 21.

"It is not so much necessary" Lees, *Modern Rhyming Dictionary*, 39.

"As Ben Blatt pointed out in early 2014" "Justin Bieber and the Beatles: They Both Liked to Rhyme the Same Words," by Ben Blatt, Slate.com, February 20, 2104, http://www.slate.com/articles/arts/culturebox/2014/02/justin_bieber_and_the_beatles_they_both_liked_to_rhyme_the_same_words.html (accessed April 1, 2016).

"Do you know Keith Richards' theory" Quoted in DeMain, *In Their Own Words*, Kindle edition.

"benign violation" Peter McGraw and Joel Warner, *The Humor Code: A Global Search for What Makes Things Funny* (New York: Simon and Schuster, 2014), 10.

"Although we were really serious" Scott Ian and John Widerhorn, *I'm the Man: The Story of That Guy from Anthrax* (Philadelphia: Da Capo Press, 2014), Kindle edition.

"Staying in the unconscious frame of mind" Quoted in Paul Zollo, *Songwriters on Songwriting* (Boston: Da Capo Press, 2003), 81.

"I saw that rhyme register" Costello, *Unfaithful Music*, 567.

"All rhymes, even the farthest afield" Sondheim, *Finishing the Hat*, xxvii.

"I've gotten to where" Paul Zollo and Tom Petty, *Conversations with Tom Petty* (New York: Omnibus Press, 2005), Kindle edition.

"Instead of always making" Pattison, *Rhyming*, Kindle edition.

"They are really false rhymes" Quoted in Alan Light, *The Holy or the Broken: Leonard Cohen, Jeff Buckley, and the Unlikely Ascent of "Hallelujiah"* (New York: Atria Books, 2012), 25.

"'Decatur' was more fun to sing" Jessica Hopper, *The First Collection of Criticism by a Living Female Rock Critic* (Chicago: Featherproof Books, 2015), Kindle edition.

"You can rhyme to a fault" Quoted in Flanagan, *Written in My Soul*, Kindle edition.

"It started 'Well, I was borned" Loretta Lynn and George Vecsey, *Loretta Lynn: Coal Miner's Daughter* (New York: Vintage, 2010), Kindle edition.

"Just because it rhymes doesn't mean" Quoted in Jake Brown, *Nashville Songwriter: The Inside Stories behind Country Music's Greatest Hits* (Dallas: BenBella Books, 2014), Kindle edition.

"So sometimes writing a song" Quoted in DeMain, *In Their Own Words*, Kindle edition.

"Rhyme is the best way" Pattison, *Rhyming*, Kindle edition.

"Rhyme is in this sense always a showcase" Quoted in Perloff and Dworkin, *Sound of Poetry*, Kindle edition.

"I hate most contemporary rhyming poetry" Kyle Dargan conversation with author in April 2012.

"An identity makes the word clear" Sondheim, *Finishing the Hat*, xxvii.

CHAPTER SIX: FIGURATIVE LANGUAGE

"awakens and enlarges the mind" Percy Bysshe Shelley, "A Defence of Poetry," http://www.bartleby.com/27/23.html (accessed September 12, 2015).

"Rapid movement during development" "Polaroid Warns Buyers Not to 'Shake It,'" Reuters/CNN.com International, February 18, 2004, http://edition.cnn.com/2004/TECH/ptech/02/17/polaroid.warns.reut/ (accessed April 20, 2016).

"fossil poetry" Ralph Waldo Emerson, "The Poet," 1844, http://www.emersoncentral.com/poet.htm (accessed April 1, 2016).

"to reveal an unexpected likeness" J. V. Brogan and Hallie Smith Richmond, "Simile," in *The Princeton Encyclopedia of Poetry and Poetics*, 1306.

"I think that I'm one of the world's best mumblers" Jim Vallance, "Cuts Like a Knife," http://jimvallance.com/01-music-folder/songs-folder-may-27/pg-song-adams-cuts-like-a-knife.html (accessed March 1, 2016).

"I got too wrapped up" Michael Jackson, *Moonwalk* (New York: Harmony Books, 2009), Kindle edition.

"They present a comparison" Robert J. Fogelin, *Figuratively Speaking* (New Haven, CT: Yale University Press, 1988), Kindle edition.

"Indisputably, the effect of crowing images" Alexander Theroux, *The Grammar of Rock: Art and Artlessness in 20th Century Pop Lyrics* (Seattle: Fantagraphics, 2013), 268.

"By the middle of the second verse" Quoted in Flanagan, *Written in My Soul*, Kindle edition.

"Effective metaphor suits the context" Cleanth Brooks and Robert Penn Warren, *Understanding Poetry* (New York: Holt, Rinehart and Winston, 1960), 277.

"Just seeing Kurt write the lyrics" Quoted in Kurt St. Thomas and Troy Smith, *Nirvana: The Chosen Rejects* (New York: St. Martin's Griffin, 2004), 89.

"To know oh no" Kurt Cobain, *Journals* (New York: Riverhead Books, 2003), 146–148.

"But what meaning *can*" Archibald MacLeish, *Poetry and Experience* (Cambridge: Riverside Press, 1961), 68.

"extended metaphor that aligns" Chris Heath, "The Mars Expedition," *Gentlemen's Quarterly*, April 2013, 201.

"Poetry begins in trivial metaphors" Robert Frost, "Education by Poetry," 1931, http://www.en.utexas.edu/amlit/amlitprivate/scans/edbypo.html (accessed April 20, 2016).

"Well, that flow" Quoted in "Drake: The AllHipHop Interview, Part II," Chuck Creekmur, Allhiphop.com, June 24, 2010, http://allhiphop.com/2010/06/24/drake-the-allhiphop-interview-part-2/ (accessed September 23, 2015).

"mock innocence makes" Quoted in Ronald L. Davis, *Mary Martin, Broadway Legend* (Norman: University of Oklahoma Press, 2008), 42.

"There is poetry in some" Charles Simic, *The Life of Images: Selected Prose* (New York: Ecco, 2015), 67.

"The sexual double entendres" Karl Hagstrom Miller, *Segregating Sound: Inventing Folk and Pop Music in the Age of Jim Crow* (Durham, NC: Duke University Press, 2010), Kindle edition.

"He played with the structure" Hook, *Unknown Pleasures*, 256.

"She can do repetitive phrases" Quoted in DeMain, *In Their Own Words*, Kindle edition.

"Redundancy in popular music" Theroux, *Grammar of Rock*, 65.

"This shift, effected by repetition" Margulis, *On Repeat*, Kindle edition.

"Miss Bolo" Charles Dickens, *The Posthumous Papers of the Pickwick Club* (1836).

"In his compelling short article" Ben Zimmer, "In Praise of the Rolling Stones and Their Zeugmoids," https://www.visualthesaurus.com/cm/wordroutes/in-praise-of-the-rolling-stones-and-their-zeugmoids/ (accessed September 12, 2015).

"'I Can't Make You Love Me' is no picnic" "Bonnie Raitt Shakes It Up," interview by Scott Simon, *Weekend Edition Saturday*, National Public Radio, May 4, 2002.

"started free-styling some poetry" Anthony Kiedis and Larry Sloman, *Scar Tissue* (New York: Hyperion, 2004), Kindle edition.

CHAPTER SEVEN: VOICE

"hoarse and insistent" Quoted in Rod Stewart, *Rod: The Autobiography* (New York: Crown, 2012), Kindle edition.

"I was blessed with distinctiveness" R. Stewart, *Rod*, Kindle edition.

"Melodies form a marriage" Jennings, *Waylon*, Kindle edition.

"sing it again, again, again" Quoted in Jonah Weiner, "Daft Punk: All Hail Our Robot Overlords," *Rolling Stone*, May 21, 2013.

"comped from a hundred different takes" "Ben Allen: Gnarls Barkley, Animal Collective, Puff Daddy?," by Alex McKenzie, *Tape On Magazine*, issue no. 76, March/April 2010.

"The respiratory system" National Center for Voice and Speech FAQ, http://ncvs.org/e-learning/faqs.html (accessed September 12, 2015).

"is the particular quality or acoustic richness" Sacks, *Musicophilia*, Kindle edition.

The emission of song is" Marco Beghelli, *Erotismo canoro*, quoted in Cavarero, *For More Than One Voice*, 117.

"The voice is our most primordial and valuable instrument" Amanda Petrusich, "The Power of the Isolated Vocal Track," *New Yorker*, February 3, 2016.

"The 'grain' of the voice is not" Roland Barthes and Stephen Heath, *Image, Music, Text* (New York: Hill and Wang, 1977), 188.

"In the vocal exercise" Cavarero, *For More Than One*, 134.

"When I sing" Grace Jones (as told to Paul Morley), *I'll Never Write My Memoirs* (New York: Gallery Books, 2015), Kindle edition.

"Singing is such an organic process" Pat Benatar and Patsi Bale Cox, *Between a Heart and a Rock Place: A Memoir* (New York: HarperCollins, 2010), Kindle edition.

"My voice wasn't a naturally loud" Juliana Hatfield, *When I Grow Up: A Memoir* (New York: Wiley, 2008), 9.

"thought like a horn" Q. Jones, *Q*, Kindle edition.

"What they had that I picked up" Quoted in Flanagan, *Written in My Soul*, Kindle edition.

"A singer is not like a saxophone" Billie Holiday and William Dufty, *Lady Sings the Blues* (New York: Broadway Books, 2011), 197.

"brings the voice energetically" Mladen Dolar, *A Voice and Nothing More* (Cambridge, MA: MIT Press, 2006), Kindle edition.

"Onstage it was amazing to see" Kim Gordon, *Girl in a Band: A Memoir* (New York: HarperCollins, 2015), Kindle edition.

"many rock vocalists reach out" Everett, *Foundations*, Kindle edition.

"A lot of people don't understand" James Brown and Bruce Tucker, *James Brown, the Godfather of Soul* (New York: Macmillan, 1986), 138.

"to sign more artists who had performing" Clive Davis and Anthony DeCurtis, *The Soundtrack of My Life* (New York: Simon and Schuster, 2013), 375.

"authorship also resides in inventive execution" Emily J. Lordi, *Black Resonance: Iconic Women Singers and African American Literature* (New Brunswick, NJ: Rutgers University Press, 2013), Kindle edition.

"I'd say material is 80 percent of a singer's career" Lynn and Vecsey, *Coal Miner's*, Kindle edition.

"If you're gonna sing the song" Zollo and Petty, *Conversations*, Kindle edition.

"We judge pre-rock singing" Jonathan Lethem, "The Fly in the Ointment," in *The Ecstasy of Influence: Nonfictions, Etc.* (New York: Vintage, 2011), 310.

"The truth is that when a singer likes the tune" Albert Murray, *Stomping the Blues* (New York: Da Capo Press, 1989), 76.

"Bessie Smith singing a good blues" Ralph Ellison to Albert Murray, June 2, 1957, in John Callahan, ed., *Trading Twelves* (New York: Random House, 2001), 166.

"The blues bears witness to" Simic, *Life of Images*, 69.

"the Poet makes himself a seer" Arthur Rimbaud, *Complete Works, Selected Letters*, trans., intro., and notes by Wallace Fowlie (Chicago: University of Chicago Press, 1966), 307.

"As a singer you impose" Quoted in Flanagan, *Written in My Soul*, Kindle edition.

"So enormously powerful" Alec Wilder, *American Popular Song: The Great Innovators, 1900–1950* (New York: Oxford University Press, 1972/1990), Kindle edition.

"The multiple authorship" "Words About Music, or Analysis versus Performance," in Nicholas Cook, Peter Johnson, and Hans Zender, *Theory into Practice: Composition, Performance and the Listening Experience* (Leuven, Belgium: Leuven University Press, 1999), 27.

"People want to hear and feel the emotion" D. Stewart, *Sweet Dreams*, Kindle edition.

"Songs are more abstract entities" John Andrew Fisher, "Popular Music," in Theodore Gracyk and Andrew Kania, eds., *The Routledge Companion to Philosophy and Music* (New York: Routledge, 2011), Kindle edition.

"People often say that a great singer" C. Davis and DeCurtis, *Soundtrack*, 194.

"No one has been able to 'keep up'" Barney Hoskyns, *From a Whisper to a Scream: The Great Voices of Popular Music* (London: Fontana, 1991), 90.

"The strongest cut on the album" Aretha Franklin with David Ritz, *Aretha: From These Roots* (New York: Villard, 1999), 211.

"In singing styles" Alan H. D. Watson, *The Biology of Musical Performance and Performance-Related Injury* (Lanham, MD: Scarecrow Press, 2009), 169.

"There was a tenderness to his voice" Nelson and Ritz, *It's a Long Story*, Kindle edition.

"no rap at all" Justin Charity, "Fetty Wap Is Not a Rapper," *Pigeons & Planes*, September 8, 2015.

"A technique heard frequently since Hoppy Jones" Everett, *Foundations*, 176.

"I mean, singing is just exaggerated speech" Quoted in Jia Tolentino, "A Chat with Dionne Osborne, the Vocal Coach Who Changed Drake's Style," *Jezebel*, November 17, 2014.

"It was mind-blowing" Quoted in Kate Sullivan, "Cons," *Spin* 18, no. 8 (August 2002): 64.

"When [Grandmaster Flash & the Furious Five's]" Kiedis and Sloman, *Scar Tissue*, 102–103.

"When I first tried to synch up" Chilly Gonzales Homepage, http://www.chilly gonzales.com (accessed September 13, 2015).

"Franklin's singing stays unusually close" Lordi, *Black Resonance*, Kindle edition.

"Song has repetition built into it" Levitin, *World in Six Songs*, 126.

"I would listen and breathe" Melissa Etheridge, *The Truth Is . . . : My Life in Love and Music* (New York: Random House, 2002), Kindle edition.

"When you sing" Lees, *Modern Rhyming Dictionary*, 18.

"As Houston's voice approached the high note" Cinque Henderson, "Anthem of Freedom: How Whitney Houston Remade 'The Star-Spangled Banner,'" *New Yorker*, January 27, 2016.

"It is a mark of skill in a lyricist" Lees, *Modern Rhyming Dictionary*, 12.

"I just wanted to come up with something unique" Quoted in Paul Edwards, *How to Rap: The Art and Science of the Hip-Hop MC* (Chicago: Chicago Review Press, 2009), 251–252.

"a 'bed of sound' upon which" Moore, *Analyzing Popular Music*, Kindle edition.

"Certain pairings of singers" Ben Ratliff, *Every Song Ever: Twenty Ways to Listen in an Age of Musical Plenty* (New York: Farrar, Straus and Giroux, 2016), 163.

"One night we were rehearsing" Quoted in Stuart L. Goosman, *Group Harmony: The Black Urban Roots of Rhythm and Blues* (Philadelphia: University of Pennsylvania Press, 2005), 187.

"As Stephen launched into the intro" Nash, *Wild Tales*, Kindle edition.

"voice was rough, husky" Nash, *Wild Tales*, Kindle edition.

"It was a conversation we were having" Carrie Brownstein, *Hunger Makes Me a Modern Girl: A Memoir* (New York: Penguin, 2015), Kindle edition.

"I worried that if they had already sung" Q. Jones, *Q*, Kindle edition.

"The truth is, everyone was given special treatment" Kenny Rogers, *Luck or Something Like It* (New York: William Morrow, 2012), Kindle edition.

"The vocal solos on 'We Are the World'" Stephen Holden, "The Pop Life: Artists Join in Effort for Famine Relief," *New York Times*, February 27, 1985.

"Even today my voice is hard to categorize" Ray Charles and David Ritz, *Brother Ray: Ray Charles' Own Story* (New York: Dial Press, 1978), 87.

"He knew from the first second he heard me" Spector and Waldron, *Be My Baby*, Kindle edition.

"I've spent my life listening to singers" Tyler, *Does the Noise*, Kindle edition.

"like a teething infant" "The Virile Man's Guide to Liking Joanna Newsom," by Andrew Wagner, *Vanity Fair*, February 23, 2010, http://www.vanityfair.com/culture /2010/02/the-virile-mans-guide-to-liking-joanna-newsom.

"When I listen back to those first EP's" Quoted in Brad Buchanan, ed., *Visions of Joanna Newsom* (Sacramento, CA: Roan Press, 2011), 40.

"Performers adapted to this new technology" Byrne, *How Music Works*, 24.

"I would sometimes comp the vocal" Shawn Colvin, *Diamond in the Rough: A Memoir* (New York: William Morrow, 2012), 118.

"Recording technology had advanced" Shania Twain, *From This Moment On* (New York: Atria, 2012), Kindle edition.

"(D'Angelo harmonizing with himself" Sasha Frere-Jones, "D'Angelo Reborn," *New Yorker*, January 12, 2015.

"The 'Rollin', rollin', rollin' on the river'" Fogerty, *Fortunate Son*, 160.

"The juxtaposition of vocal tones" Lou Reed, "Lou Reed Talks Kanye West's *Yeezus*," *The Talkhouse*, September 3, 2014.

"I don't think Future gets the technology" Quoted in "T-Pain: Future Is Not Using Auto-Tune Correctly," BET, February 14, 2013, http://www.bet.com/news/music /2013/02/14/t-pain-future-is-not-using-auto-tune-correctly.html.

"Future's voice is often likened to an android" "The Music Club, 2015—Entry 13: Why Future's *DS2* might be the album of the year, whether or not you like Future the person," by Jack Hamilton, December 23, 2015, http://www.slate.com/articles/arts /the_music_club/features/2015/music_club_2015/future_s_ds2_might_be_the_best _album_of_the_year_whether_or_not_you_like.html.

"In the beginning there was feedback" Bangs, *Psychotic Reactions and Carburetor Dung*, 156.

"We used computer-altered vocals more and more" George Clinton and Ben Greenman, *Brothas Be, Yo Like George, Ain't That Funkin' Kinda Hard On You? A Memoir* (New York: Atria Books, 2014), 129.

"Curtis Mayfield recorded *New World Order*" Fred Moten, "Post in Three Parts, Goodbye, Hello," *Harriet* (blog), Poetry Foundation, February 23, 2010, http://www.poetryfoundation.org/harriet/2010/02/post-in-three-parts-goodbye-hello/.

"the coke was fucking up my voice" Ozzy Osbourne, *I Am Ozzy* (New York: Grand Central Publishing, 2010), 140.

"There is no voice without a body" Dolar, *A Voice*, Kindle edition.

"The historical concept that black people" Miller, *Segregating Sound*, Kindle edition.

"It is here on the level of culture" Ralph Ellison, "The Little Man at Chehaw Station: The American Artist and His Audience," in John F. Callahan, ed., *The Collected Essays of Ralph Ellison* (New York: Random House, 1995), Kindle edition.

"People would listen to my songs and ask" Fogerty, *Fortunate Son*, 5.

"Yes, I changed my voice" Aerosmith and Stephen Davis, *Walk This Way: The Autobiography of Aerosmith* (New York: Dey Street Books, 2003), 161/175.

"His insecurity was forcing him" Joe Perry and David Ritz, *Rocks: My Life in and out of Aerosmith* (New York: Simon and Schuster, 2014), Kindle edition.

"I used an exaggerated black-speak voice" Tyler, *Does the Noise*, Kindle edition.

"I just want her to stop doing" Quoted in "The Playboy Conversation: Jean Grae on Iggy, Taylor, and Her New EP of Baby-Making Music," by Neil Drumming, *Playboy*, November 7, 2014, http://www.playboy.com/articles/playboy-conversation-jean-grae-interview.

"I think it's really important we all feel free" Quoted in "Iggy Azalea: The Low End Theory," by Justin Monroe, *Complex*, September 16, 2013, http://ca.complex.com/music/2013/09/iggy-azalea-interview-complex-cover-story.

"So it is not just a matter of the outsider boning up" "Authenticity, or The Lessons of Little Tree," by Henry Louis Gates Jr., *New York Times Book Review*, November 24, 1991.

"white people are the only ones" Marc Lamont Hill, appearance on *Huffington Post Live*, March 27, 2013, http://live.huffingtonpost.com/r/archive/segment/51531a8478c90a38a20000b6.

"There's a sonic preference for blackness" Imani Perry, appearance on *Huffington Post Live*, March 27, 2013, http://live.huffingtonpost.com/r/archive/segment/51531a8478c90a38a20000b6.

"Falsetto itself represents another manner" Everett, *Foundations*, Kindle edition.

"In the kinesthetic sensorium" Timothy E. Scheurer, *American Popular Music: Readings from the Popular Press*, vol. 2, *The Age of Rock* (Bowling Green, OH: Bowling Green University Popular Press, 1989), 43.

"What singles out the voice" Dolar, *A Voice*, Kindle edition.

"Even when it renders" Cavarero, *For More Than One*, 127.

"When I heard Janis Joplin" LP, *Guitar Center Sessions*, http://sessions.guitarcenter.com/lp/.

"When I sing a note" Quoted in Ian Gittins, "Diamanda Galás: 'My Performance Is Catharsis,'" *The Guardian*, April 10, 2009.

"asked me to delay" Ann Wilson, Nancy Wilson, and Charles R. Cross, *Kicking and Dreaming: A Story of Heart, Soul, and Rock and Roll* (New York: It Books, 2012), Kindle edition.

"For some" Grace Slick and Andrea Cagan, *Somebody to Love? A Rock-and-Roll Memoir* (New York: Warner Books, 1998), 223–224.

CHAPTER EIGHT: STYLE

"My music—and most music" James Brown and Bruce Tucker, *The Godfather of Soul: An Autobiography* (New York: Thunder's Mouth Press, 1986), 149.

"His dances, his language, his music" James McBride, *Kill 'Em and Leave: Searching for James Brown and the American Soul* (New York: Random House, 2016), 5.

"I was hearing everything" Brown and Tucker, *The Godfather of Soul*, 158.

"Style, of course, is everything" Jerry Lieber, Mike Stoller, and David Ritz, *Hound Dog: The Leiber & Stoller Autobiography* (New York: Simon and Schuster Paperbacks, 2010), Kindle edition.

"Style is a replication of patterning" Leonard B. Meyer, "Toward a Theory of Style," quoted in Berel Lang, ed., *The Concept of Style* (Ithaca, NY: Cornell University Press, 1987), 21.

"A musical style is a finite array" Keil and Feld, *Music Grooves*, 112.

"a constellation of styles" Fabian Holt, *Genre in Popular Music* (Chicago: University of Chicago Press, 2007), 18.

"American popular music" Weisbard, *Listen Again*, 4.

"Genre is always collective" Holt, *Genre*, 3.

"the totality of social space" Holt, *Genre*, 7.

"radio's version of what organizational theory" Gabriel Rossman, *Climbing the Charts: What Radio Airplay Tells Us about the Diffusion of Innovation* (Princeton, NJ: Princeton University Press, 2012), 71.

"A radio field structured by format" Rossman, *Climbing*, 80.

"The fact that the album" Twain, *From This Moment*, 338–339.

"Everyone has a taste biography" C. Wilson, *Let's Talk about Love*, 17.

"can make us physically well" Byrne, *How Music Works*, 321.

"One reason race has remained" Diane Pecknold, *Hidden in the Mix: The African American Presence in Country Music* (Durham, NC: Duke University Press, 2013), 12.

"We try to break down every dimension" Quoted in Sarah McBride, "Pandora's Radio Head," *Wall Street Journal Magazine*, March 11, 2010.

"[The classifications] essentially cover" http://www.tinymixtapes.com/features/tim -westergren-music-genome-project-founder.

"His musical vocabulary is outside" McBride, "Pandora's Radio Head."

"As labels have gotten more adept" Thompson, "Shazam Effect."

"People listen to Top 40" Charles Duhigg, *The Power of Habit: Why We Do What We Do in Life and Business* (New York: Random House, 2014), Kindle edition.

"when you refuse to accept the world" Paul D. Miller, Twitter post, January 21, 2016, 6:30 a.m., https://twitter.com/djspooky/status/690179650165714945.

"a slick, black, technologically advanced" Jon Kirby, "Something in the Water," in *Purple Snow: Forecasting the Minneapolis Sound* (Chicago: Numero Group, 2013).

"When you are playing most" Ratliff, *Every Song Ever*, 189.

"A lot of pop music" Costello, *Unfaithful Music*, 33–34.

"We actually found that the songs" Noah Askin. "The Recipe of a Hit Song," TEDx-INSEADSingapore, YouTube video, 11:48, posted [December 20, 2015], https://www .youtube.com/watch?v=R3UnZBpcF1o.

"The Largest Vocabulary in Music" http://lab.musixmatch.com/largest_vocabu lary/.

"The Largest Vocabulary in Hip Hop" http://poly-graph.co/vocabulary.html.

"the words or phrases chosen" Eleanor Cook, "Diction," in *The Princeton Encyclopedia of Poetry and Poetics*, 358.

"finding a great-sounding word" Fogerty, *Fortunate Son*, 163.

"I sort of have a little library of phrases" Quoted in DeMain, *In Their Own Words*, Kindle edition.

"Words in all pop genres" Simon Frith, *Sound Effects: Youth, Leisure, and the Politics of Rock 'n' Roll* (New York: Pantheon Books, 1981), 36.

"Given the relationship of redundancy" Booth, *Experience*, 13.

"Take some ordinary, everyday expression" Lees, *Modern Rhyming Dictionary*, 41.

"If you don't speak English" Quoted in "Darling Nicki: The Many Moods and Manic Genius of Hip-Hop's Killer Diva, Nicki Minaj," by Jonah Weiner, *Rolling Stone*, January 15, 2015, 41.

"The foreign tongue is first a kind" Don Ihde, *Listening and Voice Phenomenologies of Sound* (Albany: State University of New York Press, 2007), Kindle edition.

"The brilliance of rock lyrics" David Kirby, *Little Richard: The Birth of Rock 'n' Roll* (New York: Continuum International Publishing Group, 2009), 144.

"sounds like a cliché" Andrew Marantz, "Kacey Musgraves, Harper Lee, and the Home-Town Dilemma," *New Yorker*, July 22, 2015, http://www.newyorker.com/culture/cultural-comment/kacey-musgraves-harper-lee-and-the-home-town-dilemma.

"I was trying to figure out" Quoted in Flanagan, *Written in My Soul*, Kindle edition.

"It's a huge song musically" D. Kirby, *Little Richard*, 4.

"All the good pop clichés" Quoted in Flanagan, *Written in My Soul*, Kindle edition.

"Right now, I am instructed" *Billboard*, August 2015, 76.

"Those old country ballads created" Stephen Graham Jones conversation with author on July 25, 2014.

"There are a lot of people listening" Reba McEntire and Tom Carter, *Reba: My Story* (New York: Bantam, 2015), Kindle edition.

"Dave Eggers has a theory" Nick Hornby, *Songbook* (New York: Riverhead Books, 2003), Kindle edition.

"the basic melody or" A. Bruce Strauch, ed., *Publishing and the Law: Current Legal Issues* (New York: Routledge, 2013), 34.

"We were almost Jesuits" Keith Richards, interviewed by Marc Maron, *WTF*, Episode 639, September 21, 2015, http://www.wtfpod.com/podcast/episodes/episode_639_-_keith_richards.

"Epidemic of Second Thought" C. Wilson, *Let's Talk about Love*, 14–15.

"Shuffled in with sappy late-'80s cuts" Will Sheff, "Okkervil River Responds to Don Henley: Copyright Laws Kill Art," *Rolling Stone*, June 4, 2014, http://www.rolling stone.com/music/news/okkervil-river-responds-to-don-henley-copyright-laws-kill-art-20140604 (accessed April 30, 2015).

"They don't understand the law" "Don Henley of the Eagles Accuses Frank Ocean of 'Stealing' His Song," *Daily Telegraph*, June 2, 2014.

"[Henley's] song is saying" "Cover Songs," Episode 15, *Pitch* (podcast), July 1, 2015.

"(Honestly I think copyright law is garbage" Okkervil River, Twitter post, June 4, 2014, 7:08 a.m., https://twitter.com/okkervilriver/status/474190886335938560 (accessed September 13, 2015).

"Every pop musician is a thief" Quoted in Flanagan, *Written in My Soul*, Kindle edition.

"Popular music as an industry" Tara Brabazon, *Popular Music Topics, Trends and Trajectories* (Los Angeles: Sage, 2012), 195.

"The copyright of a musical composition" Byrne, *How Music Works*, 161.

"'Smells Like Teen Spirit' works" Anka and Dalton, *My Way*, 331.

"preemptive irony" Jake London, "Sucking in the Seventies: Paul Westerberg, the Replacements, and the Onset of the Ironic Cover Aesthetic in Rock and Roll (It's Only Rock and Roll but I Like It)," May 27, 2010, http://www.jawjawjaw.com/2010/05/27/sucking-in-the-seventies-paul-westerberg-the-replacements-and-the-onset-of-the-ironic-cover-aesthetic-in-rock-and-roll-its-only-rock-and-roll-but-i-like-it/.

CHAPTER NINE: STORY

"When you're writing a song" Quoted in Flanagan, *Written in My Soul*, Kindle edition.

"I know from writing lyrics" Byrne, *How Music Works*, 126.

"narrates without narrative" Theodor W. Adorno, *Mahler: A Musical Physiognomy* (Chicago: University of Chicago Press, 1992), Kindle edition.

"Like stories, music is said" Linda Hutcheon and Michael Hutcheon, "Narrativizing the End: Death and Opera," in James Phelan and Peter J. Rabinowitz, eds., *A Companion to Narrative Theory* (New York: Wiley, 2008), 442.

"the logic, principles, and practices of narrative representation" Marie-Laure Ryan, "Narration in Various Media," in Peter Hühn et al., eds., *The Living Handbook of Narratology* (Hamburg: Hamburg University, 2014), http://www.lhn.uni -hamburg.de/ (accessed September 13, 2015).

"is somebody telling somebody else" David Herman, James Phelan, Peter J. Rabinowitz, Brian Richardson, and Robyn R. Warhol, *Narrative Theory: Core Concepts and Critical Debates* (Columbus: Ohio University Press, 2012), 3.

"a multidimensional purposive communication" Herman et al., *Narrative Theory*, 3.

"Remember, the artist is telling a story" Rodgers, *Le Freak*, 228–229.

"Bruce Springsteen averages" Graham English, "Average Words per Song and the 80/20 Rule," December 26, 2007, http://i.grahamenglish.net/1163/average-words-per -song-and-the-8020-rule/.

"a song is written for the story" Quoted in Flanagan, *Written in My Soul*, Kindle edition.

"There's a theory that really" Quoted in Flanagan, *Written in My Soul*, Kindle edition.

"Then there's *my* point of view" Quoted in Flanagan, *Written in My Soul*, Kindle edition.

"We're now conditioned to expect nothing" Quoted in Flanagan, *Written in My Soul*, Kindle edition.

"His songs are deceptively simple" Quoted in Woody Guthrie, *Bound for Glory* (New York: E. P. Dutton, 1968), Kindle edition.

"love has been a dominant theme" Ted Gioia, *Love Songs: The Hidden History* (Oxford: Oxford University Press, 2015), Kindle edition.

"One of the great legacies of the Beatles" Steve Turner, *A Hard Day's Write: The Stories behind Every Beatles Song* (New York: It Books, 2005), 12.

"But were the songs that originally" Dominic Pedler, *The Songwriting Secrets of the Beatles* (London: Omnibus Press, 2001), Kindle edition.

"a revelatory distillation of experience" Audre Lorde, "Poetry Is Not a Luxury," in *Sister Outsider: Essays and Speeches* (Freedom, CA: Crossing Press, 1984), 36.

"It can really be challenging" Quoted in DeCurtis, *In Other Words*, Kindle edition.

"There are five things" Quoted in DeMain, *In Their Own Words*, Kindle edition.

"The three minute pop song" Brabazon, *Popular Music*, 72.

"When we are being told" Leo Widrich, "The Science of Storytelling," *Lifehacker*, December 5, 2012.

"allows someone to identify with another" Quoted in Daniel A. Gross, "When You Listen to Music, You're Never Alone," *Nautilus*, March 10, 2016.

"Works of art need to attract and arouse" Brian Boyd, *On the Origin of Stories: Evolution, Cognition, and Fiction* (Cambridge, MA: Belknap Press of Harvard University Press, 2009), Kindle edition.

"We must accomplish our aims" Webb, *Tunesmith*, 37–38.

"Oh, God" Quoted in Barbara Charone, "The Eagles: One of These Nightmares," *Crawdaddy!*, April 1977.

"In life, things don't simply start" Herman et al., *Narrative Theory*, 76.

"the Boy-Girl Other Half strip" William S. Burroughs, *The Ticket That Exploded: The Restored Text* (New York: Grove Press, 2014), 53.

"When drafted effectively a lyric" Webb, *Tunesmith*, 177.

"I don't think I've ever written" Zollo and Petty, *Conversations*, Kindle edition.

"Singing *is* George" Jennings, *Waylon*, Kindle edition.

"The song is about a man" George Jones, *I Lived to Tell It All* (New York: Villard, 1996), Kindle edition.

"didn't anyone bother" Philip Bailey and Keith Zimmerman, *Shining Star: Braving the Elements of Earth, Wind & Fire* (New York: Plume, 2014), Kindle edition.

"Most of the time" Peter Szendy, *Hits: Philosophy in the Jukebox* (New York: Fordham University Press, 2012), 80.

"The funny thing about 'Together Again'" Buck Owens and Randy Poe, *Buck 'Em!: The Autobiography of Buck Owens* (Winona, MN: Backbeat Books, 2013), Kindle edition.

"Well, songs are just thoughts" Quoted in Flanagan, *Written in My Soul*, Kindle edition.

"mediated reality" Quoted in Flanagan, *Written in My Soul*, Kindle edition.

"Narration reveals the finite" Adriana Cavarero, *Relating Narratives: Storytelling and Selfhood* (London: Routledge, 2000), 3.

"A song is a short story" Nelson and Ritz, *It's a Long Story*, Kindle edition.

"Most of our songs told a story" Lynn and Vecsey, *Coal Miner's*, Kindle edition.

"It is in the Scots, Irish and English" Webb, *Tunesmith*, 11.

"a story told in song" Webb, *Tunesmith*, 105–106.

"First, in these kinds of ballads" Rogers, *Luck*, Kindle edition.

"They're all *emotionally* yours" Bruce Springsteen, *Songs* (New York: Avon Books, 1998), 47.

"the melodies were uncomplicated" Springsteen, *Songs*, 274.

"When I'd write rock music" Quoted in Jeff Burger, ed., *Springsteen on Springsteen: Interviews, Speeches, and Encounters* (Chicago: Chicago Review Press, 2013), 249.

"In Bruce Springsteen songs" Nick Hornby, *High Fidelity* (New York: Riverhead Books, 1996), 136.

"The majority of popular songs express" S. Davis, *Craft of Lyric Writing*, 11.

"Usually, it's not my own voice" "Valerie June on Learning to Love 'Perfectly Imperfect' Voices," interview by Melissa Block, *All Things Considered*, National Public Radio, August 9, 2013.

"The way that a persona becomes" Moore, *Analyzing Popular Music*, Kindle edition.

"With each record I've done so far" Joanna Newsome, interviewed by Marc Maron, *WTF,* Episode 709, May 23, 2016, http://www.wtfpod.com/podcast/episode-709-joanna-newsom (accessed May 24, 2016).

"There are songs I will never sing" Judy Collins, *Sweet Judy Blue Eyes: My Life in Music* (New York: Crown Archetype, 2011), Kindle edition.

"Most of my songs were" Lynn and Vecsey, *Coal Miner's*, Kindle edition.

"This is why we have defined" Cavarero, *Relating Narratives*, 34.

"I've always been good at chronicling" Etheridge, *The Truth*, Kindle edition.

"Like many writers who present an autobiographical" Richard Tillinghast, *Poetry and What Is Real* (Ann Arbor: University of Michigan Press, 2004), 41–42.

"People often think the lyrics" Jackson, *Moonwalk*, Kindle edition.

"I used to believe that you" McEntire, *Reba*, Kindle edition.

"we tell ourselves our individual stories" Quoted in Maryemma Graham and Amritjit Singh, eds., *Conversations with Ralph Ellison* (Jackson: University Press of Mississippi, 1995), 370.

"The effect—or, perhaps, the empathetic motive" Cavarero, *Relating Narratives*, 91.

"It departs from being anything like" Quoted in Flanagan, *Written in My Soul*, Kindle edition.

"It felt invasive" Quoted in DeCurtis, *In Other Words*, Kindle edition.

"Marilyn Manson was the perfect story protagonist" Marilyn Manson and Neil Strauss, *The Long Hard Road out of Hell* (New York: ReganBooks, 1998), Kindle edition.

"A lot of people like to pass me" Quoted in DeCurtis, *In Other Words*, Kindle edition.

"For *Hi Infidelity,* we'd made four videos" Craig Marks and Rob Tannenbaum, *I Want My MTV: The Uncensored Story of the Music Video Revolution* (New York: Dutton, 2011), 43.

CONCLUSION

"I often lament that true songwriting" Rosanne Cash, ed., *Songs without Rhyme: Prose by Celebrated Songwriters* (New York: Hyperion, 2001), ix–x.

APPENDIX

"I wasn't coming up with anything specific" "Watch Wilco's New 'Born Alone' Video and Read the Story Behind Its Lyrics," by Alex Hoyt, *Atlantic*, September 7, 2011, http://www.theatlantic.com/entertainment/archive/2011/09/watch-wilcos-new-born -alone-video-and-read-the-story-behind-its-lyrics/244656/.

"the rare capacity to articulate" Raymond Williams, *Marxism and Literature* (Oxford: Oxford University Press, 1978), 210.

"When a song comes to you" Steven Tyler, *Does the Noise*, Kindle edition.

" 'Take out the papers and the trash!' " Leiber, Stoller, and Ritz, *Hound Dog*, Kindle edition.

"I wrote 'Blowin' in the Wind' " "Rock's Enigmatic Poet Opens a Long-Private Door," by Robert Hillburn, *Los Angeles Times*, April 4, 2004, http://articles.latimes.com /2004/apr/04/entertainment/ca-dylan04.

"Two decades later, Jagger" http://www.rollingstone.com/music/lists/the-500 -greatest-songs-of-all-time-20110407/the-rolling-stones-i-cant-get-no-satisfaction -20110516.

"Vincent [Youmans] and I" Quoted in Max Wilk, *They're Playing Our Song: Conversations with America's Classic Songwriters* (New York: Perseus Books, 2008), Kindle edition.

"In the ten minutes it took" John Denver, *Take Me Home: An Autobiography* (New York: Crown Archetype, 1994), 95.

Dusty Hill wrote "Tush" "ZZ Top," by Sylvie Simmons, *Kerrang!*, 1995.

"We went upstairs and wrote" Quoted in Daniel Rachel, *The Art of Noise: Conversations with Great Songwriters* (New York: St. Martin's Press, 2014), 150.

"written for a lark in ten minutes" Costello, *Unfaithful Music*, 398.

"It's a funny song" Quoted in Flanagan, *Written in My Soul*, Kindle edition.

"I did a song in eight minutes" "Young Thug: Eccentric in Chief," by Patrick Sandberg, *Dazed*, Autumn 2015, http://www.dazeddigital.com/music/article/25802/1/young-thug-eccentric-in-chief.

"[Sound engineer] Tommy Dowd" Leiber, Stoller, and Ritz, *Hound Dog*, Kindle edition.

"because it's one of those that has enough" Quoted in Margotin and Guesdon, *All The Songs*, Kindle edition.

"I sat face-to-face with him" "Meet Gina Figueroa, the Nuyorican Co-writer of 'Really Love,'" by Isabelia Herrera, remezcla.com, February 15, 2016, http://remezcla.com/features/music/gina-figueroa-d-angelo-really-love-interview/.

"Another great early pause" Jennifer Egan, *A Visit from the Goon Squad* (New York: Knopf, 2010), Kindle edition.

"I was kind of poking fun" Fogerty, *Fortunate Son*, 141.

"screams defiance at those" Pete Townshend, letter to the editor of *It* magazine, no. 112 (September 1971): 9–13, quoted in John Atkins, *The Who on Record: A Critical History, 1963–1998* (Jefferson, NC: McFarland Press, 2009), 157.

"It's like a velociraptor scream" "American Rockers Alabama Shakes Throw Everything into the Musical Stew for Sound & Color Album," by Kathy McCabe, News Corporation Australia Network, April 15, 2015, http://www.news.com.au/entertainment/music/american-rockers-alabama-shakes-throw-everything-into-the-musical-stew-for-sound-amp-color-album/news-story/723a112b75575262d6da38aabf49bd87.

"Laughing into tracks represents momentary" Ratliff, *Every Song Ever*, 133.

"The wise man never laughs" Quoted in Ellison, "An Extravagance of Laughter," in Callahan, *Collected Essays of Ralph Ellison*, Kindle edition.

"generally speaking, women" "The Barry White Effect: Men with Deep Voices Have More Children," by Gad Saad, *Psychology Today*, July 16, 2010, https://www

.psychologytoday.com/blog/homo-consumericus/201007/the-barry-white-effect-men-deep-voices-have-more-children.

"The vocal on 'Belong'" "Michael Stipe: The *Rolling Stone* Interview," by David Fricke, *Rolling Stone*, March 5, 1992, http://www.rollingstone.com/music/news/michael-stipe-the-rolling-stone-interview-19920305.

Acknowledgments

I couldn't seem to get the opening lines to the Beatles' "Paperback Writer" out of my head when writing these acknowledgments: "Dear Sir or Madam, will you read my book?/It took me years to write, will you take a look?" That supplication seems a fitting place to start because this book took far more years to write than I ever could have imagined. No one knows this better than my patient editor, Sarah Miller, who is well acquainted with the unpredictable rhythms of working and family life. Her support for me and for this book never wavered. I wish to thank her and the rest of the amazing team at Yale University Press, especially Ash Lago and Ann-Marie Imbornoni, as well as Barbara Goodhouse and Brian Ostrander of Westchester Publishing Services. Thanks also go to Robert Guinsler, my agent at Sterling Lord Literistic; Robert is a stalwart collaborator and a trusted friend.

My students at the University of Colorado, Boulder, are a source of inspiration for all the work that I do. Thanks in particular to the members of my Poetics of American Song Lyrics graduate seminar who prompted many of the ideas that I develop in this book. The Laboratory for Race & Popular Culture, which I founded in 2013, has been this book's incubator. Over the past several years, many of the lab's affiliates have contributed research, conversation, and timely critique: Jack Hamilton, Alex Corey, Caroline Rothnie, Anna Eissenberg, Hector Ramirez, Grace Rexroth, Brian Casey, Christopher Haynes, Andrew Daigle, Carlos Snaider, Adam Schuster, Nasif Islam, Israel Kalombo, Veronica Penney, Ari Gagne, Josette Lorig, Jonina Diele, and Kristina Mitchell. Particular thanks go to Dillon Mader, who helped me sift through a massive number of songs as I compiled the appendix.

This book benefited from the academic leave provided through a generous grant from the Center for the Humanities and the Arts at the University of Colorado. I am also fortunate to have the support and friendship of my colleagues here in Boulder. Thanks especially to Jeff Cox, David Glimp, Cheryl Higashida, Ruth Ellen Kocher, William Kuskin, Warren Motte, Helmut Muller-Sievers, and Paul Youngquist. Stephen Graham Jones was particularly generous, sharing his loving knowledge of country music with me during long lunchtime discussions and contributing a marvelous song list to the Appendix. My colleagues Julie Carr, Noah Eli Gordon, and Raza Ali Hasan each contributed brilliant short reflections on particular song lyrics to the appendix.

Taking my time to complete this book meant that I had ample opportunity to circulate parts of it to trusted readers. I am grateful to the following people for reading and commenting on drafts: Jane Bradley, Brian Buckley, Timothy Anne Burnside, Ed Dimendberg, Jack Meyer, Paul D. Miller, Peter Reiss, and Andy Schneidkraut. Thanks especially to the poets Kyle Dargan, Douglas Kearney, Chris Martin, and

Adrian Matejka, whose timely suggestions and kind critiques proved their great friendship.

Friendship played a significant part in the writing of this book. In that spirit, thanks to two brothers-from-another-mother, Michaeljulius Idani and Dimitry Elias Léger, for being down to roll to so many shows with me back in the day, and for reading the book in draft with such care and insight. Thanks to my friend who's known me the longest, Justin Francis, for modeling the exacting craft required to achieve excellence and for designing a remarkable book cover. Thanks to my friend and trainer Jason Hoff for our weekly lifts, which always seemed to involve extensive debates on everything from the best Van Halen lead singer (Hint: not Hagar) to the songwriting strengths and weaknesses of Whitesnake and many other discussions prompted by the songs pumped into the weight room on any given Friday morning. Thanks as well to Rhidale Dotson and the 3KP guys at AVCF for inspiring my work by keeping up the spirit in the face of adversity.

I owe a particular debt to three more readers. Ann Stockho's keen eye and careful attention to matters of structure and style helped me to transform this book into something far greater than it might otherwise have been. Jon Speese, my former student and a gifted musician, read the book as he would his own; I appreciate his numerous song suggestions and his enthusiastic support for the book's animating idea. John Callahan, my dear friend and mentor, initiated me into the conservatory of writing when I was still a teenager. Just like the jazz piano virtuosos they used to call "professors," John teaches by making music with his words. I thank him for another lesson.

Even before I knew what shape the book would take, I knew that I wanted Leland Chapin to illustrate it. Leland's wonderful compositions provide a fuller dimension to the book's themes, offering a pen-and-ink analog to the poetry of the lyrics and the music of the songs. I am inspired by his passion for art and for teaching.

Finally, I thank my family for their love and support during the long and often challenging time of writing this book. Thanks especially to my wife, Anna. Her careful and compassionate criticism of the book's early drafts prompted me to put more of myself into its pages. During the book's five-year gestation, things changed dramatically for us—particularly with the birth of our two daughters, Ava and Amaya. I dedicate this book to them and to their phenomenal mother. Oh, and thanks to the *Frozen* soundtrack for giving me a way to think about my book even while I was playing Anna and Elsa for hours with my own little princesses.

Credits

"Uptown Funk!" Words and music by Bruno Mars, Jeff Bhasker, Philip Lawrence, Devon Gallaspy, Mark Ronson, Nicholaus Williams, Lonnie Simmons, Ronnie Wilson, Charles Wilson, Rudolph Taylor, and Robert Wilson, copyright © 2014 WB Music Corp., Thou Art the Hunger, Mars Force Music, BMG Chrysalis, Way Above Music, Sony/ATV Songs LLC, Imagem Music LLC, TIG7 Publishing LLC, Trinlanta Publishing, and Taking Care of Business Music (BMI) for USA & Canada/New Songs Administration for the rest of the world. All rights reserved. Used by permission. Copyright © 2014 Imagem CV (BMI)/Songs of Zelig (BMI), Songs of Zelig administered worldwide by Imagem CV. International copyright secured. All rights reserved. Used by permission. Copyright © 2014 WB Music Corp., Thou Art the Hunger, Mars Force Music, BMG Chrysalis, Way Above Music, Sony/ATV Songs LLC, Imagem Music LLC, TIG7 Publishing LLC, Trinlanta Publishing, and Minder Music. All rights on behalf of itself and Thou Art the Hunger administered by WB Music Corp. All rights reserved. Used by permission of Alfred Music. Copyright © 2014 by Songs of Zelig, Imagem CV, BMG Gold Songs, Mars Force Music, WB Music Corp., Thou Art the Hunger, ZZR Music LLC, Sony/ATV Songs LLC, Way Above Music, Sony/ATV Ballad, TIG7 Publishing, Trinlanta Publishing, and Taking Care of Business Music, Inc. All rights for Songs of Zelig and Imagem CV administered by Songs of Imagem Music. All rights for BMG Gold Songs and Mars Force Music administered by BMG Rights Management (US) LLC. All rights for Thou Art the Hunger administered by WB Music Corp. All rights for ZZR Music LLC administered by Universal Music Corp. All rights for Sony/ATV Songs LLC, Way Above Music, and Sony/ATV Ballad administered by Sony/ATV Music Publishing LLC, 424 Church Street, Suite 1200, Nashville, TN 37219. All rights reserved. Used by permission—interpolates "All Gold Everything" performed by Trinidad James, copyright © 2015 Songs Music Publishing, LLC o/b/o Trinlanta Publishing, TIG7 Publishing LLC, and Songs MP, used with permission. *Reprinted by permission of Hal Leonard LLC.*

"Stan" Words and music by Marshall Mathers, Paul Philip Herman, and Dido Armstrong, copyright © 2000 Sony/ATV Music Publishing LLC, 8 Mile Style Music, Champion Management and Music Ltd., Cheeky Music, and WB Music Corp. All rights on behalf of Sony/ATV Music Publishing LLC and 8 Mile Style Music administered by Sony/ATV Music Publishing LLC, 424 Church Street, Suite 1200, Nashville, TN 37219. International copyright secured. All rights reserved. *Reprinted by permission of Hal Leonard LLC.* Copyright © 2000 by Submarine Music Ltd. Peermusic III, Ltd. administers on behalf of Submarine Music Ltd. Used by permission. All rights reserved. (Subject to co-publisher approval and credit.)

Index

Aerosmith
Christina Aguilera
Ray Charles / The Beatles
Beck / Shawn Colvin / Beyoncé
David Byrne / James Brown / Jay Z
Chuck Berry / Johnny Cash / Elvis Presley
Eminem / Don Henley / Paul McCartney
Kurt Cobain / Guns N' Roses / Kacey Musgraves / Common
The Rolling Stones / Waylon Jennings / Sam Smith / Areth
Elton John / Frank Sinatra / Crosby, Stills &
Taylor Swift / Burt Bacharach / Loretta Lynn / Joanna
Whitney Houston / Bruce Springsteen / Mi
Bob / Robert / Bruno Mars / Janis Joplin / Joni Mi
White Stripes / 8
Otis Reddi

31901065018956